MW00398092

come to the *Waters*

Daily Bible Devotions
for Spiritual Refreshment

James Montgomery Boice

Compiled by D. Marion Clark

BakerBooks

a division of Baker Publishing Group
Grand Rapids, Michigan

Published by Baker Books
a division of Baker Publishing Group
P.O. Box 6287, Grand Rapids, MI 49516-6287
www.bakerbooks.com

Printed in the United States of America

Library of Congress Cataloging-in-Publication Data
Boice, James Montgomery, 1938–2000.
    Come to the waters : daily Bible devotions for spiritual refreshment / James Montgomery
Boice ; Compiled by D. Marion Clark.
        p.   cm.
    ISBN 978-0-8010-1410-9 (cloth)
    1. Devotional calendars. I. Clark, Marion (D. Marion) II. Title.
BV4811.B565 2011
242'.2—dc22   2011007613

Thank you to Princeton Theological Seminary Libraries for providing access to unpublished materials in their archives of the James Montgomery Boice Collection.

11   12   13   14   15   16   17   7   6   5   4   3   2   1

To him whose Word is able to make us wise for
salvation through faith in Christ Jesus.

Introduction

"Study of the Bible must be the consuming passion of a believer's life," James Montgomery Boice exhorted worshipers in one of his fourteen sermons through Psalm 119. His congregation at Tenth Presbyterian Church, which sat under his thirty years of expositional preaching, would attest that such was the consuming passion of his life. He preached systematically through twenty-seven books and extensively through another five.

There is a plaque at Tenth Church commemorating Boice's life and ministry. It presents the passage considered the theme of his life work, Romans 11:33–36, which extols the glory of God. That is an accurate summary of his aim in ministry, to which he pointed those under his teaching ministry—to give all glory to God. But if that was his aim, the means by which he most believed in achieving that aim was to know and to obey God's Word.

I have two purposes in compiling this year-long devotional from Boice's sermons and writings. I hope this collection will keep his legacy alive for a new generation of Christians. Most of these devotions are culled from his published sermons. They give but a taste of his fuller exposition of the texts. A number of selections come from unpublished material. All but one of the Revelation devotions come from the last series of sermons he was preaching when he died. A few come from messages given in his early life before coming to Tenth, so that the body of work covers his full span of ministry.

The second purpose is the one that James Boice himself would have had for such a work, which is to aid readers in studying *the* most important book—the Bible. As helpful as the words of the expositor may be, he would have had you value much more highly the Word of God. With that in mind, each reading not only includes a Scripture text, but cites the fuller Bible reading that should go along with the devotion. Take time with each devotion to open your Bible.

An added feature of the devotional is a topical index. Boice was an expository preacher who preached through whole books of the Bible. As every preacher who follows that system knows, it led him to cover a wide variety of

7

topics. Note also a Scripture index, which lists primary Scripture references and others included in the devotions.

Though the devotional is laid out in order of the books of the Bible, you need not read them in succession. There are fifty-two psalms included, so you might read one each Sunday. Using the topical index, you could arrange a reading schedule that takes you through events of the church year.

A word about the title, *Come to the Waters*. It comes not from a devotion but a hymn written by Boice in partnership with Dr. Paul Jones, Tenth's Music Director. The "waters" are the waters of life, the gospel of Jesus Christ. As you will see time and again in the devotions, it is knowing Jesus Christ that matters above all else. Yes, we are to live with the aim of glorifying God, but that cannot be done without being cleansed by the blood of Christ and then living in Christ. Yes, the means to glorify God is to know and to obey his Word, but we will not understand the Word of God if we do not see that it is leading us to the "waters" of the gospel—to the person and work of Jesus Christ. These devotions are not intended simply to make you a better person. They are to lead you again and again to your only hope—Jesus Christ—for glorifying God.

I wish to thank Linda Boice for granting permission and providing support for the project. Terri Taylor came up with the devotional's title. Jessie Taylor compiled the topical and Scripture indexes, and Sarah Brubaker supplied the bibliography and references. My wife, Ginger, was my most fervent encourager. And I thank the editors and team at Baker Books, the publisher of most of Boice's commentaries, for accepting this work and for its final production.

D. Marion Clark
Philadelphia, PA

Good Creation
Genesis 1:1–26

And God saw that it was good.
—*Genesis 1:21*

The value of creation, declared good by God, brings us to a natural conclusion: if God finds the universe good in its parts and as a whole, then we must find it good also. This does not mean that we will refuse to see that nature has been marred by sin. But even in its marred state, it has value, just as fallen man also has value.

First, we should be *thankful* for the world God has made and praise him for it. In some expressions of Christian thought only the soul has value. But this is not right, nor is it truly Christian. The Christian view is that God has made all that is and that the material world therefore has value and should be valued by us because of this origin.

Second, we should *delight* in creation. This is closely related to being thankful but is a step beyond it. It is a step that many Christians have never taken. Frequently, Christians look on nature only as one of the classic proofs of God's existence. But instead of this, the Christian should really enjoy what he sees. He should appreciate its beauty. He should exult in creation even more than the non-Christian, because in the Christian's case there is a corresponding knowledge of the God who stands behind it.

Third, we should demonstrate a *responsibility* toward nature, meaning that we should not destroy it simply for the sake of destroying it but rather should seek to elevate it to its fullest potential. Men and women together should seek to sanctify and cleanse the earth in order that it might be more as God created it, in anticipation of its ultimate redemption.

Finally, after he has contemplated nature and has come to value it, the Christian should turn once again to the God who made it and sustains it moment by moment and should learn to *trust* him. God cares for nature, in spite of its abuse through man's sin. But if he cares for nature, then he also obviously cares for us and may be trusted to do so. This argument occurs in the midst of Christ's Sermon on the Mount in which he draws our attention to God's care of the birds (animal life) and lilies (plant life) and then asks, "Are you not much more valuable than they? . . . If . . . God clothes the grass of the field, which is here today and tomorrow is thrown into the fire, will he not much more clothe you, O you of little faith?" (Matt. 6:26, 30).

Image of God
Genesis 1:27–31

So God created man in his own image.
—GENESIS 1:27

To be made in God's image means that men and women possess the attributes of personality, as God himself does, but as the animals, plants, and matter do not. To have personality, one must possess knowledge, feelings (including religious feelings), and a will. This God has, and so do we. We can say that animals possess a certain kind of personality. But an animal does not reason as men do; it only reacts to certain problems or stimuli. It does not create; it only conforms to certain behavior patterns. It does not love; it only reproduces. It does not worship. Personality, in the sense we are speaking of it here, is something that links man to God but does not link either man or God to the rest of creation.

A second element that is involved in man's being created in the image of God is morality. This includes the two further elements of freedom and responsibility. To be sure, the freedom men and women possess is not absolute. Even in the beginning, the first man, Adam, and the first woman, Eve, were not autonomous. They were creatures and were responsible for acknowledging this by their obedience in the matter of the tree of the knowledge of good and evil. Since the fall, that freedom has been further restricted so that, as Augustine said, the original *posse non peccare* ("able not to sin") has become a *non posse non peccare* ("not able not to sin"). Still there is a limited freedom for men and women even in their fallen state, and with that there is also moral responsibility. In brief, we do not need to sin as we do or as often as we do. And even when we sin under compulsion, we still know it is wrong and, thus, inadvertently confess our likeness to God in this as in other areas.

The third element involved in man's being made in God's image is spirituality, meaning that man is made for communion with God, who is Spirit (John 4:24), and that this communion is intended to be eternal as God is eternal. Although man has a body, as do other forms of life, and a soul, as do animals, only he possesses a spirit. It is on the level of the spirit that he is aware of God and communes with him.

Here lies our true worth. We are made in God's image and are therefore valuable to God and others. God loves men and women, as he does not and cannot love the animals, plants, or inanimate matter. Moreover, he feels for them, identifies with them in Christ, grieves for them, and even intervenes in history to make individual men and women into all that he has determined they should be.

A Living Being
Genesis 2:4–7

> The LORD God . . . breathed into his nostrils the breath
> of life, and man became a living being.
> — GENESIS 2:7

The phrase translated "a living being" (actually, "living soul") in Genesis 2:7 is also used in Genesis 1:24 of the animals. But as a result of the particulars of man's creation given in the second chapter, a distinction is undoubtedly implied. Not only is man alive, he knows he is alive. Even more important, he knows from whom that life has come and of his duties to the God who breathed his own breath into him.

Man also knows that he depends on God for physical life and that he must come to him for spiritual life, as Jesus indicated (John 3:5–6). Isaiah teaches the physical dependence of man on God in a fascinating verse. It plays on the idea of man's breath by saying, "Stop trusting in man, who has but a breath in his nostrils. Of what account is he?" (Isa. 2:22). We might paraphrase Isaiah's command by saying, "Why trust in man who is able to take only one noseful of breath at a time? Trust God, whose breath is inexhaustible." The breath of God in us may be our glory, but it is still received by us only one breath at a time. We breathe in. We hold our breath. We breathe out. But then we must breathe in again or die. Nothing could better characterize our utter dependence on God.

And what if God should withhold his breath? Job answers by saying, "If it were his intention and he withdrew his spirit and breath, all mankind would perish together and man would return to the dust" (Job 34:14–15).

First Corinthians 15:45 presents this same contrast between the first Adam in his littleness and Christ in his greatness. Paul writes, "So it is written: 'The first man Adam became a living being'; the last Adam, a life-giving spirit." Adam existed by breathing in, and the breath he breathed in was from God. He could not sustain himself. Christ, on the other hand, is the One who breathes out, for he is "life-*giving* spirit." We are to live physically and spiritually only as we turn to and are united to him.

I conclude with the challenge presented from the little known book of Ecclesiastes: "Remember [God]—before the silver cord is severed, or the golden bowl is broken; before the pitcher is shattered at the spring, or the wheel broken at the well, and the dust returns to the ground it came from, and the spirit returns to God who gave it" (12:6–7). When death comes, it is too late. Now, while you still have life, come to him who is able to give eternal life, and find yourself accepted in the Savior.

The Fall

Genesis 3:1–7

She took some and ate it. . . . And he ate it.
—GENESIS 3:6

Eve sinned by being deceived; Adam sinned in utter rebellion. Both sinned out of pride. What lay at the root of the woman's determination to eat the forbidden fruit and give some to her husband, Adam, if it was not pride? What lay at the root of Adam's determination to go his own way rather than adhere to the path God placed before him, if this was not pride? In the woman's case it was the conviction that she knew what was better for herself and her husband than God did. God had said that the eating of the tree of the knowledge of good and evil would bring death. But she was convinced by her own empirical observation—after Satan had raised the doubt—that the tree would actually be good for her and that God was mistaken. In the man's case, pride is also present, for he repeated the sin of Satan, saying in effect, "I will cast off God's rule. I am too great to be bound by it. I shall declare myself autonomous. I will be like the Most High" (see Isa. 14:14).

How terrible pride is! And how pervasive; for, of course, it did not vanish in the death of the first man and woman. Pride lies at the heart of our sinful race. It is the "center" of immorality, "the utmost evil," that which "leads to every other vice," as C. S. Lewis warns us. It is that which makes us all want to be more than we are or can be and, consequently, causes us to fall short of that truly great destiny for which we were created.

This brings us back to the teaching that we are fallen beings. We are not on the way up, as today's optimistic humanists would indicate. We are not sinful by the very nature of things, as the ancient Greeks would argue. We are not even machines, as if we could be excused on the grounds of such an analysis. We are fallen. We are faithless, rebellious, filled with pride. As a result, our only hope is in that grace of God by which he sends a Redeemer, who instead of being faithless was faithful, instead of being rebellious was obedient, and instead of being filled with pride was one who actually humbled himself to "even death on a cross" (Phil. 2:8).

Judgment and Grace
Genesis 3:8–19

He will crush your head, and you will strike his heel.
—GENESIS 3:15

God passes sentence, beginning with the serpent through whom the sin originated: the serpent will crawl on its belly and eat "dust," i.e., the dust of frustration. We do not know what the serpent looked like before this judgment, though he must have been a beautiful and upright creature. Nor do we know precisely when the judgment here pronounced was executed, though it was probably at this point. What we can know is the horror of Adam and Eve as they heard the voice of God and witnessed the terrifying transformation of this once beautiful creature into the hissing, slithering, dangerous creature we know as a snake today. They must have recoiled in mortal fear, recognizing that God had every right to pronounce this same or even a more terrible judgment on them. They must have expected that he would do so, and the devil must also have expected this judgment. It was for this that he had tempted the man and the woman.

But instead—how unsearchable are the judgments and ways of God—grace intervenes. It is true that there is judgment, of a sort. The woman is given pain in childbearing; the man is to gain a livelihood through the sweat of his brow. But immediate physical death is postponed. And before even these more limited judgments are pronounced, God speaks the promise of a coming one who shall be the deliverer: "I will put enmity between you and the woman, and between your offspring and hers; he will crush your head, and you will strike his heel."

It seems to me that the fact that God does not actually say "guilty" in his words to Adam and Eve is of great importance. Had he declared our two parents to be guilty at that point, judgment in its fullest form must inevitably have followed. The man and woman would have suffered immediate banishment from God to hell, and their torment would have been endless. But God did not pronounce that verdict. He postponed it, as courts sometimes do. And when he pronounced it later, he did so not on Adam and Eve or their descendants, but on Jesus Christ who bore the punishment for all who would believe on him as Savior.

If you are in Christ by saving faith, the verdict of guilty that should have been pronounced on you has been pronounced on Christ. He bore your punishment. He "descended into hell" in your place. If you are not in Christ, that verdict remains to be spoken and indeed will be spoken against you at the final judgment.

Cain's Curse
Genesis 4:1–16

> Now you are under a curse.
> —GENESIS 4:11

If you have never come to the Lord Jesus Christ as your Savior, then you are somewhat like Cain. You are in danger, and you must flee from it. The Navy in wartime uses an expression of ships that sail into danger. They are said to be "in harm's way." That is an expression for you, if you are apart from Christ. You are in harm's way and you must get back into the safe way before you are lost forever.

There are things that will keep you from it. One is your *pride*, the very thing that got Cain into trouble in the first place. Perhaps you turn up your lips in scorn, thinking such persons weak who would cast everything aside to obtain God's kingdom. You would rather go to hell than bow like that. But that is precisely what you will do if you do not lay your pride aside and come to God on God's terms.

You may also be held back by *hate*, though you might not call it that. You think you are a paragon of virtue, but the very fact that you think so poorly of Christians should be a warning that all is not right with you and that you are encumbered with far more irritations and animosities than you imagine. Hate is a terrible thing. You do not possess it; it possesses you. It is truly the sin crouching at the door that desires to master the home's inhabitant.

Again, there are *resentment and self-pity*. No one likes these things in others, but no one is so blind to anything as these when they occur in himself or herself. Cain had killed a man, his own brother. But he was so possessed with resentment against God and others that he could not see the enormity of his crime and so actually felt sorry for himself when God punished him with far less of a judgment than he deserved.

Can you not see this? Can you not sense your danger? Sin is driving you from God, whom you think to be the cause of your misery. You are failing to see that he is actually being good to you and that his goodness is given precisely so that it might lead you to repentance.

Cain, we are told, "went out from the LORD's presence and lived in the land of Nod, east of Eden" (v. 16). Do not let it be true of you that you "went out from the LORD's presence." Flee to him and find in him the One you have needed all along.

Boice, *Genesis*, Volume 1, Baker, 1998, 260–61.

Grace Found
Genesis 6:5–8

But Noah found favor in the eyes of the LORD.
—GENESIS 6:8

Not only is sin internal as well as external; not only is it pervasive in that it affects everything we can possibly think or do. It is also *continuous*, for in God's judgment we all do "only evil *all the time*" (v. 5). From our perspective a statement like that is almost beyond belief. We would not make it of other people, even the worst of people. We certainly would not make it of ourselves. But this is God speaking—God who sees all things and sees the heart—and God is truthful.

Could a blacker picture of the utter depravity of man in his rebellion against God ever be painted? It is hard to think so. Yet just at this point, when the black thunderclouds of God's wrath against human sin are at their most threatening, a small crack appears. Grace shines through, and the promise of a new day dawns.

The older, Authorized Version says, "Noah found grace." But whether the word "grace" or the word "favor" is used to translate the Hebrew term *hën*, the significant thing is that this is the first appearance of the idea in the Bible. It is true, of course, that Adam and Eve also found grace when they sinned; justice alone would have sent them into outer darkness forever. Seth and Enoch and all the others found grace. But here for the first time, grace is explicitly mentioned. Since this is said of a time when the evil of a degenerate race was at its zenith, it indicates that so long as life lasts, regardless of the extent of the evil, there is always opportunity to find God's grace where alone it can be found, namely, in the work of Jesus Christ in dying for his people's salvation. Noah may not have known details about that future work of Christ. But he looked forward to the deliverer and ordered his life accordingly.

Notice that Noah did not earn grace. Noah found grace. He was willing to accept God's judgment on his sinful and rebellious nature and place his hope in the Savior. It is the same today. We have no claim on God. We have not earned anything but his just wrath and our eventual destruction. But we can find God's grace in Christ.

Boice, *Genesis*, Volume 1, Baker, 1998, 317–18.

Shut In by God
Genesis 7:1–24

Then the LORD shut him in.
—GENESIS 7:16

Consider these three lessons. First, when the Lord shut Noah and his family up in the ark, they were totally secure and thereby become an illustration for us of the believer's *perfect security* in Jesus Christ. The rains would come. The floods would rage. But nothing would touch these who had been sealed in the ark by Jehovah. The Lord does not place the safety of his people in others' hands. He himself throws the lock. It is said of him, "What he opens no one can shut, and what he shuts no one can open" (Rev. 3:7). The shutting in of Noah was the equivalent of our being sealed with the Holy Spirit (Eph. 4:30). Like him, we are not only saved; we are secure as well.

Second, there is a lesson of God's great *grace*. The last thing we are told in this story before the waters actually begin to come is that "the LORD shut him in." Presumably this was done at the last possible moment. Noah had been preaching God's righteousness, man's sin, and the coming of the great flood for 120 years, but no one had believed him. They were refusing to believe now. But still the door to the ark remained open, and any who wanted to could have gone inside. What great grace! What magnificent forbearance on the part of God! Since Noah had believed and had gone in, no one who stood without could say that the possibility of belief was closed to him. "Whoever willed" could come.

So also today. All who will may come. Many do not, but none of these can say that the possibility of repentance from sin and turning to Christ are beyond them.

Finally, there is a lesson in that there is an *end to grace*. Grace is great but it is not unending. If it is spurned, the day of reckoning eventually comes. For one final week the door stood open. But the week ended, the door was closed, and the flood came. The same God who opens doors is himself the door (John 10:7, 9). He also closes doors and refuses to open them—when the time for grace is gone.

For you it is not yet past, whoever you may be. This is still the day of grace, and although it will end, it has not ended yet. Won't you come while there is still time? God said to Noah, "*Come* . . . into the ark" (Gen. 7:1 KJV). At the end of the Bible we read, "The Spirit and the bride say, '*Come*!' And let him who hears say, '*Come*!' Whoever is thirsty, let him *come*; and whoever wishes, let him take the free gift of the water of life" (Rev. 22:17).

The Way of Sacrifice

Genesis 8:18–22

Then Noah built an altar to the LORD.
—*GENESIS 8:20*

Noah's offering was both a thank offering for the deliverance he and his family had received and a sin offering by which Noah confessed need of atonement for his and his family's transgressions. If life was to begin anew, it was to begin with a proper and thankful approach to God—at least so far as Noah had anything to do with it.

Noah's action provides a pattern for what sinful human beings must do to find God's favor. In a sense, we can do nothing; God has done everything. But we can at least come to God in the way God himself has appointed and be assured as we come that he will receive us and will remain faithful to us within the covenant of salvation.

As sinners we appear before God as Noah did emerging from the ark. We have been recipients of his common grace. If God had not been favorable to us, we would have perished long before now. Yet we are sinners. We merit God's judgment, just as others do. Left to ourselves the sin within will undoubtedly bring us to perdition. We will perish utterly. What are we to do? We know not what to do. But God has set a way before us: the way of sacrifice. He has shown from the earliest days of the race, going back to Eden, that, although sinners merit death for their transgressions, it is nevertheless possible for a substitute to take the sinner's place. An innocent may die. God himself showed this when he killed the animals and then clothed Adam and Eve in the animals' skins. This is the way Noah came to God after he exited from the ark. It is the way you and I must come today, though we do not actually offer sacrifices but rather look back in faith to the perfect sacrifice of the Lord Jesus Christ offered in our place. He is the lamb "slain from the creation of the world" (Rev. 13:8). He is "the Lamb of God, who takes away the sin of the world" (John 1:29).

What happens as we come to God through faith in the perfect and finished work of Jesus? We find that God is pleased, and we hear him promise that we are now his and that we shall never perish—not for this life, not for eternity. Our relationship with him "will never cease."

Boice, *Genesis*, Volume 1, Baker, 1998, 379.

Escaping God's Curse
Genesis 9:24–10:20

Cursed be Canaan!
—GENESIS 9:25

It is interesting that, in this particular branch of Ham's family, we have a reversal (probably deliberate) of God's judgment on Canaan for Ham's sin in ridiculing Noah. God had pronounced a curse on Canaan through Noah, saying, "Cursed be Canaan! The lowest of slaves will he be to his brothers." But so far as we know, in these early days God did not put this prophecy into effect until much later through Israel's invasion of the Promised Land. Instead, it is the brother of Canaan, Cush, and his descendants who determine to enslave the others.

I say this may be deliberate, for I can imagine Nimrod to have thought in this manner. He may have said, "I don't know about the others, but I regard this matter of the curse of God on Canaan as a major disgrace on my family, one that needs to be erased. Did God say that my uncle Canaan would be a slave? I'll fight that judgment. I'll never be a slave! What's more, I'll be the exact opposite. I'll be so strong that others will become slaves to me. Instead of 'slave,' I'll make them say, 'Here comes Nimrod, the mightiest man on earth.'"

This is the normal reaction of the human spirit when faced with God's curse. It says, "I'll defy it. I'll take care of my own problems." So it creates the arts, raises an army, builds its cities, and marches out to make a name for itself in defiance of God's decrees.

But God's decrees are not overturned this way. God's curse is not successfully defied. There is only one way we can escape God's curse, and that is at the point where God takes the curse on himself. There is no reason why he should do this. But he does. He comes in the person of Jesus Christ "taking the very nature of a servant [a *slave*], being made in human likeness" and thus "being found in appearance as a man, he humbled himself and became obedient to death—even death on a cross!" (Phil. 2:7–8). Thus "Christ redeemed us from the *curse* of the law by becoming a curse for us" (Gal. 3:13). And what happens? Having thus subjected himself, he is given a name that is "above every name" (Phil. 2:9) and declared to be the ruler of heaven and earth. That is our pattern: to come to Christ where the curse of God against sin is poured out, to be clothed in his righteousness, and then to learn the path of humble service to others within the human family, which is the true and only road to real greatness.

The Tower of Babel

Genesis 11:1–9

Then they said, "Come, let us build ourselves a city."
—*Genesis 11:4*

There are two different uses of the word "come" in this story. The first was spoken *by man to man against God*. The second was spoken *by God to God* (another early intimation of the Trinity) *against man*. It would not be right to end without noting that the Bible also knows a third use of the word "come" in which an invitation is extended *by God to man for man's benefit*. God says, "Come now, let us reason together. . . . Though your sins are like scarlet, they shall be as white as snow; though they are red as crimson, they shall be like wool" (Isa. 1:18). Jesus says, "Come to me, all you who are weary and burdened, and I will give you rest" (Matt. 11:28). "The Spirit and the bride say, 'Come!' And let him who hears say, 'Come!' Whoever is thirsty, let him come; and whoever wishes, let him take the free gift of the water of life" (Rev. 22:17).

What is the result when we who hear God's invitation come to him? It is just as he says! Our sins are washed away. Our burdens are lifted. Our spiritual thirst is quenched. Moreover, the effects of the curse are overturned and the proper desires of the human heart are provided for, not by man in rebellion against God, to be sure, but by the gracious and forgiving God himself from whom all truly good gifts come. The curse was the confusion of languages, but God brings blessing from the curse. He gives understanding in spite of the language barrier and even promises (Pentecost is an earnest of the fulfillment) that the nations will worship together, presumably in one voice and with full understanding of each other. The Babylonians wanted a city. Their city could not stand. But God provides his people with a city with foundations that will endure forever. Nimrod's people wanted a name. But to those who stand with God and who overcome, God promises: "Him who overcomes I will make a pillar in the temple of my God. Never again will he leave it. I will write on him the name of my God and the name of the city of my God, the new Jerusalem, which is coming down out of heaven from my God; and I will also write on him my new name" (3:12).

Abram's Call

Genesis 12:1–9

Leave your country, your people and your father's household and go to the land I will show you.
—GENESIS 12:1

God's call to Abram probably came to him on at least two occasions, which suggests that Abram started out after receiving the first call but faltered or stopped along the way at Haran (11:31). This means that, although Abram believed God enough to start out on his journey after God had appeared to him in Ur, his faith was still weak and needed much cultivation. It is a way of saying that one does not need to be a spiritual giant to become a follower of God—after all, none of us is a spiritual giant. All one has to do is begin to follow him.

You can be in one of three places spiritually. You can be an unbeliever with no awareness of spiritual things. You can be an unbeliever with a dawning awareness of spiritual things. Or you can be a believer.

If you are an unbeliever with no spiritual understanding, the life of Abram should be a message of hope for you. Before God came to him, Abram had no understanding either. He had no knowledge of the true God. He was under the influence of his pagan environment. Yet God saved him by grace. It may be that God will work in your life in a similar way, especially as you hear and try to understand the teaching of God's Word.

If you are an unbeliever who is nevertheless awakening to spiritual things and seeking to understand who God is and what he requires of you, then Abram's life is one from which you can learn. Abram responded to God because God had first taken an interest in him. He answered because God had called. In the same way, if you are awakening to the claims of the gospel, it is because God is already at work within you. You must drop anything that holds you back and respond as he speaks. You must follow as he leads.

If you are a believer in Christ, the life of Abram shows how one man heard the call of God and was willing to abandon everything for the sake of the blessings God set before him. He left his country but he found a new country and even looked beyond it to that heavenly country and that city with foundations, whose builder and maker is God. He left his people but he became the father of a new people. He left his father's house but he found room in the house of God in heaven prepared for him by the Lord Jesus Christ. So will it be for you. Those blessings are for all who set out on this pilgrimage.

Salem or Sodom?

Genesis 14:17–24

I will accept nothing belonging to you.
—GENESIS 14:23

Abram chose Salem over Sodom in the most absolute way. This is the thrust of the text. When the king of Sodom offered to share the spoils of war with him, Abram did not merely say, "That is a nice offer you made, but why don't you take half, and I'll take half?" Nor did he say, "I don't need anything now. If I ever have need of anything, I'll come down and ask you for it." No, he said, "I have raised my hand to the LORD, God Most High, Creator of heaven and earth, and have taken an oath that I will accept nothing belonging to you, not even a thread or the thong of a sandal, so that you will never be able to say, 'I made Abram rich.' I will accept nothing . . ." (vv. 22–24).

Think how absolute this is. Abram repeats the word "nothing" twice. He explains what he means, saying that it excludes even the thread of a garment or the cord that binds a sandal. He swears before God that he will take this position and stand by it.

One of the great weaknesses of the church is that so few are willing to be consistently absolute in their commitment to Christ and his kingdom. There are commitments, of course. But many are halfhearted. Christians are half-hearted in their commitment to God, in their commitment to one another, in their commitment to Christ's service.

I apply this thinking to Christian leadership. I am convinced that only a total commitment to people and to place will ever produce the kind of changes and progress we so desperately need. I like to put our need in three categories. First, we need commitment to people before programs. This does not mean that programs are unimportant. But it means that commitment to people must come first. We must want to see people develop.

Second, we need a commitment to place before promotions. So many, even in Christian work, use one job merely as a stepping-stone to another, more important position. We have to be known as those who care for and intend to remain in the place to which the Lord has called us.

Third, we need commitment to both people and place for an indefinite period of time, which means until we die—unless God clearly and forcefully leads otherwise. Without this time commitment, the other commitments are only halfhearted conveniences, and the word *commitment* means nothing.

Commitment begins, not with a city or program, but with a personal, total commitment to the Lord Jesus Christ himself. Make that commitment, and do not be halfhearted about it.

Our Great Reward

Genesis 15:1–21

> Do not be afraid, Abram. I am your shield, your very great reward.
> —GENESIS 15:1

This is a great promise. God himself was to be Abram's reward. He is your reward also. Do you seek for things? Do you think that your reward consists of what you can earn? or do? or know? If you think that, you will certainly be disappointed.

To have God as your reward means, first of all, that you share in all that God has. Abram received many revelations from God during his lifetime, and many of these had a name of God connected with them. At one point, Abram came to know God as Jehovah-jireh, which means "the God who provides." Here he came to know him as El Elyon, "the God Most High, Creator of heaven and earth." It was this God who promised to be a reward to Abram.

Moreover, he will share heaven and earth with you, if you are a believer in the Lord Jesus Christ. The Bible says that we are God's children, adding, "Now if we are children, then we are heirs—heirs of God and co-heirs with Christ" (Rom. 8:17). You are a co-heir with Christ. There is a great difference between an heir and a co-heir. If you are a single heir, you alone inherit everything. If you are one of four heirs, then you receive only one-fourth of the inheritance. If, however, you are one of four co-heirs, you inherit all, for co-heirs possess the inheritance together. In the same way, all Christians are co-heirs with Christ. All that God has is ours. We possess it jointly. And we shall enter into it one day as we receive our inheritance with Jesus.

To have God as our reward also means that we share in all that God is. We possess it in part even now. Many of God's attributes mentioned in the Bible are to be ours in Christ Jesus. Is God wisdom? We share that wisdom. Is God holy? We share that holiness. Is God almighty? We share that power.

How do you live your life as a Christian? You can live it in either of two ways. You are already secure in God; you are anchored in God's character. You have a great inheritance. But you can either rest in that or be fearful. You can watch the storms come, and say, "What will become of me then? What if I prove unfaithful?" Or you can be like Abram and grow strong in faith, resting in him who is able to keep you from falling and to present you faultless before his presence with exceeding joy. Is your faith like that? If it is not, God can teach you. Then you will grow strong in faith, giving glory to God. You will learn that what God has promised he is able to perform.

Sign of the Covenant

Genesis 17:9–14

You are to undergo circumcision, and it will be the
sign of the covenant between me and you.
—GENESIS 17:11

The same God who joined his breath and name to Abraham as evidence that he could live as God wanted him to live and do what God wanted him to do is also joined to us through the power of the Holy Spirit. His name is joined to ours as we believe in Christ and become Christians.

What does it mean to be a Christian? It means to be Christ's, to be joined to him and to take his name. If your name is Mary and you become a Christian, you become Mary Christian. If your name is James, you are James Christian. If it is Susan, you are Susan Christian—and so on. As we enter into the covenant and become Christians, we recognize that this is all of God and that our ability to do certain things, which we must do, comes not from ourselves but from God, who joins himself to us.

This is also suggested by the sign of the old covenant, which figures so strongly in Genesis 17, and by the Christian signs of baptism and the Lord's Supper, which emerge in the New Testament. So far as Abraham's sign was concerned, it is significant that Abraham did not establish it. God did. But although God established the sign, Abraham had to respond by carrying it out, as we read in the last paragraph of Genesis 17: "On that very day Abraham took his son Ishmael and all those born in his household or bought with his money, every male in his household, and circumcised them, as God told him" (v. 23).

Abraham's obedience did not mean that he was contributing anything to the covenant. In fact, it meant the opposite. The cutting away of the flesh meant the renunciation of human effort, which arises out of the flesh, and the willingness to bear about in the body the mark of the individual's identification with God.

The signs of the new covenant are similar in meaning. Baptism, the sign of initiation into the body of Christ, symbolizes three things:

1. dying to the past and to self
2. rising to newness of life in Christ
3. identification with the Lord Jesus Christ

It is in baptism that we take Christ's name and say before the entire world that henceforth we are to be known as Christians. And what of the Lord's Supper? This is the continuing sacrament of Christianity that symbolizes our constant dependence on Christ for power to live in a way that pleases him. Moreover, this is accomplished by a symbolic feeding, just as Abraham may have been encouraged to think of himself as feeding on El Shaddai. It is only by drawing on Christ that we have strength to live as God's covenant children.

God Does Right

Genesis 18:16–33

But Abraham remained standing before the LORD.
—GENESIS 18:22

Abraham's pleading that Sodom be spared destruction is a remarkable example of a prayer of intercession! It is remarkable on God's part that he would allow Abraham so to entreat him. It is remarkable on Abraham's part too. It shows the degree to which Abraham had progressed in his friendship and fellowship with God. Of course, Abraham does not get everything exactly right. When he asks, "Will not the Judge of all the earth do right?" he is almost suggesting that God might not do right or that mere human beings, including himself, might have a base on which properly to evaluate God's actions. Abraham should have known that God always does right, regardless of how his actions might appear to us. Still, he had nevertheless progressed quite a bit in knowing how to present his petitions.

Abraham's prayer suggests four great principles for our prayers. First, it is a *modest* prayer. Abraham did not demand knowledge of God's secret purposes in election, nor did Abraham think this knowledge necessary for making his petitions. We may learn from this that there is no need for us to feel hindered or restrained in praying for unconverted individuals or cities or the world just because we do not know what God's ultimate purpose may be concerning them or it. We can even be encouraged in prayer, knowing that prayer is a means of God's working and that he delights to hear and answer the intercessory petitions of his saints.

Second, it is a *humble* prayer. That is, it does not suggest even for a moment that because Abraham was a certain kind of person or had done certain things, God was under some obligation to hear him and answer his entreaties. On the contrary, Abraham said, "I am nothing but dust and ashes" (v. 27).

Third, it is a *persistent* prayer. The prayer may be read in just a few seconds, as with most scriptural prayers. But it is written in such a way as to cause us to think that Abraham rightly persisted with God in uttering these requests. Abraham intercedes for Sodom six times. Moreover, as each part of his request was granted, he seems to have been encouraged to come back and try the same approach again.

Fourth, it is a *persuasive* prayer. It was not by pleading any claim on God, for Abraham had none, as we have seen. It was persuasive in that it pleaded God's own character and glory. Abraham pleaded no merit in himself, but he argued that God must be seen and known to do right, which would not be the case if the righteous were to perish with the guilty.

Sinning "Just a Bit"
Genesis 19:15–26

But Lot's wife looked back and she became a pillar of salt.
—GENESIS 19:26

I wonder if anyone is thinking that the sins of Lot seem small. If you are thinking this way, I fear for you. Can't you see that one of the reasons why you can't sin just a little bit is precisely that you *can* sin that bit? There would be no danger if God always stepped in to stop you from doing it. But God does not stop you. There are limits to what God will permit but, nevertheless, God will let you sin. He will let the Jews construct their golden calf. He will permit David to commit adultery with Bathsheba and then murder her husband. He will allow Gomer to run off with other lovers. He will not interfere when the prodigal leaves home to squander his inheritance in a foreign country. In the final analysis, God will allow you to do what you are committed to doing—and you will have to bear the consequences of your actions.

Consider the consequences of Lot's sins on his wife. Lot may have argued at this stage of his life, as some do, that his "little sins" were hurting no one but himself. But although it may have seemed that way for a time, this was not true, and others most certainly were hurt by his actions. His daughters were hurt; the proof is in their decadent morality. But the chief example is Lot's wife, who could not seem to tear herself away from the city. Presumably she lingered behind, looked back, and was overtaken in the destruction.

If you are a Lot, I wish I could adequately press that home to you. Fathers, your sins of family neglect or drinking or sexual escapades will hurt your family. They will hurt your wife and your children. Mothers, your socializing will hurt your children, who need your love and care. Young people, the sins of your youth—your drugs, drinking, and promiscuity—will hurt everyone with whom you have contact. They will hurt your parents, who want better things for you. They will hurt your peers, for you will be part of the pattern of life that destroys them and their potential. In the future, you will be less prepared for the work you have to do. Ministers, your sin of neglect of Bible study and sermon preparation will hurt your parishioners. Employers, your sins will hurt your employees. Workmen, your halfhearted work and wasted time will hurt your company and other workers. Politicians, your sins will injure the people you are elected or appointed to represent.

Sin always has consequences, both for the individual who sins and for others. So abandon it, however small it may seem to you. Whatever it is, it is not small in God's sight, and its effects are incalculable.

Pilgrim's Regress
Genesis 20:1–18

And there Abraham said of his wife Sarah, "She is my sister."
—GENESIS 20:2

The cause of Abraham's sin was lack of faith in God. He did not believe that God could take care of him in this new situation. That lack of faith disturbed everything. When Abraham began to doubt God, thinking less of him than he should have thought, his view of himself was also altered, for he began to think more of himself than was proper. It was the old principle of the seesaw in theology. So long as our view of God is up, our view of ourselves will be down. God will be sovereign, wise, and holy. We will see ourselves as weak, foolish, and sinful. But if our view of God goes down, so that he becomes less than sovereign in our thinking, then our view of ourselves will go up and we will begin to imagine that we are generally quite able to take care of ourselves. This is what Abraham imagined. Thinking that God could not take care of him, he assumed that he would have to take care of himself, and this got him into the foolish predicament of this episode.

More than this, as his opinion of himself rose, his sensitivity to other people declined, and he began to look down on them. We see this in his attitude toward Abimelech. When Abimelech caught him in his deception, Abraham replied, "I said to myself, 'There is surely no fear of God in this place, and they will kill me because of my wife'" (v. 11). This was a slander on Abimelech, who had a great deal of reverential fear for God. Abraham was blind to this because of his own foolish pride and disobedience.

Despite Abraham's doubts about God's ability to take care of him, God's ability to do so was not altered in the slightest. He may have doubted God's grace, but God remained as gracious as he had ever been.

God showed this grace to Abraham. Abimelech must have thought of Abraham as a cowardly, hypocritical, two-faced charlatan—or worse. But this is not the way God spoke of Abraham to Abimelech. God said, "Return the man's wife, for he is a prophet, and he will pray for you and you will live" (v. 7). God was not indifferent to Abraham's sin. But the sin did not change God's view of Abraham. Abraham was still "a prophet." He was still God's man.

It is good to serve a God like that, a God who remains sovereign even when we doubt his ability to care for us, a God who remains gracious even when we sin. To serve a God like that is this world's greatest joy and opportunity. To know that he is like that is the greatest incentive you will ever have to keep from sinning.

The Names of God

Genesis 21:33–34

There he called upon the name of the LORD, the Eternal God.
— GENESIS 21:33

In this verse, we come to one of the names for God. It is *Jehovah El Olam* (meaning "The Lord, the Eternal God").

The key word in this name, *olam*, translated "eternal," originally meant that which was secret, hidden, concealed, or unknown. From the idea of an indefinite past or future, the Jews soon developed the idea of "eternity," which referred to the incalculable and unknown past and to the incalculable and unknown future. Where the word is used of God, it usually also includes his immutability, or unchangeableness. Times change, people change, needs change. *El Olam* never changes.

As you walk with God, your vision of who he is will be expanded and you will increasingly come to know him in respect to all his other names, names that you also will then both trust and cherish. There is God as our Jehovah, the God who was and is and is to come. He has been spoken of as *El Elyon*, the Possessor of Heaven and Earth. He is *El Shaddai*, the Mighty One. In Genesis 22, we find him as *Jehovah Jireh*, the God Who Provides. But what of *El Roi*, the God Who Sees Me? Or *Adonai*, the Lord? He is *Jehovah Sabaoth*, the Lord of Hosts. He is *Jehovah Nissi*, the Lord Our Banner. He is *Jehovah M'Quaddishkhem*, the Lord Who Sanctifies; *Jehovah Rohi*, the Lord Our Shepherd; *Jehovah Rophe*, the Lord Who Heals. He is *Jehovah Tsidkenu*, the Lord Our Righteousness; *Jehovah Shalom*, the Lord Our Peace. He is *Jehovah Shammah*, the Lord Who Is There. God is all these. But he is also Father, Son, and Holy Spirit. He is Alpha and Omega, the Beginning and the End. He is the Ancient of Days, seated upon the throne of heaven. He is the Child of Bethlehem, crying in a manger. He is Jesus of Nazareth. His titles are Wonderful Counselor, the Mighty God, the Everlasting Father, the Prince of Peace. He is the Judge. He is our Rock and our High Tower.

What more can we say? Our God is the Way, the Truth, and the Life. He is the source of life. He is the sustainer of life. He is Life itself. He is the Light of the World, the Bread of Life, the Good Shepherd, the Great Shepherd, the Chief Shepherd. He is the Lord of Hosts. He is the King of Kings. He is the Faithful One. He is Love. He is the God of Abraham, Isaac, and Jacob. He is the God of Moses, David, Isaiah, Elizabeth, Anna, Simeon, and John the Baptist. He is the God of Peter, James, John, Timothy, Apollos, and Paul. He is your God. He is mine. We shall never exhaust the character of our eternal God. We will never find him wanting.

Faith on Trial

Genesis 22:1–19

We will worship and then we will come back to you.
— GENESIS 22:5

As Abraham made plans to obey God and sacrifice his son, Isaac, he not only exercised faith, but worked with it, pondering the situation, trying to figure out what was happening. I think Abraham was puzzling over the problem. *How can God be true to his promise if I sacrifice Isaac?* he was asking. *What is God going to do to remain a God of honor?*

This was what Abraham was doing during the three days it took to reach the region of Moriah. The reason I think this is that the passage may suggest that he solved it on the way to Moriah. We are told that when Abraham finally saw the place in the distance, he said to his accompanying servants, "Stay here with the donkey while I and the boy go over there. We will worship and then we will come back to you."

"*We* will come back." Abraham intended to sacrifice Isaac, as God had commanded him. But by this time he was sure that the outcome would not be the end of Isaac. What had Abraham come to believe? The author of Hebrews tells us: "By faith Abraham, when God tested him, offered Isaac as a sacrifice. He who had received the promises was about to sacrifice his one and only son, even though God had said to him, 'It is through Isaac that your offspring will be reckoned.' Abraham reasoned that God could raise the dead, and figuratively speaking, he did receive Isaac back from death" (Heb. 11:17–19). Abraham had faith to expect a resurrection.

God did provide a resurrection, figuratively speaking (v. 19). But it was not until the last minute, and not before Abraham had demonstrated his total willingness to offer up his son.

Here was proof of how much a mere man would do for love of God. But I am sure you see how this incident is also a pageant of how much more God would do as an expression of his love for fallen men and women. Abraham was only *asked* to sacrifice his son; he did not actually have to do it. Even if he had, there was only a physical death involved. But when the time came for God, the heavenly Father, to sacrifice his Son, it was not a mere physical death; it was a spiritual death, one that achieved redemption for sinners. When God's hand was raised at Calvary, there was no one to call out, "Stay your hand. Do not harm the boy." When God offered up his sacrifice, the hand that was poised above Christ fell. Jesus died. Through that death, God brought life to all who trust in Christ's sacrifice. Hallelujah!

Surrendering to God

Genesis 27:27–33

I blessed him—and indeed he will be blessed!
—GENESIS 27:33

In the midst of this disgraceful episode, when Jacob stole his brother's blessing, there is a spot that stands out so brightly that one can end only by praising the wisdom and mercy of God, who brought it about. It is the conversion of Isaac from a willful rejection of the sovereign decree of God to an obedient acceptance of it.

I find the change in verse 33, after the blessing has been given. Jacob had returned to Rebekah, and Esau had appeared in the tent to offer the fruit of his hunting. "Who are you?" Isaac asks. When Esau replies, "I am your son, your firstborn, Esau," the light began to dawn within the soul of the blinded patriarch and, as the text says, "Isaac trembled violently" (v. 33).

What was happening to Isaac? It was the realization that he had tried to box with God and had been defeated, and that he would always be defeated unless he surrendered his own errant will to the Almighty. One commentator compares his self-will to a great edifice built in opposition to the revealed will of God. That structure had seemed quite substantial. Isaac was not going to let it be shaken by that contentious wife of his, Rebekah, or that sniveling sissy, Jacob. But Isaac had failed to reckon with God. When his schemes went awry, he saw that in spite of his arrogance there was nevertheless a glorious, divine will above his own.

The break came almost instantly. In verse 33 Isaac begins by saying, "Who was it, then, that hunted game and brought it to me? I ate it just before you came and I blessed him." He ends: ". . . and indeed *he will be blessed*!" "He . . . will . . . be . . . blessed." Those words were torn from Isaac's heart by the most wrenching experience of his life. But though willful and late, he had at last come out on the right side, and God never forgot that he had. This is why, years later, in the Epistle to the Hebrews, God made sure that it said, "By faith Isaac blessed Jacob and Esau in regard to their future" (Heb. 11:20). It is significant that it is all praise and no criticism. Isaac fought God's will for 137 years. But once his own will was broken, God saw the new Isaac and remembered his sins against him no more (10:17; cf. Jer. 31:34). Oh, the greatness of God! Oh, the happiness of the one who is surrendered to him!

Are you surrendered to God? Has your own selfish will been broken? Before any great work of grace, there must be the internal earthquake that Isaac experienced. If you are not God's, the earthquake must come and your own ways must crash to destruction before it.

The Gate of Heaven

Genesis 28:10–17

He saw a stairway resting on the earth, with its top reaching to heaven,
and the angels of God were ascending and descending on it.
—GENESIS 28:12

Two thousand years after Jacob's vision of the stairway reaching to earth from heaven, a Jew named Nathanael was told by his friend Philip that he had found "the one Moses wrote about in the Law, and about whom the prophets also wrote—Jesus of Nazareth, the son of Joseph."

Nathanael was skeptical. "Nazareth! Can anything good come from there?" he demanded.

Philip answered by bringing him to Jesus. For a short while Jesus and Nathanael talked, and after that Nathanael declared his belief that Jesus was indeed "the Son of God" and the "King of Israel." It is in Jesus's reply to Nathanael's confession that we have the reference to Genesis. Jesus replied, "You believe because I told you I saw you under the fig tree. You shall see greater things than that. . . . I tell you the truth, you shall see heaven open, and the angels of God ascending and descending on the Son of Man" (John 1:50–51).

In this saying Jesus clearly applies to himself the image of the heavenly stairway. That is, when Jesus spoke of the angels of God ascending and descending on the Son of Man, he was saying that he is the ladder. He is the bridge that came from heaven to earth, the only bridge by which it is possible for men and women to pass from earth to heaven.

As we read the account of Jacob's vision at Bethel, we should think of Jesus, just as we should with all the great Old Testament events. And the concluding question is this: Have you seen Jesus? Have you come to know that One who alone has bridged the gap between a holy heaven and a sinful world and who has promised to be all things to those who trust and love him? You may be lonely, as Jacob was. You may be impoverished and unemployed. You may be disgraced and dishonored. You may be fearful. Whatever you may be, I direct you to Jesus. He is the ever-present companion of the lonely. He is the wealth of the destitute, the glory of the base, the rock and fortress of the one who is afraid. He is God.

Look! I think I see heaven opening and the stairway descending. I see angels coming and going. I see Jesus himself. He is here to be your Savior. He is here to serve you. Won't you look up and see him? You will be awed by the sight and you will go away saying, "Surely the LORD is in this place, and I was not aware of it. . . . This is none other than the house of God" (Gen. 28:16–17). This very spot will be your Bethel.

Limping Forward

Genesis 32:22–32

The sun rose above him as he passed Peniel, and
he was limping because of his hip.
— GENESIS 32:31

The picture here is of the patriarch limping forward to meet Esau, limping because of the wound inflicted on his hip. I ask, is this a pitiful picture? It is not, as anyone with perception knows. It is a strong picture, for now Jacob is moving forward at the command, and in the power, of God.

This is the significance of his new name. Before this, his name was Jacob, which means "heel grasper," "cheat," or "supplanter." God forced him to confess this (v. 27). Now Jacob's name is changed to Israel. I am convinced that the meaning of this name has been misconstrued by most commentators. Israel is a compound of two words: *sarah* (meaning "fight," "struggle," or "rule") and *el* (meaning "God"). Commentators have taken this to mean "he struggles with God" or "he prevails with God" because of verse 28: "Your name will no longer be Jacob, but Israel, because you have struggled with God and with men and have overcome."

In other cases, however, of names compounded from a verb and the name of God, God is not the object of the verb. He is the subject. Thus, Daniel means "God judges," not "he judges God." Samuel means "God heard," not "he heard God." If we are to follow the same principle of interpretation here, Israel means "God rules," "God commands," or "God prevails."

But what of verse 28, which calls the patriarch Israel because "you have struggled with God and with men and have overcome"? I think the verse is ironic. With men, Jacob had contended successfully . . . and lost. He cheated Esau of the blessing but lost Esau's good will. He outwitted his blind and ailing father but lost his good name. None of these victories had brought satisfaction, and now on the banks of the Jabbok, he is bottled up between enemies. He even has God for his antagonist. However, in his battle with God, Jacob suffers a reversal of his fortunes, which is actually his victory. He loses his wrestling match with God; God touches his hip and he is permanently wounded. But in the divine logic, which is beyond our full comprehension, this loss is Jacob's victory. For at last Jacob surrenders himself. He wins by losing and is now able to go on in new strength as God's man.

I love this picture of the limping Jacob, for it describes us. We limp, so far as our own strength is concerned. In the world's eyes, we are cripples. But God's strength is made perfect in our weakness, and it is when we appear weakest that we are strong. An army like that (even a single individual like that) is invincible.

God's Man

Genesis 37:28–36

Meanwhile, the Midianites sold Joseph in Egypt.
—*GENESIS 37:36*

W hen in Rome, do as the Romans do." The gist of that saying could have been spoken to Joseph, telling him that since he was in Egypt, he might as well do as the Egyptians did and adopt Egypt's religion and morality. But Joseph retained two great things in Egypt: his character and his awareness of God's presence. Joseph was no less moral in the loincloth of the slave than he was in the richly ornamented robes given to him by his father.

Joseph was constantly aware of God's presence, and it is this that gave him his character and kept him on track. When you read Joseph's story, do you ever notice that his speech is constantly filled with references to God?

When Potiphar's wife propositioned him, Joseph replied, "How then could I do such a wicked thing and sin against *God*?" (39:9).

When Joseph had been thrown into prison and the chief cupbearer and the chief baker of Pharaoh had dreams and related them, Joseph instantly replied, "Do not interpretations belong to *God*?" (40:8).

When he appeared before Pharaoh and Pharaoh asked for an interpretation of his dream, Joseph responded, "I cannot do it, . . . but *God* will give Pharaoh the answer he desires" (41:16). When he interpreted the dream, Joseph began by saying, "*God* has revealed to Pharaoh what he is about to do" (v. 25; cf. vv. 28, 32).

When he saw his brothers later and revealed himself to them, Joseph explained the past events by noting, "It was to save lives that *God* sent me ahead of you. . . . *God* sent me ahead of you to preserve for you a remnant on earth and to save your lives by a great deliverance. So then, it was not you who sent me here, but *God*" (45:5, 7–8).

Joseph said of his sons Ephraim and Manasseh, "They are the sons *God* has given me here" (48:9).

At the very end Joseph replied to his brothers, "Don't be afraid. Am I in the place of *God*? You intended to harm me, but *God* intended it for good to accomplish . . . the saving of many lives" (50:19–20).

His last words were, "I am about to die. But *God* will surely come to your aid and take you up out of this land. . . . *God* will surely come to your aid, and then you must carry my bones up from this place" (vv. 24–25).

God! God! God! God! This was the dominant theme in Joseph's speech and life, and it is this that made him what he truly was: God's man in godless Egypt. May that same awareness make you God's true man or woman wherever his own wise plan has placed you.

Boice, *Genesis*, Volume 3, Baker, 1998, 890–91.

God's Faithfulness
Genesis 40:9–23

The chief cupbearer, however, did not remember Joseph; he forgot him.
— GENESIS 40:23

The story of Joseph's being forgotten by Pharaoh's chief cupbearer leads to certain lessons, and the first is to *stop trusting in men*, all of whom are ultimately undependable. The Bible says, "Stop trusting in man, who has but a breath in his nostrils. Of what account is he?" (Isa. 2:22). That is, "Why trust a creature who can live only by taking one breath at a time? If he misses only one breath, he dies. Trust God, who is the eternal breath from whom all our little breaths come."

At one point Joseph must have hoped in man. But his experience taught him not to trust man, and he was delivered from the bitterness that overtakes many when they do trust others and are disappointed by them.

Second, allow disillusionment with man to *turn you to the love and faithfulness of God*. Men and women may forget you, but Jesus never will. The Bible says, "If we are faithless, he will remain faithful, for he cannot disown himself" (2 Tim. 2:13).

The third lesson is to *wait for God*. It is true that God does not always work according to our timetable. When God told the cupbearer through Joseph that he would be released from prison within three days, Joseph must have been encouraged to think that perhaps his deliverance would also be only days away. But God had not told him how long his confinement would last. He knew only that he was to wait on God and that in God's own time the bars of the prison cell would be parted.

In ancient Egypt, perhaps as early as the time of Joseph but certainly long before the Christian era, there was a fable that concerned the mythical bird the Phoenix. The Phoenix was believed to have a life span of five hundred years and to be reborn at the end of that time by returning to its birthplace at Heliopolis. When the Phoenix returned to Heliopolis, it was said to have built a funeral pyre for itself and then to have been consumed on it after it had died. It then arose from the ashes to live for another half millennium. That was only a myth, of course, though it was actually believed by most persons living in the ancient world and was even used by the early Christian apologists as evidence for the resurrection. But myth or not, it is a picture of that renewal of spirit and body that always comes to God's people in his own proper time.

Boice, *Genesis*, Volume 3, Baker, 1998, 959–61.

Having Our Mind on God
Genesis 41:25–40

Since God has made all this known to you, there is
no one so discerning and wise as you.
— GENESIS 41:39

When Pharaoh placed Joseph in charge of all Egypt, he did so because of two rare qualities in Joseph. First, he noticed that Joseph was "discerning and wise." This was a recognition of Joseph's character. Second, he noticed that Joseph was one "in whom is the spirit of God."

Pharaoh perceived that this young man had something he did not have and that God was its source. This is always the case. When a man or woman is touched by God, that person will inevitably be different from those unconverted people around him or her, and the change will be strikingly for the better. Oh, at first there may be resentment that the one whom God has saved no longer has the same values or does the same things as others, things that fill the mind and time of his or her former companions. They may say, "So-and-so thinks he is too good for us" or "She's making a fool of herself with all this religious nonsense." But in time the criticism gives way to admiration and even to the appointment of such a person to a position of great honor.

Pharaoh saw this supernatural character in Joseph. Moreover, he recognized its source and knew at once that this was the man he needed to guide Egypt in the difficult times ahead.

I wonder if people see this kind of character in us and if they recognize that it is God who has given it to us. The only way we will ever have that character (and the only way that others will ever see it) is if we have our eyes on God in all things. What happens if we see circumstances apart from God? If circumstances bring adversity, we complain and consider the world and those responsible to be unjust. If circumstances bring prosperity, we boast and think that somehow we are ultimately responsible. The one character is whining and unpleasant. The other is arrogant and intolerable. But if we have our mind on God, we see God in circumstances and trust him. Adversity strengthens and mellows us. Prosperity humbles us and draws us even closer to the Lord.

Just a dream? No, rather a dream sent by God.

Just a prison? No, rather an experience that a wise and loving God has deemed necessary for our maturing.

Just a job?

Just a friendship?

Just an accident? No, rather that in which the hand of God is working for our and others' benefit. The Bible says, "Those who honor me I will honor" (1 Sam. 2:30). Learn to honor God in all things and see if he does not advance you even in the eyes of others.

Reflecting on Sin

Genesis 42:17–22

Surely we are being punished because of our brother.
—GENESIS 42:21

Solitude! It is a valuable gift of God. In solitude people meet God. One thing solitude did for these guilty brothers of Joseph was cause them to reason spiritually. They thought as most worldlings do, namely: "It's a mechanical world; God does not exist or at least he does not intervene here. Who is to say that I've sinned? Who has a right to hold me to an accounting?" Then God did intervene, and suddenly the brothers' tune changed: "Surely we are being punished *because of* our brother. We saw how distressed he was when he pleaded with us for his life, but we would not listen; *that's why this distress has come upon us.* . . . Now we must give an accounting for his blood" (vv. 21–22).

Calamity is not always a proof of past sin. Still, if calamity has come to your life and God has used it to bring the memory of your wrongdoings to mind, you know that you cannot escape the moral consequences of your sin by quibbles. Never mind that some suffer innocently! Never mind that God works in some suffering merely to bring himself glory! That is not your case. You see the connection. You know you are guilty. You know that God is not letting you escape unscathed. He is buffeting you to bring you to repentance.

I speak here of the effect of solitude to encourage spiritual reasoning. For God uses solitude to "bring us to our senses." He reminds us of the connection between sin and its consequences.

But this is not the only way God causes us to reason spiritually. He causes us to reason about salvation also, saying, "Come now, let us reason together. . . . Though your sins are like scarlet, they shall be as white as snow; though they are red as crimson, they shall be like wool" (Isa. 1:18). As the brothers of Joseph thought about their past sins, those sins rose up before them like a horrible blood-red mass. They saw no hope of cleansing. They saw only a just and terrible retribution for their wrongdoing. It is the retribution we will see if we remain unrepentant. "Sin means death!" But God continued to work in them so that in time they freely confessed their sins and found salvation through the atoning blood of him who was to come. Christ's blood washed their red sins white. And they became, not merely redeemed men, but even revered fathers of the tribes of Israel.

You may not have committed the sins Judah or any of these others committed but you have sins of your own. Perhaps God is bringing them to your mind even now. You need to confess them and find salvation through Jesus, the Lamb of God, who takes away the world's sin.

The Purge of Self-Confidence
Genesis 44:16–34

God has uncovered your servants' guilt.
—GENESIS 44:16

It was precisely at this point, when their own self-confidence and self-righteousness were broken—not a moment before—that Joseph's brothers were healed.

Notice what happened. First, their relationship to God was transformed. Before this they had been running from him while covering up their sin. When he had made his presence felt through the return of their money on their first trip to Egypt, they acknowledged that he was at work: "What is this that God has done to us?" (42:28). But it was in the form of a question. They still had not openly confessed their sin. In this later story they recognize God's hand again: "God has uncovered our sin. God has won the victory."

In my judgment, this is the point in the story at which the brothers are actually born again. Before this they were unregenerate. From this point on they are transformed individuals.

Second, there is a change in the brothers' relationships to others. This is the central thing emphasized, and it is the purpose for which Joseph had constructed his entire strategy. Here the scene of the selling of Joseph into slavery was set up again. The brothers were in a position of relative control and power. Benjamin, the favored of his father, was in jeopardy. What would the brothers do in a situation in which Benjamin's guilt seemed to be established by the discovery of the cup in his sack? The steward said, "Whoever is found to have it will become my slave; the rest of you will be free from blame" (44:10). Would the brothers save their own worthless skins at their youngest brother's expense?

Thanks to the work of God, such a thought was not now in the minds of the brothers. Years before, they willingly sold Joseph. Now there is not one of them who did not wish that the cup had been found in his sack rather than in Benjamin's. And they did not abandon him! When Benjamin was taken back to Egypt, they all returned to Egypt. They were ready to offer themselves as Joseph's slaves.

Oh glorious transformation! Glorious to God, who alone is able to bring life out of death and righteousness to a sin-scarred conscience.

If you are still trying to run from God and turn aside his gracious intervention in your life, know that God will always uncover your iniquity. The Bible says, "Your sin will find you out" (Num. 32:23). If you have not been cleansed by the blood of Christ, do so now while there is yet hope. Jesus stands ready not only to expose but to forgive, not only to condemn but to cleanse and restore to useful service.

Come to Jesus

Genesis 45:1–13

> Come close to me.
> —GENESIS 45:4

Joseph called his brothers when they would have preferred to run from him, and he called effectively. Joseph had told them who he was, and they were terrified. But he commanded them to "come close" to him; and although they must have feared that it was because he wished to harm them, to their surprise they discovered that it was not an angry master who so called, but a loving brother. Joseph had turned them from sin; they were changed men. Now he was calling them with the sweetness of a powerful and embracing love.

So also is Jesus calling you. If you hear his voice, it is because he has already made you one of his sheep. And though he could have judged you while you were yet in your sin, he has turned you from it—it is why you hear him—and now he wants you close to him.

How does Jesus call? Like Joseph, who is a type of the Lord at this point also, Jesus usually calls in secret. It is when the attendants are put out and the Lord is alone with you in the quiet of your soul that you hear the still, small voice of God. Are you quiet now? Are you listening?

Second, I am sure that Joseph called his eleven brothers by name. Later on we are told that "he threw his arms around his brother Benjamin" and that "he kissed all his brothers and wept over them" (vv. 14–15). Can we imagine his doing that without calling their names? He would have cried out, "Come here, Benjamin. Judah, don't be afraid; come. Come to me, Reuben. . . ." So on with all the brothers. Jesus calls you in the same manner. Do you hear him calling? He is not calling your neighbor. He is not calling the person seated next to you. He is not calling your husband or your wife or your children or your parents. He is calling you. Hear him. Respond to him.

Finally, he is calling you as your brother, just as Joseph called his brothers: "I am your brother Joseph, the one you sold into Egypt." You have done that and more to Jesus. But that is of no account now. Jesus is calling you as your brother, who loves you and is willing to provide for you both now and for eternity. It is not hard to win a brother's love. It is not hard to enjoy a brother's true affection. The Lord is here. He is calling. Can you not respond to his call and draw near to him as you have never done before? He is telling you of his love. All he has done in your life has been for love. Can you not tell him you know that and love him too?

Reunion
Genesis 46:28–30

Now I am ready to die, since I have seen for myself that you are still alive.
—GENESIS 46:30

Nothing makes a good parent's joy greater than the success, particularly the spiritual success, of a son or daughter. And conversely, nothing makes a parent's heart break more irreparably than the spiritual shipwreck of a willful child. You who are children, be careful to honor your parents by your moral choices. If you have any compassion for them—any love for a mother, any love for a father—do not disgrace them by disgraceful conduct. Do your very best for Christ. Use the talents he has given you. And then, when you have achieved everything you can achieve, honor them at the same time you place your crowns of achievement at the feet of Jesus.

Parents, if the success of a son or daughter is the greatest of all earthly joys, strive to be good parents. Yearn to be a good mother. Take time to be a good father. What can it profit you to be president of the company or organizer of the most successful charity in town if your son or daughter is not walking with God but is instead going to the devil in high gear?

But I acknowledge this: children have a mind of their own, and it is not always possible for a parent, even with the greatest measure of faithfulness or the most selfless outpouring of time, to keep his or her offspring godly. Children will rebel. But since that is the case, do not cease to pray for them. From your perspective the situation may seem hopeless. But remember, it is not hopeless to God. With God all things are possible.

Jacob himself is an encouragement. He raised a large family, but except for Joseph (and probably Benjamin), they were not a godly family. But then God intervened. God brought the sin of the sale of Joseph to light and achieved a conversion in these brothers. God saved them, and Jacob's joy at his reunion with Joseph was intensified by this additional great blessing. In one sense the brothers were also part of this reunion, for they too had been lost and were found. They had been dead and were resurrected spiritually.

There are parents who have died without seeing the conversion of their erring offspring. But remember that the end is not death. The conclusion is still to be told, and it will be told in the day of that final grand reunion of all the people of God in heaven. In that day the years of our lives will seem to have been few and difficult, but the best will lie ahead. In that day all tears will have been wiped away, and we will be filled with joy, being from that moment on forever with one another and forever with the Lord.

Prospering in Egypt

Genesis 46:31–47:12, 27

> They acquired property there and were fruit-
> ful and increased greatly in number.
> —GENESIS 47:27

If you were entrusted with arranging the circumstances under which the people of God could best be "fruitful and increase in number," what circumstances would you provide? Probably you would choose Canaan—a land of some depravity, to be sure, but still a land with a few righteous men, like Melchizedek. Most important, it provided room to grow. Canaan was sparsely settled. There was room for wandering shepherds like Abraham and his descendants. There, if anywhere, people could grow to be a nation.

But for 215 years the patriarchs lived in Canaan, and during that time the Hebrew clan grew to only about a hundred persons. Under nearly ideal conditions the growth was quite slow. But in Egypt, particularly in the time of persecution, the growth was rapid. In Egypt the people increased to more than two million.

This is God's way, and it is seen not only in numerical growth but in spiritual growth as well. Consider the church in China. Before the Communist takeover in 1950, there were approximately 840,000 Christians. Four decades later, after the most intense persecutions and great suffering, the church numbered about 50 million. One Chinese leader wrote in reflection, "In my opinion, the church in China is growing by leaps and bounds because it has suffered for Christ's sake and has learned that suffering is central to Christian maturity and church growth."

Let's apply this to the American church. We have a false sense of well-being in the United States, because we have inherited the legacy of an older, more godly generation. We have great buildings, successful programs, television-type personalities. But the church is stagnant. Growth, where it exists, is often artificial, and Christianity has little impact on our decaying culture.

What is the trouble? One great cause is that we are clearly too materialistic. God said that we are to be in the world but not of it. Instead, we are very much of the world and not even in it to a meaningful degree.

What will happen? I suggest that God will allow hard times to come upon the American church. We will be attacked and harassed—as we already are in some matters. We will be forced out of the mainstream of society. We will be made to pay a price for our faith so that it becomes costly rather than beneficial to follow Jesus. That is not bad. Like the church in China, it will be in such circumstances that the strength of true Christian commitment will be seen and the church will begin to be fruitful and increase in numbers again.

Christianity is not something that requires ideal conditions to survive. It thrives best in hardships. In our hardships God's strength is made perfect in weakness, and godliness springs like a root from dry ground.

God with Us

Genesis 48:12–22

I am about to die, but God will be with you.
—*Genesis 48:21*

Jacob is dying. His testimony is that God has been with him all his days. That is a great thing. But as he dies, he looks on Joseph, Ephraim, and Manasseh, who would also soon have their hard times, and says that God will be with them as he had been with him.

I address three classes of people. First, there may be some like Jacob who are nearing the end of life. You can testify that God has been faithful to you. But as you look at what you are leaving behind, you see children and grandchildren as yet unconverted. You see problems for your sons and daughters. I ask, will God be less faithful to them than he has been to you? You have trusted God with your life. Can you not also trust him with the lives of your children? Will he not also bring your grandchildren to faith?

Second, I speak to those who are children and who are witnessing the passing of a parent or older relative. You are thankful to God for that life, but you are wondering if you can live as that father, that mother, that grandparent, or uncle or aunt lived. "God was adequate for them and their problems," you say, "but can he be adequate for me?" You know the answer: God is almighty and he is unchanged. He will be with you, just as he was with the saints of old.

Finally, I speak to those who think of this in terms of contemporary leaders and their passing. Jacob was the last of the three great patriarchs. We witness his departure, and we wonder if God will have another to replace him. We see the passing of a Donald Grey Barnhouse, a C. S. Lewis, or a Francis A. Schaeffer, and we wonder if God will raise up others in their place. What will happen to that work when the minister is taken? What will happen when a person who has been greatly used in my life no longer has the strength or ability to carry on?

The answer is, God will be with you. The time is coming when each of us must pass to glory. But God is faithful. Jesus has promised to be with his church until the end of the age. His name is Emmanuel—"God with us." He will never leave us until he has accomplished all that he has spoken.

Lion of Judah

Genesis 49:8–12

> The scepter will not depart from Judah, nor the ruler's
> staff from between his feet, until he comes to whom it be-
> longs and the obedience of the nations is his.
>
> —*Genesis 49:10*

It is impossible to overlook the fact that the blessings on Judah—praise, preeminence, and prosperity—are fulfilled supremely in the Lord Jesus Christ, who was born of Judah's line and is portrayed in Revelation as *"the* Lion of the tribe of Judah" (Rev. 5:5). Jacob referred to him explicitly when he declared that "the scepter will not depart from Judah, nor the ruler's staff from between his feet, until he comes to whom it belongs and the obedience of the nations is his."

Jacob told Judah that he would be the object of his brothers' *praise.* But is this not true of Jesus in the most exalted sense? Jesus has been given "the name that is above every name" (Phil. 2:9). To him "every knee" shall bow (v. 10). Jesus Christ is the ultimate fulfillment of even Joseph's dreams, for the sun and moon and eleven stars bow to him and to no mere mortal.

We see that Jacob prophesied preeminence for Judah. But whatever *pre-eminence* Judah rightly had has been eclipsed by Jesus. Jacob thought of his fourth son as a lion, tearing his enemies apart and dominating his kingdom. Jesus has done this preeminently. In the spiritual sense there are two lions in this world. There is the Lion of the tribe of Judah, who is Jesus, and there is the devil, that "roaring lion" who prowls about seeking whom he may devour (1 Peter 5:8).

Jesus has defeated that old lion, wresting his kingdom from him and freeing all those who throughout their lives were subject to his bondage. That struggle took Jesus to the depths of the pit. But from the pit he has risen up to assume the highest place. Today Jesus is King of Kings and Lord of Lords. He is our King and our Lord. He is preeminent in the universe and must be preeminent in our lives.

Finally, Jacob spoke of *prosperity* to come through Judah. Even that physical prosperity came through Jesus, for Jesus is God and "every good and perfect gift" comes from him (James 1:17). But more important even than physical prosperity is the spiritual blessing Christ brings. Jesus brings life out of death, love out of hate, joy out of sorrow, peace out of lifelong alienation. Thus, the one who has Jesus has everything, though he loses the whole world. And the one who does not have him, though he gains the whole world, perishes.

Being Godly in a Comfortable World
Genesis 50:22–26

Then you must carry my bones up from this place.
—GENESIS 50:25

Joseph's dying words declare whose side Joseph was on. Joseph lived in Egypt ninety-three years. During that time he must have seemed to be conformed to Egypt in every outward way. He served an Egyptian king. He bore an Egyptian title. He had married an Egyptian wife. He would have shared in every honorable form of Egyptian court life, politics, and trade. Yet Joseph was no Egyptian, especially in his heart.

Most of us are like Joseph. We do not have the luxury of a detached existence. We are in the melting pot of life, and we sometimes think that, because our lives are busy and our environments secular, we cannot live for God as "spiritual" people do. If we are inclined to think that way, we should remember Joseph. Joseph was surrounded by every secular pressure. He was a citizen of the world. But his conduct throughout his entire life, as well as his dying words, proved that he did not live for the material things life can bring, but for God and his kingdom and glory. If Joseph lived like that in his circumstances, we can live for God in ours. We can endure and triumph as those whose eyes see things that are invisible.

What keeps one godly in a comfortable world? Two things!

First, the invisible must be often, if not always, in our thoughts. If we do not fill our minds with spiritual realities, secular dreams will take true religion's place and our horizons will shrink to what is now but will surely pass away. The sense of God's presence will recede. Prayer will become unreal. If we would triumph, as Joseph did, we must think of God and his kingdom often, and we must associate with and encourage others who think the same.

Second, the invisible must be always in our wishes. That is, we must look for God's kingdom and pray that it might come, as Jesus instructed. Joseph did this. All through the long years of his Egyptian service, though his body was in Pharaoh's country, his mind was in Canaan and he looked forward to that day when his bones should be carried out of Egypt and be buried there in anticipation of the final resurrection and fulfillment of God's promise. Should we do less, we to whom the promises have been made even clearer and who have in addition the sure and certain knowledge of our Lord's own resurrection? If that resurrection is uppermost in our wishes, we will live for eternity now and will make a powerful impact on earth.

Boice, *Genesis*, Volume 3, Baker, 1998, 1269–70.

Lessons from Failure

Exodus 2:11–15

He killed the Egyptian and hid him in the sand.
—*EXODUS 2:12*

There is no reason, nor is it possible, to defend Moses's murder of the Egyptian taskmaster. In his speech before the Sanhedrin, Stephen tells us that "Moses thought his own people would realize that God was using him to rescue them" (Acts 7:25). But the results were different from his expectations. First, the people rejected his leadership. Then, when Pharaoh heard of his deed and tried to have Moses killed, Moses knew he could not survive in Egypt and fled the country.

Why did things turn out as they did? The obvious answer is that Moses needed to learn some important lessons before he was ready to lead the people out. But it is also true that we need to learn these lessons too. In the providence of God, Moses's plans were permitted to go astray so that we might be encouraged and learn from our failures when the same things happen to us. Thus we learn, one, "Apart from me you can do nothing" (John 15:5). We learn what we are capable of if we go our own way instead of God's. And we learn that we can do something utterly right one moment and something utterly wrong the next. Moses's choice to identify with his people rather than to enjoy the power and pleasures of Egypt and then to kill an Egyptian to try to be his people's deliverer is one example.

And then we learn that one failure does not necessarily disqualify us from future service. God knows us. He knows that we are only dust. But he also knows what he is able to do through us in Jesus Christ.

Finally, God remembers our faith, not our failures. It is remarkable that in Hebrews 11, that great chapter about the faith of the Old Testament saints, Moses is praised for his faith three times, and not once is his sin in murdering the Egyptian mentioned. In this great summary of Moses's life and faith achievements, not once does God bring up Moses's failure.

No more will God remember your failures. God said of Israel, "I will forgive their wickedness and will remember their sins no more" (Heb. 8:12). Isaiah said, "You have put all my sins behind your back" (Isa. 38:17). Your failures as well as your sins have been forgiven because of the work of Jesus Christ. Do you believe that? Then you will not let some past failure ruin you for what God has for you to do now.

From unpublished Bible Study Fellowship lectures.

I Am Who I Am

Exodus 3:13–15

God said to Moses, I AM WHO I AM.
—EXODUS 3:14

I am who I am!" This name is linked with the ancient name for God, Jehovah. But it is more than a name. It is a descriptive name, pointing to all that God is in himself. In particular, it shows him to be the One who is entirely self-existent, self-sufficient, and eternal.

These are abstract concepts, of course, but they are very important, for it is these attributes more than any others that set God apart from his creation and reveal him as being what he is in himself. God alone possesses these characteristics. He exists in and of himself; we do not. He is entirely self-sufficient; we are not. He is eternal; in our case there was always a time before which we did not exist. This means that his existence does not depend on anybody.

God's self-existence is a hard concept for us to grapple with, of course, for it means that God as he is in himself is unknowable. Everything that we see, smell, hear, taste, or touch has origins. We can hardly think in anything but these categories. This is the basis of our science, for we argue correctly that anything we observe must have a cause adequate to explain it, and we seek for such causes. But God is beyond understanding; indeed, he is the One who is beyond us in every way. This means that he cannot be known and evaluated like other things can.

The second quality of God communicated to us in the name "I am who I am" is self-sufficiency, which means that God has no needs and therefore depends on no one. God does not need worshipers nor helpers nor defenders.

The third quality involved in the name of God is everlastingness, perpetuity, or eternity. This is a hard quality to put in one word, but it is simply that God is, has always been, and will always be, and that he is ever the same in this, his eternal being.

When we notice that God is the only truly self-sufficient one, we may begin to understand why the Bible has so much to say about the need for faith in God alone and why unbelief in God is such sin. If we refuse to trust God, what we are actually saying is that either we or some other person or thing is more trustworthy. This is a slander against the character of God. And it is folly; for nothing else is all-sufficient. On the other hand, if we begin by trusting God (by believing on him), then we have a solid foundation for all life. God is sufficient, and his word to his creatures can be trusted.

Boice, *Foundations of the Christian Faith*, InterVarsity, 1986, 101–5.

One Lamb

Exodus 12:1–13

And when I see the blood, I will pass over you.
—*EXODUS 12:13*

I am sure you have noticed in your study of the Bible how often the New Testament writers refer to the sacrifice of the lambs in Israel as an explanation of the death of the Lord Jesus Christ. The apostle Paul writes, "For Christ, our Passover lamb, has been sacrificed" (1 Cor. 5:7). Peter remarks, "For you know that it was not with perishable things such as silver or gold that you were redeemed from the empty way of life handed down to you from your forefathers, but with the precious blood of Christ, a lamb without blemish or defect" (1 Peter 1:18–19). These references are not accidental. Nor are they merely examples of the choice of a vivid Hebrew image.

Why is the death of the Lord Jesus Christ described in this way? It is described in this way because God himself took this means to explain it. In some ways it was a lesson that God had been teaching throughout all the years of man's history. As far back as in the Garden of Eden, God had killed an animal in order to clothe our first sinful parents. Here it was a one-to-one relationship—one lamb for one person. On the night of the Passover one lamb was killed for each family—one lamb for several persons. Later at Sinai, when the law was given to the newly emerged nation, God taught that on the Day of Atonement one lamb could be killed for one nation. And years later when Jesus Christ was about to begin his public ministry, John the Baptist cried, "Look, the Lamb of God, who takes away the sin of the world" (John 1:29). One lamb for all humanity. Thus one lamb for your sin, however great or heinous it may be.

Where is your sin? How is it to be judged? It can be in only one of two places. It can be on you. In that case you must bear its judgment, and you are today in the same position as a first-born Egyptian or a first-born Israelite apart from the sacrifice that God has provided. You must be judged for it. Or—and this is the glorious possibility—it can be on Jesus Christ. In that case, he has already borne its judgment. He has paid its penalty. His blood was shed. He has become your Passover. If your faith is in Christ, then the angel of death has already passed over you, and there is nothing left for you but heaven.

Boice, *The Bible Study Hour*, August 1970, 23–24.

The Presence of God

Exodus 13:20–22

By day the LORD went ahead of them in a pillar of cloud.
—*EXODUS 13:21*

The cloud in the desert was unlike any other cloud that the world had ever seen up to that time or has seen since. It was called a cloud only because the Hebrew language of the time had no other word to describe it. Its appearance was that of a cloud in the daytime, but during the night it gave forth light and warmth so that it seemed to be a pillar of fire. Generally the pillar of cloud or fire was located in the center of the camp of the Israelites. But during the first days of Israel's march from Egypt, it moved behind the people so that it provided protection against the pursuing Egyptians on Israel's rear. And later during their march it went before them to lead the way.

The cloud was not only a reminder of God's constant protection and guidance, however. It was also a symbol of God's presence. For God was with his people, and the cloud portrayed it. God spoke from the cloud. He spoke from the cloud on Sinai when he gave the law to Moses. He spoke from the cloud when it was in the camp of the Israelites standing over the Ark of the Covenant in the Holy of Holies of the Jewish wilderness tabernacle. And it was from the cloud that God spoke in judgment against the various movements of rebellion during the years of wilderness wandering. At no time in their wandering were the people of Israel able to forget—whether they wanted to or not—that the presence of God went with them and overshadowed all that they did.

I wonder if you live your life with that understanding. Do you know that your life is under the constant and righteous scrutiny of God? You should, for it is equally as true for you as it was for them. And it should change your conduct. One of the great liturgical collects of the ancient church acknowledges this truth quite clearly when it says: "Almighty God, unto whom all hearts are open, all desires known, and from whom no secrets are hid, cleanse the thoughts of our hearts by the inspiration of thy Holy Spirit that we may perfectly love thee, and worthily magnify thy name." If we really acknowledged to ourselves the truth of that statement—that our hearts and our actions are open before him—how changed some of our conduct would be.

Boice, *The Bible Study Hour*, August 1970, 26–29.

No Other Gods

Exodus 20:1–6

You shall have no other gods before me.
—*EXODUS 20:3*

These verses make three points, all based on the premise that the God who reveals himself in the Bible is the true God:

1. We are to worship God and obey him.
2. We are to reject the worship of any other god.
3. We are to reject the worship of the true God by any means that are unworthy of him, such as the use of pictures or images.

At first glance it seems quite strange that a prohibition against the use of images in worship should have a place at the very start of the ten basic principles of biblical religion, the Ten Commandments. But it is not strange when we remember that the characteristics of a religion flow from the nature of the religion's god. If the god is unworthy, the religion will be unworthy too. If the concept of God is of the highest order, the religion will be of a high order also. So God tells us in these verses that any physical representation of him is dishonoring to him. Why? For two reasons. First, it obscures his glory, for nothing visible can ever adequately represent it. Second, it misleads those who would worship him.

To avoid the worship of images or even the use of images in the worship of the true God is not in itself worship, however. We are to recognize that the true God is the eternal, self-existent, and self-sufficient One, the One immeasurably beyond our highest thoughts. We are to humble ourselves and learn from him, allowing him to teach us what he is like and what he has done for our salvation. Do we do what he commands? Are we sure that in our worship we are actually worshiping the true God who has revealed himself in the Bible?

There is only one way to answer that question truthfully. It is to ask, *Do I really know the Bible and do I worship God on the basis of the truth I find there?* This truth is centered in the Lord Jesus Christ, as seen in the Bible. There the invisible God is made visible, the inscrutable knowable, the eternal God disclosed in space and time. *Do I look to Jesus in order to know God? Do I think of God's attributes by what Jesus shows me of them?* If not, I am worshiping an image of God, albeit an image of my own devising. If I look to Jesus, then I can know that I am worshiping the true God, as he has revealed himself. Paul says that, although some knew God, they nevertheless "neither glorified him as God nor gave thanks to him" (Rom. 1:21). Let us determine that this shall not be true of us.

Boice, *Foundations of the Christian Faith*, InterVarsity, 1986, 107–8.

Satisfying God's Wrath
Exodus 32:30–35

> But now, please forgive their sin—but if not, then
> blot me out of the book you have written.
> —*EXODUS 32:32*

Moses was offering to take the place of his people as a recipient of God's judgment, to be separated from God for them. On the preceding day, before Moses had come down the mountain, God had said something that could have been a great temptation. If Moses would agree, God would destroy the people for their sin and would begin again to make a new Jewish nation from Moses (see v. 10). Even then Moses had rejected the offer. But after having been with his people and being reminded of his love for them, his answer, again negative, rises to even greater heights. God had said, "I will destroy them and make a great nation of you." Moses says, "No, rather destroy me and save them."

He must have said this in great anguish, for the Hebrew text is uneven and Moses's second sentence breaks off without ending, indicated by a dash in the middle of verse 32. It is a strangled cry, a sob welling up from the heart of a man who is asking to be damned if that could mean the salvation of the people he had come to love.

Moses lived in the early years of God's revelation to his people and at that point probably understood very little. Certainly he did not know, as we know, that what he had prayed for could not be. Moses offered to give himself for his people to save them. But Moses could not save even himself, let alone them; for he too was a sinner. He had once even committed murder, thus breaking the sixth commandment. He could not substitute for his people. He could not die for them.

But there is one who could. Thus, "But when the time had fully come, God sent his Son, born of a woman, born under law, to redeem those under the law, that we might receive the full rights of sons" (Gal. 4:4–5). Jesus's death was not just for those who believed in Old Testament times, for those who sinned in the wilderness and for their successors. It was also for us who live today, both Jews and Gentiles. On the basis of Christ's death, in which he himself received the full judicial outpouring of God's wrath against sin, those who believe now come to experience not wrath (though we richly deserve it) but grace abounding.

Grace does not eliminate wrath; wrath is still stored up against the unrepentant. But grace does eliminate the necessity for everyone to experience it, including you.

Boice, *Foundations of the Christian Faith*, InterVarsity, 1986, 254–55.

The Merciful God

Exodus 34:1–8

The LORD, the LORD, the compassionate and gracious God.
—*EXODUS 34:6*

After Moses had interceded for the people of Israel so that God would not destroy them because of their having made the golden calf, Moses made three great prayers. His first request was that he might know God (33:13). He had been with God in the mountain twice for forty days at a time but he still yearned to know God better. This is a petition every Christian should make often.

Moses's second petition had to do with God's promise to send an angel with the people. Moses judged it impossible that he should lead the people without the Lord's very own presence (v. 15). The Lord heard this request and granted it.

Moses was a remarkable man, and one of his remarkable characteristics emerged now as he added a third petition to the two that had already been granted. "Now show me your glory," he said (v. 18). As God's answer makes clear, this was nothing less than a request to see God face-to-face in all his splendor, to see him unobscured by clouds or devices like the burning bush.

God replied that he could not show his face to Moses, because no human being can see the face of God and live. But he would reveal his goodness and proclaim his name to Moses, which he did by placing him in the cleft of a rock, covering the opening with his hand, and then causing his goodness to pass by. The text says, "Then the LORD came down in the cloud and stood there with him and proclaimed his name, the LORD. And he passed in front of Moses, proclaiming, 'The LORD, the LORD, the compassionate and gracious God, slow to anger, abounding in love and faithfulness, maintaining love to thousands, and forgiving wickedness, rebellion and sin'" (34:5–7). These words unfold the meaning of "the name" of God, expressed in his mercy to all who confess their sin and come to him.

This is one of the greatest revelations of God in the Bible, and it meant a lot to Israel. Exodus 34:6 is one of the most frequently quoted passages in the Old Testament. This is where David learned that God was merciful. He learned it from this great story in the Bible. Moreover, he was wise enough to base his prayer requests on it (see Ps. 86:5). So should we! Indeed, we have even more cause to do it, because we know how merciful God has been to us through the death of Jesus Christ. The mercy of God is seen at the cross of the Savior more than at any other place. It is the ultimate expression of mercy and the means by which God saves.

Pointing to Christ
Exodus 40:17–35

And the glory of the LORD filled the tabernacle.
—*EXODUS 40:35*

If we are to approach God "in truth" (John 4:24), we must approach God Christocentrically. This means "in Christ," for this is God's way of approach to him. Jesus himself signified this when he said to his disciples, "I am the way and the truth and the life. No one comes to the Father except through me" (14:6). This is a difficult point for many to accept, of course. But it is precisely because of the difficulty that God has taken such pains to teach that this is the way of approach to him. We see this even in God's instructions given to Moses for the design of the Jewish temple.

What was the original tabernacle? It was not an edifice of great beauty or permanence. It had no stained-glass windows, no great arches. It was made of pieces of wood and animal skins. Nevertheless every part of it was significant. The tabernacle taught the way to God. Take that tabernacle with its altar for sacrifice, its laver for cleansing, its Holy Place, and its Holy of Holies, and you have a perfect illustration of how a person must approach God. The altar, which is the first thing we come to, is the cross of Christ. It was given to teach that without the shedding of blood there is no remission of sins and to direct attention to the Lamb of God who should come to take away the sins of the world. The laver, which comes next, is a picture of cleansing, which Christ also provides when we confess our sins and enter into fellowship with him. The table of the "bread of the Presence," which was within the Holy Place, speaks of Christ as the bread of life. The altar of incense is a picture of prayer, for we grow by prayer as well as by feeding on Christ in Bible study. Behind the altar of incense was the great veil, dividing the Holy Place from the Holy of Holies. This was the veil torn in two at the moment of Christ's death to demonstrate that his death was the fulfillment of all these figures and the basis of the fullness of approach to the Almighty. Finally, within the Holy of Holies was the ark of the covenant with its mercy seat upon which the high priest placed the blood of the lamb once a year on the Day of Atonement. There, symbolized by the space above the mercy seat, was the presence of God into whose presence we can now come because of the great mercy of God revealed in the death of Christ for us.

The Gospel in the Law

Leviticus 16:15–22

The goat will carry on itself all their sins.
—LEVITICUS 16:22

The meaning of Christ's sacrifice was made particularly clear in the instructions for the two sacrifices to be performed in Israel on the Day of Atonement. In the first sacrifice a goat was driven away into the wilderness to die there. That goat was first brought to Aaron or to a priest who succeeded him. The priest placed his hands on the goat's head, thereby identifying himself and the people whom he represented with the goat. He confessed the sins of the people in prayer, thereby in a symbolic fashion transferring them to the goat. Then the goat was driven out into the wilderness. The description of that ceremony states, "The goat will carry on itself all their sin." The sacrifice points to Jesus who, like that goat, "suffered outside the city gate" in order to carry our iniquities away from us (cf. Heb. 13:12).

The other sacrifice was made in the courtyard of the temple, from which blood was then carried into the Holy of Holies to be sprinkled on the ark of the covenant. The place where the blood was to be put was symbolic, as was the whole ritual. It was called the mercy seat. Being on the lid of the ark, the mercy seat was between the stone tablets of the law of Moses (within the ark) and the space between the outstretched wings of the cherubim over the ark (symbolizing the place of God's dwelling).

Without the blood, the ark with its law and cherubim paints a terrible picture. There is the law, which we have broken. There is God, whom we have offended. Moreover, as God looks down, it is the law broken by us that he sees. It is a picture of judgment, of our hopelessness apart from grace. But then the sacrifice is performed, and the high priest enters the Holy of Holies and places the blood of the innocent victim upon the mercy seat, which thus comes between God in his holiness and ourselves in our sin. There has been substitution. An innocent has died in the place of those who should have died, and the blood is proof. Wrath is averted. Now God looks in grace upon the sinner.

Who is that sacrifice? He is Jesus. We cannot say how much those who lived before the time of Christ understood about salvation. Some, like the prophets, undoubtedly understood much. Others understood little. But whatever the level of understanding, the purpose of the law was plain. It was to reveal the sin and then to point to the coming of the Lord Jesus Christ as the Savior. Before God can give us the gospel, he must slay us with the law. But as he does so, he shows us that the law contains the gospel and points us to it.

Boice, *Foundations of the Christian Faith*, InterVarsity, 1986, 224–25.

A Time for Giving Thanks

Leviticus 23:33–44

Celebrate the festival to the LORD.
—*LEVITICUS 23:39*

Our lives are filled with many responsibilities. Our days are usually taken up with useful activities. Much of our time is spent working. We have five days a week for that, and for many of us the other days are filled with work too. Sometimes our days are taken up with fighting—not physically for most of us, but for causes or sometimes even against colleagues who want to cut corners or do something that is morally questionable at work. There is also a time for us to weep for sin, and we do sin. Most of us try to avoid such times. They need to be urged upon us more often than they are.

But the day of Thanksgiving is different. Work? Yes, but not that day. You will work on another day. Fight? Perhaps, but not then. There will be other times for that. Weep? By all means, but not on Thanksgiving Day. Thanksgiving is a day to enjoy what God has given.

In the biblical context, joy is never mere frivolity, however. We rejoice because of the way God has blessed us. Therefore, when we rejoice, as we do on Thanksgiving, we also remember God's manifold past blessings. And not only blessings from the immediate past, thanking him for the bountiful display of food he has provided, but also for all the blessings of past days—for years of faithful safekeeping, for constant provision of our needs, for spiritual treasures beyond counting.

This was a feature of the Jewish Feast of Tabernacles, because the instructions to construct temporary outdoor shelters was intended to remind the people of the days of the Exodus when they had lived in the desert in tents. They were to remember how God had brought them through the wilderness and had established them in the land of promise.

So let's keep this in mind too. The problem with mere celebration is that it tends to take over and push any serious reasons for joy from our minds. That ought not to happen. We are to be joyfully thankful. But one obvious reason for it is God's physical and spiritual blessings to us, our parents, and our children over many generations.

Thanksgiving Day should be for us a spiritual Sabbath, that is, a day of rest before God. Our world is trying to secularize everything. It is even afraid to call Thanksgiving, Thanksgiving. Instead it calls it Turkey Day, which is an offense to Christians and an insult to God. Let us not allow this to happen where we are concerned. Our day is not Turkey Day, however much we may enjoy the turkey. It is Thanksgiving, thanksgiving to God, thanksgiving to our most gracious God. No God is like our God. So let us always observe our day as unto the Lord and be really thankful.

From an unpublished Thanksgiving sermon, 1996.

Jubilee

Leviticus 25:8–13

In this Year of Jubilee everyone is to return to his own property.
—*Leviticus 25:13*

Jubilee was the year, occurring every fifty years, in which all land holdings in Israel were to revert to their original family owners. Nothing in our experience exactly parallels this year of Jubilee. But the intent of those laws and the principles embodied in them are eternally valid.

1. *We are not to set our hearts on accumulating riches.* The Jubilee laws did not prohibit an industrious Jew from prospering financially. In fact, there are many promises that, if the people obeyed God, they would indeed prosper. Nevertheless, Jubilee was a curb on massive land accumulation, especially at the expense of poorer families. It was a reminder that, although wealth can be good and can be well used, there are things that are more important than riches, such as families and protection of the poor. Jubilee was a curb on greed. We need to remember this in our highly materialistic and acquisitive society.

2. *All we have, we have as a trust from God.* The Jubilee principle was based on the ultimate ownership of the land by God. Everything we have as Christians, whether land or bank accounts, a job or merely personal opportunities and talents, has been given to us by God and is to be used faithfully to serve him. We are stewards of what God has given us, and a steward is accountable to his master for what he has. Are you using what God has given you for him?

3. *"Man does not live on bread alone, but on every word that comes from the mouth of the Lord"* (Deut. 8:3). It is not enough to put worldly goods in their proper perspective or even use them responsibly as God's stewards. It is also necessary to feed on the very Word of God, since it is only spiritual food that will nourish the soul, and it is the soul, not material things, that is eternal. Jesus expressed this at the time of his temptation when he replied to Satan's suggestion that he use his divine power to turn stones into bread, saying, "Man does not live on bread alone, but on every word that comes from the mouth of God" (Matt. 4:4).

The Jubilee year began with the sounding of the trumpet. One day the trumpet call of God shall sound for us, "and the dead in Christ will rise first. After that, we who are still alive and are left will be caught up with them in the clouds to meet the Lord in the air. And so we will be with the Lord forever" (1 Thess. 4:16–17). If you are cherishing this hope, you will set light value on the possession of mere earthly things and live for God and his Word. Are you? Will you? The time to do it is now.

From an unpublished Bible Study Fellowship lecture.

The Humble Spirit
Numbers 11:24–30

I wish that all the LORD's people were prophets and
that the LORD would put his Spirit on them!
—NUMBERS 11:29

For some reason, two of the elders of Israel were not present when the Spirit of God came upon the others. They had remained in the camp. But when the Holy Spirit came upon the others so that they began to prophesy, these two men, whose names were Eldad and Medad, began to prophesy too. This was reported to Moses; and Joshua, who was with Moses and had been his aid since youth, spoke up and said, "Moses, my lord, stop them!" (v. 28). He was fearful that Moses's authority would be diminished by Eldad and Medad's prophesying, and perhaps he also feared that their words would be disruptive.

Here the truly humble spirit of Moses is apparent, even before Numbers 12:1–3. For Moses replied in classic language, "Are you jealous for my sake? I wish that all the LORD's people were prophets and that the LORD would put his Spirit on them!" (11:29).

We need to learn from Moses. It is hard for us to rejoice in another's success or prominence, especially if the person's work is in the same field as our own—because we are jealous of his or her success. Jealousy is wrong and distasteful in many situations, but nowhere more than in Christian circles and over Christian work. Yet it is prominent in the church—pastors jealous over the success of other pastors, parachurch leaders jealous over the success of other ministries, lay workers over the prominence given to other believers. This ought not to be.

We should remember Paul, who took note of the sad bickering and rivalry among the Christians of Corinth and admonished them: "So then, no more boasting about men!" (1 Cor. 3:21). When some of the Roman Christians spoke against him, hoping to add to his trouble while in prison, Paul wrote, "It is true that some preach Christ out of envy and rivalry. . . . But what does it matter? The important thing is that . . . Christ is preached. And because of this I rejoice" (Phil. 1:15, 18).

It is true that some claiming to be led by the Holy Spirit of God have brought dissension into God's church. That must be dealt with in another way. But where the true Spirit of God is at work, there Jesus Christ will always be glorified (see John 16:14), and those who love him and desire his glory will rejoice. Indeed, in our day of even greater blessing, they will rejoice that "all the Lord's people" are indeed prophets in the sense that the Holy Spirit has come upon them to bless them and their gospel witness (see Acts 2:16–18). Rejoicing in the spread of the gospel, even while under personal duress and attack, is one sure sign of a faithful minister or teacher of the Word of God.

From an unpublished Bible Study Fellowship lecture.

Eyes on God
Numbers 13:26–33

We should go up and take possession of the land, for we can certainly do it.
—*NUMBERS 13:30*

Twelve spies were sent into the Promised Land. As far as the land itself was concerned, the reports of the twelve spies agreed: it was a land flowing with milk and honey, a good land. They even brought back a huge cluster of grapes, pomegranates, and figs as proof of the land's fertility. But this is where the similarity ended. Ten of the twelve spies added, "But the people who live there are powerful, and the cities are fortified and very large. . . . We can't attack those people; they are stronger than we are. . . . The land we explored devours those living in it. All the people we saw there are of great size. . . . We seemed like grasshoppers in our own eyes, and we looked the same to them" (vv. 28, 31–33).

Of all the spies, only two, Joshua and Caleb, thought differently. Caleb said, "We should go up and take possession of the land, for we can certainly do it" (v. 30).

The people of the land were the same, regardless of who was looking at them. The difference in the reports was due solely to whether the spies had their eyes on God, as was the case with Joshua and Caleb, or whether they had forgotten God, which was the case with the ten others. Some of the people of the land were giants; Caleb later asked to conquer some of them. But when the spies kept their eyes on God, the giants shrank to manageable proportions. The two spies were right to say, "We can certainly do it." Later on in the story, they add, "The land we passed through and explored is exceedingly good. If the LORD is pleased with us, he will lead us into that land, a land flowing with milk and honey, and will give it to us" (14:7–8). On the other hand, when the ten forgot God, the giants seemed overwhelming and they appeared to be grasshoppers in their own eyes.

The people of Israel decided to follow the majority report, forgetting God and despising his promise. For this they had to wander in the wilderness for the next thirty-eight years, until all who were over the age of twenty at this time died. This was a watershed moment, a tragic one. Nevertheless, it was a great moment for Caleb and Joshua. These two stood for God and his promises, and they were still operating this way nearly forty years later, when they again stood at the border of the land.

The only thing that matters in the long run is trusting and obeying God.

Boice, *Joshua*, Baker, 1989, 21–22

Look to Jesus

Numbers 21:4–9

Then when anyone was bitten by a snake and
looked at the bronze snake, he lived.
—NUMBERS 21:9

For the Israelites to be saved from their snakebites, the only thing required was that they believe God's word about the bronze snake and look to it as he commanded them. So also are we to look to Christ for salvation.

We are to do what Charles Haddon Spurgeon, that great Baptist preacher of the nineteenth century, did the day he was saved. He was only a boy at the time, but he had gone to a service in a Primitive Methodist chapel where a layman, not the regular minister, was preaching. The man had little learning and little to say. But the result was beneficial, for he stuck closely to his text, which was: "Look unto me, and be ye saved, all the ends of the earth" (Isa. 45:22 KJV). As Spurgeon remembered it, the man did not even pronounce the words properly, but that did not matter. The layman launched into his text, and his message went like this: "My dear friends, this is a very simple text indeed. It just says, 'Look.' Now lookin' don't take a great deal of pain. It ain't liftin' your foot or your finger; it is just, 'Look.' Well, a man needn't go to college to learn to look. You may be the biggest fool, and yet you can look. A man needn't be worth a thousand pounds a year to be able to look. Anyone can look; even a child can look. But then the text says, 'Look unto *Me*.' Ay! Many of you are lookin' to yourselves, but it's no use lookin' there. You'll never find any comfort in yourselves. Look to Christ. The text says, 'Look unto *Me*.'"

At this point he noticed Spurgeon and—fixing his eyes on him as if he knew the struggle going on in the boy's heart—continued, "Young man, you look miserable and you always will be miserable—miserable in life, and miserable in death—if you don't obey my text." Then lifting up his hands as only a good Primitive Methodist could do, he shouted, "Young man, look to Jesus Christ. Look! Look! Look! You have nothin' to do but to look and live." And Spurgeon did.

Have you looked to Jesus? If you have not, is your pride keeping you from it? Those things of which you are proud may be all right before others, but they are nothing before God. Can you see that? If so, then you can also see that if they are nothing with him, they are worse than nothing for you because they are keeping you from the way that leads to life and are dragging you to eternal death. Forget them. Look to Jesus. Find Jesus and know that in finding him, you will be justified before God and he will be pleased.

The Real Battle

Numbers 33:1–4

For the LORD had brought judgment on their gods.
—*NUMBERS 33:4*

A historian might look at the story of the exodus from Egypt and say, "Moses must have been a great leader, and the victory there was his victory. He succeeded in rallying the people to the point at which they were ready to leave Egypt." Another might conclude, "No, what we have here is not a great historical genius or leader, but a mass movement of the people." But neither of these would be correct. God tells us that, if we will look at the confrontation through spiritual eyes, we shall see that the battle was not so much between Israel and Egypt, or between Moses and Pharaoh, as between Jehovah, the true God, who moved Moses and Israel, and all of the false gods of the Egyptian pantheon, backed by a host of fallen angels who had turned from God as a part of Lucifer's original rebellion.

The battle was waged with great intensity. But the result was a total and uncompromising victory for Jehovah. Through that victory the power of Egypt was broken, the people of Israel set free, and a series of stern judgments enacted against the false gods who figure prominently in the deliverance story.

This spiritual perspective on the exodus may be questioned by some. But it is set forth in a very explicit statement in this text: "the Egyptians, who were burying all their firstborn, whom the Lord had struck down among them; *for the Lord had brought judgment on their gods.*" The last phrase is a clear statement that the real battle in Egypt was not a battle between Moses and the Pharaoh or even between the Israelites and the Egyptians. It was a battle between God and the gods. And the victory of the Israelites was actually a victory over Satan in which Jehovah once again brought the history of Israel back into the line that he had previously determined.

What then are the spiritual lessons of the plagues? First, that of all the gods of this world, both demonic and imaginary, only one God, Jehovah, the God of Israel, deserves to be worshiped. He alone is the true God, and he alone is all-powerful. Second, the inevitable result of any conflict with God is always disastrous to God's adversary. Consequently, it is utter folly for anyone at any time to resist or turn his back upon God. Third, those who have been called by God and stand with him can be assured of his victory, even though it may be delayed and even though it may take great courage to stand with him. If you are so called, then you may stand with him courageously. And you may rejoice in the strength of him who has permitted us to share in his victories.

Boice, *The Bible Study Hour,* August 1970, 3–4, 17.

Found Wanting

Deuteronomy 5:1–22

Learn [the decrees and laws] and be sure to follow them.
—*DEUTERONOMY 5:1*

As we look at the Ten Commandments, we find ourselves wanting. We have not worshiped God as we ought. We have worshiped idols, albeit of our own making. We have not fully honored his name. We have not rejoiced in the Lord's Day nor served God on it. We are delinquent in regard to our earthly parents. We have killed, by anger and looks, if not in more obvious ways. We have committed adultery by thoughts and perhaps in more cases than we care to admit by acts as well. We have not been truthful. We have wished for and plotted to get that which is our neighbor's.

Moreover, it is not just we who see our sinfulness at this point, though we do see it as the commandments speak to us. It is also God who sees us. For, as the author of Hebrews states, "Nothing in all creation is hidden from God's sight. Everything is uncovered and laid bare before the eyes of him to whom we must give account" (Heb. 4:13).

What will be his reaction? Not to excuse us, certainly, for God cannot simply condone sin however much we might wish it. On the contrary, he tells us that he will by no means clear the guilty. He teaches that "the wages of sin is death" (Rom. 6:23). What shall be done? We are guilty. We stand condemned. The judgment is soon to be executed. What can we do? Left to ourselves we can do nothing. But the glory of the gospel is that we are not left to ourselves. Rather, God has intervened to do what we cannot. We are judged by the law and found wanting. But God has sent Jesus, judged by the law and found perfect. He has died in our place to bear our just judgment in order that the way might be clear for God to clothe us in his righteousness. That is why the Bible goes on to say that even though "the wages of sin is death," nevertheless, "the gift of God is eternal life through Jesus Christ, our Lord." If the law does its proper work in us, it will not make us self-righteous. It will make us Christ-righteous, as it turns us from our own corrupt works to him who is our only hope, our Savior.

The Role of God's Word

Joshua 1:1–9

Be careful to obey all the law my servant Moses gave you.
—*Joshua 1:7*

The heart of Joshua's commissioning by God was to know his Word personally. There are four parts to this commissioning.

1. *Joshua was to know God's Word.* That is, he was to read it and study it. If the law of Moses was to be Joshua's guide, as these verses clearly indicate it was, then Joshua would have to know what that law said.

2. *Joshua was to talk about God's Word.* The text says, "Do not let this Book of the Law depart from your mouth" (v. 8). Clearly, Joshua was to be conversing about the Bible in his normal day-to-day contacts with family, soldiers, friends, and others who were part of the nation.

3. *Joshua was to meditate on God's Word.* Meditation is a step beyond mere knowledge of the Scripture or mere talking about it. Meditation implies reasoning about the Word and deducing things from it. Meditation has application as a goal.

4. *Joshua was to obey God's Word in its entirety.* The last element in this list of requirements is the most important. Not only was Joshua to know, speak about, and meditate on the law of Moses, he was also and chiefly to obey it. God said, "Be careful to obey all the law my servant Moses gave you; do not turn from it to the right or to the left. . . . Be careful to do everything written in it" (vv. 7–8).

Nearly everybody wants to be prosperous at what he or she is doing, yet most fail. What is the problem? The problem is that we do not follow the divine formula for success that was given to Joshua. According to the Bible, the secret of success is to know God's Word, speak about it, meditate on it, and then, above all, do it. In God's world there is no substitute for full obedience.

This was why Joshua was so successful. Joshua was a good soldier, but he was no more brilliant as a commander than countless others who have swept across the battle plains of world history. Joshua was a leader of men, but he was no more gifted at that than many others. Joshua's great secret was that he made it his job to know the law of God and do it. That is what we need today: not increasingly clever methods, still less increasingly clever people, but obedience informed and motivated by the living and abiding Word of God.

Boice, *Joshua*, Baker, 1989, 16–18.

Rahab's Faith

Joshua 2:1–16

For the LORD your God is God in heaven above and on the earth below.
—*JOSHUA 2:11*

Rahab's experience is parallel to that of everyone who comes to God through faith in Jesus Christ today. Joshua tells us that after Rahab had helped the spies and they had agreed to spare her and her family when the city was taken, they said, "This oath you made us swear will not be binding on us unless, when we enter the land, you have tied this scarlet cord in the window through which you let us down, and unless you have brought your father and mother, your brothers and all your family into your house" (vv. 17–18). Rahab agreed and tied the scarlet cord in her window.

We are Rahab if we truly understand her story. We were part of a corrupt, degenerate society in which we each had our own reprehensible sins. But God set his hand on us. He made his great saving acts in history known to us and then brought us into contact with his messengers and representatives. He called forth faith in us, faith by which through his grace we also laid our lives on the line. In a spiritual sense, we were called to repudiate our own people and identify with God's people. As a sign of that, the blood of Christ, like a scarlet cord, was spread over our homes and lives.

And now? Now we live in an alien land between the moment of our commitment of faith and the moment of the final judgment, which will be the time of our full deliverance. In this important interim we are to stand alone for God as Rahab did: we are to be God's people in opposition to the surrounding godless culture.

What if you have not done this? Then your state is the same as that of the citizens of Jericho. You look at the surrounding walls of your great secular city and say to yourself, *Surely I am safe here. The walls are strong. This city has stood for many thousands of years.* But inside, your heart is failing you for fear, and you know that a day of certain reckoning and judgment is approaching. Why shouldn't you be like Rahab? She had nothing but a verbal report of the mighty acts of Jehovah, and even that was a selective, limited report. You have the law and the gospel, the law that condemns you for your sin and the gospel that shows you the solution to your sin through the death and outpoured blood of Jesus Christ. Why should you live any longer under God's just wrath and condemnation? Why shouldn't you believe on Christ, turn from your sinful past, and take your place with God's people?

Boice, *Joshua*, Baker, 1989, 33–34.

Consecration

Joshua 5:1–12

Joshua made flint knives and circumcised the Israelites. . . . While camped
at Gilgal, on the plains of Jericho, the Israelites celebrated the Passover.
—*JOSHUA 5:3, 10*

The consecration of the people of Israel at Gilgal was made by reenactment of the covenant signs of circumcision and the Passover. This took place after the crossing of the river but prior to the assault on Jericho.

The interesting thing about this reaffirmation of the covenant is that it was the exact opposite of what worldly wisdom would advise. Worldly wisdom would have called for an immediate attack while the people of the land were disheartened and before they could make last-minute preparations. Instead, God called for a three-day delay while Israel observed the two sacraments. Moreover, the sacrament of circumcision totally disabled the army for a time.

On the one hand, this was the moment Israel should have attacked the Canaanite forces in Jericho. On the other hand, if the armies of Jericho had known of the circumcision of the Jewish army, they should have burst from their stronghold and attacked the weakened troops. Humanly speaking, the actions of the Jews were utter folly.

But the wisdom of God is not like human wisdom, and it was far more important that the hearts of the people be right with God than that they gain a momentary military advantage. That was what the ceremonies were all about. Circumcision was the mark of the covenant; it signified membership in the covenant people of Israel, just as baptism signifies membership in the covenant community of the church today. It was a divine seal on those whom God had chosen as his people, and it was a human response to the promises of God conveyed in that election. The Passover was a meal of remembrance, just as the Lord's Supper is a sacrament of remembrance for the church of Jesus Christ today. At Gilgal the people were to remember God's covenant, promises, and past acts of deliverance, in order that they might live as his people in the days that lay ahead.

We also need to learn that lesson. Americans are always anxious to rush ahead with some program, and the larger the effort and the faster it is executed, the better. We need to learn that this is not always God's way. What we do *is* important. But what we *are* is more important still. It is more important that God have our hearts and minds than our swords.

Boice, *Joshua*, Baker, 1989, 40–42.

The Battle for Jericho
Joshua 6:15–25

When the people gave a loud shout, the wall collapsed.
—JOSHUA 6:20

If you are a Christian, you are a soldier in God's army and are engaged in a war where many enemy strongholds need to be conquered. We see them everywhere. There are fortresses of evil in our land, in the church, and, we must confess, in ourselves. They are surrounded by high walls. The gates are sealed. They are manned by strong and experienced defenders. What are we to do against such ancient outposts of God's and our enemy? The answer is that we are to assault them in the way God has told us to wage warfare: by prayer, by the Word of God, and by our testimony. When we look at evil's forces, we may think the ancient weapons of the church are inadequate and we may be greatly tempted to abandon them and use the world's tools. This is a mistake. We need to listen to God and obey faithfully to the very end. When we do, then in God's own time, the walls of Satan's strongholds will tumble.

The apostle Paul wrote, "The weapons we fight with are not the weapons of the world. On the contrary, they have divine power to demolish strongholds" (2 Cor. 10:4).

The book of Revelation says of the saints' battle against Satan, "They overcame him by the blood of the Lamb and by the word of their testimony" (Rev. 12:11).

If you are not a Christian—if you are still in arms against the Lord Jesus Christ, the rightful ruler of this world and all in it—you must remember that the victory won by the Jews at Jericho, followed by the destruction of the entire city, is a picture of what will surely come to you in the day of God's judgment. You have shut your heart against God. You have manned the battlements of your life, and although you are trembling, you refuse to repent of your sin and turn to God for his cleansing. What folly! How can you hope to stand against the only sovereign God of this universe? If you do not come to terms with God now, if you continue to hold out, you will perish in the final judgment, and your doom will be just.

The Bible says, "Kiss the Son, lest he be angry and you be destroyed in your way" (Ps. 2:12).

Rahab did that. The Bible says that the Jewish armies "burned the whole city and everything in it. . . . But Joshua spared Rahab the prostitute, with her family and all who belonged to her, because she hid the men Joshua had sent as spies to Jericho" (Josh. 6:24–25). Her position was neither better nor worse than yours, and she was saved. Why should her experience not be yours? Why should you too not escape wrath through faith in the God of Israel?

Boice, *Joshua*, Baker, 1989, 56.

Dissatisfaction

Joshua 7:16–26

When I saw in the plunder a beautiful robe, . . . two hundred shekels
of silver and a wedge of gold, . . . I coveted them and took them.
— JOSHUA 7:21

What was it that led Achan to this sad act of disobedience? It began with
dissatisfaction. Achan was dissatisfied with the way God had ordered
the affairs of his life. Achan's mind was not on the blessings that lay ahead. He
was thinking of the past and what he lacked. Achan's dissatisfaction, which
was itself a sin, gave birth to disobedience.

This is usually the case. When Satan sinned by rebelling against God, it
was dissatisfaction with his position in God's world that led him to it. He was
the creature; God was the Creator. But he wanted to be like God. He said,
"I will ascend to heaven; I will raise my throne above the stars of God; I will
sit enthroned on the mount of assembly, on the utmost heights of the sacred
mountain. I will ascend above the tops of the clouds; I will make myself like
the Most High" (Isa. 14:13–14). Dissatisfaction was the root of Satan's sin,
and it was through his rebellion against God, who had made him what he
was, that sin entered the universe.

It was the same in the case of Adam and Eve, when sin first entered the
human family. God made Eve and Adam perfect in all respects. But when Satan
called Eve's attention to the fact that she and her husband were not "like God,
knowing good and evil" (Gen. 3:5), he sowed the seed of dissatisfaction and
laid the ground for his triumph.

Is this not our case also? I am not suggesting that any follower of Christ
should be satisfied with a second-rate course of discipleship, still less with
disobedience. There is a proper form of spiritual ambition. Even the apostle
Paul said, "Forgetting what is behind and straining toward what is ahead, I
press on toward the goal to win the prize for which God has called me heaven-
ward in Christ Jesus" (Phil. 3:13–14). But this very apostle, in the same letter
in which he spoke of pressing forward to win the prize of Christ's calling, also
said, "I have learned the secret of being content in any and every situation,
whether well fed or hungry, whether living in plenty or in want" (4:12). Paul's
secret was to strive for Christ's glory rather than his own and to be willing to
achieve that end through whatever means God proposed for him.

Boice, *Joshua*, Baker, 1989, 59–60.

Wholehearted Service
Joshua 14:6—15

[Caleb] followed the LORD, the God of Israel, wholeheartedly.
—*JOSHUA 14:14*

In his wholehearted giving of himself to God, Caleb contrasts with most of the other people of Israel during this period. Caleb was given Hebron and took it, driving the Anakites from the land. Sadly, this was not true of the majority of the nation, who did not entirely drive out the Canaanites. The land was theirs, the power of the Canaanites was broken, but they did not fully possess the possessions God had given to them.

Why was this? Again here is a simple answer: they did not serve the Lord wholeheartedly as Caleb did. I think they were probably tired of fighting and just wanted a little peace for a while. They wanted to enjoy the spoils of their battles. Their religion was becoming similar to that urged on so many professing Christians today. They wanted to be "saved, safe, and satisfied." Well, saved they may well have been, and safe too. But they should not have been satisfied to the extent of abandoning their commission. There were "still very large areas of land to be taken over" (13:1), and they were not to settle down in peace and prosperity until they accomplished that.

There are other things besides giants that can get our eyes off God and his service. We can get our eyes on peace, comfort, or a thousand other things that wrongly compete for God's place.

Do you remember those verses that come immediately after that great chapter on the heroes of the faith in Hebrews? Hebrews 11 lists many of the magnificent men and women of the Old Testament, those who contended for the faith and triumphed. We are inspired by such examples, and rightly so. But immediately after their stories have been told, the author of the book applies their examples of faith to us, saying, "Therefore, since we are surrounded by such a great cloud of witnesses, let us throw off everything that hinders and the sin that so easily entangles, and let us run with perseverance the race marked out for us. Let us fix our eyes on Jesus, the author and perfecter of our faith, who for the joy set before him endured the cross, scorning its shame, and sat down at the right hand of the throne of God. Consider him who endured such opposition from sinful men, so that you will not grow weary and lose heart" (Heb. 11:1–3).

I am sure there were times when Caleb was quite weary, but he did not lose heart; he had his eyes set on God, who was giving him the victory. No more will we lose heart if our eyes are fixed on our great Savior and Lord, Jesus Christ.

Boice, *Joshua*, Baker, 1989, 105–6.

Keeping Faith

Joshua 24:14–27

But as for me and my household, we will serve the LORD.
—*JOSHUA 24:15*

What would the people of Israel choose? Verbally the choice was clear. "Far be it from us to forsake the LORD to serve other gods!" they protested. "We too will serve the LORD, because he is our God" (vv. 16, 18).

True enough! But Joshua seemed to detect a note of insincerity, or at least glibness, in this predictable and ready response. He replied, "You are not able to serve the LORD" (v. 19).

The people were self-confident. "No! We will serve the LORD" (v. 21).

"You are witnesses against yourselves that you have chosen to serve the LORD," said Joshua.

"Yes, we are witnesses," they answered (v. 22).

"Then throw away your foreign gods," said Joshua (v. 23).

"Oh, yes," they said. "We will serve the LORD our God and obey him" (v. 24).

More words were useless. So Joshua took the affirmation as given, drew up a covenant between the people and God, and recorded the fact that he had done so. Then he erected a large stone as a memorial. Joshua had fought the good fight. He had finished his race. He had kept the faith. Now there was laid up for him that crown of righteousness that the Lord, the righteous Judge, would award him on that day—and not to Joshua only, but to all who love the Lord and long for his appearing (see 2 Tim. 4:7–8).

What more can any of us do? We cannot make others' choices for them; we cannot guarantee their future. In this case, we are told that "Israel served the LORD throughout the lifetime of Joshua and of the elders who outlived him and who had experienced everything the LORD had done for Israel" (Josh. 24:31). But in the very next book of the Bible, in the second chapter where this very verse is repeated, we are told, "After that whole generation had been gathered to their fathers, another generation grew up, who knew neither the LORD nor what he had done for Israel. Then the Israelites did evil in the eyes of the LORD and served the Baals. They forsook the LORD, the God of their fathers, who had brought them out of Egypt. They followed and worshiped various gods of the peoples around them" (Judg. 2:10–12).

That may be true in our case also. A generation from now, those who follow us may utterly forsake the Lord. They may go after the evil gods of our materialistic culture. *But we must not do it!* We must say with Joshua, "But as for me and my household, we will serve the LORD."

Ready for the Gospel
Judges 7:4–8

Separate those who lap the water with their tongues like
a dog from those who kneel down to drink.
—JUDGES 7:5

In Ephesians 6:15 we are told to have our feet "fitted with the readiness that comes from the gospel of peace." In my judgment the apostle Paul is emphasizing the readiness Christians are to have to make the gospel known. Any Christian already knows the gospel; he would not be a Christian if he did not. But is he ready to share the Good News with others at any time? Are you fitted with the soldier's boots that will carry you from place to place, ready to speak about Jesus?

I think here of that interesting battle involving Gideon, one of the judges of Israel. God told Gideon to collect an army and use it to drive out the occupying Midianites. So Gideon did. He collected an army of 32,000 men. Gideon probably thought that 32,000 soldiers were barely enough for the task ahead of him, but God told him that there were actually too many. So in obedience to the Lord, Gideon told any who were afraid to fight to go home. Over 60 percent, 22,000, left. Only 10,000 remained behind. Gideon must have been shaken by that. But still 10,000 soldiers are a large fighting force—if they are good soldiers. He might have thought, *Well, I suppose we can get by with these.*

God said, "There are still too many."

How many more can we spare? Gideon must have wondered. *Fifty? A hundred?*

God told Gideon to take the army to some water where they could get a drink. He was to watch them. He was to see which ones dropped down on their knees to drink, probably putting down their shields and weapons, and which ones stood ready for battle and merely leaned over to scoop up some water with their hands.

To Gideon's dismay 9,700 men knelt down, dropping their armor. Only 300 stood at attention and scooped the water up. But God took these 300 ready individuals and used them to defeat the Midianites soundly and drive them from the land (see Judges 7).

It does not take a vast number to do God's work, but it does take men and women who are equipped and anxious to share the gospel with others. Are you kneeling (or lying down) on the job? Or are you prepared "always . . . to give an answer to everyone who asks you to give the reason for the hope that you have . . . with gentleness and respect" (1 Peter 3:15)?

Boice, *Ephesians*, Baker, 1997, 247.

Our Kinsman-Redeemer

Ruth 2:17–20

That man is our close relative; he is one of our kinsman-redeemers.
—RUTH 2:20

According to Jewish law, property should remain within a family if possible. If a Jewish person lost his or her share of the land through debt or by some other means, a near relative (if there was one) was supposed to buy the property back. This person, because of his or her close relationship to the one who had lost the property, was a "kinsman," and if he was willing and able to purchase the property and restore it to the family, he became a "kinsman-redeemer." In some cases in which there was no male heir to inherit the property after the owner's death, the duty of the kinsman extended to marrying the widow in order to raise up heirs.

A kinsman-redeemer had to fulfill three qualifications:

1. He had to be a close relative (a stranger would not do).
2. He had to be willing to take on this responsibility (nobody could be compelled to do this work).
3. He had to be able to pay the ransom price; that is, he had to have sufficient means at his disposal.

These three conditions were fulfilled in the case of Jesus Christ, and they are best illustrated in the story of Ruth and her redeemer Boaz. Naomi realized that God was arranging circumstances so that Boaz could perform the duties of a kinsman-redeemer for her, in regard to her inheritance, and for Ruth, in regard to raising up an heir. When Ruth called him her kinsman-redeemer, Boaz was delighted, for it meant that Ruth was interested in him and had not, as he said, "run after the younger men, whether rich or poor" (3:10). As it turned out, there was another relative who was interested in the land but was unable to fulfill the obligation to Ruth, so Boaz willingly bought the land and married Ruth.

In redeeming us, Jesus did exactly what this beautiful story illustrates: (1) he became our kinsman by the incarnation, being born in the town of Bethlehem, (2) he was willing to be our Redeemer, because of his love for us, and (3) he was able to redeem us because he alone could provide an adequate redemption price by dying. We rightly sing:

> There was no other good enough
> To pay the price of sin;
> He only could unlock the gate
> Of heaven, and let us in.

The redemption of Ruth may not have cost Boaz a great deal, at the most only money, but our redemption cost Jesus Christ his life.

How God Chooses
1 Samuel 16:1–13

Man looks at the outward appearance, but the LORD looks at the heart.
—1 SAMUEL 16:7

In the first mention of David in the Old Testament, he appears not as a hero but as a youth who was for the most part overlooked by his family. This, of course, is a main point of the passage. For it is apparent, even in the most casual reading, that the author is emphasizing that the choice of David to be king was not man's choice but God's.

This is the first great principle of any spiritual blessing. The choice must be God's. If the choice were left to you or me to choose Israel's king, we would choose Saul or Eliab, Jesse's oldest son. And we would choose wrongly. Only God can choose properly. Hence, we shall experience blessing only in those actions and those deeds that originate with him.

Some people question why God cannot bless actions that originate with man. But the answer is made perfectly clear in the story. It is because only God can see a situation correctly. God knows what is in the heart of man. God knows the end from the beginning.

"The LORD does not look at the things man looks at. Man looks at the outward appearance, but the LORD looks at the heart." These words are not only a statement of the clearness of God's vision and his capacity to judge, they are also a statement of our limitations. And, of course, this is the crux of the problem. It is not just that God can see clearly. It is that God *alone* can see clearly. At best we see only the outward appearances.

The choice of a person for any spiritual work must be God's. Not only are you and I unable to see a man's heart, there is also the fact that even if we could see it, we cannot assess it properly, due to sin. Like a bad camera lens, sin distorts and inverts our vision.

There is an application here that we should not miss. If we really cannot see as God sees, and if we cannot assess the heart as God assesses it, then it must follow that, when God chooses people for spiritual work, the people themselves may come from what are to us the most unexpected places. We will not often find them among the great of the earth or those who commend themselves to us for their intellect, bearing, or outstanding qualities of leadership. When we look for capable leaders, we look up. God says, "When I look for a man who is to serve me faithfully, I look low down" (see 1 Cor. 1:27–29).

Boice, *Ordinary Men Called by God*, Kregel, 1982, 104–6.

David's Secret
2 Samuel 5:1–10

David became greater and greater, for the LORD God of hosts was with him.
—2 *SAMUEL 5:10 NASB*

David's secret of success was that he kept his eyes on the Lord. David looked to the Lord and obeyed.

Let me illustrate this by a story. One summer, when I was just a boy, my family and I were in California with Dr. Donald Grey Barnhouse on one of the *Eternity* magazine tours. In the course of the tour, a day came when we were free from other activities. So a number of us went to an amusement park. In this amusement park there was a very large barrel, about seven feet in diameter and about thirty feet long. It lay on its side and revolved. The challenge was to walk through this barrel without falling down and tumbling about in the bottom. This was a challenge to us all, but it was particularly a challenge to Dr. Barnhouse. He started in. He was in about two or three yards when his feet began to get higher than his center of gravity and down he went. There he was, rolling around in the bottom of this barrel.

The man who ran the barrel, and who sat at a little desk at one end of it, shut the barrel off, and Dr. Barnhouse came out again. He was very upset that he had not made it to the other end. So he said, "I'm going to do it again. Start it up." The man who controlled the barrel said, "Wait a minute. First, you should know that there is a secret for walking through the barrel. Do you see that mirror at the other end of the barrel?" "Yes." "What do you see in the mirror?" "I see you," Dr. Barnhouse replied. "That's right," the operator said, "you see me. Now this time, when you start through the barrel, forget that the barrel is turning, and instead of looking at the barrel, look at me in the mirror. That will give you a true sense of the vertical. And you will be able to adjust your steps and keep from falling." So the barrel was started. And this time, Dr. Barnhouse and all the rest of us walked through triumphantly.

What was the secret? The secret was in keeping our eye on the man in the mirror who ran the barrel. You already see the point of the story. Who is it who runs the affairs of this life with all its ups and downs, crises, joys, and disappointments that we all experience? The answer is God! Who has it all under control? God! How, then, is the Christian to get through the affairs of this life without losing his balance spiritually? By keeping his eyes on God!

Boice, *The Bible Study Hour*, August 1971, 15–16.

The God Who Knows
2 Samuel 7:18–29

What more can David say to you? For you know
your servant, O Sovereign LORD.
—*2 SAMUEL 7:20*

Because God knows all things, he knows the worst about us and yet has loved us and saved us. In human relationships we often fear that something in us might come to light to break the relationship. Otherwise why would we be so careful to put our best face with other people? But God already knows the worst about us and nevertheless continues to demonstrate his love. He "knows our frame" and "remembers that we are dust" (Ps. 103:14 NKJV). We needn't fear that something within us will rise up to startle God, that some forgotten skeleton will come tumbling out of our closet to expose our shameful past, or that some informer will speak out against us to bring shame. Nothing can happen that isn't already known to God.

Not only does God know the worst about us, he also knows the best about us, even though that best may be unknown to any other person. There are times in our lives when we do very well at something and yet find that we go unnoticed. Or we do as well as we possibly can but we fail. What we have done is therefore misinterpreted. There is comfort in knowing that God, who knows all things, also knows us and knows that we really did do the best of which we were capable. And he does not judge us. He does not condemn us.

God knows what he is going to make of us. He knows the end we have been made for and he is most certainly going to bring us to it in his own proper time. That end is spelled out in Romans 8:29. "For those whom He foreknew, He also predestined to become conformed to the image of His Son" (NASB). God is determined to make us like Jesus Christ.

We get discouraged in the Christian life, and with good cause. We take a step forward and fall half a step back. We succeed once but then we fail twice. We overcome temptation but we also fall in temptation, sometimes over and over again. We say, "Oh, I'm not making progress at all. I'm doing worse this year than last year. God must be discouraged with me." But God is not discouraged with us. That is the point. God knows everything. So while it is true that he is fully aware of our failures and victories, few as the victories may be, he is also aware of far more than that. He is aware of what we will one day be when by his grace we are fully conformed to the image of Jesus Christ. It is a sure thing. So we should take confidence in that, even though the discouragements are many and real. We have a great destiny.

Boice, *Foundations of the Christian Faith*, InterVarsity, 1986, 138–40.

Not Alone

1 Kings 19:9–18

> Yet I reserve seven thousand in Israel—all whose knees have not
> bowed down to Baal and all whose mouths have not kissed him.
> —*1 KINGS 19:18*

Have you ever felt that you have seriously tried to serve God and have done so for many years, but that it is difficult? Have you felt that, although *everything* may not be against you, at least *no one* is standing with you or serving with you to share the burden?

Elijah felt that. He had stood against the wickedness of King Ahab. He had been used of God to declare a rainless period of three years. He had confronted the Baal priests, calling down fire upon an altar. After this the prophets of Baal were killed, and the period of drought in Israel ended.

We would expect that the triumph would have left Elijah thankful and exhilarated. But this was not the case. Like so many of us after the end of some great struggle of our lives, Elijah felt let down and discouraged. Ahab and his evil wife, Jezebel, threatened to kill him for having killed the false priests, and Elijah had to flee. The next time we see him, he is in a cave at Mount Horeb in Sinai, where he had fled for his life.

Elijah prayed to God: "I have been very zealous for the LORD God Almighty. The Israelites have rejected your covenant, broken down your altars, and put your prophets to death with the sword. I am the only one left, and now they are trying to kill me too" (v. 10).

He repeated the same self-pitying complaint: "I have been very zealous for the LORD God Almighty. The Israelites have rejected your covenant, broken down your altars, and put your prophets to death with the sword. I am the only one left, and now they are trying to kill me too" (v. 14).

At this point God revealed that he had chosen another king to replace Ahab: Jehu the son of Nimshi. He had chosen another man to help and eventually succeed Elijah as Israel's prophet: Elisha the son of Shaphat. Elijah was to anoint both to these roles. Then God said: "Yet I reserve seven thousand in Israel—all whose knees have not bowed down to Baal and all whose mouths have not kissed him."

Today you may seem to be alone in your determination to live for God in this wicked, spiritually hostile world. You may believe that everything and everyone is against you. But this is not the case. You are not alone. God is with you—he alone is greater than any opponent you may face—and in addition to God himself there are also thousands who have not and will not bow their knees to the pagan gods of our culture. Let that encourage and lift your spirits.

No Substitute for Obedience

2 Kings 5:1–18

So he went down and dipped himself in the Jordan seven times, as the man of God had told him.
—2 KINGS 5:14

The thing that most honors God and that God most delights to honor is obedience. And it is to be an obedience to the end. I highlight this because of our frequent failure to continue on this path. I think of what must have happened after the Syrian general Naaman had been told by Elisha that he would be cured of his leprosy if he bathed in the Jordan River seven times. We know he did not like the idea, because he protested about the inferiority of the Jordan River to the rivers of his own country. "I thought that he would surely come out to me and stand and call on the name of the LORD his God, wave his hand over the spot and cure me of my leprosy. Are not Abana and Pharpar, the rivers of Damascus, better than any of the waters of Israel? Couldn't I wash in them and be cleansed?" Naaman asked (vv. 11–12).

It must have been a great trial to this proud general to wash in Jordan's muddy waters *seven* times, and I can imagine him objecting to his servant who, in this story, had more spiritual sense than Naaman had. After he had bathed once, Naaman would have protested: "Look, I bathed in the river, but I am just as I was before. Nothing happened."

"The prophet said you had to bathe seven times," the servant would have answered.

After the second immersion, the protest would have been the same. There was not even the slightest hint that the method was working. Not a single spot had cleared up. The only difference was that the general was wet and muddy. So on after the third washing and the fourth and the fifth and the sixth. "Nothing is happening," the angry Naaman would have declared.

"You've only dipped yourself in the water six times," the servant would have said. "The prophet said seven." It was only after the seventh washing, after total obedience to the very end, that "his flesh was restored and became clean like that of a young boy" (v. 14).

We need to learn the lesson that Naaman the Syrian learned in the muddy Jordan River. Not only is there no substitute for obedience to God, there is no substitute for obedience in all particulars—to the very end. And when God does not act as quickly as we think he should or in precisely the way we are convinced he should act, we are still not justified in pulling back or adopting an alternative procedure. We need to listen to God and obey faithfully to the very end. When we do, then in God's own time, the walls of Satan's strongholds will tumble.

Boice, *Joshua*, Baker, 1989, 54–55.

If God Be for Us

2 Kings 6:11–17

> Do not be afraid. . . . Those who are with us are
> more than those who are with them.
> —2 KINGS 6:16

It is having a God like this that transforms opposition for God's people. For it is not that we do not face spiritual enemies. We do! It is rather that we have a God who is greater than any circumstances and all enemies and who promises to be with us, bless us, and keep us through everything.

When the servant of Elisha saw the Aramean armies, he was terrified. We can see him dropping his water jug, running back up the path to the city, bursting through the gates, finding Elisha, and exclaiming, "Oh, my lord, what shall we do?" (v. 15).

Elisha was calm. "Don't be afraid," he answered. "Those who are with us are more than those who are with them." At this point Elisha asked God to open the eyes of the servant, and when God did so, the young man saw the hills full of horses and chariots of fire all around Elisha. The end of the story shows how, when the armies of Aram began to move against Elisha, God struck the soldiers with blindness and Elisha led them in their blind state into the armed city of Samaria, where they were captured by Israel's king.

What is it that surrounds us? Is it the world with all its temptations and ensnarements? The flesh with its lusts? The devil with his malicious hatreds and eternal enmity against God? It does not matter: "*Those who are with us are more than those who are with them.*"

"But I am in sore straits, O Lord, and in misfortune; no one regards me, no one gives me anything, all blame me and speak ill of me."

"*Those who are with us are more than those who are with them.*"

"But Lord, Joseph is no more and Simeon is no more, and now they want to take away Benjamin."

"*Those who are with us are more than those who are with them.*"

"But I don't see those who are on our side, Lord."

It doesn't matter. "*Those who are with us are more than those who are with them.*"

The one who is above all and who is on our side is alone sufficient; and if he is for us, who can be against us?

"He who did not spare his own Son, but gave him up for us all—how will he not also, along with him, graciously give us all things? Who will bring any charge against those whom God has chosen? It is God who justifies. Who is he that condemns? Christ Jesus, who died—more than that, who was raised to life—is at the right hand of God and is also interceding for us" (Rom. 8:32–34).

For the Glory of God

1 Chronicles 16:23–30

For great is the LORD and most worthy of praise.
—*1 CHRONICLES 16:25*

A number of you have asked what you can do for me in my illness. You can do what you are doing, which is to pray. For what should you pray? Should you pray for a miracle? Well, you're free to do that, of course. My general impression is that the God who is able to do miracles—and he certainly can—is also able to keep one from getting the problem in the first place. So although miracles do happen, they're rare by definition. A miracle has to be an unusual thing. I think it's far more profitable to pray for wisdom for the doctors and then also for the effectiveness of the treatment.

Above all, I would say pray for the glory of God. If you think of God glorifying himself in history and you say, "Where in all of history has God most glorified himself?" He did it at the cross of Jesus Christ, and it wasn't by delivering Jesus from the cross, though he could have. Jesus said, "Don't you think I could call down from my Father ten legions of angels for my defense?" But he didn't do that. And yet that's where God is most glorified.

If I were to reflect on what goes on theologically here, there are two things I would stress. One is the sovereignty of God. That's not novel. I have always talked about the sovereignty of God. God is in charge. When things like this come into our lives, they are not accidental. It's not as if God somehow forgot what was going on, and something bad slipped by. God does everything according to his will.

But what I've been impressed with mostly is something in addition to that. It's possible, isn't it, to conceive of God as sovereign and yet indifferent? God's in charge but he doesn't care. But it's not that. God is not only the one who is in charge; God is also good. Everything he does is good. And what Romans 12:1–2 says is that we have the opportunity by the renewal of our minds—that is, how we think about these things—actually to prove what God's will is. And then it says, "His good, pleasing, and perfect will."

Is that will good, pleasing, and perfect to God? Yes, of course, but the point of it is that it's good, pleasing, and perfect to us. If God does something in your life, would you change it? If you'd change it, you'd make it worse. It wouldn't be as good. So that's the way we want to accept it and move forward.

Now our call to worship: I am going to read from 1 Chronicles chapter 16 . . .

James Boice's last words to his congregation.

Blessings of Sovereignty
1 Chronicles 29:10–13

> Yours, O LORD, is the greatness and the power and
> the glory and the majesty and the splendor.
> —1 CHRONICLES 29:11

Knowledge of the sovereignty of God derives great blessings. What are they? First, it inevitably *deepens our veneration of the living and true God*. Without an understanding and appreciation of these truths, it is questionable whether we know the God of the Old and New Testaments at all. For what is a God whose power is constantly being thwarted by the designs of men and Satan? What kind of a God is he whose sovereignty must be increasingly restricted lest he be imagined to be invading the citadel of man's "free will"? Who can worship such a truncated and pitiable deity? On the other hand, a God who truly rules his universe is a God to be joyfully sought after, worshiped, and obeyed.

Second, such knowledge of God *gives comfort to all who are in the midst of trials, temptation, or sorrow*. Temptations and sorrows do come, as we know. They come to Christians and non-Christians alike. The question is: how shall we meet them? Clearly, if we must face them with no clear certainty that they are controlled by God and are permitted only for his own good purposes, then they are meaningless and life is a tragedy. On the other hand, if God is still in control, then these circumstances are known to him and have their purpose.

Third, an understanding of the sovereignty of God will *provide encouragement and joy in evangelism*. How can one evangelize without this confidence? How can one propose to take a message that is so obviously unpalatable to the natural man or woman and have any hope of moving him or her to accept it, unless God is able in his sovereign grace to take such a rebellious sinner and turn him in spite of his own inclinations to faith in Jesus? If God cannot do that, how can any sane human being hope in himself to do it? On the other hand, if God is sovereign in this as in all other matters—if God calls whom he will and calls effectively—then we can be bold in evangelism, knowing that God by grace may use us as channels of his blessing. Indeed, we can know that he will use us. For it is by human testimony that he has determined to bring others to him.

Finally, a knowledge of the sovereignty of God will *afford a deep sense of absolute security*. If we should look to ourselves, we would have no security at all. For all about us—the lust of the flesh and eyes, and the pride of life—is stronger than we are. Yet, when we look to the strength of our God, we can be confident. To know the true God affords great security even in insecure times.

Boice, *Foundations of the Christian Faith*, InterVarsity, 1986, 122–23

If My People

2 Chronicles 7:12–16

If my people . . . will humble themselves and pray and
seek my face and turn from their wicked ways, then I
will hear from heaven and will forgive their sin.

—2 CHRONICLES 7:14

Do you feel the need to confess your sin to God? What then do we need to do? The answer is no mystery. It is clearly stated in this verse. These are the steps to God's blessing.

1. *We must humble ourselves.* By nature we are not humble. It is only when we come before God that we are genuinely humbled, for it is then that we see ourselves as the sinful and rebellious creatures we really are.

2. *We must pray.* We do not naturally pray. Why? Because we believe we are self-sufficient. This is why God often has to bring us very low. It is often only in the depths of life, when everything is crumbling around us, that we are willing to turn from ourselves to God and ask him for the help we need.

3. *We must seek God's face.* To seek God's face means to seek his favor rather than the favor of the world around us and to seek his will rather than our own. To seek God's face means a radical change in the use of our time, talents, resources, and lifestyle.

4. *We must turn from our wicked ways.* If we do not think we have wicked ways, we will not turn from them—and we are fooling ourselves. When God brings the reality of our sin home to us, we will find ourselves distressed by sin and unwilling to rest until we confess it to God, find his forgiveness, and turn from everything that is displeasing to him. *Everything!* Not just the "great" sins. Not just the sins that have obviously gotten us into trouble or that offend others. All sins. God does not ask for 50 percent of what we are or look only for 60 percent righteousness. He wants all of us, and he insists on genuine holiness. We cannot serve God and sin too.

Is it difficult to repent? It certainly is! Nothing is harder or goes more against the grain of our sinful natures, but it is necessary for personal happiness and God's blessing. The promise is that if we will repent of our sins, then God will hear from heaven (he never turns a deaf ear to the repentant), forgive our sin (how much we need it), and heal our land.

Boice, *Nehemiah*, Baker, 1990, 104.

Method of Prayer

Nehemiah 1:1—11

I mourned and fasted and prayed before the God of heaven.
—*NEHEMIAH 1:4*

There is an acrostic for prayer that you have probably heard: ACTS. In this acrostic, *A* stands for adoration, *C* for confession, *T* for thanksgiving, and *S* for supplication. Each of these is present in Nehemiah's model prayer.

The first is *adoration*. It is expressed in this sentence: "O LORD, God of heaven, the great and awesome God, who keeps his covenant of love with those who love him and obey his commands . . ." (v. 5). It is a short statement but it acknowledges several great attributes of God: his sovereignty, love, and faithfulness.

The second element in Nehemiah's prayer is *confession of sin*. "I confess the sins we Israelites, including myself and my father's house, have committed against you. We have acted very wickedly toward you. We have not obeyed the commands, decrees and laws you gave your servant Moses" (vv. 6–7).

Nehemiah knew that the sin of the Israelites had caused the judgment of God that resulted in the destruction of Jerusalem. If Jerusalem were to be restored, it would need to be restored upon the basis of a confession of these sins. So Nehemiah is specific about them. Note that Nehemiah recognizes the principle of solidarity—he is one with the people, so his sins are their sins and theirs are his. Furthermore, Nehemiah recognizes that he is himself a sinner. There is no sin of the people that led to the fall of Jerusalem of which he is not guilty or is not capable of having done in the same circumstances.

The third element in this prayer is *thanksgiving*. It is expressed in Nehemiah's review of God's promises: "Remember the instruction you gave our servant Moses, saying, '. . . even if your exiled people are at the farthest horizon, I will gather them from there and bring them to the place I have chosen as a dwelling for my Name.' They are your servants and your people, whom you redeemed by your great strength and your mighty hand" (vv. 8–10).

The final element in the ACTS acrostic is *supplication*, which Nehemiah employs as a conclusion to his prayer: "O Lord, let your ear be attentive to the prayer of this your servant and to the prayer of your servants who delight in revering your name. Give your servant success today by granting him favor in the presence of this man" (v. 11).

A leader sees the needs of others and grieves over them. Nehemiah saw the need and wept. But even more important than his tears was the fact that Nehemiah prayed. More important than his friendship with people was his friendship with God, since it is God alone who is able to change hearts, move kingdoms, and provide for our many needs.

Boice, *Nehemiah*, Baker, 1990, 18–21.

Getting Right
Nehemiah 5:1–13

What you are doing is not right. Shouldn't you walk in the fear of our God?
—NEHEMIAH 5:9

We must ask of ourselves: What good is it to build great evangelical institutions, constructing walls against the "evil" of our opposing, secular world, if within the walls the so-called people of God are indistinguishable from those without? What good is it to preserve a separate "Christian" identity if Christians behave like unbelievers? To put it in sharp terms, we need to stop calling the world to repent until we repent ourselves.

Of what should we repent? There are scores of things, but a thoughtful consideration of this chapter of Nehemiah suggests two of them.

1. *Disobedience to the revealed law of God.* The nobles of Nehemiah's day were disobeying the teachings of Exodus, Leviticus, and Deuteronomy. Why is it that so many within the evangelical church take the revealed law of God so casually? It is no surprise that the world does this. The world does not receive the Bible as God's Book. But we do. We even maintain that it is inerrant "in the whole and in its parts." How then can we take it so lightly? How can we say, as I have heard many so-called evangelicals say, "But that [specific teaching] was for that day, not today." Or, "Well, we have to be realistic. Life just doesn't fit those clear-cut categories." We play loose with the Scriptures and we need to repent of it. We need to become people of the Book—in fact and not just in our profession.

2. *Putting our personal prosperity before other people's well-being.* That is what these nobles were doing. They were enriching themselves at the expense of poor people. May I suggest that the evangelical church has been doing this too—or at least enriching itself while disregarding its poorer members. The only times in history in which the church has been really godly and really strong have been times when it was out rubbing shoulders with the poor and helping them. Revival has always borne fruit among the masses. But most of us do not even know the poor. We will give contributions to help them, sometimes—if we are not asked for too much. But we are not a church of the poor. We are not even a church of the masses. We need to repent of our elitist dispositions.

What is our problem? Isn't it our love of money, the very thing that was causing the officials of Nehemiah's day to exploit those around them? Don't we put the good life for ourselves first, at whatever cost?

We need to repent of such wickedness. We need to get right within the walls before we build the walls higher.

Boice, *Nehemiah*, Baker, 1990, 64–65.

Under Covenant
Nehemiah 9:3–10:29

In view of all this, we are making a binding agreement.
—*NEHEMIAH 9:38*

Things changed radically in Jerusalem under the governorship of Nehemiah and the pastoring of Ezra. The people had been spiritually dead. Now they revived, and the changes that came transformed their nation and culture permanently.

What were the steps of this revival? The first stage was the reading, teaching, and hearing of the Word of God. The result of this was that the people were awakened to their sin. This was the second stage of the revival.

Ah, but many people have expressed sorrow for sin and acknowledged their distress without changing. That is why the third stage of this revival is so critical. The third stage is a formal commitment to change, expressed in a covenant. The text refers to it as "a binding agreement" to which the leaders, Levites, and priests formally affixed their seals, the equivalent of a signature.

The Christian church is of a divided mind about covenants. On the one hand, there are those who distrust them, primarily because they rightly distrust any human ability to keep covenants. "Whenever you promise God that you will do something, you are sure to break that promise," they argue. That is generally true, of course. At the very least, the reservations of these people warn us that none of us should subscribe to a covenant or covenants lightly.

On the other hand, it is impossible to write off all formal commitments. The very act of becoming a Christian is something of a covenant, for when we repent of our sin and turn in faith to Christ as our Savior, we also promise to follow him and serve him as our Lord. When we are baptized, we enter into a covenant. When we join a church, we make a covenant. In our church the promise is "to make diligent use of the means of grace, to share faithfully in the worship and service of the church, to give of your substance as the Lord may prosper you, and to give your whole heart to the service of Christ and his kingdom throughout the world." Why should other important spiritual steps be any different? Why should we not frequently determine to change for the better—and covenant to do so?

I suggest that you formally covenant to put God first in everything you do: order your marriage or family according to the Bible's standards, set aside one day in seven to worship and serve God in the company of other Christians, tithe your income for the Lord's work—and do whatever else God puts it upon your mind to do for him. And make it a lifetime commitment!

Boice, *Nehemiah*, Baker, 1990, 107, 113–14.

God's Favor

Esther 5:1–3

He was pleased with her and held out to her the
gold scepter that was in his hand.
—ESTHER 5:2

Esther became King Xerxes's queen after being taken from the home of her cousin and guardian, Mordecai, to live in Xerxes's palace. A great enemy of the Jews named Haman hatched a plot against the Jews in which Xerxes unwittingly signed a decree that would result in death for all the Jews in Persia. Mordecai got a message to Esther, telling her about the plot and saying that she must go to the king and tell him what was about to happen and prevent it.

Alas, there was a problem. It was a law of the Persians that no one could approach the king unbidden. If a person approached the king in the inner court without being summoned, there was only one result: death—unless the king held out his golden scepter to that person and thus spared his or her life. Even Queen Esther could not approach him without danger of being put to death.

Mordecai explained to Esther that she had undoubtedly been brought to her royal position "for such a time as this" (4:14). Esther agreed to go to the king. She spent three days in prayer and fasting, asking the Jews through Mordecai also to fast and pray with her. Then, at the end of her period of preparation, she put on her royal robes and stepped into the king's inner hall. The king was sitting on his throne, facing the entrance. When he saw Esther, he was so pleased with her beauty that he stretched out the scepter that was in his hand and thus accepted her. So Esther had access to the king, and through her, the Jews were eventually spared.

This is what has happened to us through the work of Jesus Christ and the application of that work to us in our justification.

But the parallel is not exact, and for us the result is even more wonderful. Esther was beautiful, and the king was pleased with her. But in our case, sin has made us highly offensive to God and we have not even tried to approach him. Still God has loved us. He sought us when we were far from him. He sent his Son to die for us, taking the punishment of our sin upon himself. Now, because of Christ's work, we have been brought into the palace where we enjoy God's favor and have continuing access to him.

The author of Hebrews puts it this way: "Therefore, brothers, since we have confidence to enter the Most Holy Place by the blood of Jesus, . . . let us draw near to God with a sincere heart in full assurance of faith, having our hearts sprinkled to cleanse us from a guilty conscience" (Heb. 10:19, 22).

Sudden and Certain Justice
Esther 7:3–10

So they hanged Haman on the gallows he had prepared for Mordecai.
—ESTHER 7:10

Mordecai was a Jew who worked in the court of Xerxes, the king of Persia. Haman was a high official. Most people deferred to Haman, bowing to him almost as if he were the king. Mordecai would not do this. Therefore, Haman hated him for the perceived affront and plotted to get him killed. Haman did this by a particularly nasty bit of anti-Semitism, telling the king that there was a race of people in the kingdom who did not obey the king's laws and were subversive. He got the king to approve a secret, sudden uprising against the Jews, while he himself prepared a gallows on which he planned to hang his great enemy, Mordecai.

Since Esther was present in the palace at this strategic moment, God used her to alert Xerxes to what was really going on and to expose Haman. Xerxes, Esther, and Haman were at dinner when she did this. She told the king of a person who was plotting to destroy both her and her family. The king couldn't believe someone would try to kill his queen. "Who is he?" he demanded. "Where is the man who has dared to do such a thing?" (v. 5).

Esther pointed to the man sitting next to her, saying, "The adversary and enemy is this vile Haman" (v. 6).

Haman must have been struck with terror like a man turned to stone. He was exposed—suddenly, and there was no escape. The king was furious, and that very day Haman was hanged on the gallows he had prepared for Mordecai. Poetic justice? Yes. But even more important than that: sudden and certain justice, just like that which will come on all who despise God and reject his Son and our Savior, Jesus Christ.

In the last chapter of Paul's letter to the Thessalonians, the apostle writes of the wicked, saying, "While people are saying, 'Peace and safety,' destruction will come on them suddenly, as labor pains on a pregnant woman, and they will not escape" (1 Thess. 5:3).

Whom Do You Trust?

Job 1:1–22

Have you not put a hedge around him?
—Job 1:10

God promises to shield the believer against Satan. A main point in Job's situation is that God had placed a hedge around him. Satan could do nothing to him until God permitted the hedge to be lowered a little in order to demonstrate Job's character; and God did this only with the full knowledge that Job would triumph and that all Job had lost would be restored.

Satan had charged that Job worshiped God merely for what he could get out of it. God had prospered Job. If God would allow Satan to take away Job's possessions, Job would curse God to his face. In presenting this argument, Satan makes an interesting admission. He admits that God is protecting Job: "Have you not put a hedge around him and his household and everything he has?" Presumably Satan had tried to attack Job before, but the hedge was in the way, and he was not able to do it. He makes his slander against both Job and God, but in doing so he admits both his weakness and God's faithfulness to those who trust him.

God replies that he is going to put the matter to a test. He is going to lower the hedge so that Satan may attack Job's possessions, but it is still going to remain high enough to protect Job personally. Satan goes off, lays waste the property, and kills the children. Job gets up, displays evidence of mourning, but says, "'Naked I came from my mother's womb, and naked I will depart. The LORD gave and the LORD has taken away; may the name of the LORD be praised.' In all this, Job did not sin by charging God with wrongdoing" (Job 1:21–22).

Satan made another accusation. He said that, although Job valued his possessions, he valued his life even more. It was not love of God that kept Job faithful; it was fear. Job was afraid for his health. God answers by lowering the hedge still further. Satan may touch Job's body but he may not take his life. Accordingly, Satan proceeded to afflict Job with boils. Job mourned the day he was born. But in all this, "Job did not sin in what he said" (2:10).

We are no different from Job, except that most of us do not have the strength of character he had. We are God's, as he was, and God is also our protector. God is our shield not only against our enemies but against Satan, the greatest enemy of all. There is nothing that Satan will ever be able to do to you that will not first pass through the will of God, who allows it only in order to bring about a spiritual victory.

Our Powerful Redeemer

Job 19:23–27

I know that my Redeemer lives.
—JOB 19:25

The word *redeemer* in Hebrew is *goel*. It refers to a relative who performs the office of a redeemer for his friend. We must visualize a situation such as this. A Hebrew has lost his inheritance through debt. He has mortgaged his estate and, because of a lack of money to meet the debt, he is about to lose it or has already lost it. In such a situation it is the *goel*'s duty, as the next of kin, to buy the inheritance; that is, to pay the mortgage and restore the land to his relative.

This is what Job refers to in his great expression of faith in his divine Redeemer, and it is why this passage must refer to Job's own resurrection. As Job speaks these words, he is in dire physical condition. He has lost family and health. He must have imagined that he is about to lose his life too. He will die. Worms will destroy his body. But that is not the end of the story. For his body, like land, is his inheritance; and there is One who will redeem it for him. Years may go by; but at the latter day the Redeemer will stand upon earth and will perform the office of a *goel* in raising his body. He will bring Job into the presence of God.

A second duty of the *goel* was to redeem by power, if this should be necessary. Abraham performed this duty toward his nephew Lot when Lot had been captured by four kings in a war. Abraham pursued the kings and recovered the prisoners and spoil. This is what the Lord Jesus Christ is to do, is it not? He will attack in power—we speak rightly of resurrection power—and will break death's hold. Now we look forward to the redemption of our bodies in that great and final resurrection.

Finally, the *goel* also had a duty to avenge a death. Imagine that an Israelite has been struck by a sword and is dying. The *goel* comes and learns who it is who has struck his friend and relative. Immediately he snatches up his own sword and dashes off to avenge the murder. Our Christ is likewise our avenger. We are dying men but we have a redeemer. Thus, we read of his future activities and triumph: "For he must reign until he has put all his enemies under his feet. The last enemy to be destroyed is death. . . . 'Where, O death, is your victory? Where, O death, is your sting?' The sting of death is sin, and the power of sin is the law. But thanks be to God! He gives us the victory through our Lord Jesus Christ" (1 Cor. 15:25–26, 55–57).

The Right Path
Psalm 1:1–6

Blessed is the man who does not walk in the counsel of the wicked.
—*PSALM 1:1*

When most people think of the results of upright or godly living, they think of rewards. That is, they think that if they do what God tells them to do, he will reward them, but that if they do not, they will be punished. But what the psalmist actually says here is quite different. He is talking about "blessedness," the blessedness of the man "who does not stand in the way of sinners" but whose "delight is in the law of the LORD." His point is that this is not a reward but rather the result of a particular type of life.

The poet uses two images to show the result of these two ways. The first is a fruitful tree. It describes the man who delights in the law of God and draws his spiritual nourishment from it as a tree that draws its nourishment from an abundantly flowing stream. The land about might be quite dry and barren. The winds might be hot. But if the tree is planted by the stream, so that it can sink its roots down and draw nourishment, it will prosper and yield fruit. This is the godly man.

The second illustration the psalmist uses is chaff, to which he compares the wicked. The wicked are like chaff in two senses. Chaff is worthless and chaff is burned. This pictures the futile, empty, worthless life of the godless, as well as their inevitable judgment.

If only those who are running away from God could see this! But they cannot, because they will not listen to God and the world is shouting the exact opposite of the Bible's teaching. The world says that to be religious is foolishness. Religious people never have any fun or accomplish anything, the wicked say. If you want to amount to something and enjoy yourself doing it, get on the fast track of sin, reach out for whatever you want, and take it. Be happy. That is what the world teaches. But it is all a lie, which is exactly what Paul calls it in Romans 1 where he analyzes this fast downward spiral (see v. 25).

In Eden, the devil told Eve that if she disobeyed God by eating of the forbidden tree, her eyes would be "opened" and she would be "like God, knowing good and evil" (Gen. 3:5). But she did not become like God; she became like Satan. And her eyes were not opened; they had been open. Now she (and her husband) became blind to spiritual realities.

Do not believe the devil's lie. Do not follow the world when it tries to draw you from righteous living by beguiling falsehoods.

God Our Shield

Psalm 3:1–8

> But you are a shield around me, O LORD; you be-
> stow glory on me and lift up my head.
> —PSALM 3:3

The first stanza of Psalm 3 is an expression of the crisis that has come into the psalmist's life because of the enemies who have risen up against him. The second stanza is a quiet expression of his confidence in God. What has produced this abrupt but obvious change? The answer is that he has turned his attention from his enemies to God.

When a believer gazes too long at his enemies, the force arrayed against him seems to grow in size until it appears to be overwhelming. But when he turns his thoughts to God, God is seen in his true, great stature, and the enemies shrink to manageable proportions.

This principle was illustrated by the difference between the ten and the two spies when they were sent into Canaan at the time of the Jewish conquest. Ten of the spies were overwhelmed with the stature of the Canaanites, especially the descendants of Anak, who were giants. They said, "We can't attack those people; they are stronger than we are. . . . We seemed like grasshoppers in our own eyes" (Num. 13:31, 33). The other two spies, Caleb and Joshua, said, "We should go up and take possession of the land, for we can certainly do it" (v. 30).

What was the difference? Had they seen different things? No. The land was the same. Both groups had seen the giants. But the ten looked only at the giants and forgot about God, with the result that they seemed in their own eyes to shrink to the size of grasshoppers. The two kept their eyes on God, and for them it was the giants who appeared small.

So also with David. As soon as David turned his thoughts to God, he was reminded of how strong God is, and his foes, even the formidable armies then flocking to the side of his rebellious son Absalom, seemed manageable. He tells us three things about God. First, God was a "shield" around him. God had been a shield for him on earlier occasions; he would prove himself to be so again. Second, God would "lift up" his head, even when he was severely cast down. Sin beats us down; God always lifts us up. We can expect God to do that for us, even if we do not see him doing it right now. Third, God "an-swers" the psalmist when he cries aloud to him. God always answers, though not always at once and not always as we wish.

If you are not fully aware of what you have in God—a shield against foes, a lifter-up of your drooping head, a responder to prayer—this is a good time to think about it.

In God's Thoughts
Psalm 8:1–9

What is man that you are mindful of him, the
son of man that you care for him?
—PSALM 8:4

Psalm 8 begins with a celebration of the surpassing majesty of God, and this places men and women within a cosmic framework. It is a way of saying from the outset that we will never understand human beings unless we see them as God's creatures and recognize that they have special responsibilities to their Creator.

The first thing that is asserted about man in Psalm 8 is his insignificance in the vast framework of creation. This grows out of the opening verses. For when the psalmist thinks of the glory of God exceeding the greatness of creation and thus thinks of creation, he is struck with how small man is by comparison.

I suppose this beautiful section of the psalm grew out of David's memory of lying in the fields at night staring at the stars, in the days when he cared for his family's sheep. Not many of us have this experience today. Most of us live where light from a city blocks out most of the stars' light. But if you live in the country, you know how majestic the heavens really are. This was especially true for David. In the east the air is very clear, and, for those who look up at them, the stars seem to be almost overwhelming in number and to hang nearly within reach of the outstretched arm of the observer. "What is man that you are mindful of him?" asked David when he recalled the stars' vast array.

Sometimes we experience this emotion too. True, we do not often have David's opportunities to lie back and wonder at the heaven's greatness. But we have our scientific knowledge and know, at least mathematically, much more than he. We know that the earth, which is vast enough, is only a small planet in a relatively small solar system toward the outer edge of one of the billions of solar systems in the universe. And we know something of the distances. We know that light coming to us from the most distant parts of the universe takes billions of years to get here.

How small we are in this vast cosmic setting! How astonishing that the God of this vast universe, the God who made it and orders it, should think of us and care for us!

Praise the Lord!

Psalm 9:1–20

I will praise you, O Lᴏʀᴅ, with all my heart; I will tell of all your wonders.
—Pꜱᴀʟᴍ 9:1

The tone of Psalm 9 is set by the first two verses, which declare David's intention of praising God verbally, with words and in song, and with his whole heart. Here we need to apply David's example to ourselves, for it is often the case that we do neither of these things. We do not praise God with our lips very much, if at all. And when we do, if we do, we praise him halfheartedly. In many churches the hymns are rather mumbled than sung, and no one under any circumstances actually praises God in words. It is more often true that Christians complain of how God has been treating them, carry on excessively about their personal needs or desires, or gossip. This should not be. Christian worship should be more like the exuberant worship of ancient Israel than it is.

Let me tell you about one thing I have started to do as a result of my study of the psalms. Recognizing that they are open in their praise of God (as well as emotive in their articulation of pain or grief), I decided to make a point every day of acknowledging God's goodness in some area to some person. That does not seem like much. But when I began to think along these lines, I realized how much time frequently went by without my having praised God for anything. And I discovered something else. Once I had begun to make a point of acknowledging God's goodness, I began to think of his goodness more often, and I actually developed a more positive and spiritual frame of mind. This is not mere psychological conditioning, though it works that way perhaps. It is actually a recognition (not always easy to achieve) that God is constantly active in our lives and that, as the apostle Paul put it, "in all things God works for the good of those who love him" (Rom. 8:28).

Later in the psalm David appeals for mercy so that "I may declare your praises" (Ps. 9:14). It is a way of saying that man's chief end is not to enjoy this life or even to escape the punishment due us for our many sins, but to praise God.

"What is the chief end of man?"

You know the answer: "Man's chief end is to glorify God and to enjoy him forever" (*Westminster Shorter Catechism*, question and answer 1). And those are not separate things. To glorify God is to enjoy him, and the enjoyment of God always results in the praise of his people. We never come closer to our true and ultimate destiny as redeemed persons than when we do that, just as David has done so beautifully in this psalm. So praise the Lord! Praise the Lord always and with your whole heart!

What Can the Righteous Do?

Psalm 11:1–7

For the LORD is righteous, he loves justice; upright men will see his face.
—*PSALM 11:7*

What can the righteous do? David looked around at the wicked. He looked up to God. Now he looks ahead, to the future, concerned at this point not with the destiny of his enemies but with his own destiny and that of all who trust God. This verse means: *because* "the LORD is righteous [and] loves justice, upright men will see his face."

This last phrase is an anticipation of nothing less than the beatific vision, the ultimate aspiration of the Old Testament saints: to see God face-to-face. Strangely, many commentators seem reluctant to admit this, pleading the incomplete and uncertain view of the afterlife Old Testament believers are supposed to have had. But although Old Testament understandings are obviously less developed than those of the New Testament, based as the latter are upon the resurrection and explicit teaching of Jesus, and although the idea of seeing God's face could mean only that the light of his favor will shine upon the upright, it is nevertheless hard to suppose that David is not thinking here of the believer's ultimate reward and bliss. Why? He has just spoken of a future judgment on the wicked: "On the wicked he will rain fiery coals and burning sulfur" (v. 6). What is called for now is a parallel statement of what the same all-seeing and just God will do for those who are righteous.

They will see God! How glorious!

Remember how Moses asked this favor of God and was told he could not see him? God said, "I will put you in a cleft in the rock and cover you with my hand until I have passed by. Then I will remove my hand and you will see my back; but my face must not be seen" (Exod. 33:22–23). "You cannot see my face, for no one may see me and live" (v. 20).

Yet this is what the Old Testament believers continued to seek. They pray for it many times in the Old Testament. Wishful thinking? Something nice, but actually impossible? Not at all. Because, when we come to the end of the New Testament, to the letters of the apostle John, who gazed often on the face of the earthly Jesus, we find him promising, "When he [that is, the heavenly, glorified Jesus] appears, we shall be like him, for *we shall see him as he is*" (1 John 3:2, italics added). The upright really will see God's face.

My God Is My Rock

Psalm 18:30–50

It is God who arms me with strength and makes my way perfect.
—*PSALM 18:32*

David describes in common terms what God's intervention meant to him personally. It meant, in short, that God provided for his every need.

The terms are physical. First, his feet: "He makes my feet like the feet of a deer; he enables me to stand on the heights" (v. 33). The words are almost identical to the ending of the book of the minor prophet Habakkuk (Hab. 3:19). Second, his hands: "He trains my hands for battle" (v. 34). Third, his arms: "My arms can bend a bow of bronze" (v. 34). Fourth, his ankles: "You broaden the path beneath me, so that my ankles do not turn" (v. 36). Interspersed with these acknowledgments are verses that say that God armed him with strength (v. 32) and gave him his own shield of victory (v. 35). As a result, David was always able to achieve a full victory over all his enemies.

Verses 37–42 describe the extent of these victories. They were complete and total. Then, lest the reader get the impression that somehow this was David's own achievement, verses 43–45 make clear that his victories were due to God's intervention and provision.

David was a king and a military commander, so he needed strength for and victory in battle. We do not usually need these things. But the principle holds true for us anyway, since, whatever we need, God, the same God, provides it. Is it wisdom? God is the source of wisdom, and we are told to pray for it. "If any of you lacks wisdom, he should ask God, who gives generously to all without finding fault, and it will be given to him" (James 1:5). Is it peace in the midst of trouble? God is the source of peace. Jesus said, "Peace I leave with you; my peace I give you" (John 14:27). Is it love? Joy? Patience? The Bible says, "The fruit of the Spirit is love, joy, peace, patience, kindness, goodness, faithfulness, gentleness and self-control" (Gal. 5:22–23). Paul wrote, "And my God will meet all your needs according to his glorious riches in Christ Jesus" (Phil. 4:19).

Wise people have found this to be true and have therefore learned to turn to God for their needs, rather than turning to the false promises of the surrounding evil world.

There is another interesting thing about these verses. David begins by saying, quite rightly, "As for God, his way is perfect" (Ps. 18:30). But then, just two verses further on, he adds, ". . . and [he] makes my way perfect" (v. 32). So it is! A life well-ordered is a life that follows after and is obedient to the Lord.

Responding to God

Psalm 19:1–14

O LORD, my Rock and my Redeemer.
—*PSALM 19:14*

The final three verses of this psalm are the climax of the psalm. For in them the psalmist applies what he has been learning to himself. They show that he has been learning.

His response to God's self-revelation falls into two categories.

The first is *prayer* that God will forgive his sin and deliver him from additional transgressions. Sometimes we treat forgiveness lightly, asking God to forgive us but not really thinking that we are sinners, at least not serious sinners, and treating forgiveness almost as a basic human right. It is clear that David does not do this. He is aware of sin's subtle nature and complexity, dividing it into categories: errors, which are wrongs innocently committed; hidden faults, that is, faults unknown to himself because so deeply ingrained in his personality, certainly not hidden to God; and willful sins, which are sins of deliberate presumption. The latter are probably equivalent to "great transgression" in verse 13. The psalmist also knows that he can never be fully aware of these sins in order to seek forgiveness unless God reveals their presence to him by the written law.

We remember the prayer of the tax collector in Jesus's well-known parable, for although it is less detailed, it contains the same essential elements. The tax collector prayed, "God, have mercy on me, a sinner" (Luke 18:13). We know this man was coming to know God and was really praying to God, because he saw himself to be a sinner, as David also did. The Pharisee did not.

The second part of David's response to God's revelation of himself is an *appeal* to God as his Rock and Redeemer. We are not only led to see ourselves as sinners when we study the Bible. The Bible also leads us to the One who is our only deliverer from sin. And, wonder of wonders, he is the same one who has revealed himself gloriously in the heavens. The heavens tell us that he exists and that he is all-powerful. The Bible shows that he is our Redeemer from sin, that is, the one who is able to break sin's bonds and set us free, and that he is the Rock upon which the redeemed man or woman can build and be kept from transgressions.

The Suffering Savior

Psalm 22:1–18

My God, my God, why have you forsaken me?
—PSALM 22:1

The suffering One cries out to God, believing that he has been forsaken by him, asking why he has been forsaken, and asserting that God is silent. He receives no answer (see Matt. 27:46).

The idea that Jesus could be forsaken by God has been so disturbing to so many people that various theories have been invented to explain it. Some have supposed that Jesus was referring to the psalm only to call attention to it, as if to say that what he was suffering was what the psalm describes. Others have argued that Jesus felt forsaken, when in fact he was not. In the final outcome, of course, Jesus was not forsaken. This is what the psalm as a whole shows. However, according to the teaching of the New Testament, Jesus was indeed forsaken by God while he bore the sin of his people on the cross. This is the very essence of the atonement—Jesus bearing our hell in order that we might share his heaven. To be forsaken means to have the light of God's countenance and the sense of his presence eclipsed, which is what happened to Jesus as he bore the wrath of God against sin for us.

How could this happen? How could one member of the eternal Trinity turn his back on another member of the Trinity? I do not know. I cannot explain it. But I believe that this is what the Bible teaches, so great was the love of God for us and so great was the price Jesus willingly paid to save us from our iniquities.

Now I ask, is this atonement, so poignantly described, for you? The hymn writer Charles Wesley asks:

> And can it be that I should gain
> An interest in the Savior's blood?
> Died he for me, who caused his pain?
> For me, who him to death pursued?

That possibility was so wonderful to Wesley that he composed his entire hymn around it, describing such love as "amazing" and the death itself as a "mystery" beyond the ability even of angels to fathom. Wesley knew that it was indeed for him that Christ died and that his only hope of salvation lay in that atonement.

> 'Tis mercy all, immense and free;
> For, O my God, it found out me.

The question is whether it has found out you. Have you trusted in Jesus personally? Will you do it? All you have to do is tell him that you trust him, saying, "Thank you, Jesus, for dying for me. I am ready to follow you as my Lord and Savior." If you will pray that prayer, you will find that Jesus has indeed made atonement for your sins. He was forsaken so you might never be forsaken. He bore your sins so that you might not have to suffer for them.

Boice, *Psalms*, Volume 1, Baker, 1994, 193–94, 196–97.

The Shepherd's Psalm
Psalm 23:1–6

The LORD is my shepherd . . .
—*PSALM 23:1*

Psalm 23 is a masterpiece throughout. But if ever a psalm could stand almost on a single line, it is this one, and the line it can stand on is the first. In fact, it can stand on only part of a line, the part which says, "The LORD is my shepherd."

What an amazing juxtaposition of ideas! The word LORD is the English translation of the great Old Testament personal name for God, first disclosed to Moses at the burning bush, as told in Exodus 3, and then repeated more than four thousand times in the pages of the Old Testament. The name literally means "I am who I am." It is an inexhaustible name, like its bearer. Chiefly, it refers to God's timelessness, on the one hand, and to his self-sufficiency, on the other. Self-sufficiency means that God needs nothing. He needs no wisdom from anyone else; he has all wisdom in himself. He needs no power; he is all-powerful. He does not need to be worshiped or helped or served. Nor is he accountable to anyone. He answers only to himself.

Timelessness means that God is always the same in these eternal traits or attributes. He was like this yesterday; he will be like this tomorrow. He will be unchanged and unchangeable forever.

He is the great "I am."

On the other side of this amazing combination of ideas is the word *shepherd*. In Israel, as in other ancient societies, a shepherd's work was considered the lowest of all work. If a family needed a shepherd, it was always the youngest son, like David, who got this unpleasant assignment. Shepherds had to live with the sheep twenty-four hours a day, and the task of caring for them was unending. Day and night, summer and winter, in fair weather and foul, they labored to nourish, guide, and protect the sheep. Who in his right mind would choose to be a shepherd?

Yet Jehovah has chosen to be our shepherd, David says. The great God of the universe has stooped to take just such care of you and me. This is an Old Testament statement, of course. But Christians can hardly forget that the metaphor was also taken up by Jesus and applied to himself, thus identifying himself with Jehovah, on the one hand, and assuming the task of being the shepherd of his people, on the other.

"I am the good shepherd; I know my sheep and my sheep know me—just as the Father knows me and I know the Father—and I lay down my life for the sheep" (John 10:14–15). So we are not stretching the twenty-third psalm to see Jesus as our shepherd and to apply the psalm to ourselves.

What We Seek

Psalm 27:1–14

Though my father and mother forsake me, the LORD will receive me.
—*PSALM 27:10*

David seeks from God what a child seeks from his or her parents. We look to a parent to receive, listen to, guide, and protect us, don't we? Well, that is exactly what David is seeking from God.

We seek acceptance. In the world, we experience much rejection. Parents reject children; children reject parents. We are rejected by spouses, erstwhile friends, potential employers, and others in dozens of diverse situations. But God does not refuse us. David prays, "Do not hide your face from me, do not turn your servant away in anger. . . . Do not reject me or forsake me" (v. 9), and he knows, even as he prays, that God will not forsake him. God has accepted him in the past. He will continue to accept him.

We seek to be heard. Sometimes children talk to us only because they want to be listened to, and unfortunately many parents are too busy to listen. Is God ever too busy to listen when we speak to him? Never! God is a true, listening parent, a parent who says: "Ask and it will be given to you; seek and you will find; knock and the door will be opened to you" (Matt. 7:7).

We seek guidance. Which of us knows the way to walk so we will be kept out of sin and make progress in the way of righteousness? No one! We no more know how to live our lives for God than children know how to avoid danger and care for themselves. They need to be taught, as do we. In God we have one who can be turned to for guidance. David prays, "Teach me your way, O LORD; lead me in a straight path because of my oppressors" (Ps. 27:11).

We seek protection. The fourth thing a child looks for in a parent is protection, and David is certainly seeking this of the Lord because of his many enemies. They are the background of the psalm. They are the bullies of the neighborhood, and David needs the protecting presence of God just as a small child needs his father in such circumstances.

What are we to do when answers to our prayers are delayed? We simply need to wait. "Wait for the LORD; be strong and take heart and wait for the LORD" (v. 14). If some wealthy person promised to give you an expensive gift, wouldn't you wait for it expectantly? If you were in trouble and a king were coming to your aid, wouldn't you be alert for his appearance? God is just such a generous benefactor and powerful king. He is well worth waiting for.

Boice, *Psalms*, Volume 1, Baker, 1994, 242–44.

God's Protection

Psalm 33:1–22

The eyes of the LORD are on those who fear him.
—*PSALM 33:18*

God protects his people, foiling the plans of their enemies and turning back their enemies' attempts to harm them.

It occurs to me, as I think about these words, that many deliverances are probably unknown to us because they are turned back before they even come within our vision. I think this is important. In our prayers we usually remember the many tangible blessings God has given to us: families, homes, health, work, friends, special things that are important just to us, and the privileges we have as citizens of a democratic nation. We also think of less personal but nevertheless tangible blessings worldwide: that the world is more or less at peace, that other peoples are currently achieving or rediscovering their freedoms, that the gospel is widely proclaimed in our day. But while we remember these things, let us not forget to thank God for the things we do not have, the things we are spared because of his faithful and effective care. We do not know what these are specifically but we can think of the categories.

Have we been spared severe sickness during the past year? We should be thankful for that. Not everyone has been. If we have been spared, we should thank God for it.

Have we been kept from serious accidents? That should be a cause of our most grateful thanksgiving.

Have we been delivered from people who would harm us at work? In our homes? On the streets? If you have been preserved from harm by such enemies, it is the Lord's doing and you should acknowledge it.

And what about temptations? The Bible tells us that "God . . . will not let [us] be tempted beyond what [we] can bear" (1 Cor. 10:13). This implies that there are temptations that God turns aside before they can reach us. If he did not, we would certainly have fallen into them. That we continue on the path of discipleship and righteousness is a result of God's care of those who are his people.

Seeking Judgment
Psalm 35:1–28

May those who seek my life be disgraced and put to shame . . .
—PSALM 35:4

Is it right to ask God to judge our enemies, as David did? Let me suggest the following.

First, remember that David was not writing as a private citizen but as the king and chief justice of Israel. The bearing for us of David's position as king is that, while we must be careful about asking God to judge those who have offended us personally, there is nothing wrong with asking for justice on behalf of others who have been wronged. In fact, we should be vigorous in the pursuit of such justice. Usually, our problem is not that we are too vindictive at this point, but rather that we do not care about justice for other people much at all.

Second, in a more subdued way, there is also a sense in which we can pray along these lines for ourselves. This is because we *are* sometimes unjustly slandered, and it is right for truth to triumph.

But we have to be extremely cautious how we do this. For one thing, we are seldom entirely innocent of wrong ourselves. We must therefore always pray with a humble and contrite heart, asking God to reveal whatever fault may lie in us and so lead us in the way of righteousness. Again, while we properly appeal to God for justice, we are not authorized to take matters into our own hands and so try to do to the other person what he or she has done to us. Judgment is a prerogative of God. We should follow the apostle Paul's counsel: "Do not take revenge, my friends, but leave room for God's wrath, for it is written: 'It is mine to avenge; I will repay,' says the Lord. On the contrary: 'If your enemy is hungry, feed him; if he is thirsty, give him something to drink. In doing this, you will heap burning coals on his head.' Do not be overcome by evil, but overcome evil with good" (Rom. 12:19–21).

Still further, although our enemies may be vicious now, it is true that God may convert them. We should never despair of their conversion. The apostle was himself a fierce persecutor of the early Christians, but after his conversion he became the church's greatest missionary.

Finally, we can apply the words of this psalm to the devil, for he is described in Scripture precisely as David describes his enemies. He is our great foe, "a roaring lion looking for someone to devour" (1 Peter 5:8) and a slanderous "accuser of our brothers" (Rev. 12:10). Thank God, we have a powerful champion and advocate in King Jesus. It is not wrong for us to pray for his help for the confounding of Satan's devices and to rejoice in anticipation of the devil's ultimate and certain fall.

Four Blessings
Psalm 36:1–12

For with you is the fountain of life; in your light we see light.
—*PSALM 36:9*

David lists four ways in Psalm 36 in which the righteous are uniquely blessed.
Satisfaction. David does not use the word *satisfaction*, but this is what he means when he speaks of the righteous feasting on the "abundance" of God's house. What is "God's house" in this psalm? Some writers see the phrase as a reference to the temple, which can indeed be called the house of God. But there is nothing in the context to suggest this. Others suppose it to be a reference to heaven, in line with Jesus's saying, "In my Father's house are many rooms" (John 14:2), or his stories about guests feasting in the king's great hall. In my judgment, the "house" David speaks of here is the world in which we live and in which God's blessings are poured out. The reason I say so is that a present feasting is spoken of, not a future one. These verses describe a present and continuous enjoyment of God's bounties.

Joy. Our word for the second blessing is joy, though the word David uses here is *delights*. The interesting thing about David's word is that it is the plural of the word *Eden* and undoubtedly looks backward to the joys of our first parents before the fall.

Life. Verse 9 adds two more blessings of the righteous—life and light. Their fullness begins to be hinted at by the apostle John in the prologue to his Gospel, when he writes of Jesus, "In him was life, and that life was the light of men" (John 1:4). The prologue makes clear that the life spoken of is both physical, since "without him nothing was made that has been made," (v. 3), and spiritual, since "to all who received him, to those who believed in his name, he gave the right to become children of God—children born not of natural descent, nor of human decision or a husband's will, but born of God" (vv. 12–13).

It is hard to doubt that John was thinking of Psalm 36:9 as he composed the prelude.

Light. "In your light we see light." Where is the light of God to be found so that we might walk in light and grow as children of light? A glimmer is seen in nature. It is what the heathen have but reject, according to Romans 1. A steady beam is seen in the Old Testament, pointing onward to him who is himself the Light. The full glory of God's light is in the gospel we proclaim. Yet the fullest revelation awaits the day when we shall see God in his glory and be like Jesus, whom we will encounter face-to-face (see 2 Cor. 3:7–18).

Boice, *Psalms*, Volume 1, Baker, 1994, 312–13.

Wait for the Lord
Psalm 37:32–40

Wait for the LORD and keep his way.
—*PSALM 37:34*

In the long run the righteous will be exalted and protected, and the wicked will be brought down. Therefore, the psalmist commands us to: "Wait for the LORD and keep his way."

In Psalm 1 the author used an attractive metaphor for the life of the person who lives by God's Word. He said he will be "like a tree planted by streams of water, which yields its fruit in season" (v. 3). In Psalm 37 the same metaphor reappears. But here it is used in reverse, the wicked being compared to a green tree which flourishes for a time but soon passes away and is seen no more (vv. 35–36). This is not what we would naturally expect. Earlier in the psalm the wicked were compared to pretty flowers of the field, which do not last long. That seems right. But it is hard to think of a great tree suddenly passing away, unless perhaps it is cut down, which may be what the psalmist is thinking.

Nothing in the Bible is a mistake, of course. So in this case I imagine the image of the tree to be teaching that there are times when the wicked do so well that they seem indistinguishable from the righteous. Their security seems equally assured. They flourish. But we are taught not to judge by appearances but by the Word of God. Proverbs 3:5–6 says, "Trust in the LORD with all your heart and lean not on your own understanding; in all your ways acknowledge him, and he will make your paths straight."

This is what Psalm 37 encourages us to do and what the child of God will experience if he or she trusts in the Lord, delights in the Lord, commits his or her way to the Lord, is still before the Lord, and refrains from anger. The one who does those things will end as the psalm itself does, with meek objectivity, reiterating that the Lord helps, delivers, and saves those who trust him.

"But I can never become like that," someone protests. "It is not my nature to be meek."

Perhaps not. Perhaps none of us is meek by nature. But we can become meek if we will commit our way to God and learn from him, just as the psalm advises. Or to put it in New Testament terms, we are to learn from Jesus, who said, "Come to me, all you who are weary and burdened, and I will give you rest. Take my yoke upon you and learn from me, for I am gentle [that is, meek] and humble in heart, and you will find rest for your souls" (Matt. 11:28–29).

Boice, *Psalms*, Volume 1, Baker, 1994, 328–29.

Up from the Pit

Psalm 40:1–17

He lifted me out of the slimy pit.
—PSALM 40:2

What is your slimy pit? Some people are caught in the mud and mire of sin. David himself was an example of this at one point in his life. He began his descent into this pit by staying home from battle in the season when kings were supposed to be at war. While enjoying himself in Jerusalem, he saw a woman named Bathsheba bathing herself on the roof of a home close to the palace. David brought her to the palace, slept with her, and then, when he learned she was pregnant, arranged to have her husband Uriah abandoned in battle so that he was killed by enemy soldiers. David continued nearly a year in this condition. The story is in 2 Samuel 11.

Maybe you are caught in just such a sin. Perhaps one sin has led to another. You know what is happening but you can't get out of it. That is no surprise. Sin is like that. Romans 1 describes the downward pull of sin on all people. When you are caught in this way, there is no point beyond which you may not go. You need help. Where is your help to come from if not from God?

Some people have a very different kind of pit from which they need to be lifted. It is the pit of personal defeat, whether at work or school or in the home or in some other setting or relationship. Some people would say that their entire lives have been one long and unending defeat. They have never succeeded at anything.

I do not want to trivialize your discouragement. But I can tell you this. God does have things he wants you to succeed at, and he will enable you to succeed at those, even though they may be different from what you are doing now. The place to begin is where David began. He began by laying his problem before the Lord. There was a time early in his life when he could have spoken very graphically of his defeats. No matter what he did, he was unable to please King Saul, and Saul in his hatred and jealousy of David ruthlessly hounded the young man from place to place. It was many years before the Lord intervened to remove Saul and eventually bring David to the throne. If you are defeated, bring your defeats to God. Wait on God. David "waited patiently for the LORD." That is how Psalm 40 begins (v. 1). If you wait patiently, you too will learn that God has important things for you to do, and he will give you significant victories in his own perfect time.

Our Refuge
Psalm 46:1–11

The LORD Almighty is with us; the God of Jacob is our fortress.
—*PSALM 46:11*

The conclusion and proper application of Psalm 46 is this statement in verse 11. Who is he, this God who is his people's refuge? The answer is given in the two names of God in this refrain.

First, he is "the LORD Almighty." The words are literally "the LORD of Hosts (Jehovah Sabaoth)." "Hosts" refers to the armies of Israel, on the one hand, and to the angelic armies of God, on the other. This makes the name especially apt in this psalm, since the psalm is based on a historical deliverance of the people from earthly armies, whatever their origin, and also looks forward to a final deliverance when God will subdue the hostile forces of rebellious man forever.

We have a wonderful insight into the power of God's hosts in the story of Elisha at Dothan. The city of Dothan had been surrounded by the armies of Ben-Hadad of Syria in an attempt to capture Elisha, and they were discovered early in the morning by Elisha's young servant. When he saw the soldiers and chariots positioned around the city, he rushed back inside and cried out to Elisha, saying, "Oh, my lord, what shall we do?" (2 Kings 6:15). Elisha prayed that God would open the eyes of his servant to see the heavenly hosts protecting him, and when God did, the servant saw that the hills were filled with horses and chariots of fire around Elisha. Elisha reminded his servant that "Those who are with us are greater than those who are with them" (v. 16).

Second, God is the God of Jacob. Jacob was the third of the three Jewish patriarchs and the least outstanding of the three. He was a schemer, as his name implies. It took him a lifetime to learn to trust God. Yet the God of Abraham was his God no less than he was the God of Abraham. This is your God too, if you have come to him through faith in Jesus Christ. And if he is your God, then he is with you at all times, which is what this important couplet says.

On the day he died, John Wesley had already nearly lost his voice and could be understood only with difficulty. But at the last with all the strength he could summon, Wesley suddenly called out, "The best of all is, God is with us." Then, raising his hand slightly and waving it in triumph, he exclaimed again with thrilling effect, "The best of all is, God is with us." Is the Lord Almighty with you? Is the God of Jacob your refuge? Make sure that he is. The storms of life will come, and the greatest storm of all will be the final judgment. Make Christ your refuge now, while there is still time.

King of All the Earth

Psalm 47:1–9

How awesome is the LORD Most High, the great King over all the earth!
—*PSALM 47:2*

From the very beginning God had said that he purposed to bless all nations and all peoples through Abraham and his descendants, particularly through his one great descendant, the Messiah, Jesus Christ. And that is what he has done and is doing. He is building Christ's spiritual kingdom with people from all nations and races.

There were times when the Jewish people thought in exclusively ethnic or nationalistic terms, as nations generally do. They thought that the blessings of God's kingdom were for them alone. But the psalmist knew differently, and so did that great Jewish theologian, Paul, who wrote that Abraham "is the father of all who believe but have not been circumcised [that is, Gentiles], in order that righteousness might be credited to them" (Rom. 4:11). And again, "The promise comes by faith, so that it may be by grace and may be guaranteed to all Abraham's offspring—not only to those who are of the law but also to those who are of the faith of Abraham. He is the father of us all. As it is written: 'I have made you a father of many nations'" (vv. 16–17).

Someone asked me whether the kingdom of God is past, present, or future. It is impossible to describe the kingdom of God as being merely past, merely present, or merely future. It is all of these and more, for it is also internal and external. It involves willing compliance as well as forced compliance. This is because the kingdom of God is God's rule, and God rules everywhere and all things. The only meaningful question is, Are you a member of that kingdom? Are you a part of it? Am I?

There is only one way to become a willing part of God's kingdom, and that is by personal surrender to the claims of Jesus Christ, the divine Son of God and Savior of his people. It is to bow before him, for he is the only true "KING OF KINGS AND LORD OF LORDS" (Rev. 19:16).

In this age God is building his kingdom by calling out a people to himself. They are from every imaginable people, nation, condition in life, and race—Americans and Africans and African Americans; tribal people, street people, and sophisticated urban dwellers; working men and men without work; judges and those who have been judged; all types of people. And he is turning them into men and women in whom the kingdom of Jesus Christ is present and in whom his loving, winsome, and upright character can be seen. There is nothing in life more important or more wonderful than belonging to that kingdom.

Cleansed by the Blood

Psalm 51:1–19

Blot out my transgressions.
—PSALM 51:1

"B lot out" refers to removing writing from a book, perhaps removing an indictment. Here is an illustration. There are certain ancient Bible manuscripts called palimpsests. They are pieces of papyrus (or some other ancient book material) that at one time contained a different text. But because this text was no longer needed and the material on which it was written was expensive, someone rubbed out the old writing, turned the sheet sideways, and wrote new words. This is what David wanted and what we all desperately need. The books of our lives have been written upon with many sins, and these stand as a terrible indictment against us. Unless something is done, they are going to be read out against us at the last day. But God can and will do something, if we ask him. God will rub out the ancient writing, turn the pages sideways, and write over the newly prepared surface the message of his everlasting compassion through the work of Jesus Christ.

This is not possible without great cost, of course. This is taught in the four words that begin verse 7, words that I think are the most important in the entire psalm: "Cleanse me with hyssop."

Because of its shape and structure, hyssop was used as a small brush. In the ceremonies of the temple it was used to sprinkle blood. The author of Hebrews indicates that hyssop was used in the enacting of the covenant in Moses's day: "When Moses had proclaimed every commandment of the law to all the people, he took the blood of calves, together with water, scarlet wool and branches of hyssop, and sprinkled the scroll and all the people. He said, 'This is the blood of the covenant, which God has commanded you to keep.' In the same way, he sprinkled with blood both the tabernacle and everything used in its ceremonies. In fact, the law requires that nearly everything be cleansed with blood, and without the shedding of blood there is no forgiveness" (Heb. 9:19–22).

David understood this and when he asked God to cleanse him with hyssop, he meant, "cleanse me by the blood. Forgive me and regard me as cleansed on the basis of the innocent victim that has died."

That is how we must come to God too. We need forgiveness badly. But "without the shedding of blood there is no forgiveness." It is only on the basis of the shed blood of Jesus Christ, the Son of God, that we may find God's mercy. Have you found mercy? Your sin may be as great as David's, even greater. But however great it is, you will find God to be wonderfully merciful if you will come to him as David did.

Cast Your Cares on God

Psalm 55:1–23

Cast your cares on the LORD.
—*PSALM 55:22*

This statement is the verse picked up by the apostle Peter and commended to us in the fifth chapter of his first epistle: "Cast all your anxiety on him because he cares for you" (1 Peter 5:7). Peter was a great worrier, and not without cause. But as he grew older he learned not to worry but rather to do what he then also commended to others, to cast his cares on God.

Why should we do that? Isn't this just another form of escapism? No. In fact, it is the exact opposite. It is learning to cast our cares on God that enables us not to run away but to stand tall and carry on with the task God has assigned us. Casting our cares on God enables us to be steadfast. The last verses of this psalm give three reasons why we should cast our cares on God.

First, "he will sustain you." When we are down, it is natural to think that we will never be able to bear up under the troubles that are pressing in from every side. We are sure we will be beaten down. But that is not the case. The Bible says, "No temptation has seized you except what is common to man. And God is faithful; he will not let you be tempted beyond what you can bear. But when you are tempted, he will also provide a way out so that you can stand up under it" (1 Cor. 10:13).

Second, "he will never let the righteous fall." The apostle Peter was sure he was going to fall when he was trying to walk toward Jesus over the water of the Sea of Galilee. He looked at the waves and began to sink. "Lord, save me!" he cried (Matt. 14:30). This is exactly what David has been praying in this psalm. He wants to be saved. And the Lord did it. He saved David, just as he saved Peter and all who cast their cares upon him. David is not exaggerating when he says, "The LORD . . . will never let the righteous fall."

Third, "[God] will bring down the wicked." Evil persons may succeed for a time, but it is the promise of God as well as the judgment of history that they soon perish and are destroyed, just as they had sought so hard to destroy other people.

The bottom line is the psalm's last sentence: "But as for me, I trust in you"— that is, in God. That is David's final testimony. Is it yours? If you are focusing on the evil around you, you may not be able to say, "But as for me, I trust in you." But you will be able to say it, if you have really cast your cares on God.

Trust in God
Psalm 56:1–13

In God I trust; I will not be afraid.
—PSALM 56:4

There are two parts to David's confidence:
    1. *Confidence in God.* The first is that he is confident in God. He trusts God. Not man! Not circumstances! Not his own cunning, as useful as that seemed to have been at Gath, the occasion for writing this psalm (see 1 Sam. 21:10–15)! He trusts God: "In God I trust." It is because of this that he could ask, "What can man do to me?" and expect the answer, "Nothing."

So let me ask, Do you trust God? If you are a Christian, you have trusted him in the matter of your salvation. That is the greatest thing. God has saved you from sin, hell, and the devil. If you are a Christian, you believe he has done that. But if he has done that, can you not also trust him in lesser things like loneliness or even those sometimes dangerous circumstances that cause fear and desperation?

    2. *Confidence in the Word of God.* There is another aspect to David's confidence in God—it is based upon the Word of God. What is this "word of God" to which David refers? Clearly it is the entire self-revelation of God in Scripture given up to that time—the Pentateuch (the first five books) and possibly Joshua and Judges. This is only a portion of our Bible, but it was enough to make God's character and desires for his people known. David therefore praises God for his Word, recognizing it as one of the greatest of all God's good gifts to men and women.

It may also be the case, however, that David is thinking specifically of the words of God that were brought to him by the prophet Samuel, assuring him that he would be king over Israel (see 1 Sam. 16:1–13). That must have seemed a long way off when David was in Gath or hiding in the cave of Adullam. But no matter! It was the word of God, and though the fulfillment of that word might be long delayed, it was nevertheless absolutely certain. Therefore, it was not only in God but also in the specific words of God that David trusted.

You and I do not have individualized revelations from God delivered to us today by God's prophets. We have the Bible. But the Bible we have is more extensive than David's. It contains all we need to know about spiritual things. Equally important, we have the Holy Spirit to give us understanding of what has been written as well as the ability to apply it to specific areas of our lives.

Lessons for Victory
Psalm 60:1–12

With God we will gain the victory.
—*Psalm 60:12*

What lessons is David learning as he reflects, first on his people's defeat by Edom and second on the promises of God to give an eventual victory? It seems to me that there are two of them.

1. *Only God can give victory.* There were a number of well-fortified cities in Edom, the source of the country's strength and great pride. But when David speaks of *"the* fortified city"(v. 9), he can only mean Petra, the most inaccessible and apparently impregnable mountain stronghold of Edom. Only God could give victory over a fortress like that, and David knew it. So he cries to God, acknowledging that "the help of man is worthless" (v. 11).

2. *We must ask for it.* David was also learning that, although only God can give victory, we must nevertheless ask for it. And so he did, anticipating God's positive answer.

These lessons are applicable to us in terms of the spiritual battles we are called to fight. We are members of the kingdom of the Lord Jesus Christ, and our task is to advance his kingdom in this spiritually hostile world. The apostle Paul said, "For our struggle is not against flesh and blood, but against the rulers, against the authorities, against the powers of this dark world and against the spiritual forces of evil in the heavenly realms" (Eph. 6:12). How can we gain this victory? Not by ourselves, or even with the help of other Christians. In this battle "the help of man is [truly] worthless" (Ps. 60:11). We need God to fight with us and on our behalf.

The second lesson applies to us too: we must ask for God's help. The book of James says, "You do not have, because you do not ask God" (James 4:2). Jesus expressed the other side of James's words when he said, "Ask and it will be given to you; seek and you will find; knock and the door will be opened to you" (Matt. 7:7). We can ask for many things wrongly and so fail to receive them. But the one thing we can be sure of receiving is victory on behalf of the gospel. Do you remember Nebuchadnezzar's vision that troubled him so much? It was a vision of a great statue representing in sequence all the many great kingdoms of this world. At the end of the vision a rock "not cut by human hands" struck the statue and destroyed it, and then grew up to become "a huge mountain" that "filled the whole earth" (Dan. 2:34–35). That rock is the Lord Jesus Christ, and that mountain is his kingdom, which is destined to triumph.

If you believe that, then this is the banner around which you must rally and on behalf of which you can confidently fight.

Singing Praise
Psalm 61:1–8

Then will I ever sing praise to your name.
—*PSALM 61:8*

David began this psalm feeling at "the ends of the earth," far from God. But as he thought about God and prayed to him, he drew closer to God and grew in confidence until he ends actually expecting to be established in Jerusalem, his capital, for many days and many generations. That is something to praise God for. And that, quite naturally, is how the psalm ends: "Then will I ever sing praise to your name and fulfill my vows day after day" (v. 8).

Shouldn't that be true for you as well? It is not only David who had such a great God, or those who lived with him in this Old Testament period. His God is our God, and it is our privilege to know him even more intimately than David did, for we know him in the Lord Jesus Christ. Jesus is the Rock that is higher than we are, infinitely higher. He is very God of very God, as the creeds say. He is the Rock of Ages. But he is also the Rock that has been cleft for us, crucified, that we might be saved from sin.

> Rock of Ages, cleft for me,
> Let me hide myself in thee.

Jesus is our refuge, but not only a refuge from human enemies and foes. He is a refuge from the wrath of God to be poured out at the final judgment. He is our tower that we can run into and be safe. He is our tabernacle. The apostle John used this very word when he wrote, "The Word became flesh and made his dwelling among us" (John 1:14). In the Greek the words "made his dwelling" are literally "tabernacled." Jesus is the one who said of the city of Jerusalem, "O Jerusalem, Jerusalem, you who kill the prophets and stone those sent to you, how often I have longed to gather your children together, as a hen gathers her chicks under her wings, but you were not willing" (Matt. 23:37). But he has gathered *us* to himself.

Sometimes we need to feel we are at "the ends of the earth" before we can discover how wonderful Jesus is. That is what the great Augustine was thinking of when he wrote, "They that are godly are oppressed and vexed in the church or congregation for this purpose: that when they are pressed, they should cry; and when they cry, that they should be heard; and when they are heard, that they should laud and praise God." We will be happy Christians if we learn to do just that.

The Shining Face of God
Psalm 67:1–7

May God be gracious to us and bless us and make his face shine upon us.
—*Psalm 67:1*

The language of this verse is drawn from the great Aaronic blessing of Numbers 6. The text says that God told Moses to have Aaron bless the people, saying, "The LORD bless you and keep you; the LORD make his face shine upon you and be gracious to you; the LORD turn his face toward you and give you peace" (vv. 24–26).

A shining face is the opposite of an angry or scowling face, and a face turned toward someone is the opposite of a face turned away in indifference or disgust. A shining face implies favor, the favor of the one whose face is shining, and it implies the friendliness of warm personal relationships too. So what is meant by this blessing is something more than what we normally think of when we ask God to "bless us." Usually all we mean is that we want God to help us to succeed at something or enable us to make money or give us the job, house, or car we desire. But although such forms of material blessing are not excluded by the Aaronic benediction, they are only part of it—and a lesser part at that. More desirable is that God would himself enter into a gracious personal relationship with his people.

The greatest blessing will be to see God. Do you remember the prayer of Moses, found in Exodus 33? Moses made three requests in that prayer: first, that God would teach him his way so that he might know him and continue to find favor with him; second, that God would remain with the people and never take his presence from them; and third, that he might look on God's face and see his glory (vv. 12–18). God granted the first two of those requests but he told Moses, "You cannot see my face, for no one may see me and live" (v. 20).

This is profoundly true, of course. No sinner, however devout or pious, as Moses was, can possibly look upon the face of God and survive that holy, piercing sight. But one day we shall! We shall look upon God in the day when all his redeemed people, drawn from every tribe and tongue and nation and purged of even the slightest taint of sin, stand before his throne to sing praises to the almighty God and to the Lamb. In that day God's face will shine upon us in the fullest measure—we will see him "face-to-face"—and the ultimate beatific vision anticipated by Psalm 67 will be ours. In that day our joy will be even greater because great multitudes from all the nations of the earth will be praising God with us.

Poor and Needy

Psalm 70:1–5

Yet I am poor and needy; come quickly to me, O God.
—*Psalm 70:5*

The last verse of Psalm 70 is what I call the psalmist's most basic belief or persuasion. It has two parts: (1) he is "poor and needy," and (2) God is his "help and . . . deliverer."

The height of faith is not to presume on what God will or will not do but to be convinced precisely of what David is convinced: that we are needy, that we cannot help ourselves, and that God is the only one who can help us.

Many people get off base on the very first of these two points because they assume, as virtually all unbelievers do, that human beings are perfectly able to help themselves. In other words, they are not "poor"—they have great natural resources—and they are not "needy," certainly not in spiritual areas! If they are going to get to heaven, it will be by their own efforts. They are the master of their soul. They are the captain of their fate. According to one public opinion poll, over 60 percent even of so-called evangelical Christians believe that the saying "God helps those who help themselves" is in the Bible!

Those who know their Bible don't want anything to do with that false teaching. They know that they can't help themselves. So they say with David, who by all outward appearances was a rich and very powerful man, "Yet I am poor and needy; come quickly to me, O God." Above all, they confess their utter need of God in salvation. They know that there is no salvation to be found anywhere except in Jesus Christ.

The second part of David's confession is important too, for it is only this that makes the prayer hopeful. David knew his weakness and need but he also knew God's grace and greatness. Therefore, even though he is weak, he turns to God strongly. And though needy, he comes to the one who is able to satisfy his need. Do you know that? Do you know God as the one who offers deliverance from the penalty and power of your sin through the work of Jesus Christ? The very name *Jesus* means "Jehovah saves." It is Jesus's work as Redeemer to set his enslaved people free.

This is not weak faith, but great faith, crying out to God urgently because the need is great.

Faithful and Righteous
Psalm 71:1–24

My tongue will tell of your righteous acts all day long.
—PSALM 71:24

To deal with the limitations of old age, David looks to the past to remind himself of God's faithfulness and power. He looks to the future to remind himself of the work yet to be done. Then, having done both of those things, he turns to the present and begins to do exactly what he has been talking about. He bears witness to God now. What he praises God for chiefly is his righteousness (vv. 19–21) and faithfulness (vv. 22–24).

1. *God's righteousness.* The word *righteousness* is used in different ways in the Bible, most notably of that divine righteousness that is imparted to us in justification. That is not the way the word is used here, nor characteristically in the psalms. Here it refers to God's right dealings, to the fact that everything he does is just, that no one can fault him. The word appears in this sense throughout the psalms ascribed to David. Again and again he calls God a "righteous God" and speaks of "your righteousness." (There are not many psalms from which this word or the idea represented by this word is missing.) This is a great testimony, that a person has lived a long time and has found by his or her own experience that God does all things rightly or justly. Therefore, (1) God can be trusted, and (2) it is wise to conform one's life to God's will and standards. That is a great and important testimony to pass to the next generation.

2. *God's faithfulness.* In one sense the entire psalm has been about God's faithfulness: his faithfulness in the past, and the prayer of the psalmist that God will remain faithful to him in his old age. Here at the end the theme is the same, for it is the last and chief thing David wants to declare to those who are to come. He wants them to know that God is an utterly faithful God and can be trusted to remain so.

> "Great is thy faithfulness," O God my Father,
> There is no shadow of turning with thee;
> Thou changest not, thy compassions, they fail not;
> As thou hast been thou forever wilt be.
>
> "Great is thy faithfulness! Great is thy faithfulness!"
> Morning by morning new mercies I see:
> All I have needed thy hand hath provided—
> "Great is thy faithfulness," Lord, unto me!

If you have known God at all, you have found that he is indeed a God of great faithfulness and know that this must be your testimony.

Pleading with God

Psalm 74:1–23

Rise up, O God, and defend your cause.
—PSALM 74:22

Psalm 74 is a model for prayer because of the way it pleads with God. Or, as Charles Spurgeon said, it is an example of how we can pray to God with arguments. The psalmist wants God to take his hand out of his pocket and act boldly to rebuke his enemies and reestablish his people in their land (vv. 9–11). But the psalm is not merely a plea that God would do this. It is also a listing of reasons why he should.

1. God should act because the people who are suffering from his harsh but righteous judgment are but sheep (v. 1). That is, they are poor, silly, and defenseless things.
2. God should act because he has already purchased these poor people for himself (v. 2). That is, he has already expended a great deal of effort on them, and they were no better when he first redeemed them than now.
3. God should act not merely because the people have suffered, but because his temple has been devastated and the prescribed formal worship of God by his people has ceased (vv. 3–8).
4. God should act because the people's case is hopeless otherwise (v. 9). Signs and prophetic speaking have to come from God.
5. God should act because the mocking by Israel's enemies is really a mocking of God (vv. 10–11). It is his name that is being reviled, and his name must be honored above all else.
6. God should act because he has acted powerfully and with wonderful compassion in the past (vv. 12–17). It is his nature to make his greatness known. Why should he not do so again? Why should he not do so now?
7. God should act because he has entered into an everlasting covenant with his people (v. 20), and the terms of that covenant call for God to be with them forever. True, the people have been unfaithful. But "what if some did not have faith? Will their lack of faith nullify God's faithfulness? . . . Let God be true, and every man a liar" (Rom. 3:3–4).
8. God should act because it is fitting that his enemies be rebuked and the poor and needy praise his name (v. 21).
9. God should act because it is his cause and not a mere man's that is in jeopardy (vv. 22–23). It is God's purposes that are being opposed by Israel's enemies.

If you are having trouble praying about something important in your life, why not do what Asaph, the author of this psalm, does? Make a list of why God should answer your prayer and plead those reasons. Either God will answer, or you will find that your prayer is not a good one and you will pray for something better.

Reasoning from God's Attributes
Psalm 77:1–20

Your ways, O God, are holy. What god is so great as our God?
—*PSALM 77:13*

What Asaph the psalmist remembers about God when he reflects on the years of his working is in the stanza comprising verses 13–15. This is all about God, just as the opening stanzas of the psalm were mostly about Asaph. Here he muses on the attributes of God as seen in Israel's history. He recalls three matters.

1. *God is holy.* The holiness of God is a rich concept, having to do more with God's transcendence than his uprightness. Yet it embraces his moral qualities, and here "holy" must refer to the fact that whatever God does is upright. This has been true in the past. Therefore, it must be true in the present too. However matters may seem to the poet from his personal perspective in history, his review of the past teaches him that God can always be trusted to do the right thing. This is true of all his "ways," including those in which the poet himself is called to walk.

2. *God is great.* In the previous stanza Asaph had reflected on God's "deeds" and "miracles" (v. 11), his "works" and "mighty deeds" (v. 12). This leads him to ask, "What god is so great as our God?" with the implied answer, "No god at all," and to repeat that Israel's God "performs miracles," "display[s his] power" (v. 14), and bares his "mighty arm" (v. 15). This is important because it tells us that God is not only an upright God ("Your ways, O God, are holy," but also that he is able and does put all his holy decrees into action. In other words, nothing frustrates him, nothing turns him aside from his perfect, right, and moral path.

3. *God is caring.* How do we know that God is caring? It is because he "redeemed" the people, meaning that God delivered them from their bondage under the slave lords of Egypt (v. 15). Therefore, if God is caring as well as powerful or sovereign, he can be counted on to work in each detail of history for his people's good. And this means that even allowing the psalmist to fall into the depression with which the psalm began is not carelessness on God's part, but rather a part of his total loving plan. This is practical theology of the best sort, for it reasons from the immutable character of God to the purpose for his acts in history and takes comfort from such truths.

Confession
Psalm 79:1–13

Deliver us and forgive our sins for your name's sake.
—PSALM 79:9

Every true prayer should have within it a confession of the worshiper's sins. This is not some morbid preoccupation. It is an inevitable result of prayer that is truly prayer to God. This is because God is holy, and we are not. So if we are really praying to him, we will be aware of his holiness, and his holiness will convict us of our sinful state. This is how we know that the prayer of the tax collector in Jesus's parable was a true prayer and the prayer of the Pharisee was not. The Pharisee began his prayer with "God" but he went on to talk about himself and how good he was. Jesus said he was praying "to himself." The tax collector prayed, "God, be merciful to me, a sinner," and Jesus said that he was heard and went home justified (Luke 18:9–14).

This has bearing on Psalm 79, for one of its most important features is an acknowledgment of sin. There is an acknowledgment of the sins of the fathers, since it was for their sins that Judah was overrun and Jerusalem destroyed (v. 8). But there is also acknowledgment of the people's own and present sins, for the psalmist prays, "Deliver us and forgive our sins for your name's sake."

This is important. The people were suffering the destruction of their entire civilization—politically, economically, socially, and religiously. Yet there is not the slightest suggestion that they did not actually deserve it, or even that they did not deserve having it continue as long as it had. Instead of excusing their sins, the psalmist acknowledges them and pleads for forgiveness (actually "atone for our sins").

What is he thinking of when he mentions atonement? The only atonement he knew was that made at the temple by the high priest when sacrifices were offered up, particularly on the Day of Atonement. That temple was now gone. How could atonement for sin be made? I do not know what the psalmist was thinking of but I do know how God did it. God did it, not by causing the temple to be rebuilt and the sacrifices to be reinstituted—though the temple was rebuilt in the days of Ezra and Nehemiah, and the offerings were begun again—but rather by sending Jesus Christ to be the perfect and only sufficient sacrifice. That is why, when Jesus died, the veil of the temple was torn in two from top to bottom, indicating that the way into the presence of God was now open for all who would come through faith in his sacrifice.

Boice, *Psalms*, Volume 2, Baker, 1996, 657.

The Purpose of Judgment
Psalm 83:1–18

So that men will seek your name, O LORD.
—*PSALM 83:16*

Psalm 83 includes an impassioned appeal to God to overthrow and destroy Israel's enemies (vv. 9–17). What are we to say about this? The first observation made by the psalmist is that God had destroyed Israel's enemies in this way in the past. Asaph was saying, "O Lord, as you have delivered us in the past, so deliver us again. Show yourself to be as powerful in our day as you have been for the generations that have preceded us." Second, the psalmist says that it is God's cause that is in danger, and therefore it is God's battle—not that of the people.

The final observation is the most important of all. It is the way the psalm ends. It calls for judgment—that is true—but it ends by stating the purpose for that judgment: "so that men will seek your name, O LORD." And in the last verse: "Let them know that you, whose name is the LORD—that you alone are the Most High over all the earth" (v. 18).

In other words, although desiring deliverance and judgment, the ultimate desire of the psalmist is that other people, even the Jews' enemies, might come to know and obey the true God.

That is precisely why we do not rush to calls for judgment. Judgment will come. The God of all the universe will do right (see Gen. 18:25). But this is still a day of grace, when men and women may still repent of their sin and seek after God that they might find him and be rescued from the wrath to come.

Let me end by going back to the beginning of the psalm and reminding you of the greatest "non-answer" to that prayer in all history. The first verse of Psalm 83 says: "O God, do not keep silent; be not quiet, O God, be not still." One day many centuries after this was written, the Son of God was hanging on a cross outside the city of Jerusalem, where he had been encircled and condemned by his cruel enemies, and he in a sense prayed this prayer. He cried to God, "My God, my God, why have you forsaken me?" (Matt. 27:46; Mark 15:34). God did not answer. He did not intervene to save Jesus from his enemies or rescue him from the cross.

It was good God did not answer, for God's silence to Christ's forsaken cry meant our salvation from the Father's wrath, and it meant that we have the gospel and not just judgment to proclaim.

When Righteousness and Peace Meet

Psalm 85:1–13

Love and faithfulness meet together; righteousness and peace kiss each other.
—PSALM 85:10

Verse 10 is one of the great poetic sections of the Psalms. It is generally understood as pointing to the work of Jesus Christ in making atonement for our sins by which alone God is able both to satisfy the demands of his righteousness or justice and at the same time to show mercy to those who have fallen short of his just standards. This may be part of what is involved. But the picture painted by verses 10–13 is larger and more comprehensive than that. They are actually looking forward to an ideal state and time when the harmony that is in God will also pervade and dominate God's creation.

The devil is the great disrupter. He has brought disharmony to the universe. God brings harmony. In these verses four great attributes of God meet together—love, faithfulness, righteousness, and peace—and then, like conquering generals, they march side by side to a victory that is the sure and certain hope of God's people. The verses suggest three harmonies.

1. *The harmony in God.* When we speak of mercy and truth as well as righteousness and peace being reconciled in God because of the work of Jesus Christ, we imply that somehow they are in conflict. But the qualities in God are never in conflict, and the psalm is certainly not speaking of a conflict. On the contrary, love and faithfulness, righteousness and peace are always at home in God, and it is from this divine harmony that all other harmonies come. We have peace only when we rest in him.

2. *Harmony between heaven and earth.* The second harmony is between God and man, which is what verse 11 suggests when it speaks of faithfulness springing from the earth and righteousness looking down from heaven. We may see this as God's gift of righteousness from above and our response of faith reaching up to receive God's righteousness and then issuing in faithfulness. But the picture is probably not as specific as this. The verse is better seen as pointing to a state in which God's people live in faithful obedience to God and are blessed by him. When that happens salvation has indeed come to a people and the glory of God dwells in their land.

3. *A harmony in man.* The third harmony is in man himself. For these qualities—love, faithfulness, righteousness, and peace—are attributes of God that can be shared with man and therefore can and must appear in those who are God's people. Moreover, when they appear in us, we find that we are at peace not only with God but also with ourselves and one another. In fact, we become peacemakers in an otherwise cruel, warring, and disharmonious world.

Where Sin Leads

Psalm 90:1–17

You have set our iniquities before you, our secret sins in the light of your presence.
—PSALM 90:8

The third section of Psalm 90 (vv. 7–12) recognizes that man's greatest problem is not just his frailty—that is, that he exists for only a short bit of time and is then no more. It is that he is also a sinner and is subject to the just wrath of God. In fact, it is sin that is the cause of his death and misery. Moses, the author of the psalm, must have been thinking of the fall of Adam and Eve when he wrote this (remember that he also wrote Genesis 3), as well as of his own sin in striking the rock and of God's judgment, which kept him from the Promised Land. "We are consumed by your anger and terrified by your indignation. You have set our iniquities before you, our secret sins in the light of your presence. . . . Who knows the power of your anger? For your wrath is as great as the fear that is due you" (vv. 7–8, 11).

This is a profound set of statements. Not only has Moses set the weakness of man and the shortness of his life against the grandeur and eternity of God, he has also traced man's mortality to its roots, seeing death as a judgment for sin. We might think that he would contrast man's sin with God's holiness, just as he has contrasted man's mortality with God's eternity. Instead, he is trying to show that death is linked to sin and is caused by it. We die because Adam sinned (see Rom. 5:12–21) and because we sin ourselves.

Are you aware that sin always leads to death? To the death of dreams, hopes, plans, relationships, health, and eventually even to that ultimate spiritual death that is a separation from God forever? If you are aware of this, you will not treat sin lightly, as many do. You will say with David, "Who can discern his errors? Forgive my hidden faults" (Ps. 19:12). You will pray, "Keep your servant also from willful sins; may they not rule over me" (v. 13). You will strive to live an upright life before God.

The Rewards of Trust

Psalm 91:1–16

I will protect him, for he acknowledges my name.
—*Psalm 91:14*

In the last three verses of this psalm, God promises three things to those who trust him.

1. *Protection for the one who is in danger* (v. 14). Psalm 91 speaks throughout of the many dangers that threaten God's people, but its central message is that God will rescue and protect from all such dangers those who trust him. Those who have trusted God know this and praise God constantly for his help and protection.

2. *An answer for the one who is in trouble and prays to God about it* (v. 15). One of the great blessings of following hard after God is knowing that, when we call upon him, he will hear and answer us. These verses say that God will deliver and honor such a person. They also say that God will be with the believer "in trouble," which is a way of acknowledging that God does not always lift a Christian out of troubles. Sometimes it is his will that we endure them and profit from them. We are told in Romans that we acquire hope, develop character, and learn perseverance from what we suffer (Rom. 5:3–4). When we go through such circumstances, God goes through them with us. He sustains us in our sufferings.

3. *Long life and salvation for the one who seeks God's satisfaction* (v. 16). Long life is a blessing frequently promised to the righteous in the Old Testament (Exod. 20:12; Deut. 30:20; Pss. 21:4; 23:6; Prov. 3:2, 16), but the promise is not necessarily for a prolongation of days but rather for a complete or full life. Here there is the added promise of a "salvation" in heaven, yet to come.

These verses also make the point that the promises are for those who trust in or love God. Therefore, they are blessings that some believers miss out on, simply because they are always fretting and do not trust God as they should. Here the psalmist quotes God as saying that the blessings are for those who love God and acknowledge his name (v. 14), call upon him (v. 15), and seek satisfaction in what he alone can provide (v. 16).

Do you do that? Or are you still trying to find satisfaction in the world? Do you love the world more than you love Jesus?

A Rule of Law and Justice

Psalm 93:1–5

Your statutes stand firm; holiness adorns your
house for endless days, O LORD.
—*PSALM 93:5*

Psalm 93 closes with two characteristics of God's kingly rule: it is a kingdom of law and it is a kingdom of holiness or justice.

1. *A rule of law.* God's rule is a rule of power. It is also a rule of law, which is what the important word "statutes" in verse 5 refers to. God's statutes are his decrees, above all his laws.

What this means is that God rules his people by his Word. By reminding us that the statutes of God "stand firm," like the world and even the throne of God itself, the psalmist is saying that those of us who profess to know God and confess him as our God must know and obey his statutes too—if we would be actually ruled by him.

Let me put it another way. The Lord Jesus Christ rules his church by guiding its destiny sovereignly, of course. But the way he specifically rules his people within his church is by the teaching of the Scriptures. It is there that we learn what he would have us do and what he would have us be. We cannot claim to be ruled by Jesus Christ unless we know what he has told us to do in the Bible and are doing it.

2. *A rule of justice.* There are two obvious ways that human rule can be perverted. It can be by the whim of those in power and not by law. Or even if it is by law, it can be by unjust laws that exist only to legitimize the oppression of the weak by those more powerful. God is guilty of neither of these perversions. First, his rule is by law. Second, it is according to holiness or justice, for the law of God is perfectly upright, which is what the last sentence of the psalm asserts: "Holiness adorns your house for endless days, O LORD."

Everything associated with God is holy, from which it follows that we must be holy too. If we are not holy, how can we adorn the house of God? We cannot! We do the very opposite. We dishonor it—and the God we profess to serve. If we strive to live holy lives, as we must, then we honor God and prove that he is indeed ruling us as his holy people. Peter wrote, "But you are a chosen people, a royal priesthood, a holy nation, a people belonging to God, that you may declare the praises of him who called you out of darkness into his wonderful light" (1 Peter 2:9).

Why Worship God

Psalm 95:1–7

Come, let us bow down in worship.
—PSALM 95:6

Psalm 95 gives two important reasons we should worship God.

1. *Because God is such a great God* (vv. 3–5). Appreciation can be shown to many people, praise to others. Worship belongs to God only. Yet we cannot worship God until we have a proper sense of who he is. Verses 4–5 begin by teaching that he is the Creator of all things: "In his hand are the depths of the earth, and the mountain peaks belong to him. The sea is his, for he made it, and his hands formed the dry land."

This is the starting place. That God is the Creator of everything is the first reason for the call to worship in verses 1–2.

2. *Because God is our own dear Shepherd* (vv. 6–7). This stanza uses God's relationship to his people as a second reason why we should worship God and as a reason for the psalm's second call to worship in verse 6. Here the worship of God is made personal, for we are reminded that God not only made the caves and the mountains, the seas and the dry land; he made us too. What is more, he cares for us, if we are numbered among his people. Using a common but beautiful pastoral image, the psalm says that we are God's sheep, "the flock under his care" (v. 7).

What Christian can read this without thinking of Jesus's use of the same image in John 10: "I am the good shepherd. The good shepherd lays down his life for the sheep. . . . I know my sheep and my sheep know me—just as the Father knows me and I know the Father—and I lay down my life for the sheep. . . . My sheep listen to my voice; I know them, and they follow me. I give them eternal life, and they shall never perish; no one can snatch them out of my hand" (John 10:11, 14–15, 27–28).

We owe God worship because he is God and has created us. But even more, we owe him worship because he has given his life for us, has called us to faith, and now keeps and preserves us with a power that nothing either in heaven or earth can shake. We are the sheep of Jesus's hand, and nothing will ever snatch us out of Jesus's hand.

The Doctrine of Creation

Psalm 98:1–9

Let the sea resound, and everything in it, the world, and all who live in it.
—PSALM 98:7

The psalmist is suggesting that nature is not yet all that God has predestined it to be and is in a sense waiting for its true fulfillment. This understanding of creation is radically different from the way the world looks at nature. The world makes either one of two errors where the cosmos is concerned. Either it deifies nature, virtually worshiping it. Or the world regards nature as evolving toward perfection, accompanied by the human race, which is also evolving.

The apostle Paul in Romans 8:19–21 gives us a very different picture. He pictures something staring off into the distance. But it is not man who is on tiptoe looking off into the distance. It is creation itself, and what creation is earnestly looking for, as it looks beyond itself, is the "glorious freedom of the children of God," which it will share. Creation wants to praise God, and will, according to Paul's teaching and this psalm.

The other error of the world is seeing in nature some kind of perfecting principle, almost like saying, "The world is not God yet, but it is on the way." In cosmic terms this is the principle of evolution. In human terms it is the principle of inevitable perfection: "Every day in every way I am getting better and better." In other words, I may not be God yet, but I will be, given time. Of course, a lot of time has gone by and man seems to be as much unlike God as he ever was.

The Christian's perspective is far more balanced and more mature than this or anything the world can devise. The Christian doctrine of creation has three parts.

1. *This is God's world.* God made it, and it is his. As a result, we must respect the world and not abuse it. We must treat it responsibly.

2. *The world is not what it was created to be.* It has been subjected to troubles as the result of God's judgment on man at the time of the fall. It has been subjected to frustration, bondage, and decay, according to Paul's teaching in Romans.

3. *The world will one day be renewed.* I think of the way C. S. Lewis developed this idea in *The Lion, the Witch, and the Wardrobe.* In the first section of that book, when Narnia was under the power of the wicked Witch of the North, the land was in a state of perpetual winter. Spring never came. But when Aslan rose from the dead, the ice began to melt, flowers bloomed, and the trees turned green. It is poetical writing but it describes something that will happen. The rivers will indeed clap their hands. The mountains will indeed sing. And we will all join in. Hallelujah!

The Lord Is Good

Psalm 100:1–5 .

> For the LORD is good and his love endures forever; his faith-
> fulness continues through all generations.
> —*PSALM 100:5*

This final verse of Psalm 100 invites us to thank God because of who he is. It tells us three things about him.

1. *God is "good."* The gods of the heathen were not good. They were self-ish and capricious. You could never know when they might turn against you and do you harm. Not so our God. The God of the Bible is and has always been good. When he created the world and all that is in it, he saw that it was "good" (Gen. 1:4–31). When he gave us his law, that law was "good" (Rom. 7:12). When he reveals his will to us, his will is "good, pleasing and·perfect" (12:2). The word *gospel* means the "good news." The very word *God* is a shortened form of "good."

2. *God is "love."* This love "endures forever." God is many things. He has many attributes. But nothing lies so much at the very heart of God as love. Nothing so endears him to his people.

3. *God is "faithful."* In the midst of a rapidly changing world it is a comfort to know that God himself is unchanging. He is today what he was for our fathers and mothers—and what he was for Paul and Mary and Joseph and David, indeed for all the patriarchs of the faith back to and including our first parents. Moreover, he can be counted on to remain as he has been.

Has God been good in the past? Of course! Then he will always be good. You need never worry that he might cease to be good or change his good ways.

Has God been loving? Of course. Then he will always be loving. His very nature is love. You need never worry that he will cease to love you.

Has he seen you through difficult times? Very few Christians have avoided such difficult times altogether. Yet those who have gone through them testify that God has kept them securely. Well, then, he will do it for you also, whatever may come. Has anyone ever had greater reasons to thank God than we who are his redeemed people, who know him not only as our Creator but also as our loving Shepherd and Lord? Then let us shout with gladness: "Enter his gates with thanksgiving and his courts with praise; give thanks to him and praise his name. For the LORD is good and his love endures forever; his faithfulness continues through all generations" (Ps. 100:4–5).

All God's Benefits

Psalm 103:1–22

Praise the LORD, O my soul, and forget not all his benefits.
—PSALM 103:2

Why should a person praise God? Because of "all his benefits." David lists what he means by God's benefits in verses 3–5.

1. *Forgiveness of sins* (v. 3). This is the greatest of all gifts that we can receive from God, and the first we need to have. It is true that we need to remember to thank God for our homes and jobs and wealth and all our material possessions. But where would we be if we were to acquire all these things and lose our souls? The forgiveness of our sins is the greatest benefit any of us can ever receive from God, and we can receive it only because God gave his Son over to death on the cross to procure it for us.

2. *Healing* (v. 3). The second thing the writer is thankful for is healing, indeed healing of "all" his diseases. This verse has played an important but unwarranted role in some systems of theology that stress what is called "healing in the atonement," meaning that if we have been saved from sin by Christ, we have been healed or have a right to be healed of any physical affliction too. This is bad theology, because it is simply not true that those who have been forgiven for sin are spared or have a right to be spared all diseases. Believers do get sick, and many passages teach that God has his purposes in the sicknesses.

What does the sentence mean then? David is saying that when we are healed, as we often are, it is God who has done it. He is the healer of the body as well as of the soul. Therefore, such health as we have been given is a sure gift from God. God should be praised for it.

3. *Redemption from the pit* (v. 4). When David says that God redeems our lives from the pit, he is saying that God brings us back from the very brink of death. The "pit" is Sheol, where the dead go when they die. As far as he himself is concerned, he does not mean that God has rescued him from Sheol by taking him to heaven, for he is not in heaven yet. He means that God has redeemed him by sparing him from death, presumably by healing his diseases.

4. *Satisfaction with good things* (v. 5). And it is not a matter of a mere rescue either, as if our lives are spared but, so far as anything else is concerned, our lives are miserable. No. God satisfies us with good things "so that [our] youth is renewed like the eagle's." Hasn't that been your experience? Can't you praise God for an abundance of good things that he has graciously brought into your life?

Heed These Things

Psalm 107:1–43

Whoever is wise, let him heed these things and consider the great love of the LORD.
—*PSALM 107:43*

I suggest four uses of the doctrine Psalm 107 teaches, that even for the
righteous God sends sorrow as well as joy, hardship as well as material
blessing—yet is not arbitrary.

1. *Reverence for God.* Since God's ways are not our ways and his ultimate
   purposes in life are usually beyond our finding out, we must revere him
   and be humble.
2. *Looking for things that are eternal.* Looking beyond the seen to the
   unseen and eternal is faith. Although there are ups and downs in this
   life, the end of all things for God's people is not down but up.
3. *Calling sinners to repentance.* Although the ways of God in this life are
   not always within our understanding, nevertheless we do discern some
   important patterns, and one of them is that arrogance, strife, self-love,
   greed, and other forms of wickedness are generally punished, while
   virtue is frequently rewarded.
4. *Thanksgiving.* Believers should thank God for being what he is and acting as he does—and not only when things are going our way or we have
   it easy.

Alexander Duff was an eloquent pastor and missionary pioneer, the first
sent to India by the Presbyterian Church of Scotland. On October 14, 1829,
he and his wife set out for the Indian subcontinent on a ship called the Lady
Holland, and four months later, at midnight on the 13th of February 1830,
the ship ran aground while attempting to navigate the Cape of Good Hope.
The pounding surf soon destroyed the ship, washing everything it held away,
but miraculously all the passengers and crew made it safely to land.

Nothing remained of their belongings, but as one sailor walked along the
shore looking for food and fuel, he came upon two books, a Bible and the
Scottish Psalm Book. He found the name of Alexander Duff in both of them,
so he brought them to the missionary. Duff had been transporting eight hundred books to India, where he hoped to (and later did) establish a college, but
of those eight hundred books only these two remained. In spite of this loss,
Duff at once opened the Bible to Psalm 107 and read it to the other survivors,
concluding with the words: "Whoever is wise, let him heed these things and
consider the great love of the LORD."

Can you do that? What matters most in life is not the number or severity of
the perils from which we are delivered, but whether we are actually in the hands
of that greatly loving God. If we are in his hands, we can "heed these things,"
"consider the great love of the LORD," and then praise him as Psalm 107 does.

Fighting for Christ

Psalm 110:1–7

You will rule in the midst of your enemies.
—*PSALM 110:2*

Christ is ruling from his throne in order to extend his kingdom throughout the whole world through the witness of his followers. Two phrases here show us what Jesus's reign is like.

1. *"In the midst of your enemies."* Here is a king who rules in the midst of his enemies. His is a spiritual rule that infiltrates the hostile powers of this world in a nearly invisible fashion. Moreover, it is a rule that he exerts indirectly, as it were, not by coming in power himself (though he will also do that in judgment at the end of time) but through his people, the church.

Our calling, though, is not to Christianize society, as if the secular world could be made Christian. Rather, we are to fight for Christ's spiritual kingdom. How? Paul pointed out the right way: "Though we live in the world, we do not wage war as the world does. The weapons we fight with are not the weapons of the world. On the contrary, they have divine power to demolish strongholds" (2 Cor. 10:3–4).

What are our weapons? First, *participation*. Christians need to participate in secular life rather than merely shoot at secular people and what secular people are doing from the sidelines. Participation is implied in Paul's words "though we live in the world" and in the psalm's equivalent expression "in the midst of your enemies." Second, *persuasion*. Persuasion is opposed to coercion. Informed by God's Word, Christians must endeavor to persuade others of the truth: "We demolish arguments and every pretension that sets itself up against the knowledge of God, and we take captive every thought to make it obedient to Christ" (v. 5). Third, *prayer*. We pray because we know that even with the best of scripturally informed arguments, without God's specific supernatural intervention, the world will neither understand nor heed what we are saying.

2. *"Your troops will be willing"* (Ps. 110:3). Those who are enlisted in Christ's service have enlisted willingly. This army is composed entirely of volunteers. True, these soldiers were not always willing—they were once as hostile to Christ and his kingdom as others still are—but they were made willing by that gentle working of Jesus's grace in their lives. Perceiving his sacrifice of himself for them and loving him for it, they have now made themselves willing sacrifices for him.

Are you willing? Have you presented yourself to Jesus as a living sacrifice? I hope you have. If not, perhaps what you need is a new vision of the exalted Lord Jesus Christ. When Isaiah saw the Lord seated on a throne, high and exalted, he heard the voice of the Lord saying, "Whom shall I send? And who will go for us?" Isaiah could only answer, "Here am I. Send me!" (Isa. 6:1–8).

The Caring God
Psalm 113:1–9

He settles the barren woman in her home as a happy mother of children.
—*PSALM 113:9*

Some modern, more pedantic scholars suggest that verse 9 is a weak ending to Psalm 113. They fail to see how a psalm calling for praise of the exalted God can properly end on a reference to God's provision for "the barren woman."

But that is exactly the point of the psalm. What is most praiseworthy about God, according to the psalmist, is that, although he is infinitely exalted above everything, even the heavens, he nevertheless stoops to raise the poor from the dust, the needy from the ash heap, and even the barren woman from the disgrace her barrenness brought her in those days.

This psalm ends by saying that the great, exalted God of the Bible is not only concerned about needy people in general but also with the individual. He cares about you. He cares for you and me personally. He cares for us specifically in two ways.

1. *He saves us from our sin one by one.* Not everyone has the experience in this life of being raised from the dust to a throne or from an ash heap to sit with princes, but all who are saved by Christ are lifted from the pigsty of this decadent world to sit with Jesus in his glory and rule with him. It happens one by one! In our sin you and I have been the lowest of the low, but God has raised us up through faith in Jesus Christ. Has that been your experience? Do you know Jesus not as some great Savior in general, but as your own personal Savior and Lord?

2. *He rescues us when we are cast down.* Downtrodden individuals are not a collective mass, though this is how society generally regards them. They are individual people who have suffered specific defeats or setbacks. They are not discouraged in some general way. God knows each of these persons individually. He knows you. If even the very hairs on your head are numbered (Luke 12:7), God clearly cares for you and knows exactly what you are suffering. Moreover, he is able to do something about it. He is able to lift you up and seat you with princes.

Has life cast you down? Turn to God who is able to lift you up and trust him to do it. Then do as the psalm finally says: Praise the Lord!

Repaying the Lord

Psalm 116:1–19

How can I repay the LORD for all his goodness to me?
—*PSALM 116:12*

Without suggesting that there is any intrinsically valuable thing we have to give God, the psalmist does suggest ways we can respond to God's goodness. First, we need to tell others about God's mercy to us. In the very last verses of Psalm 116, the psalmist speaks of thanking God and calling on him "in the presence of all his people, in the courts of the house of the LORD." He means that we should give public testimony to God's redeeming grace.

Second, we need to "lift up the cup of salvation and call on the name of the LORD" (v. 13). This metaphor is based on the libation or drink offering prescribed in Numbers 28:7. In the postbiblical period the rabbis said there were to be no sacrificial gifts without libations, noting that the two are joined in Joel 1:9. They also said that the words of Judges 9:13 ("wine, which cheers both gods and men") were to be pronounced as a blessing over the cup. But there is a big difference between the drink offering of Numbers 28 and what the psalmist says here. In Psalm 116 the writer is not talking about *giving* God anything, though that might be expected from his question ("How can I repay the LORD?"). Instead he talks about *taking* something, that is, the cup of salvation. It is a profound insight: the only way we can repay God from whom everything comes is by taking even more from him.

"I will lift up the cup of salvation" is immediately joined to "and call on the name of the LORD," because we receive God's gift and then go on in the same relationship, forever asking and receiving from him.

Jesus and the Twelve must have sung Psalm 116 at the Last Supper after Jesus had instituted the communion service with its "cup of salvation." That cup represented the blood of Jesus, which was poured out as an atonement for our sins. It speaks of giving all the way, 100 percent. "Salvation comes from the LORD" (Jonah 2:9), but it is also a cup that needs to be taken by us, which is what we symbolize by taking it at the Lord's Supper. It is a spiritual cup, and the way it is taken is by faith, by believing that Jesus is truly the Son of God and our Savior.

The Lord Is God

Psalm 118:1–29

The Lord is God.
—*PSALM 118:27*

The last three verses of Psalm 118 are a powerful summary and application of the psalm: "The LORD is God, and he has made his light shine upon us. With boughs in hand, join in the festal procession up to the horns of the altar. You are my God, and I will give you thanks; you are my God, and I will exalt you. Give thanks to the LORD, for he is good; his love endures forever."

These verses make three powerful statements about God and about our right relationship to him.

1. *"The LORD is God."* In verse 27 the word "LORD" is the proper name Jehovah, or Yahweh. The verse is saying that it is Jehovah, the God of the Old Testament, who is truly God, not one of the other competing gods of this rebellious, evil world. This is the great issue of religion, not, Is there a god? (the Bible says it is only the fool who questions this—Ps. 14:1), but rather, Who is the true God? In this verse the psalmist says that Jehovah is the true God and that he has revealed this to us by making his light shine on us. This is the God who is being worshiped at the altar in Jerusalem, he and none other.

2. *"You are my God."* This God is the psalmist's own personal God, not merely the God of Israel, even less a God who is the result of some abstract philosophical speculation. Jehovah is his God, one in whom he has placed his own personal trust and to whom he has made a personal commitment. Is this God your God?

3. *"The LORD . . . is good."* In verse 29 the psalmist calls on the people among whom he is bearing witness to thank God because this true God "is good." The psalm began and now also ends with these words, drawing us back to consider the experience of the psalmist (and ourselves) once again.

The writer found that God is good because God had been good to him. He had been oppressed, but God had freed him from his oppression. He had been attacked, but God had delivered him from his enemies. He had been about to fall, but God had raised him up and given him important work to do, testifying to God's goodness. Is it any different for those who have been saved by Jesus Christ? We too have been freed from sin, delivered, and given work to do. If that is your case, thank God and get to work.

Studying the Word of God
Psalm 119:161–76

I obey your statutes, for I love them greatly.
—PSALM 119:167

Study of the Bible must be the consuming passion of a believer's life. This is because it is only by the study of the Word of God that we learn what it is to obey God and follow Jesus. If you want to know God as he speaks to you through the Bible, you should do the following.

1. *Study the Bible daily.* We should discipline our lives to include regular periods of Bible study, just as we discipline ourselves to have regular periods for sleep, eating our meals, and so on. These things are necessary if the body is to be healthy and if good work is to be done. In the same way, we must feed regularly on God's Word if we are to become and remain spiritually strong.

2. *Study the Bible systematically.* The best system is a regular, disciplined study of certain books of the Bible as a whole. The psalmist did this. The proof is the great variety of terms he uses for the Scriptures. As he saw it, the Bible embraces the law, statutes, ways, precepts, decrees, commands, words, and promises of God. He did not want to neglect even one of them.

3. *Study the Bible comprehensively.* There should be an attempt to become acquainted with the Bible as a whole. This means reading it comprehensively. Paul told Timothy, "*All* Scripture is God-breathed and is useful for teaching, rebuking, correcting and training in righteousness" (2 Tim. 3:16).

4. *Study the Bible devotionally.* Nothing is clearer in this psalm than the close, indissoluble link between knowledge of God and study of the Word of God, between loving God and loving the Bible. In reading the Bible, we study to know God, hear his voice, and be changed by him as we grow in holiness. Furthermore, we must memorize important sections of Scripture. As Christians we need to allow the Word of God to become a part of us. To have that happen, we must memorize it.

5. *Study the Bible prayerfully.* The best way to study the Bible is to encompass the study in prayer. Before we begin to read, we should say, "Lord God, I am turning to your Word. I cannot understand it as I should. I need your Holy Spirit to instruct me and draw a proper response from me. What I understand I want to obey. Help me to do that for Jesus's sake." Then we must study the passage, and when we find something that pertains to our lives, we must stop and acknowledge it prayerfully. Without regular, personal Bible study and prayer, we are not really walking with Christ as his followers, and we are certainly not obeying him in specific areas.

Heavenly Jerusalem

Psalm 122:1—9

Our feet are standing in your gates, O Jerusalem.
—*PSALM 122:2*

We look for the heavenly Jerusalem still to come, for we are still pilgrims. We have not yet fully arrived, and our eyes are fixed not even on the church, as wonderful as it can be, but on the heavenly "city with foundations, whose architect and builder is God" (Heb. 11:10).

We catch a glimpse of that city in Revelation, where the Holy City, the New Jerusalem, descends from heaven. It is no mere copy of the earthly city that had been destroyed for its sins. It is a glorious new city described in what we would call surrealistic terms. "It shone with the glory of God, and its brilliance was like that of a very precious jewel, like a jasper, clear as crystal. It had a great, high wall with twelve gates, and with twelve angels at the gates. On the gates were written the names of the twelve tribes of Israel. . . . The wall of the city had twelve foundations, and on them were the names of the twelve apostles of the Lamb" (21:11–14).

When John looked for the city's temple, he did not see one, because "the Lord God Almighty and the Lamb are its temple." Moreover: "The city does not need the sun or the moon to shine on it, for the glory of God gives it light, and the Lamb is its lamp. The nations will walk by its light, and the kings of the earth will bring their splendor into it. On no day will its gates ever be shut, for there will be no night there. . . . Nothing impure will ever enter it, nor will anyone who does what is shameful or deceitful, but only those whose names are written in the Lamb's book of life" (vv. 22–27).

A river of life is in the city, flowing down from the throne of God. It causes trees to bear fruit, and their leaves are for "the healing of the nations" (22:2). John's description ends by glancing at God's servants, those who see God's face and bear his name on their foreheads. They dwell in perpetual light and reign with him "forever and ever" (v. 5).

These descriptions bear ties to reality, for heaven is a real place, not merely an idea; yet they are also clearly symbols, all with a rich biblical history, pointing to the glories, joys, and eternal security of those who are truly God's people. What really matters is that we are going there. Christians are pilgrims who know that God is able to keep them from falling and at last to present them before his glorious presence with great joy (see Jude 24).

Our Help

Psalm 124:1–8

Our help is in the name of the LORD, the Maker of heaven and earth.
—*PSALM 124:8*

The final verse of Psalm 124 is an echo of Psalm 121:2. Similar verses occur throughout the psalms, and many worship services have begun with these words or others like them. Job Orton (1717–1783) reported in the late eighteenth century that the French Protestants always used this verse to begin their public worship. Rightly so, for these words direct our thoughts to God, who is the only sure help of his people and the only rightful object of our true devotion. There are three important emphases in this verse.

1. *"Our help is in the name of* the LORD." Others may offer to help us, but we dare not turn to them since they do not have what we need. Only the Lord, the Maker of heaven and earth, is adequate for us in our weakness. He is omniscient; he always knows what we need and knows it perfectly. He is omnipresent; he is always there when we need him. He is omnipotent; he can do what needs to be done. He is loving and gracious; he always has our spiritual best interest at heart. With a God like this why should we ever trust other gods or lean so much on other people?

2. *"Our* help *is in the name of the* LORD." Everything we need or can possibly need is in God, but particularly we rejoice that our *help* is in God, since we are so helpless. Spurgeon observed that in God we have help "as troubled sinners," being delivered from the punishment and guilt of our sin. We have help "as dull scholars," being taught to know and understand God's Word. We have help "as trembling professors," being witnesses to his gospel, God giving us words to speak and blessing our testimony in the lives of others. We have help "as inexperienced travellers" on life's journey, being guided on the right paths and kept from perilous pitfalls and wasteful detours. We have help "as feeble workers," being unprofitable servants at best, but God is blessing the work of our hands and making it of lasting value.

3. "Our *help is in the name of the* LORD." The help that is to be found in God is *our* help—not someone else's, but our very own help. We have tested God's Word and have found God to be everything he has described himself as being. We look to the past and testify, "The Lord has helped me." We look to the present and assert, "The Lord is my help even this very day." We look to the future and affirm, "The Lord will be my help forever."

Victory through Suffering
Psalm 129:1–8

> Plowmen have plowed my back and made their furrows long.
> —PSALM 129:3

Psalm 129:1–3 describes Jesus, the Messiah, as well as the Jews from whom he came. Jesus was beaten literally. Like Israel, Jesus might well have said, "They have greatly oppressed me from my youth." Jesus would certainly have added, "but they have not gained the victory over me" (v. 2).

How could they? Jesus is God, the sovereign Ruler of the universe. Therefore, although Satan and the united kings of the earth should gather together "against the LORD and against his Anointed One" (Ps. 2:2), God the heavenly King only laughs at them, for he has rescued us from sin by Christ's death, raised Jesus from his dark tomb, and lifted him to glory, therefore announcing triumphantly, "I have installed my King on Zion, my holy hill" (v. 6).

Because Jesus lives, we also live, and because he has been victorious, we shall be victorious too. Victory is not gained by avoiding our share of this world's oppression. Jesus said, "In this world you will have trouble," but added, "Take heart! I have overcome the world" (John 16:33). We must triumph as he did, enduring oppression and ultimately passing through the portal of death to resurrection.

Often in the long course of history, Christians have been forced to cry, as Israel did, "They have greatly oppressed me from my youth!" However, underneath that cry and sometimes even over it, we also hear the confession, "But they have not gained the victory over me."

Why is this pattern of oppression and suffering so necessary? The answer is, So the world might know that our power is not from ourselves, but from God. The apostle Paul was repeatedly imprisoned, beaten, stoned, shipwrecked, starved, and threatened, but here is what he wrote to the believers at Corinth to encourage them: "We have this treasure [the gospel] in jars of clay to show that this all-surpassing power is from God and not from us. We are hard pressed on every side, but not crushed; perplexed, but not in despair; persecuted, but not abandoned; struck down, but not destroyed. We always carry around in our body the death of Jesus, so that the life of Jesus may also be revealed in our body. For we who are alive are always being given over to death for Jesus' sake, so that his life may be revealed in our mortal body" (2 Cor. 4:7–11).

There is a forceful Christian battle cry, composed in Latin and placed next to the burning bush: *Nec tamen consumebatur*! It means, "Yet not consumed." God's people may be oppressed but they are never consumed and so can cry, "Thanks be to God! He gives us the victory through our Lord Jesus Christ" (1 Cor. 15:57).

Forgiveness
Psalm 130:1–8

But with you there is forgiveness; therefore you are feared.
—PSALM 130:4

Let me mention four things about God's forgiveness.

1. *God's forgiveness is inclusive.* Verse 4 sets no limits on what sins are forgiven. It says, "There is forgiveness," forgiveness for any sin by anybody. Murder, adultery, lying, stealing, coveting, failing to keep the Lord's Day, taking the name of God in vain, whatever it may be. There is forgiveness with God. You may be utterly ignorant of the Bible. You may not know a single item of theology. Know this at least: "There is forgiveness" with God.

2. *God's forgiveness is for now.* You do not have to hope that somehow you might have forgiveness at the last day, at the final judgment, but need to stand in trembling uncertainty until then. You do not have to work for it or earn it; you could never earn it anyway. There is forgiveness now, at this very moment; and it is for you, whoever you may be, wherever you are, or whatever you have done. At this very moment you can pass from death to life and know that your sins have been forgiven forever.

3. *God's forgiveness is for those who want it.* It is there, but you must ask God for it and trust him to give it to you. The writer of the psalm is confessing his sin, not covering it up. He is asking God for mercy. He is believing, or trusting, God, for he says, "With you there is forgiveness." Thousands of people confess this each week in the words of the Apostles' Creed: "I believe . . . in the forgiveness of sins." Have they actually asked God for forgiveness? Many do not even know what the words mean. Do not be among those unbelieving masses. Come to God and ask him for the forgiveness you need and he provides.

4. *God's forgiveness leads to godly living.* Such forgiveness leads to a heightened reverence for God. It is what verse 4 teaches when it adds to forgiveness the words "therefore you are feared." Fear—a holy reverence of God—is the essence of true religion. It is what is drawn from us when we know that we have been loved and saved by God in spite of our sin and former disregard of him.

The true and inevitable effects of forgiveness are love and worship and service. By these effects you can measure whether you have actually confessed your sin, believed on God, and been forgiven or are merely presuming on forgiveness without any genuine repentance or faith. Those who have been forgiven are softened and humbled and overwhelmed by God's mercy, and they determine never to sin against such a great and fearful goodness. They do sin, but in their deepest heart they do not want to, and when they do, they hurry back to God for deliverance.

The Omniscience of God
Psalm 139:1–24

O LORD, you have searched me and you know me.
—*PSALM 139:1*

Here is what appreciation of the omniscience of God should do for every Christian.

1. *It should humble us.* I think here of Job, who questioned the troubles he experienced. We might expect God to explain things to Job. Instead, we find God rebuking Job for presuming to think that he could understand God's ways. At the end Job is completely humbled. He replies to God: "Surely I spoke of things I did not understand, things too wonderful for me to know. . . . Therefore I despise myself and repent in dust and ashes" (Job 42:3, 6).

If we ever begin to appreciate the perfect knowledge of God and by contrast our own pathetic understanding, the first effect this will have on us will be humility. We will be embarrassed to think that we ever supposed we could contend with God intellectually.

2. *It should comfort us.* God knows the worst about us and loves us anyway. He knows the best about us even when other people do not and blame us for things that are not our fault. Job expressed his comfort in God's knowledge, saying, "He knows the way that I take; when he has tested me, I will come forth as gold" (23:10).

3. *It should encourage us to live for God.* In Psalm 139 David has been reflecting on the omniscience of God, and it has led him to ask God to help him lead an upright life. He knows that God will do it precisely because God knows him so well.

We know very little. We do not even know ourselves, but God knows us. He knows our weaknesses and our strengths. He knows our sins but also our aspirations toward a godly life. He knows when isolation will help us grow strong but also when we need companionship to stand in righteousness. He knows when we need rebuking and correcting but also when we need teaching and encouragement. If anyone can "lead me in the way everlasting," it is God. Moreover, since I know he knows me and wants to help me, I can be encouraged to get on with upright living.

4. *It should help us to pray.* Jesus encouraged his followers to pray to God confidently, expecting answers. "When you pray, do not keep on babbling like pagans, for they think they will be heard because of their many words. Do not be like them, for your Father knows what you need before you ask him" (Matt. 6:7–8).

God's knowledge of what we need is so perfect that he often answers even before we pray to him. "Before they call I will answer; while they are still speaking I will hear," wrote Isaiah (Isa. 65:24). Who can be terrified by a God who knows and answers us like that?

Walking by Faith
Psalm 141:1–10

Let the wicked fall into their own nets, while I pass by in safety.
—PSALM 141:10

I n the last stanza of Psalm 141 (vv. 8–10), David concludes his prayer or, we could say—making the link between prayer and worship—the time of worship ends. The service is now over. We hear the benediction and are about to go back out into the world. What should have happened to us as a result of the time spent with God? David suggests that, having been with God and having prayed to God, we should leave with our eyes still fixed on God. In the world there are dangers. Snares have been set by the wicked, traps by evildoers; but if our eyes are fixed on God, we will be able to walk safely through these many dangers and temptations.

There is a scene from *Pilgrim's Progress* by John Bunyan that has always struck me forcefully. Pilgrim is making his way up a steep path by night toward the Porter's Lodge. He comes to a place where two lions are chained by the path, one on his right and the other on his left. He does not know they are chained, and he is afraid and about to turn back when the porter calls to him, saying, "Fear not the Lions, for they are chained, and are placed there for trial of faith where it is, and for discovery of those that have none. Keep in the midst of the Path, and no hurt shall come unto thee." So Pilgrim presses forward, keeping on the straight path by fixing his eyes on the porter and refusing to look at the lions lunging at him from the sides of the path. This is the image David paints. He is fixing his eyes on God as he makes his way through the dangers of life.

One day Jesus will have destroyed those dangers. Hebrews applies the words of Psalm 8 to him: "You crowned him with glory and honor and put everything under his feet. . . . At present we do not see everything subject to him. But we see Jesus . . ." (Heb. 2:7–9). Therefore, "Let us fix our eyes on Jesus, the author and perfecter of our faith. . . . Consider him who endured such opposition from sinful men, so that you will not grow weary and lose heart" (12:2–3). This is the secret of an effective godly life as well as the point at which all true worship should begin and end.

Anticipated Blessing
Psalm 144:1–15

Blessed are the people of whom this is true; blessed
are the people whose God is the LORD.
—PSALM 144:15

The final section of Psalm 144 anticipates the blessing the king expects God to give his kingdom after those who are threatening him are defeated. The psalm's prayer for deliverance is a confident prayer leading to the vision of future blessing. David is sure that when the deliverance is given, the blessing will be realized.

The blessing begins with the family as the foundation of any strong society (v. 12). It advances to the people's prosperity (v. 13), then to the security of the city (v. 14). Finally, the blessing is anchored in its only adequate source, God, which is why the psalm ends by saying that the greatest blessing of all is to have Jehovah as one's God.

How different this blessing is from the world's way of thinking! Most people want the blessings of these last verses but they suppose they can have them without God. People are not made to be alone. People need people, and most people dream of a loving, supportive family in which they can prosper and attain their potential, but without God the family has no strength and relationships are frequently destroyed. The collapse of the American family in our day is one proof of the effects of godlessness. People also want to prosper. Who does not? They want their work to go well and their bank accounts to grow, but even when this happens, they are still insecure and find that things alone do not satisfy them. Finally, people want to be safe, but when the culture is crumbling, as ours is, they know they are not secure and that violence and even death can strike them from nearly any source at any moment.

Having Jehovah as our God does not in itself immediately guarantee these blessings, for we live in a fallen world. Even David did not experience uninterrupted blessings. The families of believers also fail, as David's did; we do not always live utterly free from want; we are often in physical danger, as David was when he wrote this psalm. But we are blessed by God all the same. Besides, to know God is the greatest of all blessings, and knowing and serving God is the best and surest path to every other blessing.

Blessing
Psalm 146:1–10

Blessed is he whose help is the God of Jacob,
whose hope is in the LORD his God.
—PSALM 146:5

Verses 5–9 of Psalm 146 form a beatitude, presenting the blessings of God.
1. *The Lord is our hope* (v. 5). God alone can save us. God saves us from
our enemies and ultimately from all human calamities and from sin through
the work of Jesus Christ.

2. *The Lord remains faithful forever* (v. 6). God remains faithful to us after
he has saved us. The faithful can remain faithful to God because God is faithful to them.

3. *The Lord sets prisoners free* (v. 7). Verses 7 and 8 take us to Jesus's announced purpose of his mission (Luke 4:18, quoting from Isa. 61:1–2) "to
preach good news to the poor . . . proclaim freedom for the prisoners and recovery of sight for the blind, to release the oppressed." As far as we know, Jesus
never literally freed anyone from prison. That fact and the context here show
that the deliverance in both places must be spiritual, a deliverance from sin.

4. *The Lord gives sight to the blind* (v. 8). Again, we are reminded of Jesus
when the psalmist describes God as giving sight to the blind. The greatest
blindness of all is blindness to the truth of God disclosed in Scripture. When
Jehovah gives sight to the blind, the blind recognize the Bible to be true and
place their faith in Jesus.

5. *The Lord lifts up those who are bowed down* (v. 8). Many things in life
push us around or knock us down, but God cares for us and lifts us up again.

6. *The Lord loves the righteous* (v. 8). Why does God grant such blessings?
The answer is because he loves us. It is not because we have made ourselves
righteous. God has made us righteous in Christ, and even that is because he
loves us.

7. *The Lord watches over the alien* (v. 9). God watches over the defenseless
and protects them from the wicked.

In the last verse of this psalm the writer says that the God he has been
describing and praising will reign "for all generations." It follows that God
also must be praised from generation to generation.

Will you put your hope in God and worship God as the only utterly trustworthy being in this universe? If you will not, your only alternative is despair
and cynicism, for people will always let you down. The politicians will let you
down. The intellectuals will let you down. The scientists will let you down.
"Salvation comes from the LORD," said Jonah, and he was right (Jonah 2:9).
God alone is utterly good, utterly powerful, and utterly trustworthy. Why
settle for less? God is the only being about whom we can honestly and truly
say, "Hallelujah."

Always Praising Him
Psalm 150:1–6

Praise the LORD.
—*PSALM 150:1*

Psalm 150 answers four questions about worship. First question: Where should we praise God? Answer: Everywhere, in heaven and on earth. Second question: Why should we praise God? Answer: Because of everything God is and for all he has done. Third question: How should we praise God? Answer: With everything we've got.

Now at last, question four: Who should praise God? Answer: Everything and everybody. "Everything that has breath," says the psalmist (v. 6).

This is exactly what will happen. At the moment, we see God insulted, blasphemed, denied, and ignored. We see Christ rejected. But one day "every knee [will] bow," whether willingly or not (Phil. 2:10). As far as the saints are concerned, the apostle John wrote in Revelation: "Then I heard every creature in heaven and on earth and under the earth and on the sea, and all that is in them, singing: 'To him who sits on the throne and to the Lamb be praise and honor and glory and power, for ever and ever!'" (Rev. 5:13).

What a great choir! What a great song! What a great privilege. It will be ours if we have placed our faith in Jesus Christ, the Lamb of God who has indeed taken away the sin of those who trust him.

At Tenth Presbyterian Church, it is our custom to read through the psalms consecutively. When we get to the end, we just go back and start again. There is a sense in which we should be doing that now. If we have actually come to the place where we have echoed the praise of that great heavenly choir that sings "to him who sits on the throne and to the Lamb" and if we are repeating the final words of the Psalter that cry, "Let everything that has breath praise the LORD," we will want to go back to the first psalm and seek ever more intently the blessing that comes from meditating on and delighting in God's Word. "Blessed is the man . . . [whose] delight is in the law of the LORD, and on his law he meditates day and night" (Ps. 1:1–2).

We cannot praise God without meditating on his Word, for we will only praise God as we come to know him, and the only way we will come to know him is through his self-disclosure in the Bible and by our meditating on it.

It works the other way too, for we cannot miss seeing that the Psalter begins with Bible study and ends with endless praise. It doesn't even end with a doxology, though it could. It does not end with an amen. It ends with a call to praise God, which is itself our great doxology to which we add our own sincere and loud "Amen."

"Let everything that has breath praise the LORD. Praise the LORD."

Knowing God

Proverbs 9:10

The fear of the LORD is the beginning of wisdom, and
the knowledge of the Holy One is insight.
—PROVERBS 9:10

Knowing God is always knowing God in his relationship to us. Consequently, according to the Bible, knowledge of God takes place only where there is also knowledge of ourselves in our deep spiritual need and where there is an accompanying acceptance of God's gracious provision for our need through the work of Christ and the application of that work to us by God's Spirit. Knowledge of God takes place in the context of Christian piety, worship, and devotion. The Bible teaches that this knowledge of God takes place, not so much because we search after God—because we do not—but because God reveals himself to us in Christ and in the Scriptures.

Such knowledge is of vital importance. First, only through the knowledge of God can an individual enter into what the Bible terms *eternal life*. Jesus indicated this when he prayed, "Now this is eternal life, that they may know you, the only true God, and Jesus Christ, whom you have sent" (John 17:3).

Second, knowledge of God is important because it also involves *knowledge of ourselves*. On the one hand, knowledge of ourselves through the knowledge of God is humbling. We are not God nor are we like him. He is holy; we are unholy. He is wise; we are foolish. He is strong; we are weak. On the other hand, such knowledge of ourselves through the knowledge of God is also reassuring and satisfying. For in spite of what we have become, we are still God's creation and are loved by him. No higher dignity has been given to women and men than the dignity the Bible gives them.

Third, the knowledge of God also gives us *knowledge of this world*: its good and its evil, its past and its future, its purpose and its impending judgment at the hand of God. The world is a confusing place until we know the God who made it and learn from him why he made it and what is to happen to it.

A fourth reason the knowledge of God is important is that it is the only way to *personal holiness*. The knowledge of God leads to holiness. To know God as he is, is to love him as he is and to want to be like him.

Finally, the knowledge of God is important in that it is only through a knowledge of God that *the church and those who compose it can become strong*. In ourselves we are weak, but as Daniel wrote, "The people who know their God shall stand firm and take action" (Dan. 11:32 KJV).

So let us learn about God and come to know God in the fullest, biblical sense. This is true wisdom for everyone. It is the special duty and privilege of the Christian.

Boice, *Foundations of the Christian Faith*, InterVarsity, 1986, 23–24.

The Limits of Human Wisdom
Ecclesiastes 1:1–18

Everything is meaningless.
—*ECCLESIASTES 1:2*

Ecclesiastes is a short book; it has only twelve chapters. Yet Ecclesiastes is a high point of the wisdom literature in the sense that it shows the limits of man's earthbound wisdom, just as Job shows the limits of man's knowledge. Ecclesiastes is essentially a sermon on one text: "'Meaningless! Meaningless!' says the Teacher. 'Utterly meaningless! Everything is meaningless.'" As anyone can tell just by looking at the subheads in the New International Version, the preacher develops the text to make these points:

1. Wisdom is meaningless.
2. Pleasures are meaningless.
3. Wisdom and folly are meaningless.
4. Toil is meaningless.
5. Advancement is meaningless.
6. Riches are meaningless.

But if God is sovereign over the affairs of his creation, if he has a single supreme purpose in all he does, and that purpose is a good purpose because he is a good God, then how are we to understand Ecclesiastes?

The answer is that this book shows us the limits and hence the folly of human wisdom apart from revelation. Apart from what God is doing in Jesus Christ and in our lives, the last part of which is at best only partially revealed to us, everything is indeed "meaningless." There is more, of course. There *is* what God is doing, what he reveals. But before we can see those things, we need to see that there is no meaning in anything apart from them. One of the great proofs of our lack of wisdom is that we do not see even this fundamental point of earthly wisdom clearly.

Even Christians don't. Otherwise, why would they spend so much of their time and energy working for things that do not satisfy at any significant level and, in fact, will never do so?

Why do they spend their time acquiring houses and cars and television sets and fine furniture, which will eventually depreciate and decay?

Why do they work for increasingly larger paychecks and bank accounts, which they will not be able to take with them to heaven when they die?

Why do they yearn for earthly recognition, which can vanish in a flash?

Why do we do these things? We do them because we have not learned even the rudimentary earthly wisdom of Ecclesiastes, let alone the infinitely more profound wisdom of the revealed counsels of God. Yet we presume to suppose that we can criticize God for what he is doing in our lives. We think that we could tell him how to do things better, if we only had the chance. What folly! What utter folly! We who think we are teachers need to learn again the first principles of the oracles of God.

Vision of God
Isaiah 6:1–8

I saw the Lord seated on a throne, high and exalted.
—ISAIAH 6:1

The vision contains four elements. The first element is that of sovereignty, embodied in the picture of "the Lord seated on a throne, high and exalted." It is a dramatization of the fact that he and he alone is in control of things and is always in control of them.

The second thing that Isaiah saw was God's train (or robe), and he noticed that it filled the entire temple. This suggests that there is room for no one else at the highest pinnacle of the universe. It is not just that Jehovah reigns, therefore, but also that no one else reigns beside him or in opposition to him.

The third element in Isaiah's vision was a sight of those angelic beings that wait on God to do his bidding. He says each had six wings: "With two wings they covered their faces, with two they covered their feet, and with two they were flying" (v. 2). In saying that they covered their face, he is saying that they were *reverent*, for they did not consider themselves worthy even to gaze upon God. In saying that they covered their feet, he speaks of *self-effacement*. "Seraphim" probably means "the burning ones," so they are glorious also, as is God. Yet they did not want any eyes to settle on them, but on God only. Finally, he speaks of the wings that they used to fly. This speaks of *service,* for they used these to do God's bidding.

Then here is a picture of what is required to serve God: humility, self-effacement, and readiness to respond. And here is a reminder of the resources that are available to God in accomplishing his purposes and protecting those whom he has promised to protect. All the glory and power that surrounds the court of our Lord is also available for the defense of those who are his servants.

The fourth thing that Isaiah noticed was the worship given to God by these hosts of heaven. "They were calling to one another: 'Holy, holy, holy, is the LORD Almighty; the whole earth is full of his glory'" (v. 3). Worship means to acknowledge God's worth, that is, to take up his attributes and to remember them before him one by one. The attribute of God that most impressed these angelic beings was holiness.

Actually, Isaiah had three visions. The first was a vision of God. The second was a vision of himself, for having seen God in his holiness, he recognized afresh that he was a sinner. Finally, there was a vision of service. This came about when Isaiah confessed his sin, was cleansed of his sin by God, heard God's voice saying, "Whom shall I send? And who will go for us?" and then responded, "Here am I. Send me" (v. 8). So should it be for us.

Four Gifts for Christmas

Isaiah 9:6–7

And he will be called Wonderful Counselor, Mighty
God, Everlasting Father, Prince of Peace.
—ISAIAH 9:6

Four names for Jesus are given here. They are great names, for they describe who the incarnate Son of God is and they do so in terms of his gifts to us. By describing him as a Wonderful Counselor, the verse tells us that he is the source of divine spiritual wisdom, which we need. By calling him the Mighty God, it tells us that he will empower us for life's tasks. Everlasting Father unfolds the gift of sonship. Prince of Peace highlights the gifts of peace both between ourselves and God and internally.

As I think about these gifts, I am impressed at how well they correspond to the needs of the human heart. Suppose, even apart from the biblical revelation, that we should conduct an opinion poll to find out what men and women feel they most need. Suppose we should ask, "What do you feel are your greatest needs?"

"Well," people would say, "we have minds. So we have a need to know things rightly, to understand. We need wisdom. We also have wills, and because we have wills, we want to achieve something. We want our lives to make a difference. To do that we need power. We are also individuals, but we sense that we are not meant to be alone. We want to belong somewhere. We need satisfying relationships. We are also conscious of having done wrong things. We need to be forgiven. We need somebody to deal with our guilt." Isn't that what we would find if we should poll people and analyze their basic experiences? Aren't those the things we really need?

As I look at these gifts, I find that they speak to each of those needs.

> To know the truth! Jesus Christ is the truth, and he is for us a Wonderful Counselor.
>
> To achieve something worthwhile! Jesus is the Mighty God who enables us to do that. We accomplish worthwhile things through his power.
>
> To belong to someone! Jesus answers this need, because he is our Everlasting Father. Through him we are brought into God's family.
>
> To be forgiven and at peace! Jesus is the Prince of Peace. He has made peace for us by his death.

Four gifts for Christmas. They are the greatest gifts that anybody can give or we can have, and they are all in Jesus. They are for us. They are for you, if you will have them.

Boice, *The King Has Come*, Geanies House, 1992, 26–27, 35–36.

Common and Special Grace
Isaiah 26:7–11

Though grace is shown to the wicked, they do not learn righteousness.
—*ISAIAH 26:10*

Jesus once compared his ministry to that of John the Baptist. John was an austere figure who lived in the desert and preached a sober message of repentance from sin. Jesus moved among the masses and participated in such joyful affairs as weddings. But the people did not listen to either John or Jesus. So Jesus said: "To what can I compare this generation? They are like children sitting in the marketplaces and calling out to others: 'We played the flute for you, and you did not dance; we sang a dirge and you did not mourn.' For John came neither eating nor drinking, and they say, 'He has a demon.' The Son of Man came eating and drinking, and they say, 'Here is a glutton and a drunkard, a friend of tax collectors and "sinners."'" (Matt. 11:16–19).

People do not respond to common grace. It does not matter whether common grace expresses itself in the good things of life that should lead us to seek out and thank God who is the source of all good things, or whether it expresses itself in bad things, like natural disasters, that are intended as a warning of the even greater disaster of God's final judgment. The wicked respond to neither, as Isaiah says. Therefore, if anyone is going to be saved from sin and brought to true faith in God and obedience, it is going to be by *special grace* and not by *common grace*, that is, by the electing grace of God, which reaches down to regenerate lost sinners and turns them from their destructive ways.

People are always fickle until God brings true stability into their lives through the gospel. If anything of any permanence is to happen—if lives are to be changed, if the seed of the Word is to fall into good soil and bear fruit, and do it year after year—it will only be through the special electing and regenerating grace of God.

Common grace saves no one. But although common grace saves no one, the special grace of God operating by the preaching and teaching of the Word of God does.

Boice, *Amazing Grace*, Tyndale, 1993, 27–28.

Prophetic Truth
Isaiah 48:1–6

I foretold the former things long ago.
—*ISAIAH 48:3*

The Old Testament records numerous prophecies that were shown to be fulfilled in later history, including those about the coming of the Messiah. In considering future prophecies, we need to take notice of three conclusions. First, if such prophecies have been fulfilled as the Bible and history reveal them to have been fulfilled, then the God of the Bible is the true God and we should worship him. This is the conclusion that must be reached if we take God's own challenge through the prophet Isaiah seriously: "'Present your case,' says the LORD. 'Set forth your arguments,' says Jacob's King. 'Bring in your idols to tell us what is going to happen. Tell us what the former things were, so that we may consider them and know their final outcome. Or declare to us the things to come, tell us what the future holds, so we may know that you are gods'" (Isa. 41:21–23).

Second, if these prophecies have been fulfilled, as we know them to have been fulfilled, then the Bible is a supernaturally trustworthy and totally authoritative book. God himself stands behind this book. It follows that we can trust the Bible for what it has to say about own condition and about God's plan of salvation through the death and resurrection of Jesus Christ.

Finally, if the biblical prophecies about past events have come true and if we may, therefore, expect the biblical prophecies about future events to come true, then the future is bright for those who are believers in the Lord Jesus Christ and are his followers. One day the rays of the sun will rise on that last and future world that has been spoken of so much by our contemporaries. But it will not be a world devastated by an atomic holocaust, as some are predicting. It will not be a world decimated by the inevitable encroachment of worldwide famine about which others are warning. It will not be a dehumanized world composed of machines and the men who serve them. These things may come. The Bible even predicts that some of them will come. But this will not be the end. The Bible teaches that there is a future beyond them when the Lord Jesus Christ, the Messiah who came once to suffer and who will return again, will reign in righteousness and will establish a social order in which love and justice prevail.

Boice, *The Bible Study Hour*, September 1972, 6–10.

Deliverance in Zion
Isaiah 63:1–6

It is I, speaking in righteousness.
—ISAIAH 63:1

Who is this warrior described in Isaiah 63:1? He is none other than the Lord Jesus Christ, returning to Jerusalem in the day of his wrath after having subdued the nations. He is the great "I am," speaking in righteousness. He is the Judge and Savior (see v. 4).

The time is coming when God is going to sort things out and punish unrighteousness. If we were to look at this past period in the history of Edom and Israel, we might conclude that Edom will escape and Israel will always suffer. Here is Edom: a nation of sinners, but in power, impregnable in Petra. Here is Israel: chosen of God but disciplined because of sin—her city overthrown, her people scattered. A person might look at this and say, "Well, that's the end of Israel! Off they go to Babylon! They're never going to come back from that captivity. Who ever heard of a captive nation rising and repossessing their land? It has never happened before; it is certainly not going to happen in this case." Yet God brings Edom down, and he exalts his people.

In this world the ungodly often seem to flourish; the godly are stricken. But God says that, in the ultimate working of his plan, the ungodly are going to be punished—the Day of the Lord will come upon them—while those who are his people will be lifted up and blessed in Jesus Christ.

If the Day of the Lord has not yet come, it is in order that God might show grace to more people. In the apostle Peter's day, skeptics were saying that because things seemed to continue as they have been from the beginning, therefore there is no judgment. But Peter answered, "The Lord is not slow in keeping his promise, as some understand slowness. He is patient with you, not wanting anyone to perish, but everyone to come to repentance" (2 Peter 3:9). God is delaying the ultimate working out of his judgment on many nations until those whom he will call to faith in the Lord Jesus Christ do come. This is the day of his grace.

If you are not a believer in Christ, God tells you to believe in him now. Run to Mount Zion for salvation! Run to Jesus! If you are a believer, then do as Israel will do and possess your great possessions.

This People, This Place

Jeremiah 32:36–41

They will be my people, and I will be their God.
—*JEREMIAH 32:38*

Here are three principles to guide us in ministry to the city or wherever God has called us to serve.

1. *People before programs.* The problem rises when we come with our programs and we want to impose them on the people. We ought to be working the other way around. We ought to be concerned for the people, and out of a concern for the people come the programs. How do we figure out if a program that is already in place but is not going well is really the program needed? Do we get angry at the people? Sometimes we get impatient, and we think *people should be behind this thing more.* When we are thinking that way, we are thinking programs first.

2. *Place before promotions.* There ought to be a commitment to *place.* Not everybody has to have the same commitment to place, but it ought to be true for some. It takes time to make an impact, and it certainly takes time to make an impact in a church where you are in the business of developing character and discipleship. Therefore, a commitment to place takes priority over our own opportunity. This means that we don't move on simply because we have a nice opportunity.

3. *A permanent commitment.* We are not to be committed to one place "for the time being." We are not to leave unless the Lord absolutely prods us out of the place, and even then only after we have talked with others who have the same commitment to place to make sure it isn't just restlessness on our part.

There are challenges in each of the areas. If you talk about *people,* well, the problem about people is that they aren't nice; they are sinners. We are too, and we're not nice, and we all get tired of that. The problem about *place* is that grass is always greener somewhere else. You begin to think you've had about enough of this and you just want to go someplace else. And when we talk about *permanence,* well, the problem there is we just get tired. Especially as you get older you get tired because you face the same battles that you faced twenty years ago. You haven't solved all of the problems, and you have to keep fighting, and you just get worn out.

But God does not get worn out. God is committed to the place, and the people, and forever and ever! And if that's our God, then by the grace of God who empowers us to do what he does and to be like Jesus Christ, we can do the same thing. It is that kind of commitment that God honors and blesses, and I'd like to commend it to you.

From an unpublished talk at Briarwood Presbyterian Church.

A New Spirit
Ezekiel 36:23–29

I will . . . put a new spirit in them.
—*EZEKIEL 11:19*

While studying in Basel, my wife and I participated in a Bible study that met in our apartment. There was a girl in the study for whom we had been praying for some months prior to her attending. She had been converted years before in England under the ministry of Stephen Alford, but as the result of an unhappy engagement to the wrong man, she had turned on Christianity and had become entangled by one of the pseudoreligious sects that are flourishing in our day. While we had been praying, the Lord had been working, and one Friday night she turned up on our doorstep just as the Bible study was to begin. She was included that night and the nights that followed. This particular evening we had come to Paul's great chapter on love in 1 Corinthians 13. And as we studied this passage together, thinking over all the aspects of this new life to which the Christian has been called, this girl made a comment that showed the Lord was working in her life. She said, "When you read over all these things and realize what it means to be a Christian, you begin to realize that you could never be one without God's help." And she prayed that night along these lines.

Now it is exactly for this reason that God has given us his Holy Spirit. You see, man is separated from God by his sin, and God has removed that sin for all who will come to him in the righteousness of Christ. But God is not satisfied that sin be removed in this judicial way alone. He is also anxious that believers actually live righteously in this world. And he has given us his Spirit that we may do so. The Holy Spirit will teach us what God would have us do. He will move us to want that perfect will of God. And he will empower us to live in accordance with it. Ezekiel knew this truth and expressed it six hundred years before the sending of the Holy Spirit at Pentecost. "I will . . . put a new spirit in them; I will remove from them their heart of stone and give them a heart of flesh. Then they will follow my decrees and be careful to keep my laws. They will be my people, and I will be their God" (Ezek. 11:19–20).

Unpublished talk, source unknown.

Decision Making
Daniel 1:1–16

But Daniel resolved not to defile himself with the royal food and wine.
—DANIEL 1:8

W hat is your reaction to Daniel's decision? Remember that Daniel was a young man at this time—probably between fifteen and seventeen. It was at this young age that he was taken away from his own country and culture, plunged into the strange but exciting life of the great world capital, and lured to loyalty by the best of all possible educations and by provision of the very food served to Nebuchadnezzar. Yet Daniel refused to partake of this food. As I say, what is your reaction to that? Do you find it a very little thing? Do you see Daniel's decision as the immaturity and foolishness of youth? Would you have acted as Daniel and his friends did in these circumstances, or would you have gone along with your great benefactor's desires? Would you have said, "After all, why should we live by Jewish dietary laws while in Babylon? Let's eat and drink. It's just a small thing"?

Well, it was a small thing. Yet that is just the point. For it is in the small matters that great victories are won. This is where decisions to live a holy life are made—not in the big things (though they come if the little things are neglected), but in the details of life. If Daniel had said, "I want to live for God in big ways, but I am not going to make a fool of myself in this trivial matter of eating and drinking the king's food," he never would have amounted to anything. But because he started out for God in small things, God used him greatly.

It is particularly in youth that the most significant and life-forming decisions are made. Are you a young person? Then you should pay close attention to this point. Most young people want their lives to count, and most Christian young people want their lives to count for God. Youth dreams big. That is right. You should dream big. But youth is also often impatient and undisciplined, and young people are tempted to let the little things slide. You must not do that if you are God's young man or God's young woman. God will make your life count, but this will not happen unless you determine to live for him in the little things now. You know what Jesus said: "Whoever can be trusted with very little can also be trusted with much, and whoever is dishonest with very little will also be dishonest with much" (Luke 16:10). Being wholly given over to God now is the essential and best possible preparation for future service.

Boice, *Daniel*, Baker, 1989, 22.

The Sovereignty of God
Daniel 2:19–23

Praise be to the name of God for ever and ever; wisdom and power are his.
—DANIEL 2:20

The theme of Daniel's prayer is the sovereignty of God. The prayer has three parts.

First, there is praise to God for two of his most important attributes: wisdom and power. How appropriate is the ascription of wisdom to God in these circumstances—when Daniel needed to know the king's dream and its meaning! The wisest of the Babylonians, the magicians, enchanters, sorcerers, and astrologers, had been shown to be inadequate. They had confessed, "There is not a man on earth who can do what the king asks. . . . No one can reveal it to the king except the gods" (vv. 10–11). That was true. But there is a God in whom is hidden all wisdom, and this is disclosed in the story.

The second attribute for which Daniel praised God is power, that is, his sovereignty. In our natural state none of us likes this attribute of God. This is because we want to be sovereign ourselves. We want to be powerful, to control our lives. This was true of Nebuchadnezzar, the greatest ruler of the time. As the story unfolds, even Nebuchadnezzar subjects himself to God and confesses openly, "He does as he pleases" (4:35).

The second part of Daniel's prayer is the acknowledgment that God imparts both wisdom and power to mankind. He imparts power, for "he changes times and seasons; he sets up kings and deposes them" (2:21). He imparts wisdom, for "he gives wisdom to the wise and knowledge to the discerning. He reveals deep and hidden things; he knows what lies in darkness, and light dwells with him" (vv. 21–22). No doubt the greatest portion of this wisdom, wisdom of spiritual things, is reserved for God's people. But there is a general wisdom given to nonbelievers too, just as political power is given to nonbelieving as well as believing rulers. The important thing is the recognition that this comes from God. It makes all the difference in the way we live our lives when we know that God and not man is ultimately in charge of circumstances.

Finally, in the third part of his prayer, Daniel praises God for the wisdom and power he had imparted to him personally. You and I have not been given Daniel's special ability to know and understand dreams. But wise as Daniel was, we have a wisdom greater even than his since it has been given to us to know and believe on Jesus Christ personally. The Bible says that in Christ "are hidden all the treasures of wisdom and knowledge" (Col. 2:3). So to know Jesus as Savior and Lord is to be wise. If you have that knowledge, do you thank God for it, as Daniel did? Do you praise him for the wisdom that has made you wise unto salvation?

Boice, *Daniel*, Baker, 1989, 30–32.

Faith in the Furnace
Daniel 3:1–30

> If we are thrown into the blazing furnace, the God we serve
> is able to save us from it, and he will rescue us.
> —DANIEL 3:17

There were three things that gave Shadrach, Meshach, and Abednego the strength to stand firm in this great test of their commitment.

1. *They knew that God was sovereign.* Nothing is clearer in their response to King Nebuchadnezzar than this. This is no airy, speculative abstraction. This is faith in the furnace. It is a firm conviction of the sovereignty of God in the midst of all things contrary. These men knew that God is sovereign, and therefore it was not foolish but wise for them to entrust their lives to him in this matter.

2. *They knew the Scriptures.* If we are to do the right thing in similar circumstances, we must know the Word of God, because only the Word of God will cut through such ambiguity. Shadrach, Meshach, and Abednego triumphed because their minds were filled with Scripture and because they kept coming back to Scripture as the only fully trustworthy and inerrant authority in all matters.

3. *They were willing to die for their convictions.* It is possible to believe in a sovereign God and know from Scripture what that sovereign God requires and yet fail to do the right thing because you are unwilling to pay the price of obedience. Many fail because they will not pay the price of a loss of popularity or loneliness or ridicule or persecution or economic hardship. Only those who are willing to pay such prices make a difference.

Some people do pay for their faith by dying. But in other cases God intervenes to spare his servants. He spared Shadrach, Meshach, and Abednego. When Nebuchadnezzar peered into the furnace, he saw them walking around in the fire, unbound and unharmed. And he also saw a fourth person who looked "like a son of the gods" (v. 5).

It is not difficult to know who that fourth person was. He was Jesus Christ in a preincarnate form. It is a vivid portrayal of the fact that God stands with his people in their troubles.

God does go with his people in their trials. Countless believers have testified to that. So let us be confident in the promise of that presence and be strong. Let us stand for the right and do it. Let us refuse to compromise. Let us stand with unbowed heads and rigid backbones before the golden statues of our godless, materialistic culture. Let us declare that there is a God to be served and a race to be won. Let us shout that we are determined to receive God's prize, which is far greater than this world's tinsel toys, and that we are servants of him before whom every knee will bow.

Boice, *Daniel*, Baker, 1989, 45–47.

Weighed on the Scales
Daniel 5:18–31

You have been weighed on the scales and found wanting.
— DANIEL 5:27

The day is coming—it may not be far off—when you and I and all persons are going to stand before the judgment seat of God. God is our king, but you are a rebellious subject. God is righteous, but you are a sinner. You are to be weighed in that judgment, and the judgment of God written over you is going to be the judgment of God on Belshazzar's Babylon: MENE, MENE, TEKEL, PARSIN.

Mene means that God is going to number your deeds to show that you have failed to achieve his standards. We are told in Revelation of a great book in which the deeds of men and women are recorded. This book will be opened on the day of judgment, and the evil you have done will be poured out on one side of God's scales. That is what the word *tekel* signifies. All the lies, all the hypocrisies, all the self-seeking, all the harm done to others—all this will fill the scale. You will be weighed. And as you stand there, that great scale of God is going to go crashing down on the side of your just doom and condemnation.

Then God is going to speak the word *peres*: divided. The Greek word for judgment means "divided," for God's judgment is a final dividing of the ways. One way leads to life; the other leads to the outer darkness of hell "where there will be weeping and gnashing of teeth" and "eternal punishment" (Matt. 25:30, 46).

What will you say in that day? How will you respond when God measures your deeds, weighs your character, and declares you wanting?

Left to yourself there will be nothing for you to do and nothing to say in response. But God has done something at the point of your inability. God has sent the Lord Jesus Christ to die in your place, taking the full punishment of your sin upon himself. Jesus has made it possible for God to apply his righteousness to your account. You have no righteousness of your own—not as God counts righteousness. But God takes those scales, brushes your evil deeds aside as having been punished on your behalf in Jesus Christ, and on the other side of the scale, he places his own character. The scales swing back, and you are justified on the basis of Christ's righteousness.

You must trust him. You must turn from unrighteousness. Will you? There is no better time to do it than right now.

Boice, *Daniel*, Baker, 1989, 63–64.

The Practice of God's Presence
Daniel 6:1–10

Three times a day he got down on his knees and prayed, giving thanks to his God, just as he had done before.
—*DANIEL 6:10*

I like those last words: "just as he had done before." This was a pattern
with Daniel. The outside world may have been changing, but God had not
changed and Daniel was not going to allow his relationship to God to change
regardless of the shifting circumstances.

I want you to see two things about Daniel at this point. First, Daniel was
the smallest of all possible minorities at this time—a minority of one—but
although he was only one man among many hostile enemies, *he was the one
man who knew the true state of affairs in this struggle*. Darius did not know
what was going on. He had not even been able to see through the strategy
of the administrators and satraps, and he perceived nothing of the spiritual
struggle. The conspirators did not understand the situation. They did not
know Daniel's God, and they thought it would be an easy thing to get Daniel
executed.

At this time Daniel probably did not even have the support of his three
friends, for they are not mentioned as they were in the incident involving Nebuchadnezzar's dream (see 2:17–18). Either they had been transferred to other
parts of the empire or they had died; Daniel was now elderly. Here was one
man standing alone in the midst of an utterly pagan culture. All were against
him. Any who knew his convictions would have laughed at them. Yet in all
this vast empire Daniel was the one man who really had it together. He knew
that there was a true God, and he knew who that true God was. He knew
that God was powerful. He knew that God could deliver him, if he chose to
do so. Above all, he knew that obeying and serving the one true God had to
be the supreme goal in his life.

That leads to the second important thing about Daniel, namely, *what he
knew he practiced openly*. Some people maintain their belief in God privately
and confess him if asked. But they do not want to offend anyone. They do
not want to be seen as religious. So they back off. They retreat. They privatize
their convictions. Daniel did not do that, and in this he showed true greatness.
Instead of hiding his convictions, he knelt before his window in the sight of
Babylon and prayed as he had always done.

We need more Daniels. We need more people who are willing to bring their
awareness of God and his laws off the reservation, who are willing to open
their windows and honor him before a watching world.

Boice, *Daniel*, Baker, 1989, 70–71.

The Way of the Righteous
Daniel 12:1–3

Those who are wise will shine like the brightness of the heavens.
—*DANIEL 12:3*

This combination of ideas—purification, refinement, spotless living, and shining with the brightness of the heavens—speaks of the actual personal righteousness of God's elect people, which by the blessing of God inevitably leads others to believe in God and become like God themselves. It is what we are called upon to be and do as the end approaches.

Whenever the Bible speaks of the people of God shining like the stars (or whatever), it is speaking of their showing forth the character of God by their own acts of righteousness as a result of spending time with him. After Moses had spent time with God on the mountain, his face shone with a transferred brilliance—so much so that the people asked that he cover his face with a veil until the glory of God, visible in his face, should subside (Exod. 34:29–35; 2 Cor. 3:7–18). Moses revealed God's glory as a result of having spent time with him, and this is what Paul picks up in 2 Corinthians to argue that we also are to reflect God's glory to others.

We do not always do it well. We are like the moon. When the sun goes down and the moon comes up, the moon shines. But it does not shine by its own light. It shines only by reflecting light from the sun. Sometimes it is a full moon, and the sky is filled with light. At other times it is a new moon, barely visible. Or else it is a tiny quarter, and we cannot tell whether it is a waxing or a waning quarter. Our job is to reflect the light of God's glory so that people living in our own dark age might see the light and be drawn to its true source.

Those who shine with God's glory will lead many to righteousness, as the angel told Daniel they would. Is that what you are doing in this age? Are you wise in spiritual things because you have filled your mind with God's written revelation? Do you spend time with God? And because you have spent time with God, do you reflect his character to our darkened world? Do you lead others to Christ? Are you God's witness? This is what God has given us to do. It is our commission and task and opportunity.

Boice, *Daniel*, Baker, 1989, 123–24.

Spiritual Adultery

Hosea 1:1—11

Go, take to yourself an adulterous wife.
—HOSEA 1:2

You may not have sunk so low as Gomer, Hosea's wife. You may not have been so unfaithful as to deny God and seek other gods, committing spiritual adultery with them. But you have certainly flirted with other gods. You have taken the overpowering love of your great bridegroom and lover Jesus Christ with less obedience and respect than he deserves. You have been half-hearted in your love. You have given God a tip in the offering plate on Sunday mornings, and you have allowed his name to pass your lips lightly—"Oh, yes, I'm a Christian"—while actually living for yourself in this materialistic and self-serving age. You have had a chance to show what it really means and what an honor it is to be the bride of Christ. But you have disgraced that name, in small ways if not in large ones, and you know that you are scarcely the stainless, wrinkle-free, holy and blameless bride he merits (Eph. 5:27). If this is the case, learn what it means to be Christ's bride. Learn what a horror spiritual adultery is and flee from it to Christ. Lie in his arms. Tell him of your love. Do not continue in disobedience, allowing little infidelities to become those great spiritual adulteries that bring chastisement.

If you are not a Christian, you have never known a love like this. Because you have not experienced a love like this, you may be wondering if it really exists or if it is possible for one like yourself to be loved by God in this way. If this is your case, you should know that what you feel of your own inadequacies is true of all who are brought into God's spiritual family. We were all in fellowship with God once . . . in Adam. Since then we have gone our own way. We may be described as Scattered, Not-Pitied, Not-God's-People. It is for people like us that Christ died. If you are touched by this story and sense that Christ died for you, then do not let thoughts of your own inadequacies or past sins hold you back. Run to him. Believe on him. Know for yourself that Christ's love really is as this story describes it.

The apostle Peter wrote to Christians telling them, in clear reference to the story of Hosea, "Once you were not a people, but now you are the people of God; once you had not received mercy, but now you have received mercy" (1 Peter 2:10).

That is the story of all who have ever been saved: Scattered! Not-Pitied! Not-My-people! But now: Planted! Pitied! The People of God!

A Door of Hope

Hosea 2:14–23

Therefore I am now going to allure her.
—*HOSEA 2:14*

Chapter two of Hosea presents a series of "therefores" in which the hand of God's judgment has been pressed down ever more firmly on Hosea's rebellious and errant wife. But just as we are expecting further trouble, God opens the hand of his grace and sends forth hope. He says, "Therefore I am now going to allure her; I will lead her into the desert and speak tenderly to her. There I will give her back her vineyards, and will make the Valley of Achor a door of hope" (vv. 14–15).

"Achor" means "troubling," and the phrase that contains it ("the Valley of Achor") means "the valley of troubling." How can such a place be hopeful? How can the destructive troubling be changed? We cannot change it certainly. But there is one who can and who does. God sets hope before us when all seems most lost. He does it by taking our trouble on himself. Do you remember those words of our Lord in the final hours prior to his death as he thought ahead to all that would take place on Calvary? He said, "Now my heart is troubled, and what shall I say? 'Father, save me from this hour'? No, it was for this very reason I came to this hour" (John 12:27). Again we are told that "Jesus was troubled in spirit" (13:21). Why was Jesus troubled? He was troubled in our place. God troubled him with our sin that we might be saved from it and be brought back to God. It is on the basis of his death for that sin that he can now say to us, "Do not let your hearts be troubled and do not be afraid" (14:27; cf. v. 1).

He not only removes our trouble; he restores us to God: "'In that day,' declares the LORD, 'you will call me "my husband"; you will no longer call me "my master." . . . I will betroth you to me forever; I will betroth you in righteousness and justice, in love and compassion. I will betroth you in faithfulness, and you will acknowledge the LORD. . . . I will show my love to the one I called "Not my loved one." I will say to those called "Not my people," "You are my people"; and they will say, "You are my God"'" (Hosea 2:16, 19–20, 23).

There is no greater promise than that. No wider door of hope could possibly be set before us. If you think all is hopeless, hear God as he speaks these words to your heart: "I will betroth you to me forever. . . . I will respond. . . . I will plant. . . . I will show my love to the one I called 'Not my loved one.'" Come to him and allow him to restore the years of your life that have been lost.

The Greatest Love Story
Hosea 3:1–3

Love her as the LORD loves.
—HOSEA 3:1

After Gomer left Hosea, she sank lower and lower in the social scale of the day until she became a slave and was sold in the capital city of Samaria. When the time came for her to be sold on an auction block, Hosea was told by God to buy her.

One man started the bidding: "Twelve pieces of silver!"

"Thirteen!" said Hosea.

"Fourteen pieces of silver!"

Hosea's bid was "Fifteen!"

The low bidders were beginning to drop out, but one man continued bidding: "Fifteen pieces of silver and a bushel of barley!"

Hosea said, "Fifteen pieces of silver and a bushel and a half of barley!" The auctioneer looked around and, seeing no more bids, said, "Sold to Hosea for fifteen pieces of silver and a bushel and a half of barley."

At this point Hosea *owned* his wife. He could do anything he wished with her. Yet at this point Hosea's love, which is an illustration of God's love for us, burned brightest. Instead of seeking vengeance, he put Gomer's clothes on her, led her away, and claimed that love from her that was now his right. Moreover, as he did so, he promised no less from himself.

Here is the way he puts it: "The LORD said to me, 'Go, show your love to your wife again, though she is loved by another and is an adulteress. Love her as the LORD loves the Israelites, though they turn to other gods. . . .' So I bought her. . . . Then I told her, 'You are to live with me many days . . . , and I will live with you'" (Hosea 3:1–3).

Does God love like that? Yes! God steps into the marketplace of sin and buys us out of sin's bondage by the death of Christ. When we see Hosea standing in the marketplace under orders from God to purchase his wife, who had become an adulteress and a slave, we recognize that this is the measure of God's love.

We are Gomer. We are the slave sold on the auction block of sin. The world bids for us. But when all seemed lost, God sent Jesus Christ, his Son, into the marketplace to buy us at the cost of his life. If you can understand it as an illustration, God was the auctioneer. He said, "What am I bid for these poor, hopeless, enslaved sinners?"

Jesus said, "I bid the price of my blood."

The Father said, "Sold to the Lord Jesus Christ for the price of his blood." There was no greater bid than that.

So we became his, and he took us and clothed us, not with the dirty robes of our old unrighteousness, which are as filthy rags, but with the robes of his righteousness. That is how God loves us. That is what Jesus did on your behalf.

Admitting Guilt

Hosea 5:13–15

Then I will go back to my place until they admit their guilt.
—HOSEA 5:15

What happens when we do not turn to God even after he sends trouble to get our attention? In that case, says God, he reluctantly pours out on us the greatest judgment of all: *He leaves us.* He turns away from us. He abandons us to precisely what we want: "Then I will go back to my place until they admit their guilt. And they will seek my face; in their misery they will earnestly seek me." I can think of no more horrible judgment than to be abandoned by God in the very depths of our wretchedness and misery.

Yet that is our hope, for even at this point God is being good to those who are his. He will hide his face. We will grope in our darkness. But even this, dreadful as it is, exists only "until" we admit our guilt and turn to him. Thus it is that even in the darkest hour there is a glimmer of hope and love in God's judgments.

What happens when we do turn to him? We feared his omniscience because it meant exposure of ourselves as we truly are. We have done everything possible to avoid admitting our guilt. But when we finally come to God and allow him to remove the robes of our self-righteousness, to which we have clung so desperately, we find that he is waiting with the blood of Christ to cleanse our sin, the oil of his Spirit to anoint our wounded bodies, and the robes of his own righteousness to clothe us. When Adam and Eve sinned, they ran from God when they heard his voice in the garden. But God sought them out, confronted them in their sin, and then clothed them with skins of animals that he himself killed. When Hosea found Gomer, she was exposed on the auction block of Samaria, naked in the sight of all the people. But Hosea purchased her for himself and clothed her again. So it is with us. We have hidden from God. But in Christ we can now stand before him. We can be known and yet clothed at the same time. Indeed, we can cry with Isaiah: "I delight greatly in the LORD; my soul rejoices in my God. For he has clothed me with garments of salvation and arrayed me in a robe of righteousness, as a bridegroom adorns his head like a priest, and as a bride adorns herself with her jewels. . . . The Sovereign LORD will make righteousness and praise spring up before all nations" (Isa. 61:10–11).

Repentance That Does Not Count

Hosea 6:1–3

Come, let us return to the LORD.
—HOSEA 6:1

The essential elements of a true confession are missing in Hosea 6:1–3. First, there is no *reference to sin*. There is acknowledgment of the consequences of Israel's sin: injury and the absence of God himself. But there is no acknowledgment of the sin that caused them. There is nothing of the acceptable prayer of the tax collector, referred to by Jesus, who cried out, "God, have mercy on me, a sinner" (Luke 18:13).

A second missing element is a *personal relationship with God*. This is seen in the mechanical way the people conceive of God's restoring them. Voltaire, the French atheist, once said sarcastically of God's forgiveness, "Forgiveness? That's his job!" That glib rejoinder is on Israel's tongue in these verses. True, God has judged them. But he will restore them again. That's the way he always does it. They have been down for two days, but they will rise on the third. The sun sets; the sun also rises. God will be like that with his people.

It is always an error to presume thus on God. We try to force him into our little boxes, thinking that in that way we can somehow control him and get him to do what we want. But God cannot be thus controlled, and it is the case rather that he conforms us to his wishes. We are never in greater danger than when we assume that he will always forgive us as long as we go through the outward forms of repentance. An example of genuine repentance is at the end of Hosea. We read: "Return, O Israel, to the LORD your God. Your sins have been your downfall! Take words with you and return to the LORD. Say to him: 'Forgive all our sins and receive us graciously, that we may offer the fruit of our lips.' This is a true confession, and where it occurs God promises, 'I will heal their waywardness and love them freely'" (Hosea 14:1–2, 4).

That is the secret—"Take *words* with you and return to the LORD. Say to him: 'Forgive all our *sins* and receive us *graciously*.'" First, confession of sin. Second, an appeal to God on the basis of his abundant grace.

It is the same in the New Testament. "If we claim to be without sin, we deceive ourselves and the truth is not in us. If we confess our sins, he is faithful and just and will forgive us our sins and purify us from all unrighteousness" (1 John 1:8–9). "If you confess with your mouth, 'Jesus is Lord,' and believe in your heart that God raised him from the dead, you will be saved. For it is with your heart that you believe and are justified, and it is with your mouth that you confess and are saved" (Rom. 10:9–10).

Repentance That Does Count

Hosea 14:1–9

Take words with you and return to the LORD.
Say to him: "Forgive all our sins."
—*HOSEA 14:2*

There are three things that make this confession a true one, things lacking in the false repentance of chapter 6. First, there is an *awareness of sin* and that in two ways: (1) that sin is sin and (2) that it is serious. We see this in the word that is used for sin, literally "iniquity" (v. 1). It is an ugly word but it rightly describes sin's nature, which is ugly. True repentance begins with an acknowledgment that sin is sin and that it is ugly and terribly offensive in God's sight.

The second thing that makes the confession a true repentance is its *turning from specific sins*. In this case it is a repudiation of those foreign alliances, which the people have trusted, and the idols, which they made in the days of their apostasy. To repent of one's own, specific sin is so difficult that it is actually impossible apart from the grace of God.

The third element in the true repentance of these verses is an *appeal to the grace of God*. This is involved in verse 2: "Forgive all our sins and receive us graciously." It means that we must come to God solely on the basis of his grace, not imagining that in spite of our sins there is nevertheless some merit in us to commend us to God—not even the fact that we have repented of our sins and appeal to his mercy.

There is probably nothing that is harder for us to do. It is hard to admit that we are sinners and that sin is serious. It is harder to admit to specific sins and turn from them. Hardest of all is to admit that apart from these sins there is still nothing in us to commend us to God or compel him to be favorably disposed toward us. What we usually do, even when we are confessing our sin, is immediately rush on to remind God that, although we have sinned, there are nevertheless other areas in which we have been true to him. This is not true repentance. We only truly repent when we admit, as the old Anglican collect has it, that "there is no health in us."

How do we repent? Hosea hits on something important when he answers, "With words." "Take words with you and return to the LORD." We must not merely assume that God knows of our repentance, though he does if we are repentant. Rather, we must express our repentance verbally. Without this open confession, we can never be fully sure that we have done what God requires. But "if we confess our sins," we can know that "he is faithful and just and will forgive us our sins and purify us from all unrighteousness" (1 John 1:9).

Restoration

Joel 2:18–27

I will repay you for the years the locusts have eaten.
—JOEL 2:25

A blessing that God says will follow genuine heart repentance is restoration of the lost years. This is a special blessing. Many of us have run from God and have wasted many years. It is only by returning to God that the loss of those years can be made up.

When we disregard God and run away from him, we enter upon a downhill course. We do not think this will happen when we start out. But it does happen, because God has established this as one of the laws governing spiritual disobedience, and he is faithful to his laws. When we disregard God, life inevitably goes downhill. We miss our opportunities. We fail in small and then in greater things. We become hardened by sin. We increasingly live for ourselves and disregard others. We lose friends. Eventually we are all alone and are totally miserable in our loneliness. God can change all that. We cannot undo what is done. Sin is sin, and the effects of sin often continue for long periods. But God can restore what the locusts have eaten. Opportunities may have been lost, but God can give new and even better opportunities. Friends may have been alienated and driven away, but God can give new friends and even restore many of the former ones. God can break the power of sin and restore a personal holiness and joy that would not have been dreamed possible in the rebellion.

Are you one whose life has been destroyed by the locusts of sin? Has sin stripped your life of every green thing, so that it seems a spiritual desert? If so, you need to return to the one who alone can make life grow fruitful again. Only God can restore the years that have been eaten away.

Do you ask where you can find him? There is only one place. That is in the Bible, where he has made himself known. If you do not know the Bible, then you are not worshiping the one true God who is found there, but rather a God of your own making or imagination, whatever you may call him. You must ask: *Do I really know the Bible? Am I worshiping God on the basis of the truths I find there?* Those truths are centered in Jesus Christ, who is the theme of the Bible. In him the invisible God is made visible. In him the immaterial God is revealed in space and time. It is said of some that "although they knew God, they neither glorified him as God nor gave thanks to him" (Rom. 1:21). Let us determine that this shall not be said of us. We see God in Jesus. Let us know him as God, love him as God, serve him as God, worship him as God.

The Day of the Lord

Amos 5:18–20

Will not the day of the LORD be darkness, not light—
pitch-dark, without a ray of brightness?
—*AMOS 5:20*

Consider what Amos teaches about this coming day of judgment. When Amos says that the Day of the Lord is going to be a day of darkness, he especially means that God's blessing will be withdrawn and men and women will be *without the Light of life.*

The second characteristic of the Day of the Lord is *isolation.* While we have light, we see one another and feel we are with one another, even though space separates us physically. In the dark, we cannot see. We feel isolated. That is what it means to be in the dark spiritually. It is to be alone without Christ.

The third characteristic of the day of God's judgment is that it is *inescapable.* This is what Amos suggests in verse 19, in his picture of a man trying to escape a fierce lion. In the context of his prophecy, the lion is the Lion of Judah. He is the God-lion. This is God in the day of his wrath on the ungodly. God is inescapable.

The final characteristic of the Day of the Lord is *utter hopelessness.* There will be no glimmers of light in that day, says Amos. The state of the lost will be one of utter hopelessness, as it always is for those who set themselves against God.

There is only one bright point in this portrait of the coming great darkness: the Day of the Lord has not come yet. There is hope for those who will turn to Christ.

If judgment is inevitable, then the only logical thing is to flee to the place where it has already been poured out, that is, to the cross of Calvary. Only there may a guilty sinner find shelter. Augustus Toplady knew this hope. Toplady lived in England in the 1700s. He was in a field when suddenly a storm swept down out of the sky. He was far from a village and had no shelter, but he saw a large rock ahead of him and thought there he might escape some of the storm's violence. When he got to the rock, he saw that it had been split open. There was a crack into which he could fit. He went in and was sheltered from the storm. While waiting there, he thought of God's coming judgment and of the fact that Jesus, the Rock of Ages, was broken by God so that sinners like ourselves, who hide in him, might be safe. Struck by this thought, he found a playing card that had been lying at his feet and wrote, "Rock of Ages, cleft for me, let me hide myself in thee."

Are you hiding in that Rock? There is no other shelter. It is only there where you can safely meet God.

At Ease in Zion

Amos 6:1–8

Woe to you who are complacent in Zion.
—AMOS 6:1

Suppose you are a Christian who is at ease in Zion. What follows from the pride that has made you complacent? The first thing is that you become *insensitive* to the needs of others. You are at ease; others are not. Your needs are met; others lack many of life's necessities. If you would, you could help many out of your resources. But you are not willing to do that because you think *you* deserve everything you have.

The second thing that happens is that you become *irresponsible*, not only in regard to the needy but also where your own family, neighbors, church, city, or government is concerned. There is work to be done, much work. But you have opted out because it is much easier to enjoy your abundance, isolated from the very real problems around you, than to sacrifice your ease for the good of others.

Third, the situation is dangerous, and you become *oblivious* to the danger. An old expression says, "Idle hands do the devil's work." It is in periods of idleness that we get into trouble.

Are you at ease in Zion? Have you said to yourself, *I've done my bit for God and the church. It's time to quit now. There are younger people who can do the work. Let them do it. I don't have to do anything?* If you are saying that, you are on the road to great trouble.

Wake up from such lethargy! Look about you! See the work that most needs to be done and get on with it! It is in such work that you will be most like the Lord Jesus Christ, your Master, who "humbled himself and became obedient to death—even death on a cross!" (Phil. 2:8). It is only people like that whom God honors.

I am applying these truths to Christians. But suppose you are not a Christian. Suppose you have rejected the one who died for your salvation. What shall we say of you? If the plight of the Christian is dangerous, what of your danger? If the Christian is irresponsible, are not you even more so? If he is insensitive, you are doubly insensitive, for you are insensitive not only to the needs of other people but also to your own. Jesus was talking about you when he said, "What good is it for a man to gain the whole world, yet forfeit his soul?" (Mark 8:36). He meant that a person who has accumulated things but neglected his relationship to God is a fool because he has made a bad bargain. Wake up and turn to Jesus! To be at ease in Zion when your eternal destiny is not settled is the most foolish of all life's follies, and the end is the greatest of tragedies.

Your Brother's Keeper
Obadiah 10–15

You should not look down on your brother.
—OBADIAH 12

The sin of unbrotherliness has small beginnings but it grows. First, there is the sin of *standing aloof* when your brother stumbles. This first offense leads to a second one—*looking down on* your brother in the day of his misfortune. The third stage is *rejoicing over* fellow Christians who have fallen. Christians talk about other Christians and can even be happy that the other one has sinned. Somehow it makes them appear better. The fourth state is *boasting*. This grows from pride. If we saw ourselves on the same level as others, we would mourn with them and turn to God in humble thanksgiving that we have been spared, though our sins are also many.

What we think inevitably issues in actions. The Edomites actually caught Jews who were escaping from Jerusalem and delivered them back into the hands of their enemies. It sounds terrible and it is. But this is something of which Christians are sometimes also guilty through their treatment of Christians who have sinned or erred in some doctrine. I may be wrong in this but I believe that there are some Christians who spend more time serving the enemy by delivering fellow believers into the hands of unbelievers than they do serving God. Our duty to other believers is to build them up (Eph. 5:12) and restore them if they have sinned (Gal. 6:1).

But there is this to add. There was a day when two kings confronted one another for the first time. One was an earthly king. His name was Herod Antipas. The motto of his reign was: "What will it profit *me*?"

The other king was Jesus. He was the King of Kings, who, according to his divine nature, was the supreme King over all the kings of this earth. But he did not want the throne until you and I could share it with him. To make that possible he would die.

Herod said, "What does it profit *me*?"

Jesus said, "What can I do that will be the greatest possible benefit to my brethren?" God vindicated Jesus! Jesus went to the cross. He died. But his death was followed by a resurrection, and today he lives to enable those who believe on him to behave as he did and bring a true, supernatural brotherhood to this world. For his part, Herod went on with his revelry but soon was banished to Lyons, France, where he died in misery.

This is the choice before you: to go Herod's way or Jesus's way. You cannot do both. If you drift, the way will be Herod's. You will live for self. You will end up thinking yourself better than others and mistreating them. If your life is to be different from that—and your end as well—you must follow Jesus.

Ironic Conversions

Jonah 1:1–16

At this the men greatly feared the LORD.
—*JONAH 1:16*

Jonah 1:16 seems to mean that the sailors were converted. It means that in an ironic way God was already accomplishing his purposes in spite of the prophet Jonah's stubborn rebellion.

The fact that the sailors were saved is evident in practically every word used. To begin with, this is the third time that the men are said to have *feared* something or somebody. The first was the storm (v. 5). The second was the disclosure that Jonah was a Hebrew who worshiped Jehovah (v. 10). This time they are said to have feared Jehovah himself. There is a progression.

Moreover, they were worshiping *Jehovah*. Earlier, when we were told of their prayers, we read: "All the sailors were afraid and each cried out to his own god" (v. 5), that is, to idols. Now, after Jonah has been thrown overboard and the wind has stopped, we are told that they prayed to Jehovah, Jonah's God. And how did they worship? Well, they performed a sacrifice and they made vows. Also they made their vows *after* they had been delivered, not before. This was not a foxhole conversion.

This is a great irony. We remember that Jonah was running from God because he did not want God to save the heathen in Nineveh. But the first great event in the story was the conversion of the heathen sailors.

This carries us further in the lesson about God's sovereignty. What God is going to do, he will do. If he has determined to save Mary Jones, God will save Mary Jones. If he has determined to save John Smith, God will save John Smith. But notice, God can do this through the obedience of his children, as he does later with Nineveh through Jonah, in which case they share in the blessing. Or he can do it through his children's disobedience, as here, in which case they miss the blessing. Either way, God blesses those whom he will bless. But the one case involves happiness for his people while the other involves misery. Which will it be in your case? Will you resist him? Will you refuse his Great Commission? Or will you obey him in this and in all matters?

Perhaps you are not yet a Christian. If not, then learn from God's grace to the sailors. You have not yet perished in your godless state, because God, who made the sea around you and the dry land on which you walk, preserves you. Do not remain indifferent to him. Turn to him. Approach him on the basis of the perfect sacrifice for sin made once by his own Son, Jesus Christ, and follow him throughout your days.

Prayer from the Depths
Jonah 2:1—9

From inside the fish Jonah prayed to the LORD his God.
— *JONAH 2:1*

Jonah's prayer has four characteristics of all true prayer. The first is *honesty*. He acknowledged his trouble and that it was God who had caused it. Then there is *penance*, which means "confession," "self-abasement," or "mortification showing sorrow for and repentance of sin." The third characteristic of Jonah's prayer was *thanksgiving*. Jonah was thankful that God had turned him from rebellion and had caused him to call on the name of the Lord once again.

One final characteristic of Jonah's prayer is the most significant of all. *Jonah is now ready to take his place alongside the ungodly.* Earlier he had said, "I am a Jew, and I do not want to preach to the heathen" (see 1:9). Now he was willing to take a place beside them as one who needed God's mercy.

We find this in a parallel between verse 9 of this chapter and verse 16 of chapter 1. Verse 9 says, "I, with a song of thanksgiving, will *sacrifice* to you. What I have *vowed* I will make good." The earlier verse says, speaking of the sailors, "At this the men greatly feared the LORD, and they offered a *sacrifice* to the LORD and made *vows* to him." The heathen sailors learned to approach God as he must be approached—through the blood of an innocent victim sacrificed for sin and through a personal commitment expressed in a vow. Jonah, the prophet of the Lord, also approached through the sacrifice (promising to do in the future what he could not do in the fish) and made a vow.

It is hard to miss the point. Jonah, despite his earlier protestations, came to God, not as a Jew who deserved special privileges or concessions, but as a sinful human being who was one with all other sinful human beings and who needed God's grace.

It is thus with us all. If you come to God claiming privileges, boasting of your own special achievements and therefore expecting God to accept you or acknowledge you on the basis of your own merit, you have no hope of salvation. On the other hand, if you come to God, admitting that you deserve nothing from him but his just wrath and condemnation, if you place your faith in his Son, the Lord Jesus Christ, who willingly became your sacrifice, and if you promise to serve him and be his faithful disciple till your life's end, then he saves you and brings you into a deep experience of the grace of God.

No one has ever truly repented till he or she has acknowledged that there is nothing in any person that can possibly commend him or her to God. And no one has ever been saved who has not come to God on the basis of the sacrifice that he alone has provided.

Wideness in God's Mercy

Jonah 4:1–11

Should I not be concerned about that great city?
—JONAH 4:11

God asks Jonah a final question with which the book closes. God said: "You have been concerned about this vine, though you did not tend it or make it grow. It sprang up overnight and died overnight. But Nineveh has more than a hundred and twenty thousand people who cannot tell their right hand from their left, and many cattle as well. Should I not be concerned about that great city?" (vv. 10–11).

Jonah had been sorry for the vine. So God does not talk to him about the adult population of the city, who undoubtedly deserved the judgment Jonah was so anxious to have fall on them. God talks about the cattle, who were innocent, and the smallest children, designated as those who could not yet discern between their right hand and their left. Was God not right to show mercy for their sake, if not for the adult population? Does not even Jonah's compassion for the vine vindicate God's judgment?

The book ends with a question, a question that has no written answer. This is not a mistake. It ends on a question in order that each one who reads it might ask himself or herself the same question: Is God not right? Is he not great for showing mercy?

The lessons of the book of Jonah are many. There are lessons that concern Jonah himself. He is a type of practically everything: a type of Christ (who was buried but who rose again), a type of Israel, a type of all believers (for we all run away from God at times and need to be disciplined). There are lessons that concern Nineveh and the true meaning of repentance. There are lessons relating to the doctrine of God's sovereignty over men and nature.

But greater than all these lessons is the lesson of the greatness of the mercy of God. How great is God's mercy? We have a hymn that says, "There's a wideness in God's mercy, like the wideness of the sea." But even that is not wide enough. The real measure of the wideness of the mercy of God is that of the outstretched arms of the Lord Jesus Christ as he hung on the cross to die for our salvation. That is the wideness of God's mercy. That is the measure of the length to which the love of God will go.

How can we, who have known that mercy and benefited from it, be less than merciful to others? How can we do less than love them and carry the gospel to them with all the strength at our disposal?

A Mighty Ruler
Micah 5:2–5

Out of you will come for me one who will be ruler over Israel.
— MICAH 5:2

The prophecy of a ruler becomes quite personal. For the issue is not merely whether the one born in this small Judean town so long ago really was a great ruler, but whether he is your ruler. The question is, Are you his subject? Have you bowed your knee to him in proper homage?

You say, "I have never bowed before anyone. I run my own life." If that is so, then you are opposed to Christ, regardless of what sentimental feelings you may or may not have at Christmastime. God regards your opposition to the rightful rule of his Son Jesus Christ over you as a matter of personal derision.

Another may say, "I believe that Jesus is a mighty ruler, even that he is (or may be) God, and I am willing to have him as my Lord someday. But not now, especially not at Christmas. There are so many things to do, so many good times to be had, so many sins to be indulged. I'll come to him later." If you are saying this, your folly may be even greater than those who would rebel against him entirely, because you are self-deluded. You will never come to him at that rate. Your sins will take you further and further from him, and eventually you will perish.

A third person says, "But Christ is my Lord. It is just that I want to run my own life now. I want to do what seems best to me to do." According to Jesus, those who go their way, rather than his, are not his true disciples. We have a saying that is quite true: Either Jesus is Lord of all, or he is not Lord at all. You cannot profess to be his disciple without following him in all things and always.

If this mighty ruler from the tiny town of Bethlehem is not your ruler, then what you need is to be reborn. Or to put it another way, Jesus needs to be born in you. Jesus was born in Bethlehem when he came to earth the first time. But now he also needs to be born in your heart, wherever you may live.

Invite Jesus into your heart now. Confess your sin, thank him for his great love and grace in dying for you, and promise to follow him from this time onward as your Lord.

If you do that, the angels who sang in the skies above Bethlehem at Christ's birth will burst into praise once again. For Jesus said that there is joy in heaven over even one sinner who repents of sin and turns to him.

Boice, *The King Has Come*, Christian Focus Publications, 1992, 45–47.

Judgment
Nahum 3:1–7

"I am against you," declares the Lord Almighty.
—*Nahum 3:5*

This is a dreadful thing. It is terrible to have the great God of the universe say, "I am against you." But it is not only to Nineveh that he speaks those words. He speaks them to all who sin against him, whether in Nineveh, Rome, New York, Philadelphia, or wherever the sinner may be. If God says that to you, you should know that it is a terrible thing to fall into the hands of such an angry God.

These judgments, recorded so vividly in the pages of the Word of God, are not given to us to titillate our minds by comparing them with their eventual fulfillment in history. God records these judgments to show us that he is a God of judgment as well as of love and that judgment upon the wicked will surely come. The Judge of all the earth does right. What is right where you are concerned? If you have gone your way, spurned God's law, sought out your own corrupt devices—justice demands your eternal condemnation. God must and will judge you. In terms of that great judgment, which is hell, the fall of Nineveh is almost insignificant.

Earlier in the collection of Minor Prophets, there is another book concerned with Nineveh: Jonah. Jonah was told to go to Nineveh and preach a message of utter and lasting destruction (Jonah 1:1–2; 3:1–2). On that occasion the city turned from its sin, and Nineveh was spared.

If you are not yet a believer in the Lord Jesus Christ, you are in a position similar to Nineveh on the earlier occasion. Judgment hangs over you because God is a God of justice, and justice will be done. But this is the day of God's grace. Judgment, though imminent, has not yet come. There is still time to turn from your sin and embrace him who said, "Come to me, all you who are weary and burdened, and I will give you rest" (Matt. 11:28).

God tells you about judgment so you might turn from your sin and seek his face at the cross of his Son, the Lord Jesus Christ. Deliverance is to be found at this cross, because God poured out his judgment there. The cross is your shelter, if you will have it so. It is only as we stand beneath it that we are protected from that greatest of all judgments, which is yet to come.

Waiting for an Answer

Habakkuk 1:12–2:1

I will stand at my watch.
—HABAKKUK 2:1

Habakkuk has gone as far in his reasoning as he can. Now he needs to know more if he is to make progress. So he waits to see what God will say to him.

This is worth looking at in detail, for it answers the question: *How* do we leave a problem with God? What should our frame of mind be?

First, we should *detach ourselves from the problem*. Habakkuk suggests this when he says he will go to a watchtower. A tower is something set apart from or detached from the common press of life. So Habakkuk is saying, "I have been down in the valley with my problem and have not been able to solve it. Now I am going to draw apart for a while and leave it with God. I am going to detach myself from the difficulty."

Second, we should *expect God's answer*. Just because we have left something with God and have ceased worrying about it does not mean that we should forget about it entirely. Here again Habakkuk's image of the watchtower is helpful. The tower is detached from the crowds of people below, but the person who enters it does so in order to keep an eye on the landscape. He has work to do, and that work is to watch to see what will happen. Habakkuk says that he "will stand at" his watch and "look to see" what God will say to him.

How do we look for God's answer? How does God speak? The primary way is through Scripture. Sometimes God directs us by what used to be called "intimations," deep personal feelings concerning the way we should go. He frequently directs us by what we call "open or closed doors." That is, God provides an opportunity for service or takes it away. Still, the primary way of knowing God's direction or answer to our perplexities is through Scripture. Anyone who has made a habit of reading the Word of God regularly knows how that happens. We have a problem, have been unable to solve it, and have left it with God. It may be that we have even forgotten about it temporarily. But one day we are reading a passage of the Bible and suddenly a verse leaps out at us and we recognize at once that it contains the solution to what has troubled us. It is God's answer to the problem we previously left with him.

The final point is that we should *be persistent in our expectation*. Habakkuk also implies this by his image. He says that he is going to stay in his watchtower until God answers his question. God likes that kind of tenacity. I think that is the kind of persevering attitude God honors.

Living by Faith
Habakkuk 2:4–5

His desires are not upright—but the righteous will live by his faith.
—HABAKKUK 2:4

The way of the righteous is the way of faith in God. The way of the wicked is the way of drawing back from faith in God. The first submits to God and trusts God. The second submits to no one. The person who chooses the second way is arrogant. He says, "I don't need religion. I can take care of myself. I can do without God."

If what we need is God, as the Bible claims, and if we turn to things instead of God, as we so often do, these other things will inevitably disappoint us no matter how much we have or how fervent our misplaced devotion to them may be. What do you turn to for strength and security in life? Is it money? Do you think that if you only have enough money you will be all right? Is it other people? Do you think that somehow your friends will help you get by? Is it success? Fame? Your own strength and ability, whatever they may be? Do you think that if you get all these in order, somehow you will manage?

They will not be enough! You and I are made in the image of God, destined for fellowship with God. If we will not have God, then there will always be a vacuum—a terrible, hellish vacuum—in our lives.

The challenge presented to us here is that choice. Will it be the world's way, the way of the ungodly with its emptiness, frustration, and eventual ruin? Or will it be God's way, the way of faith in him who alone is worthy of that faith? Joshua presented the choice to the people of his day. He had come to the end of his life and was soon to die. But before he died, he brought the people together and reminded them of all God had done for them from the time he first called Abraham out of Ur of the Chaldeans to the day he brought them out of Egypt into the Promised Land. At the end he said, "If serving the LORD seems undesirable to you, then choose for yourselves this day whom you will serve, whether the gods your forefathers served beyond the River, or the gods of the Amorites, in whose land you are living. But as for me and my household, we will serve the LORD" (Josh. 24:15).

Joshua was saying what Habakkuk later said in other language. Though the world should rise up against us, the righteous will live by faith. It is by faith in the righteous God alone that we can stand against it.

A New Song
Zephaniah 3:14–20

The LORD, the King of Israel, is with you.
—*ZEPHANIAH 3:15*

Assuming that you are God's child and are growing in holiness, what follows? In chapter three of Zephaniah, what follows is a song of joy. That is, you are invited to sing and shout aloud, because: "The LORD has taken away your punishment, he has turned back your enemy. The LORD, the King of Israel, is with you; never again will you fear any harm."

There is a double cause for singing in that statement. First, if you are one who has come to serve the Lord only and who is going on with him in holiness and service, you can know that your sins have been forgiven and that God has turned back your great enemy, the devil. The Lord said something like this when his disciples had returned from one of their itinerant preaching trips, rejoicing that God had given them power over sickness. Jesus replied, "Do not rejoice that the spirits submit to you, but rejoice that your names are written in heaven" (Luke 10:20). Second, if you are truly the Lord's, then you can know that he is with you and that you will never again need to fear any harm. This makes us think of Psalm 23:6: "Surely goodness and love will follow me all the days of my life, and I will dwell in the house of the LORD forever." Or Matthew 28:20: "Surely I am with you always, to the very end of the age."

I know of nothing greater to sing about than that, because it is God's reversal of the fall, which opened the sluice gate of misery on the human race. When Adam and Eve sinned, the first thing they were aware of (in addition to their own psychological nakedness) was that a barrier now existed between themselves and God. Before this they had been willing to meet with him. No doubt the times of such meeting were the most blessed of their existence. But when they sinned and then later heard God walking in the garden in the cool of the day, they hid from him. When God called them and began to confront them with their disobedience, they tried to hide behind excuses. Adam blamed Eve, and she blamed the serpent. As punishment for their sin, God sent them from the garden, which in a certain sense was also sending them away from him.

What joy to have that reversed! What joy to have our sin forgiven and the lost relationship between us and the Holy God restored!

A Day to Remember
Haggai 1:1–15

The whole remnant of the people obeyed the voice of the LORD their God.
—*HAGGAI 1:12*

From time to time the preaching of the Word of God strikes home, and a life is genuinely changed. When that happens in large numbers, you have a revival.

This happened under Haggai's preaching. We recall from our study of the earlier prophets that the warnings given to the Jewish people before God's judgment by the Assyrian and Babylonian invasions generally went unheeded. Micah had some success. But for the most part the people could not have cared less about the prophets' warnings. To our joy we see a different kind of response from the people of Judah under Haggai's ministry. They had been negligent of God's work. They had invented flimsy excuses as to why they were inactive. But they were not basically hostile to God or his commandments, as the people living before the exile had been. They really wanted to please God. So when the word of the Lord came to them by Haggai, they recognized it as a true word of God and did what God commanded.

The chapter concludes: "So the LORD stirred up the spirit of Zerubbabel son of Shealtiel, governor of Judah, and the spirit of Joshua son of Jehozadak, the high priest, and the spirit of the whole remnant of the people. They came and began to work on the house of the LORD Almighty, their God, on the twenty-fourth day of the sixth month in the second year of King Darius" (vv. 14–15).

There is an interesting note in that last verse, where we are told that the people resumed the work on the twenty-fourth day of the month. If we compare that with the first verse of the chapter, where we are told that Haggai began to preach on the first day of the month, we find that the change came about in just twenty-three days. Haggai spoke on August 30, 520 BC. The work began on the twenty-first of September.

I wonder if there is a date like that in your life or if today might possibly become that day. I do not mean the day of your conversion; you may or may not have a known day for that. I mean the day in which you finally got the priorities of your life straightened out and determined that from that time on you would put God and his work first in everything. You need to do that. You need to ask yourself these questions: *Is my own comfort of greater importance to me than the work of God? Am I making increasing efforts to get ahead financially but finding greater and greater disappointment in my life?* If the answer is yes, just turn around and get on with God's business. Obey him. Put him first in your life.

No Shortcuts
Zechariah 4:6–10

"Not by might nor by power, but by my Spirit," says the LORD Almighty.
—ZECHARIAH 4:6

This message to Zerubbabel has several parts: first, a general principle: "'Not by might nor by power, but by my Spirit,' says the LORD Almighty"; second, a reference to obstacles: "What are you, O mighty mountain?" (v. 7); third, a promise that Zerubbabel will complete the temple construction: "The hands of Zerubbabel have laid the foundation of this temple; his hands will also complete it. Then you will know that the LORD Almighty has sent me to you" (v. 9).

This is where the vision encourages us. Zerubbabel was a man beset by many problems in his attempts to carry God's work forward. He was fighting lethargy, smallness of vision, and lack of faith within Israel. Without, he was fighting the determined opposition and evil cunning of God's enemies. These forces undoubtedly did seem like a "mighty mountain" before him. They were an obstacle human power could not remove. But God urged him to be strong in completing his task, knowing that the Lord himself would reduce the mountain to level ground. The victory would be won by God's Spirit, not by human power.

There were no shortcuts, however. The work still had to be done: the stones still had to be laid. Any worthwhile work always begins small and progresses from that point to become bigger. As I counsel with people in our day, many of them young people, I am convinced that one of their biggest problems is that they expect shortcuts. They want a simple principle that will explain all the Bible and eliminate the need for concentrated and prolonged Bible study. They want an experience that will set them on a new spiritual plateau and eliminate the need for hard climbing up the steep mountain paths of discipleship. They want a fellowship that has all the elements of a perfect heavenly fellowship without the work of building up those elements by their own hard work and active participation. This is not the way God has ordered things. He could have given shortcuts but he has not. Even Zerubbabel, who was the leader of Israel at this time and who in this vision receives a promise that he will live to see the completion of the temple—even Zerubbabel, who is promised the fullness of the Holy Spirit to complete his work—even Zerubbabel still had to take his plumb line in hand and work away at the mountain one day at a time.

It was about four years after this that the temple was completed. Those four years contained much hard, grueling work, often hindered by Zerubbabel's internal and external enemies. Should it be easier for us? Should we expect shortcuts? On the contrary, victories will be won now as then only by those who advance toward them one step at a time.

The Shepherd-King
Zechariah 9:9–10:12

See, your king comes to you, righteous and having salvation.
—*Zechariah 9:9*

Zechariah tells of four things the Shepherd-King does.

1. *The Shepherd saves his people* (9:14–17): "The LORD their God will save them on that day as the flock of his people" (v. 16).

2. *The Shepherd provides for his people* (10:1–2). In the past Israel had looked to idols for the blessings God stood ready to give the people if they had only asked him. In those days they were like sheep without a shepherd, lost and oppressed by their enemies. In the latter days, about which these verses speak, the people will ask God for blessings and will find them.

3. *The Shepherd purifies his people* (10:3–5). Israel's lack of a true shepherd in verse 2 leads to the thought that the people were nevertheless afflicted by false shepherds, whom the true Shepherd now intends to punish. Who are these false shepherds? Probably all false prophets, kings, or other leaders, both Jew and Gentile, are meant.

Ultimately, there is only one true leader: the Lord, the Shepherd of Israel. That is why verse 4 must refer to the Messiah. In one sense, it could refer to whatever good rulers God himself brings forth from Judah. But in the ultimate sense, only Jesus of Nazareth is the "cornerstone" (a sure foundation), the "tent peg" (intrinsic strength), and the "battle bow" (a conquering warrior).

4. *The Shepherd gathers his people* (10:6–12). The last section of Zechariah 10 tells how the Great Shepherd of Israel will restore the people by regathering them from the distant reaches of the earth. The prophecy must concern a yet future day. The regathering may have begun with the reestablishing of the modern state of Israel. This will be a great regathering in which the scattered flock of the Messiah is returned to its own land and to great material and spiritual blessing.

I argue here, as elsewhere, that verses like these refer to a literal future blessing upon a regathering and believing Israel. This is their meaning. Nevertheless, it is true that we who have been brought to faith in Jesus Christ as Savior can see ourselves in the points of this prophecy. Has the Lord not done each of these great things for us? He has saved us by his death. He has provided for us and encourages us to come to him in prayer, asking for anything we lack. He is purifying us. He is also gathering us—both Jew and Gentile—from the farthest reaches of this world.

The Lord is not merely the Shepherd-King of Israel. He is our Shepherd too. Praise God that we have such a Shepherd!

Holy to the Lord
Zechariah 14:20–21

On that day HOLY TO THE LORD will be inscribed.
—*ZECHARIAH 14:20*

On that day HOLY TO THE LORD will be inscribed on the bells of the horses, and the cooking pots in the LORD's house will be like the sacred bowls in front of the altar. Every pot in Jerusalem and Judah will be holy to the LORD Almighty, and all who come to sacrifice will take some of the pots and cook in them. And on that day there will no longer be a Canaanite in the house of the LORD Almighty" (Zech. 14:20–21).

What is Zechariah talking about here? Why horse bells and cooking pots? The point is that the people and city will be so holy that even these insignificant things will be fully dedicated to the Lord. All of life will have the glory and enjoyment of God as its object.

Have you ever thought of holiness in terms of your destiny as a child of God? You are not holy now. You are sinful; the more you live, the more you will be aware of it. But your destiny is holiness. God has determined that we are to be holy through the work of the Lord Jesus Christ.

We think of things relationally today. Because God is a person and we are like him in having personalities, we think of our destiny in terms of our relationship to God. We look forward to the day when we will be able to express our love to him fully and know the full measure of his love to us. This is not wrong, of course; we are persons, and our future is to be enfolded in the all-embracing love of God. But this is not the way the Bible speaks of our destiny. It is not the love relationship that is emphasized. The Bible emphasizes that which is the basis of all other experiences: holiness. The reason why our relationship to God is not all it should be is that we are not holy. The reason why our relationships with other people are not all they should be is that we are sinful. We need holiness. On the day that we pass from earth to heaven, we will be holy, for we will be like Jesus, since we will see him as he is (1 John 3:2).

Then we must strive to be holy now. That is what 1 John 3 emphasizes. It says that we will be like Jesus, but immediately after this it says, with reference to this present life, "Everyone who has this hope in him purifies himself, just as he is pure" (v. 3). We emphasize so many other things. Instead of these, we must find and fulfill God's emphasis, knowing that one day HOLY TO THE LORD will be inscribed on us and we will be the Lord's holy people forever.

God's Challenge
Malachi 3:6–12

"Test me in this," says the LORD Almighty.
—*MALACHI 3:10*

Not merely our money or time, but our whole selves—body, soul, and spirit—are God's, and therefore we are to honor God wholly with all we are. Paul wrote, "You are not your own; you were bought at a price. Therefore honor God with your body" (1 Cor. 6:19–20). He said, "Therefore, I urge you, brothers, in view of God's mercy, to offer your bodies as living sacrifices, holy and pleasing to God—this is your spiritual act of worship" (Rom. 12:1). That is the essence of it. So long as we are thinking legalistically about giving in terms of financial percentages and portions of the week, we will be exactly like the self-righteous sinners of Malachi's day. We will do little and think it much. We will resent God who, in our judgment, should do more for us. On the other hand, if we give God ourselves as living sacrifices, then the most we give will seem to be little and we will be overwhelmed that God is willing to use us in his service.

Will you try it God's way? Will you put God to the test? This is what God challenges the people to do in Malachi 3:10–12. The text has four parts.

First, God calls for obedience: "Bring the whole tithe into the storehouse, that there may be food in my house." All spiritual relationships with God start with obedience.

Second, God issues a challenge: "Test me in this."

Third, God accompanies his call and challenge with a promise: "See if I will not throw open the floodgates of heaven and pour out so much blessing that you will not have room enough for it. I will prevent pests from devouring your crops, and the vines in your fields will not cast their fruit."

Fourth, God speaks of the ultimate result: "Then all the nations will call you blessed, for yours will be a delightful land."

Are you bold enough to accept this challenge personally? Usually we try to shy away from anything as tangible as this, for we are afraid that our faith or testimony will be shaken if we try it and God does not come through. But it is not my idea to put God to the test with obedience. This is God's challenge. It is God who says, "Test me in this . . . and see . . ."

Why not obey God in this matter? Why not put God first in the use of your financial resources, your time, above all in what you do with yourself—and see if he will not "throw open the floodgates of heaven and pour out so much blessing that you will not have room enough for it"?

The Unchanging God
Malachi 3:13–18

> Then those who feared the LORD talked with each
> other, and the LORD listened and heard.
> —MALACHI 3:16

A reminder of these concluding verses is this. Just as the situation among the people had remained unchanged, so too God was unchanged. The Lord had stated this explicitly earlier: "I the LORD do not change" (v. 6). But verses 14–18 make the point again by bringing some of God's immutable attributes before us as the book closes. God is unchangeable in his knowledge; he knows the faithful and the faithless, the righteous and the wicked. God is unchangeable in his holiness; his standard remains the righteousness that the law embodies (see Mal. 4:4). God is unchangeable in his judgments; though postponed, the reality of judgment still looms before the wicked (vv. 1–3). God is unchangeable in his promises; he still speaks of a day of blessing in which the hearts of the fathers will be turned to their children and the hearts of the children to their fathers (v. 6).

Men and women wish that they could get God to change. They do not like him for his godly attributes: sovereignty, holiness, omniscience, justice, wrath—even love, because it is a holy love. But they could endure these perfections if it were possible to think that given time God might change in some of them.

We could endure God's sovereignty if we could think that given a bit more time God's grip on the universe might weaken and another strong personality might take over. Perhaps we could take over. Maybe men could be sovereign.

We could endure God's holiness if we could think that given a bit more time his tough moral standards might change. What we are forbidden to do now, we might be able to do then. We could wait to sin.

We could endure omniscience if given the passage of years it might be possible for God to forget. We could wait for him to become senile.

We could endure his justice if with the passage of time it might become more of an abstract ideal than a reality.

We could even endure his love if it could cease to be the perfect and properly jealous love the Bible describes it to be.

But God does *not* change. God is the same today as he has always been; he will be the same in what we would call billions of years from now. God will always be sovereign. He will always be holy. He will always be omniscient. He will always be just. He will always be loving. It is appropriate that we be reminded of this in the closing pages of the Old Testament.

Name of All Names

Matthew 1:18–25

> And you are to give him the name Jesus, be-
> cause he will save his people from their sins.
> —*MATTHEW 1:21*

What a name this was!

Jesus is the Greek form of the Hebrew name Jehoshua, Jeshua, or Joshua, and it means literally "Jehovah is Salvation." So the message to Joseph centered primarily on the great work Jesus was to do. Jesus was to be the agent of God's salvation, and his work was to "save his people from their sins," as the angel explained clearly.

But there is more in the name Jesus even than this. The name also means that Jesus is the Savior-God himself, as indicated by Matthew's reference to Isaiah's prophecy of the virgin birth and to the name Immanuel, which means "God with us" (see vv. 22–23). It is as the incarnate Son of God that Jesus achieved our salvation, and it is as the eternal God-man that he now represents us and intercedes for us before the Father.

The Bible lists many names for Jesus. He is the First and the Last, the Beginning and the End, the Alpha and the Omega, the Ancient of Days.

He is King of Kings and Lord of Lords.

He is the Anointed One, the Messiah.

He is the Prophet and the Priest.

He is the Savior, the Only Wise God our Savior.

He is our Wonderful Counselor, the Mighty God, the Everlasting Father, the Prince of Peace.

He is the Almighty.

He is the Door of the Sheep, the Good Shepherd, the Great Shepherd, the Chief Shepherd, the Shepherd and Bishop of our souls.

He is the Lamb, the Lamb without Spot or Blemish, the Lamb Slain from before the Foundation of the World.

He is the Logos, the Light, the Light of the World, the Light of Life, the Tree of Life, the Word of Life, the Bread That Came Down from Heaven, the Spring—if a person drink of it, he will never thirst again.

He is the Way, the Truth, and the Life.

He is the Resurrection, the Resurrection and the Life.

He is our Rock, our Bridegroom, our Beloved.

He is our Redeemer.

He is the One Who Is Altogether Lovely.

He is the Head over all things which is his body, the church.

He is God with Us, Immanuel.

But above all, he is Jesus. Jesus.

We love him for that name, because he came to save his people from their sins.

Boice, *The King Has Come,* Christian Focus Publications, 1992, 54, 61–62.

The Gifts of Faith

Matthew 2:1–12

Then they opened their treasures and presented him
gifts of gold and of incense and of myrrh.
—*MATTHEW 2:11*

It is easy to see why gold is an appropriate gift for Jesus Christ. Gold is the metal of kings. When gold was presented to Jesus, it acknowledged his right to rule. In presenting the gift of incense, the wise men pointed to Christ as our great High Priest, the one whose whole life was acceptable and well pleasing to his Father. Just as gold speaks of Christ's kingship and incense speaks of the perfection of his life, so does myrrh speak of his death. Myrrh was used in embalming. Christ was to suffer, to die for sin. It was myrrh that symbolized this aspect of his ministry.

In coming to Christ we must come with our faith. Moreover, there is a sense in which by faith we too may present our gifts of gold, incense, and myrrh.

Begin with your myrrh. Myrrh is not only a symbol of Christ's death but also of the spiritual death that should come to you for your sin. Lay it at Christ's feet, saying, "Lord Jesus Christ, I know that I am less perfect than you are and am a sinner. I know that I should receive the consequence of my sin, which is to be barred from your presence forever. But you took my sin, dying in my place. I believe that. Now I ask you to accept me as your child forever."

After you have done that, come with your incense, acknowledging that your life is as impure as the life of the Lord Jesus Christ is sinless. The Bible teaches that there is no good in man that is not mixed with evil. But it also teaches that Christ comes to live in the believer so that the good deeds produced in his or her life may become in their turn "a fragrant offering, an acceptable sacrifice, pleasing to God" (Phil. 4:18).

Finally, come with your gold. Gold symbolizes royalty. So when you come with your gold, you acknowledge the right of Christ to rule your life. You say, "I am your servant; you are my Master. Direct my life and lead me in it so that I might grow up spiritually to honor and to serve you accordingly." Have you done that? Have you come believing in all that the myrrh, incense, and gold signify? If you have, you have embarked on a path of great spiritual joy and blessing. For those are the gifts of faith. They are the only things we can offer to the one who by grace has given all things to us.

Boice and Ryken, *The Christ of Christmas*, P&R Publishing, 2009, 126–34.

The Baptism of Jesus
Matthew 3:1–17

Jesus came from Galilee to the Jordan to be baptized by John.
—MATTHEW 3:13

Since John's baptism was a baptism unto repentance and Jesus had no sin of which to repent, how is it that he sought baptism by John? And why did he seek this, as he said to John, "to fulfill all righteousness"? How could baptism add anything to the already perfect righteousness of Jesus Christ?

The best way to understand Jesus's words is by understanding what is the primary significance of baptism, which is not immersion or sprinkling but the idea of identification, which is what I think the word *baptizo* primarily means. In Christian baptism we are identified with Jesus in his death and resurrection so that his death becomes our death and his resurrection our resurrection. In Jesus's baptism by John, Jesus identified himself with us in our humanity, thereby taking on himself the obligation to fulfill all righteousness so that he might be a perfect Savior and substitute for us.

The last two verses of chapter 3 record the testimony of God the Father to Jesus. We might call it God's authenticating seal on the outward sign of John's water baptism of Jesus. This was an impressive testimony for two reasons. First, the entire Trinity was present: the Father who spoke from heaven, the Son of God who was baptized, and the Spirit of God who was seen descending like a dove on Jesus.

The second reason involves the words that were spoken. "A voice from heaven [that is, God's voice] said, 'This is my Son, whom I love; with him I am well pleased'" (v. 17). Any Jew who knew the Old Testament would immediately have a setting for these words. The first part of the sentence ("This is my Son") comes from Psalm 2:7, where God declares of his Messiah, "You are my Son." The second part of the sentence ("with him I am well pleased") comes from Isaiah 42:1, at the beginning of the prophecies of God's suffering servant who would atone for Israel's sin (42:1–9; 49:1–7; 50:1–11; and 52:13–53:12). So here, in the words of God himself, we have verification of the essential message of John the Baptist and Christianity itself, described earlier, namely, that Jesus is the Son of God, the Messiah, and that his work was to save his people from their sins.

I ask you these questions: Do you love Jesus? And are you well pleased with him? The Father certainly is; that is what these words state clearly. If the Father is pleased with Jesus, shouldn't you be? If you are not, you are far from being a true Christian. If you are, surely you will want to follow Jesus in faithful obedience and point others to him, as John the Baptist did.

Jesus and the Devil
Matthew 4:1–11

Then Jesus was led by the Spirit into the desert to be tempted by the devil.
—*MATTHEW 4:1*

From the temptations of Jesus and how he overcame them, there is direct application for our lives when we are tempted and must stand against Satan's wiles. Let me summarize by three statements.

1. *We face the same battle.* The devil is not omnipresent as God is. Satan cannot be everywhere tempting everyone at all times. He has probably never tempted you directly. But this does not mean we do not face spiritual battles every day. We do. Paul wrote about these battles in his letter to the Ephesians, saying, "For our struggle is not against flesh and blood, but against the rulers, against the authorities, against the powers of this dark world and against the spiritual forces of evil in the heavenly realms" (Eph. 6:12). These battles are so fierce that Paul warned us to be ready for them by arming ourselves with God's armor. We must be fully equipped for the struggle.

2. *We have the same choice.* As Jesus did, we have the choice of trusting God and sticking to the path he sets before us or distrusting God and seeking to win victories for God or ourselves in the world's way. What will it be? Will we go God's way? Or will we follow the world, the flesh, or the devil? Joshua challenged the people of his generation, saying, "Choose for yourselves this day whom you will serve, whether the gods your forefathers served beyond the River, or the gods of the Amorites, in whose land you are living. But as for me and my household, we will serve the LORD" (Josh. 24:15).

3. *We can have the same victory.* The Bible says, "No temptation has seized you except what is common to man. And God is faithful; he will not let you be tempted beyond what you can bear. But when you are tempted, he will also provide a way out so that you can stand up under it" (1 Cor. 10:13). What is that path to victory? The temptation of our Lord points the way: "It is written! . . . It is written! . . . It is written!" As Paul told the Ephesians, the only offensive weapon we have is "the sword of the Spirit, which is the word of God" (Eph. 6:17).

Remember Christ's example. Here is Jesus—the holy Son of the almighty God, the one in whom neither Satan nor man could find any wrong or gain even the tiniest foothold. Jesus's eyes were always on the glory of his Father. He lived in the closest possible communion with him. But if Jesus, your Lord and Savior, needed to know Scripture in order to resist Satan and win the victory over him, how much more do you and I need it to win a corresponding victory!

Following Jesus
Matthew 4:12–25

Come, follow me.
—MATTHEW 4:19

The words "follow me" occur thirteen times in the Gospels. But in addition, there are scores of references in which one person or another is said to have followed Christ. Why are these two words so important? They are important because they teach important truths about what it means to be Christ's disciple.

1. *Obedience.* The words "follow me" are an imperative, a command—which is why those commanded to follow Jesus did in fact immediately leave their nets, boats, counting tables, or whatever else was occupying them and follow Jesus. Without obedience there is no genuine Christianity. Those who are truly Christ's sheep both hear and obey his call from the beginning and thus enter a life in which obedience is a chief characteristic.

2. *Repentance.* When Jesus called Matthew, he called one who knew he was a "sinner." Jesus emphasized repentance (Matt. 9:13), but the need for repentance is no less evident in the calls of the other disciples. It is impossible to follow Christ without repentance. How could it be otherwise? Jesus is the holy, sinless Son of God. Anyone who is following him, therefore, must by definition turn his back to sin and set his face toward righteousness. Christians do sin, but when they do, they must confess their sin and turn from it, being restored to fellowship again.

3. *Submission.* In one of his most important sayings about discipleship, Jesus describes submission as putting on a yoke. This suggests a number of things, but chiefly it suggests submission to Christ for work assigned. *Submit* comes from the Latin words *sub* (meaning "under") and *mitto* (meaning "to put" or "place"). Therefore, submission means being placed under the authority of another. How could it be otherwise if the one we are following is our true King and Lord, and we are truly his disciples?

4. *Trust.* It is impossible to follow Christ without trusting him, for a lack of trust will cause us to deviate from the path he takes or cause us to choose to leave him. By contrast, it is impossible to genuinely trust Christ and not follow him, since a failure to follow means a person is committed to some other goal or is trusting some other thing or person.

5. *Perseverance.* Following Christ also involves perseverance because following is not an isolated act, done once and for all and never to be repeated. Rather, it is a lifetime commitment that is not fulfilled until the race is won, the final barrier crossed, the crown received, and all rewards laid gratefully at the feet of Jesus. Following Jesus is not only a door to be entered but a path to be followed, and the true disciple proves the reality of his discipleship by following that path to the end. A true disciple is one who follows Christ to the end of everything.

Mourning That Leads to Action

Matthew 5:1–12

Blessed are those who mourn, for they will be comforted.
—MATTHEW 5:4

The second beatitude can refer to sorrow aroused by the suffering of others. Christianity is partly caring for other people. And it should produce a sound social conscience. In fact, if it does not, we have some reason to doubt our Christianity. For John said, "We know that we have come to know him if we obey his commands. The man who says, 'I know him,' but does not do what he commands is a liar, and the truth is not in him" (1 John 2:3–4). What were Christ's commandments? Well, there were many. But among them were these: "Love your enemies and pray for those who persecute you" (Matt. 5:44); "So in everything, do to others what you would have them do to you, for this sums up the Law and the Prophets" (7:12). "Give to everyone who asks you" (Luke 6:30); "Be merciful, just as your Father is merciful" (v. 36); "In the same way, let your light shine before men, that they may see your good deeds and praise your Father in heaven" (Matt. 5:16). An awareness of the sin of the world should produce a mourning for its evils in Christ's followers.

It follows from this that the Christian church should never stand aloof from the great social movements of the day or, worse yet, be critical of them. Christians should be in the vanguard of social reform. And they should be there from a heartfelt love of humanity and from an acute awareness of the horror and destructiveness of man's sin.

I believe that this often has been true in past periods of church history. Lord Shaftesbury was one of the great Christian social reformers, but there were others: Calvin, Oberlin, Wilberforce, Moorehouse. And it would be proper to include in this list most of the pioneers of the modern missionary movement—William Carey, Robert Moffat, David Livingstone, John Paton, and others—all of whom combined an evangelistic zeal with social action.

To each of us, therefore, the second beatitude is a call to involvement in the social arena—in the struggle of minorities for true equality; the plight of underpaid workers; pollution of our natural resources; education; ethical problems in politics, medicine, and business; and other contemporary problems—just as Christians were formerly active in the war against slavery, child labor, lack of freedom of the press, and immorality. We should mourn for such things. And we should mourn deeply enough to do something about them.

Boice, *The Sermon on the Mount*, Zondervan, 1972, 30–31.

True or Empty Claims
Matthew 7:1–23

Not everyone who says to me, "Lord, Lord,"
will enter the kingdom of heaven.
—*MATTHEW 7:21*

Jesus contrasts those who profess to follow Jesus—they call him "Lord, Lord"—yet do not do what God requires, and those (the contrast is implied) who do the will of God and thereby prove that their discipleship is genuine (vv. 21–23). This contrast describes hypocrisy. It is professing faith in Jesus Christ while actually rejecting or disobeying him. Two important matters are worth noting.

1. *This person has the right doctrines.* He calls Jesus "Lord, Lord," confessing Jesus's deity and professing that he is his master. But he is not following Jesus as his master. There were times in Jesus's ministry when people called him Lord, meaning perhaps no more than "Sir." *Lord* was a title of respect. But here a great deal more is involved, for it is Jesus who is speaking, and he is using the word with the richest possible meaning. In the Old Testament, *Lord* is usually translated "Jehovah," a name for God. In New Testament settings the equivalent word is *kyrios*, the title by which citizens of the Roman Empire addressed the emperor as a god. What Jesus is saying is that there will be people in the church who will confess his divinity but who will not be saved. They will be on the expansive road to hell.

Can that really be? Certainly, it can! A person can sit in the pews of a church for years, firmly believing that Jesus is God, that he died on the cross for sin, and even that he is returning one day to judge the world, yet never have come to the point of actually trusting that same Jesus Christ as his Savior.

2. *This person has prophesied and done miracles.* Jesus declares: "Many will say to me on that day, 'Lord, Lord, did we not prophesy in your name, and in your name drive out demons and perform many miracles?'" (v. 22). Jesus does not deny they did miracles. He accepts their profession as a fact. But he also does not deny their self-deception. Their hypocrisy has escalated to a point at which they have actually fooled themselves. They believe their deceptions. But neither eloquent teaching nor miracles prove one to be a true disciple, and these persons are exposed as "evildoers."

These apparent Christians are not condemned because their teaching was wrong or their miracles spurious but because they did not practice what they preached. They were bearing bad fruit, even when they were professing to be good.

So beware, especially if you sense you are a nominal Christian only. There are many paths to hell, many of them religious, but there is only one way to heaven, and that is through trusting in Jesus Christ.

Spiritual Sickness
Matthew 8:1–17

He took up our infirmities and carried our diseases.
—MATTHEW 8:17

W̶e need to look at the miracle stories not as simple stories about Jesus's ability to make sick people well, but for what they teach us about sin and its cure. When we do this, we find four unmistakable lessons.

1. *We are spiritually sick.* Even worse, we are dying because of sin. This is why Matthew begins with the leper's healing; lepers were considered as good as dead. Yet the same point is made in the other stories. The centurion's servant was dying, and as far as Peter's mother-in-law is concerned, we should remember that in ancient times, before antibiotics and aspirin, more people died from fever than from any other single cause. The point is that we are all perishing in sin, and there is no human remedy that will save us. Without God and the power God alone has to heal us, we will perish eternally.

2. *We need a Savior.* And Jesus is that Savior. Matthew summarizes his account of the first three healings by citing Isaiah 53:4. That verse expresses a link between the healing of disease and the healing of sin's sickness, but it also comes from a passage that prophesies the coming messianic Savior. Jesus is that Savior, and his authority both to heal and to forgive human sin is proof of it. There is no other Savior, because no other speaks or heals with such power.

3. *Faith is necessary.* Faith is the channel by which the salvation of God comes to us. Did the leper have faith? He did. He believed that Jesus could heal him. The only question was whether Jesus would choose to do so. As for the Roman centurion, he understood that Jesus spoke with the authority and power of God. This is what you and I need too, if we are to be saved from sin. Our condition is desperate. Jesus is the physician who alone can save us, but we must have faith in him. Do you? Faith is the one thing we need, the one thing that really matters.

4. *The stakes are life or death.* This is the most important matter you will ever be asked to consider, for at stake is your life or your death: the life of God to be enjoyed in part now, though more fully later and forever, or the way of death that is bad enough now but will become indescribably tragic and inescapable when you pass from this phase of your existence to eternity. Jesus describes spiritual death as being "thrown outside, into the darkness, where there will be weeping and gnashing of teeth" (Matt. 8:12). Those are frightening words, but I think Jesus knew what he was talking about. Don't you?

If you do, why don't you turn from your sin and believe on him now as your Savior?

Teaching, Preaching, and Healing
Matthew 9:35–38

> Jesus went through all the towns and villages, teach-
> ing . . . preaching . . . and healing.
> —*MATTHEW 9:35*

What was Jesus doing at this time? Verse 35 tells us that Jesus was doing exactly what he had been doing all along.

1. *Jesus taught in their synagogues.* This is the point at which Jesus always began, and it is where we must start if we are to model our ministry after his. The people he saw were "harassed and helpless, like sheep without a shepherd" (v. 36), and the reason they were helpless is that they did not know the Bible. They should have known it; they possessed the Old Testament, and their teachers should have been teaching it to them. But they were like people today. They had not been taught and they did not have the inclination to seek out Bible truths themselves. What they needed to know and what Jesus certainly taught them was who God is, what God has made us to be, how we have fallen short of God's righteousness and corrupted his image within us, and how we need a Savior who can save us from sin and from ourselves.

2. *Jesus preached the good news.* This teaching leads to the "good news," of course, which is what Jesus "preached" to them. Preaching is not the same thing as teaching. Teaching is instruction; it has to do with content, and it is primary. Preaching contains instruction but it is more than instruction. It is also proclamation, an announcement of what the listeners must hear and to which they must respond. Preaching is the point at which teaching becomes personal. The word that is used for "preaching" is the same word used for what a king's herald does. A herald speaks for the king, making his decrees known. In this case, the proclamation was about the kingdom of God and his anointed King, Jesus, who is the Christ. This decree was good news, and the good news was that the awaited King, who is also the Savior, whom we need to save us from our sins, had now come.

3. *Jesus healed their diseases.* These were literal diseases, of course. His power to heal disease was one evidence that he was the Messiah. But the healing of physical disease is linked to and illustrates the far more important healing that has to do with sin. What we need most is forgiveness of our sins and reconciliation with God, which is what Jesus accomplishes. This is the *really* good news of the kingdom.

Today we have the power of the Holy Spirit to bless our words about Christ and bring those who hear our message to repentance and faith in him. In that sense our work is like that of Jesus. We teach the Bible, preach the gospel, and heal sin-sickness, as the Holy Spirit blesses our words and brings people to Christ.

Deciding for Christ

Matthew 10:17–42

Whoever finds his life will lose it, and whoever loses his life for my sake will find it.
— *MATTHEW 10:39*

The last verses of Jesus's discourse (vv. 17–42) focus on a person's relationship with Jesus in two ways. First, they focus on the disciple himself and
whether he remains true to Jesus or not. Second, they focus on people who
receive or reject his followers.

Jesus says that a person who would be his disciple must value him more than:

- A favorable judgment by this world's rulers: "Whoever acknowledges me
  before men, I will also acknowledge him before my Father in heaven. But
  whoever disowns me before men, I will disown him before my Father in
  heaven" (vv. 32–33).
- The love of one's own family: "Anyone who loves his father or mother
  more than me is not worthy of me; anyone who loves his son or daughter
  more than me is not worthy of me" (v. 37).
- Even life itself: "Anyone who does not take his cross and follow me is
  not worthy of me. Whoever finds his life will lose it, and whoever loses
  his life for my sake will find it" (vv. 38–39). There is no higher demand
  or more exalted calling.

The point of all these verses is the necessity of deciding for Christ and
remaining faithful to Christ until the end. We cannot drift along and expect
that everything will turn out all right. To fail to decide for Christ and live for
Christ is to be against him. It is to perish.

What extraordinary teachings these are! They show Jesus's amazing self-
understanding, for who but a man who knew himself to be God could make
such statements? If Jesus is not God come in the flesh, this is either an example
of an incredible insanity or else a hideous attempt to deceive other persons.
Which is it? If Jesus was insane, ignore him. It is the only rational thing to do.
If he was attempting to deceive other people, expose him. Fight his lies for the
sake of those who might be taken in and harmed by them. On the other hand,
if Jesus is who he claimed to be—if he is the true Son of God—then Jesus
speaks the words of God and must be both believed and obeyed. If Jesus is
the Son of God, these are the most important words you will ever hear since
your eternal destiny hangs on your acceptance or rejection of them.

A Gospel Invitation
Matthew 11:25–30

Come to me, all you who are weary and burdened.
— *MATTHEW 11:28*

It is difficult to think of an invitation more important or more gracious than this. There are several reasons why this invitation is so gracious.

1. *The invitation is for everyone.* Jesus's words are for people of all ages, all nationalities, and all temperaments, and he calls people exactly as they are. We should emphasize this because we tend to think that Jesus's call is for people who are somehow "suited" for religion or perhaps have "earned" a gospel invitation. But it is precisely here that the universal offer must be stressed, as it was by Jesus. Following Christ is, in a certain sense, the hardest thing anyone can ever do. But at the same time, it is possible for everyone, because Christ himself gives us the will to persist in our calling.

2. *The invitation is for those who are burdened by sin.* The phrase "weary and burdened" does not refer to physical weaknesses or to what we might call the burdens of a difficult life, though it may include them. It chiefly refers to a sense of sin's burden and the need of a Savior. The people who were thus burdened believed that Jesus could lift sin's weight and turned to him to do it. These people listened to him, trusted him, and found salvation.

3. *The invitation is to learn about Jesus.* When Jesus called his disciples to "follow" him, he was comparing Christianity to a path in which his followers were to walk, he going ahead of them. When he challenged his disciples to "learn from me," he was comparing Christianity to a school in which he was to be both the subject matter and the teacher. This is the school in which every true believer has matriculated and in which a lifelong course of study is prescribed.

4. *The invitation offers rest for tired people.* In fact, it offers rest twice. There is a rest that is given: "Come to me, all you who are weary and burdened, and I will *give* you rest." That rest comes instantly when we first trust in Christ. Then there is a rest that is found: "Take my yoke upon you and learn from me, for I am gentle and humble in heart, and you will *find* rest for your souls" (v. 29). That rest comes as we increasingly learn to follow Jesus in our daily lives.

Jesus is the only rest you or any other poor, struggling, burdened soul will ever need. Why not turn to him right now? Turn from all inferior teachers to the one who alone can teach true godliness and whose teaching will save your soul.

God's Servant

Matthew 12:15–21

Here is my servant whom I have chosen.
—MATTHEW 12:18

Matthew sums up who Jesus was and indicates the nature of his ministry by quoting a well-known messianic passage from Isaiah (42:1–4; Matt. 12:18–21).

This is the longest quotation from the Old Testament in Matthew but it is not a word-for-word quotation. Rather it is an interpretation. The verses quoted contain four great predictions:

1. The Messiah will bring justice to the earth (v. 18).
2. The Messiah will not cry out like a demagogue but instead will go about his work quietly and humbly (v. 19).
3. The Messiah will not trample on the weak or those who are poor in spirit (v. 20).
4. The Messiah will bring salvation to the Gentiles (v. 21).

What an amazing set of predictions! Yet Jesus did precisely these things. His actions, however, did not fulfill the expectations of his day. The Jews of Christ's day wanted a Messiah who would drive out the Romans and establish a revived Jewish state. The disciples themselves had such thoughts even after the resurrection (see Acts 1:6). Jesus went about his work quietly, teaching and at last dying for his people. The benefits of his atonement were offered to the Gentiles. As far as justice is concerned, this is something that is being proclaimed now through the church and will be realized perfectly in power when Jesus comes again.

D. A. Carson writes, "What is pictured is a ministry so gentle and compassionate that the weak are not trampled on and crushed till justice, the full righteousness of God, triumphs," as it certainly will in the end.

If you are a Gentile, you have benefited from that prophesied messianic ministry. If you have been buffeted by life ("a bruised reed") or if you are weak in faith ("a smoldering wick"), you are in a position to benefit also. Have you been buffeted? Is your faith weak? If so, be encouraged. Jesus did not come to snuff out anything that is weak but instead to fan the smoldering wick into a flame and to straighten and strengthen the bent rod. Aren't you glad he did not come to execute justice at this time? That will happen. Justice will be done. Judgment is inevitable in a universe ruled by a just and holy God. But today is the day of God's grace, and we live because Jesus is the Savior. He alone saves, strengthens, and keeps all who will repent and turn to him.

The Open Heart

Matthew 13:1–23

> But the one who received the seed that fell on good soil is
> the man who hears the word and understands it.
> —*MATTHEW 13:23*

The open heart receives the gospel like good soil receives seed. This soil produces a good crop. Three minor points might be made.

1. Only a portion (in the parable, one-fourth) of the preaching of the gospel bears fruit—in Christ's or any other age. We should remember that even Jesus did not get all people to believe on him, though many did, and if this is so, we must not think we have failed when people reject our message. On the other hand, we should be encouraged in our witnessing by knowing that some *will* believe.
2. The only sure evidence of a genuine reception of the Word of God in a person's life is spiritual fruit. Although we are not saved by our good works, the total absence of them indicates that we have never been truly saved.
3. The presence of fruit is the important thing, not the amount of it, at least in most cases.

But these points are all less important than the main one, namely, that it is only the open heart that receives the preaching of the gospel and is saved. Not the hard heart. Not the shallow heart. Not the strangled heart. The only heart that ever receives the truth of the gospel and is saved is the heart that opens itself to Jesus and his teaching.

Which leads to these most important questions: Do you have an open heart? Are you receptive to God's truth? Have you allowed the teaching of the Bible to settle down into your life so that you have turned from sin, placed your whole faith in Jesus, and begun to produce the Holy Spirit's fruit? You may say, "I'm afraid not. I wish my heart were like that, but I'm afraid it is hard or shallow or strangled by this world's goods. What can I do? Is my case hopeless?"

No, it is not. It is true that you can do nothing, any more than soil can change its nature. But although you can do nothing, there is one who can: the divine Gardener. He can break up the hard ground, uproot the rocks, and remove the thorns. That is your hope—not you, but the Gardener. In other words, said Jesus, "With God all things are possible" (Matt. 19:26). And so they are! Not just for someone else either. They are possible for *you*, if God does the work. What you need to do is turn to Christ and allow him to give you an open heart that will receive the gospel. Admit that you have a hard, calloused, grasping, covetous, or even frivolous heart, and ask him to save you anyway.

Pursuing the Prize
Matthew 13:44–46

> When he found [a pearl] of great value, he went away
> and sold everything he had and bought it.
> —*MATTHEW 13:46*

What did the two men in the parables in these verses do when they came upon treasure? First, they recognized the value of what they had found. Second, they determined to have it. Third, they sold everything to make their purchase. Fourth, they acquired the treasure. Having recognized the value of their discovery and having sold everything in their desire to have it, the man who discovered the treasure and the merchant who discovered the pearl then made their purchase. They acquired that on which their desires had been set.

This speaks of individual appropriation. It tells us that salvation does not consist merely in seeing the value of Christ's work and wanting it for oneself. Christ must actually become ours by faith, which is the means of appropriation. Faith has three elements. There is an intellectual element, in which we recognize the truths of the gospel. There is an emotional or heart element, in which we find ourselves being drawn to what we recognize. There is also a volitional element, in which we actually make a commitment to him whom the gospel presents. Salvation is a personal matter. People are not saved by Jesus en masse. They are saved one by one as by the grace of God they recognize their need and come to Jesus, trusting that he is who he claimed to be (the Son of God) and that he did what he claimed he would do (provide for our salvation through his death on our behalf). The man in the field did not allow someone else to buy the treasure, hoping that he might share in it. The merchant did not form a cooperative to acquire the pearl of great price. Each made the purchase for himself.

Do not think, if you are teetering on the brink of decision, that having renounced everything for Jesus you will one day find yourself disappointed at what will have proved to be a bad bargain. You will not find yourself coming back with your treasure or pearl, hoping to get your property back. It is never that way. In the exchange described by these parables, the men who made their purchases received a bargain. They made the deal of their lives, their fortune, and they were happy.

So it will be for you. You are not called to poverty in Christ but to the greatest spiritual wealth. You are not called to disappointment but to fulfillment. You are not called to sorrow but to joy. How could it be otherwise when the treasure is the only Son of God? How can the outcome be bad when it means salvation?

Faltering Faith
Matthew 14:22–33

> But when he saw the wind, he was afraid and, begin-
> ning to sink, cried out, "Lord, save me!"
> —MATTHEW 14:30

True faith involves an actual trust in Jesus as the Son of God and Savior. It means that a person actually commits himself or herself to Jesus. To use the image of the story, it means stepping out toward him in faith.

Peter's action demonstrates this well. He believed that the figure he saw on the water was Jesus and that Jesus had power to call him and hold him up as he walked toward him. And he could! As long as Jesus told him to come and as long as he kept his eyes on the Savior!

When Peter looked around and became aware of the fierce wind and saw the rolling waves, he became afraid and started to sink. His faith faltered at this point. But it is important to recognize that Peter's faith did not fail utterly. He had lost faith in Jesus's ability to keep him above the water but he still trusted Jesus at some level since he immediately called out to him for help. "Lord, save me!" he said.

This incident is an illustration of true but faltering faith, which is what the faith of most of us is like. If Peter had no true faith at all, his act of getting out of the boat would have been mere foolishness or bravado, and when he began to sink, he would have started to flail his arms about, desperately trying to get back into the boat. He would not have cried out to Jesus. The fact that he cried out is proof that he really did trust Jesus. On the other hand, his faith was weakened by the waves, just as our faith is often undermined by difficult circumstances or by tragedies in life. When Jesus rebuked him, it was not for having no faith at all but for having little faith. "You of little faith," Jesus said, "why did you doubt?" (v. 31).

Now note this: it was when Peter was in trouble that he was driven to Jesus and was closest to him. It is exactly the same with us, and it is why Jesus permits storms to come into our lives too. As long as life is going along smoothly, we may be genuinely trusting Jesus for our salvation as true Christians, but our faith can be somewhat distant, abstract, or even peripheral. We trust Jesus, true enough, but if the truth be told, we also trust ourselves and our abilities. We may even trust ourselves more than we trust Jesus. Let trouble come, and suddenly we are confronted with our own lack of ability and weakness, and we are driven to Jesus simply because we have nowhere else to turn. It is in times such as these that faith in Jesus grows strong.

Clean Hands or Clean Heart
Matthew 15:1–20

What comes out of his mouth, that is what makes him "unclean."
—*MATTHEW 15:11*

D o you stand before God with clean hands only, that is, with mere ceremonial religion, or do you come with a new, clean heart?

Washing our hands in a religious way is not the issue today, of course, but the principle applies in other areas. For some this type of ceremonial religion means good works, perhaps giving money to help the poor or donating time to charity. A person like this supposes that he will be accepted by God for these works. Another person thinks in terms of religious observance, so she is faithful to attend church services. Another person places weight on standing or sitting for prayers, how he holds his prayer book, or whether he crosses himself on entering a church. My mother is a strong Christian today but she says that, when she looks back to her catechetical instruction in preparation for her first communion, all she can remember is how she was told to hold her prayer book and when she was to sit down and stand up.

If you have been understanding religion in these or similar ways, you may have discovered that ceremonial things do nothing to change the nature of your heart. Regardless of how often you go to church, it is still the case that out of your heart come such sins as "evil thoughts, . . . false testimony [and] slander," or even such sins as "murder, adultery, sexual immorality [and] theft" (v. 19).

You have two problems. You need forgiveness for your sins and you need a new heart that will enable you to stop sinning and begin to serve God. Where can forgiveness be found? Where can a new heart be acquired? The good news is that Jesus came to give you both. He died on the cross so you might have forgiveness, he bore the punishment for your sins in your place, and he rose again to impart the Holy Spirit, who is the source of new life. It is God alone who can give you a heart capable of loving and serving him.

Do you want a new heart? The only place you will ever get it is from God the Father and from Jesus, who made the gift possible. Come to God. Ask Jesus for it. The Pharisees would not come, which is why they perished in their sins.

The Great Confession
Matthew 16:13–20

"But what about you?" he asked. "Who do you say I am?"
—MATTHEW 16:15

Jesus asked his disciples two probing questions.

First, "Who do people say the Son of Man is?" (v. 13). The disciples would have been in a better position than Jesus to have known what people were saying about him, but Jesus did not need to elicit this information from his followers. These identifications were standard speculations for anyone who stood out above the common people. The surprising thing is that no one was suggesting that Jesus was the Messiah.

Now Jesus asked his second question: "But what about you? Who do you say I am?" It was at this point that Peter spoke for the rest and gave his classic answer: "You are the Christ, the Son of the living God" (v. 16). Peter's answer did two things, both forcefully. First, it identified Jesus as the Messiah, the one who was to reign forever on the throne of his great ancestor David. Second, and even more important, it identified Jesus as divine: "the Son of the living God." It is that combination of ideas that makes Peter's confession so important, for he was confessing that Jesus was no mere man but God himself come to save his people.

In the Greek text this is as forceful as any confession could be. It is only ten words, but in it the definite article occurs four times, like this: "You are *the* Christ, *the* Son of *the* God, *the* living One." This was so true and so important a confession that Jesus pointed out that it was not in the same category as other things Peter was in the habit of blurting out, most of which were wrong. He told Peter, "Blessed are you, Simon son of Jonah, for this was not revealed to you by man, but by my Father in heaven" (v. 17). It was the result of a specific divine revelation.

So also today. The first and most important thing any person needs to understand about Jesus is that he is the Son of God, "very God of very God," as one of the ancient creeds puts it. That is because the value of his work, dying for sin, depends on who he is. If he is not God, his death would have no more value than any other person's death. But because he is God, his death has infinite value and is able to take away sins.

Do you see that? Can you believe it? If you can, it is because God has revealed it to you. It is because he is blessing you by bringing you from death to spiritual life, just as he was blessing Peter. Salvation is God's work from the beginning to the end.

Overcoming Failure
Matthew 17:1–23

But they could not heal him.
—MATTHEW 17:16

There are always valleys. But as far as failures are concerned, although we will certainly also have those, we do not need to have as many as we do or experience them so often. Fortunately, Matthew 17 has provided pointers to the way we can overcome many of our failures.

1. *Listen to Jesus.* On the mountain in the excitement of the moment, Peter thought he had to say something, so he blurted out his idea about constructing three shelters for Jesus, Moses, and Elijah. God told him to be quiet and listen to Jesus. That is exactly what you and I need to do. There is a time to speak, but we must listen to Jesus first, because it is only as we do that we will be able to say anything worthwhile.

2. *Take up the cross.* We like the glory, but we are not nearly so enthusiastic about cross-bearing. Yet what Jesus told his disciples repeatedly is that there is no crown without a cross. John the Baptist had to suffer, Jesus had to suffer, and so do we. It is only through much self-denial that we can be Christ's followers.

3. *Know your weakness.* We all have failures in our Christian lives, and one reason God allows so many of them is so we will learn that "apart from me [Jesus] you can do nothing," as Jesus said (John 15:5). We should remember Peter. Peter had a high opinion of himself. When Jesus explained that the disciples would abandon him at the time of his arrest, Peter was sure he would not do so. "Even if all fall away on account of you, I never will," he said (Matt. 26:33). But he did. He even denied the Lord three times. Like us, Peter needed to learn how weak he was and that if he was to stand, it had to be by Jesus's strength.

4. *Keep your faith personal.* The final lesson is that there can be no substitute for a personal faith in God, who is personal. Are the doctrines of the Bible important? Of course they are. We do not know who God is, how sinful we are, or what God has done to save us in Christ apart from God's own revelation in Scripture. But knowledge alone saves no one. Christianity does not consist merely in collecting information. Is service important? Yes. The Bible says not only that we are ordained to salvation but also that we are ordained to good works (Eph. 2:10). We must do them. But the most important thing is that we get to know God, that we develop a personal relationship with him, and that we serve him because we love him.

Listen to Jesus. Take up your cross. Know your weaknesses. But above all, keep your faith personal. It is that relationship, more than anything else, that will keep you from these failures.

Childlike Humility
Matthew 18:1–4

Who is the greatest in the kingdom of heaven?
—*MATTHEW 18:1*

The disciples had been asking about greatness in the kingdom they believed Jesus would establish. They assumed that greatness was all they had to worry about. They assumed they would be in the kingdom. But Jesus explains that unless they possessed a nature that was entirely different from what they were betraying by their question, they would not even enter the kingdom. Forget about who was going to be most important, Jesus said. What they needed to worry about was being there at all!

To enter the kingdom people must possess the humility of children, but to do so they need to be radically changed. People are not humble by nature. We are self-seeking, selfish, and driven by pride. What do we need if we are to become humble, trusting what God has done for our salvation and not what we can accomplish for ourselves? We need to "turn" or "be converted," which is God's work. We need to pray the prayer of Jeremiah 31:18: "Turn me, and I shall be turned, for you are the LORD my God" (my translation). Did the disciples get it? Were they actually turned and changed to become like little children? As long as Jesus was with them, they didn't get it. But when he died, they did, for they understood at last that he had given himself for them and had bought their salvation at the cost of his own life. And they really were changed.

It is beautiful to see. The disciples were all guilty of this self-advancing spirit. But among the many who were guilty, James and John stand out as the most guilty because of their compliance with the efforts of their mother to get them the first places. Yet think what happened to them! At one time Jesus called them "Sons of Thunder," no doubt because of their arrogant, boisterous attitudes (Mark 3:17). They were changed when they finally got their minds off themselves and onto Jesus.

We are not told much about James, but he must have changed. We do not hear of him struggling for prominence after the crucifixion and resurrection of the Lord, and he eventually died for Jesus, being executed by King Herod (Acts 12:1–2). John lived to be a venerable old man, known at last as the "apostle of love." He spoke humbly when he said, "This is how we know what love is: Jesus Christ laid down his life for us. And we ought to lay down our lives for our brothers" (1 John 3:16). If Jesus can turn a "son of thunder" into an "apostle of love," he can conquer your pride and teach you humility so that you can become like one of Jesus's "little children." He needs to, if you are to belong to his kingdom.

Serving God to the End

Matthew 19:30–20:16

So the last will be first, and the first will be last.
—MATTHEW 20:16

What Jesus had in mind when he told the provocative parable of the workers in the vineyard is suggested by the most important verse that both introduces the story and ends it: "But many who are first will be last, and many who are last will be first" (Matt. 19:30). The important word here is *many*, for the teaching is not that every person who begins early with God and works for him throughout a lifetime will inevitably be last or that everyone who begins late will inevitably be first. That will be true for *many* people, but it will not be true for all.

Many who begin early will lose their reward or not even come to faith in Christ because they approach God in a false or mercenary spirit, on the basis of their merit and not on the basis of God's grace. Many who enter last will be first because, although they begin late, they nevertheless recognize that their status is due to God's grace alone and praise God for it. But neither of those cases is true for everyone.

It is not necessary either to start early and finish last or start last and finish first. In fact, neither is best. The truly desirable thing is to start early and work with all the might you have, not for reward but out of genuine love for our Master, Jesus Christ, and when you have finished still to say, "I am nevertheless an unprofitable servant." It is such people whom God delights to honor.

Daniel was such a person. He was carried off to Babylon at a very early age. He was immersed in the splendors of the great Babylonian court and was trained for high position and responsibility. He could have been swept away by the temptations. But Daniel decided at that early age not to "defile himself" (Dan. 1:8). He determined to serve God, and he was still there decades later as an old man serving God and hearing God say, "Go your way till the end. You will rest, and then at the end of the days you will rise to receive your allotted inheritance" (12:13).

Daniel served God for seventy years.

Moses served God for eighty years.

Abraham served God for a hundred years.

Enoch served God for three hundred years.

This is the challenge I put before you, especially if you are young. Do not wait to serve God. Do not wait until the ninth or eleventh hour of your all-too-brief life. Start now. Serve now. Keep at your service year after year. And when you come to the end, you will not say, "What am I owed for my service?" You will say, "What a joy it has been to serve my gracious and loving Lord!"

Who Is Jesus?

Matthew 21:1–11

The whole city was stirred and asked, "Who is this?"
—MATTHEW 21:10

Matthew ends his account of the triumphal entry by telling us that when Jesus entered Jerusalem, "the whole city was stirred," as it had been thirty-three years earlier when the Magi came to inquire, "Where is the one who has been born king of the Jews?" (2:2–3). Here they ask, "Who is this?" The crowds answered, "This is Jesus, the prophet from Nazareth in Galilee" (vv. 10–11).

The crowd was calling the man who was entering Jerusalem on a donkey the Messiah, for that is what the shouts of praise meant. John tells us that they called him "the King of Israel" explicitly (John 12:13).

Significant? Yes, but not good enough. They were still thinking of a powerful political ruler, the kind who could marshal an army and drive out the occupying Romans. And the people were shallow even in their confession of Jesus as the King and Messiah of Israel. In a few days they would be singing an entirely different tune as they beseeched Pilate, the Roman governor, "Crucify him! Crucify him!" (Matt. 27:22–23).

Who is Jesus? This is the time to get your answer to that question straight, in case you have never done it before. Matthew has presented Jesus as God's King. He was rejected by many but believed on by a few. Where do you stand on this issue? Is Jesus the King? Is he the Son of God? Is he the Savior? Have you trusted him for the salvation of your soul?

If you are still hesitating with your answer, let me take you through the possibilities. First, eliminate the one impossible idea that Jesus was merely a good man. Whatever he might be, he was certainly not just a good man, for no good man could honestly make the claims he made. Jesus presented himself as the Savior of the human race, claiming to be God. Is he? If so, he is more than a mere man. If not, then he is at best mistaken (consequently, not "good") and at worst a deceiver.

Is he a deceiver? Is that the explanation we have for one who was known for being "meek and lowly," who became a poor itinerant evangelist in order to help the poor and teach those whom others despised? Somehow the facts do not fit. We cannot face the facts of his life and teaching and still call Jesus a deceiver. What then? If he was not a deceiver and not just a good man, only one possibility is left. Jesus is who he said he is. He is the one the Gospels, including Matthew, proclaim him to be. He is the Christ, the Son of God, the Savior. Do you believe that? If you do, now is the time to turn from your sin, trust Jesus for your salvation, and follow him.

Unprepared
Matthew 25:1–13

And the door was shut.
—MATTHEW 25:10

Here are two lessons from this parable of the ten virgins.

1. *Being prepared for judgment is not transferable.* No person can get by on another's faith. You cannot be saved by the life of Christ in someone else. Many people delude themselves along these lines. They do not have true faith in Christ, but they have been exposed to it over a period of years and suppose that, in the time of Christ's judgment, they will be able to appeal to God's work in the life of someone close to them.

"What right do you have to come into my heaven?"

"Well, I don't really know how to answer that, Lord. But consider my mother. She was a godly woman, and I learned a lot from her."

"I didn't ask that," the Lord replies. "I asked, What right do *you* have to enter my heaven?"

"Look at my Sunday school teachers, Lord! They were godly people; they certainly went out of their way to teach me. They prayed for me too. Don't forget them!"

Jesus replied, "What right do *you* have to enter heaven?"

This helps us understand why the wise women refused to give their oil to the five who were foolish. Their refusal seems uncharitable. But the story is not about charity. Rather, the parable reveals that when Christ returns, each person must stand on his or her own. Your mother's faith will not save you. Your wife's faith will not save you. You will not be saved by the spiritual life of your son or daughter. The questions will be, Where do *you* stand? Are *you* alive in Christ? Are *you* ready?

2. *Lost opportunities cannot be regained.* The foolish women set out to buy oil, but the bridegroom came, and they were too late. So it will be when Christ returns in judgment. Those who are ready will be taken in to the marriage feast, and those who are not ready will be shut out.

Do not say, "I will turn to Christ later. I will repent after I enjoy a few more years of sin. There is always time for Jesus." You do not know that. Today may be the last time you will hear the gospel. And even if it is not—even if you do hear it again and again—it will be no easier for you to turn to God later. In fact, the opposite is the case. The fact that you have rejected the free offer of God's grace now will harden you so that you will find it much more difficult to repent later. Millions who once heard the gospel and postponed a decision have since perished in their sins. The only wise thing is to come to Jesus now. The Bible says, "Now is the time of God's favor, now is the day of salvation" (2 Cor. 6:2).

Doing Good
Matthew 25:31–46

Whatever you did for one of the least of these brothers of mine, you did for me.
— MATTHEW 25:40

The works Christians perform do not save them, but the works are evidence that Christians love and trust Jesus. And here is a point worth noting. The evidence of a credible Christian profession is not how many great works have been performed for Jesus, how many churches have been built or sermons preached or millions of dollars given to Christ's cause. The proofs of conversion are not "great" things at all. They are little things, as most people think of them: sharing food with a brother who is hungry, giving water to a sister who is thirsty, welcoming a stranger, offering clothes to one who needs clothing, caring for the sick, or visiting a person who is in prison.

It is because these are little things that the righteous do not even remember having done them. They ask Jesus, "When did we see you hungry and feed you, or thirsty and give you something to drink? When did we see you a stranger and invite you in, or needing clothes and clothe you? When did we see you sick or in prison and go to visit you?" (vv. 37–39).

It is also because these are little things that the unrighteous did not do them. They might have done them if someone important, such as Jesus, had been there. But they hadn't seen anyone like that. "Lord, when did we see you hungry or thirsty or a stranger or needing clothes or sick or in prison, and did not help you?" (v. 44). Of course, they only delude themselves by such comments, because they would not have helped even an important person in a truly selfless way. They would have done it only for what they could have gotten in return.

Let's notice one other thing as well. The wicked are condemned in this story not because of some great positive evil they have done but for their simple neglect of doing good. Or to put it in other terms, the people spoken of here are not the great sinners of the world, like Adolf Hitler or some serial killer. They are the good people who occupy the pews of churches and serve on philanthropic boards. Therefore, when the judgment comes, they are astonished. They are like the foolish virgins who cannot understand why the groom will not open the door for them or the servant who cannot perceive why the Lord is not satisfied by his zero-growth performance.

It is not refraining from doing evil that marks the Christian who loves and trusts Jesus, but the active desire to do good. And that desire comes from receiving the life of the Lord Jesus Christ within, which is regeneration.

A Lasting Memorial

Matthew 26:6–16

> What she has done will also be told, in memory of her.
> —*MATTHEW 26:13*

An interesting twist to the story of Mary anointing Jesus is that it was a memorial for him, in view of his death and burial, though what she did actually became a memorial to her. Think how many great deeds of the many great kings, generals, tycoons, and other brilliant men of this world have been forgotten. People try to erect great monuments to themselves, but what they have done is hardly remembered by succeeding generations. But Mary's selfless, loving, extravagant act lives on as a memorial to her and a witness to the greatness of her Lord.

Do you want to be remembered? Then do as Mary did. Leave off building monuments; build the lives of other people. Share your possessions and give yourself to others. Remember that Jesus said, "Whoever wants to save his life will lose it, but whoever loses his life for me will find it. What good will it be for a man if he gains the whole world, yet forfeits his soul?" (Matt. 16:25–26).

That is what happened to Judas. This disciple spent three years in the closest possible association with the only perfect man who ever lived. Yet in the end he turned his back on Jesus and gave him up to be murdered. It was a horrible deed, and Judas experienced a horrible end. But it is not altogether different from the decisions of those who turn their backs on Jesus today and whose end is the same as the betrayer's. Like Judas, many seek the world and its pleasures and forfeit their souls.

How could Judas have missed learning what was truly valuable and giving up everything for it? I do not know but I know that millions are doing just that today. Let me remind you that it is possible to be quite close to Jesus Christ, to sit in a Christian church listening to good sermons, to hear good Bible teaching on radio or television, to have Christian parents or Christian friends who live consistent and effective Christian lives and bear strong testimonies to the gospel of God's grace, and yet fail to love Christ and never reach the point of making a personal commitment to him as your Lord and Savior. You can be that close to Jesus Christ and yet be lost.

It would be a tragedy for that to be true in your case, but it is not necessary, especially if you have understood who Jesus is and what he came to earth to do. Like Mary, you need to look deeply into his eyes and learn to love him as the one who loves you and gave himself for your salvation.

The Lord's Supper
Matthew 26:17–30

This is my blood of the covenant.
—MATTHEW 26:28

In some ways, it is a pity that debate about the literal or nonliteral meaning of Christ's words has been so fierce, since it has tended to obscure the equally important (probably far more important) teachings about Jesus's death that we have here. Think how many important doctrines are taught by Jesus's words and this sacrament.

1. *A vicarious atonement.* Jesus died in our place as our substitute, taking our guilt on himself and bearing the punishment for our sins. This was the meaning of the Passover, which was being observed that very week when Jesus was teaching, and it is what is symbolized by the breaking of the bread. As the bread was broken, so would Jesus's body be broken, but not for himself. It would be broken for those who would trust him as their Savior.

2. *A new covenant.* Jesus's linking of the old covenant and the new covenant makes clear that his death was the fulfillment and end of the millions of blood sacrifices that had been used to seal and maintain the old covenant. There would be no more need for sacrifices once he had died for our sin.

3. *The forgiveness of sins.* The fact that Jesus spoke of the forgiveness of sins is an indication that he was thinking of Jeremiah 31 as well as Exodus 24. But these words make an additional point. To be forgiven by God is our great need, for it is only as our sins are forgiven and we are clothed with the righteousness of Christ that we can stand before a holy God. It is by the blood of Christ alone that we are cleansed from sin's defilement.

4. *Particular redemption.* Jesus did not say that his blood would be poured out for everyone for the forgiveness of their sins, but "for many" (Matt. 26:28). Jesus's blood made an actual atonement for transgressions. His sacrifice actually propitiated God on their behalf. His death secured their justification, and by his stripes they all were truly healed. Particular redemption means that Christ's death was not for all, but Jesus's words also teach that it was not merely for a few but for many. Many have come. Many more are yet to come. There are many with whom we have yet to share the gospel.

5. *Eternal security.* Christ's words also teach the truth of eternal security, for he stated as an unchallengeable fact that one day he would drink wine with his disciples ("with you," v. 29) in his Father's kingdom. How could Jesus be sure? Obviously because his death would accomplish their salvation so completely and perfectly that not even Peter's public denial of the Lord would undermine it.

Boice, *The Gospel of Matthew*, Volume 2, Baker, 2001, 561–63.

Judging Jesus
Matthew 26:57–68

He has spoken blasphemy! Why do we need any more witnesses?
— MATTHEW 26:65

Jesus's claims matched what the Old Testament taught about the Messiah.

1. The Messiah was to have been born in Bethlehem, as Jesus was (Micah 5:2; Luke 2:1–7).
2. The Messiah was to be virgin born, as Jesus was born of Mary, who was a virgin at the time (Isa. 7:14; Matt. 1:24–25; Luke 1:26–30).
3. The Messiah was to be of David's line, and Jesus was descended from King David (2 Sam. 7:12, 16; Isa. 11:1–2; Matt. 1:1–16; Luke 3:23–37).
4. The Messiah was to be preceded by a figure like Elijah, and John the Baptist filled that role (Mal. 3:1; 4:5; Matt. 17:12–13; John 1:19–23).
5. The Messiah was to do many great works, and Jesus had performed the works that had been prophesied (Isa. 61:1–2; Matt. 11:1–6; Luke 4:16–21).
6. The Messiah was to make a public entry into Jerusalem riding on a donkey, as Jesus had done (Zech. 9:9; Matt. 21:1–11).
7. The Messiah was to be betrayed by a close friend, and Jesus was so betrayed (Ps. 41:9; Matt. 26:14–15; 27:3–8).
8. The Messiah was to be despised and rejected by his people and to be familiar with suffering, and Jesus was (Isa. 53:2–3).

What about Jesus's claim to be God's Son?

1. There are scriptural references precisely to the kind of unique Son of God Jesus claimed to be (Ps. 2:7; Isa. 9:6).
2. The Old Testament speaks of God becoming flesh (Isa. 7:14).
3. There are passages in which Jehovah is said to have appeared among men (Gen. 16:13; 18:13, 17, 26; Dan. 3:25).

These passages contain references to the appearance of God on earth in human form and suggest that Jesus was the one. Their absence from the trial exposes the closed minds and jealous hearts of those who were Christ's judges. These leaders were not substantially different from millions of careless people in our day. Christ is proclaimed as God's unique Son, but millions reject that claim and turn their backs on the defense. There is a defense. It is presented regularly in countless Christian churches, on radio and television, in books, magazines, and other forms of communication. But they will not hear it. They will not go to church. They will not read Christian books.

Yet the important thing is not what they are doing; it is what you are doing. Have you considered Christ's claims? Have you pondered his defense? If not, I challenge you to do so now. In the last analysis, it is not Jesus who is on trial. That is past; it is over. You are the one who is on trial, and the question before you is, What will you do with Jesus?

Passing Responsibility
Matthew 27:11–26

It is your responsibility!
— *MATTHEW 27:24*

Pilate was trapped by his own scheming. He had miscalculated. But his stubborn character still came through. He was caught, but he did not want to be defeated by the Jews' religious rulers whom he obviously despised. "What shall I do, then, with Jesus who is called Christ?" he demanded.

"Crucify him," they answered.

"Why? What crime has he committed?" asked Pilate. He understood very well that Jesus had done nothing at all to merit punishment, certainly not crucifixion.

They had no answer. There was none. All they could do was cry louder, "Crucify him! Crucify him!"

Matthew indicates that the situation was getting out of hand, that "an uproar was starting" (v. 24). The leaders were stirring it up, of course. It was part of their plan. It was the thing Pilate had to avoid at all costs. But the leaders were doing something else too, according to John's version of the story. They were badgering Pilate with the threat of an unfavorable report of his conduct to Caesar. "If you let this man go, you are no friend of Caesar. Anyone who claims to be a king opposes Caesar," they said (John 19:12). That tipped the scales, of course, for although Pilate may actually have feared Jesus a bit—perhaps Jesus was a kind of god (the ancients believed in such things) and might actually do him harm—and although Pilate feared the hatred of the religious leaders and the fickleness of the crowds even more, Pilate feared the emperor most of all and dared not risk his disfavor. So at last he called for water and washed his hands before the crowd. "I am innocent of this man's blood," he said. "It is your responsibility!"

How ironic! Innocent? That is precisely what Pilate was not. All the water in the world could not wash the guilt of Jesus Christ's blood from his hands, as countless generations since have realized. There was another great irony too. When Pilate told the Jews, "It's your responsibility," he was saying precisely what they had said to Judas earlier: "What is that to us? That's your responsibility" (Matt. 27:4). They had not escaped their guilt by passing it off on Judas, and neither could Pilate escape his guilt by passing it off on them. They were all guilty. And so are we! Though we cannot wash away the stains of Christ's blood by any acts of our own or by ceremonial washings, by the blood of Christ we can indeed be cleansed. His death takes away our sins. "What can wash away my sin?" It is a searching question to which there is only one answer: "Nothing but the blood of Jesus!"

The Burial's Significance

Matthew 27:57-61

> [Joseph] placed [the body] in his own new tomb.
> —MATTHEW 27:60

Jesus's burial has theological significance for us. This point strikes us when we study what is said about the grave in the Old Testament and about the burial of Jesus in the New Testament. Old Testament texts speak of the grave with dread. Examples include Genesis 37:35 ("In mourning will I go down to the grave") and 2 Samuel 22:6 ("The cords of the grave coiled around me"). Often the word translated "grave" in our Bibles is *Sheol*, which has overtones of hell, as in Psalm 116:3 ("the anguish of the grave") or Job 10:21, which calls it "the land of gloom and deep shadow." To say that Jesus not only died but was also buried in the grave means that he descended as low as he could go in order to raise us up to heaven.

Yet there is more. In Romans, Paul speaks of Christians being buried with Jesus in his death, just as they are raised with him in his resurrection. He does this while discussing the Christian life, explaining why believers cannot continue in sin. For example, "We were . . . buried with him through baptism into death in order that, just as Christ was raised from the dead through the glory of the Father, we too may live a new life" (Rom. 6:4).

When theologians work out these parallels, they have little trouble showing how we have been crucified with Jesus, raised with him, or even made to ascend into heaven with him. But they have trouble with the burial. How were we buried with Christ? they ask. What does this add that is not already covered by our death to sin?

I suggest that the reason burial is an important step even beyond death is that burial puts the deceased person out of this world permanently. A corpse is dead to life, but in a sense it is still in life, as long as it is around. When it is buried, when it is placed in the ground and covered with earth, it is removed from the sphere of this life permanently. It is gone. That is why Paul, who wanted to emphasize the finality of being removed from the rule of sin and death, emphasizes it. He is repeating but also intensifying what he said about our death to sin earlier. "You have not only died to it," he says. "You have been buried to it." To go back to sin once you have been joined to Christ is like digging up a dead body.

I do not think the Gospel writers had this in mind when they wrote about Christ's burial, but guided by the Holy Spirit, they were laying down as a detail of history what Paul in particular would later unfold in its full theological significance.

Boice, *The Gospel of Matthew*, Volume 2, Baker, 2001, 630–31.

See the Grave

Matthew 28:1–10

Come and see the place where he lay.
—MATTHEW 28:6

Think for a minute about why we should see the grave and how we may profit by it.

First, we see the grave that we might understand *the condescension of the Lord Jesus Christ*. The Lord Jesus Christ is not just a man for whom such a death would be natural. Jesus is the Lord! Jehovah! The Savior! Christ! Messiah! He is the one who dwelt with God in all eternity—who was God, equal to God, equal in all power and glory—yet laid aside the glory to take upon himself the form of a man in order that he might die to save us. Oh, the condescension of such a God who would come from the glories of heaven to this earth and then die and lie in such a tomb! When we look at the grave, we see there the love and condescension of our Lord.

We see something else too. We see *the horror of our sin*, for our sin placed him there. He did not die for his own sin; he was sinless. He died in our place. When we see the place where the Lord lay and say, "It is my sin that brought him to that end," we begin to develop a proper awareness of sin and hatred for it.

The third reason we should see the tomb is that we might be reminded of *where we also will lie*. Unless the Lord comes for his own before that moment, we too must die. There is a time when we will be separated from all that we now know. We will leave friends and loved ones behind. We will leave our material possessions. The tomb teaches us that there is a life beyond this life for which we must prepare.

Fourth, we look at the tomb to see that *Jesus is not in it now*. He is risen! He has conquered death! That is the one great evidence for the resurrection. In all the reports we have, whether in the New Testament or those preserved indirectly by secular writers such as Josephus or in the Jewish Talmud, there is not one instance of any attempt to deny that the grave was empty.

Finally, looking at the tomb reminds us not only that Jesus rose from the dead, but that *we shall rise also* if we are united to him. Jesus came, as the Scriptures say, "to save completely" (Heb. 7:25) those who believe on him. We are saved, not just in spirit in order to have fellowship with God; not just in soul in order to be transformed during the days of our earthly life, but in body also. The salvation Jesus brings is complete. So we look to the empty tomb to see that one day we too shall rise and shall be with him.

Boice, *The Christ of the Empty Tomb*, P&R Publishing, 2010, 190–92.

The Great Commission
Matthew 28:16–20

Go and make disciples of all nations.
—*Matthew 28:19*

Notice that the word *all* occurs four times in these verses.

1. Jesus possesses *all* authority. This is no weak authority, because the one who spoke it is no weak master. He is the risen Lord, and "*all* authority in heaven and on earth" has been given to him (v. 18).

He is not merely talking about an acknowledgment of his earthly authority in heaven. Rather, his authority is superior to and over all other authorities whether spiritual, demonic, or otherwise. Consequently, we do not fear Satan or anyone else while we are engaged in Jesus's service.

Second, Jesus announces that he has authority over everything on earth. He has authority over us, his people, and over those who are not yet believers. That is, his authority extends to the people to whom he sends us with the gospel. No one is outside the sphere of his authority or is exempt from his call. This is also a statement of Jesus's ability to bring fruit from our efforts, for it is through the exercise of his authority that men and women actually come to believe and follow him.

2. Jesus sends us to *all* nations. The Jewish disciples who had followed Jesus through the days of his ministry and who were being commissioned formally to his service were not to limit their operations to Judaism, but were to go to all the people of the world with this gospel. Whenever the church has done this, it has prospered. When it has failed to do this, it has stagnated and dried up. Why? Because discipleship demands evangelism; it is an aspect of our obedience as Christ's followers, and Jesus blesses obedience. That evangelism, furthermore, is to lead converts to the point of baptism "in the name of the Father and of the Son and of the Holy Spirit." At some point a person's commitment to Jesus as Savior and Lord must become public and he must unite with the church, which is Christ's visible body, both of which baptism effects.

3. We are to teach people *all* he has commanded (v. 20). Christ commanded us to teach converts "to obey everything" (or *all* things), which means that for all Christians a lifetime of learning must follow conversion and membership in Christ's church.

4. As we do, we are to know that Jesus will be with us *all* the days, or always. The final universal of Matthew 28:18–20 is "*al[l]*-ways" or, as the Greek text literally says, "all the days, even to the consummation of the age." This is a great, empowering promise, and it is wonderfully true. In the first chapter of Matthew, Jesus was introduced as "Immanuel"—which means "God with us" (Matt. 1:23). Here, in the last verse, that very same promise is repeated. Jesus will be with us as we go.

Boice, *The Gospel of Matthew*, Volume 2, Baker, 2001, 646–49, 651.

Celebrating Sunday
Mark 2:23–3:6

The Sabbath was made for man, not man for the Sabbath.
— MARK 2:27

How should we *celebrate* Sunday? Consider the first question of the Westminster Shorter Catechism: "What is the chief end of man?" The answer given is: "Man's chief end is to glorify God and to enjoy him forever." *Joy* is to be the first characteristic of the Lord's Day. May I suggest that you are not really celebrating Sunday at all if you do not enjoy it?

The second important characteristic of the Lord's Day should be *activity*. Jesus said that real worship is done "in spirit and in truth" (John 4:24). Truth involves content. Thus, worship is above all else an active, rational activity. It must engage the mind.

The second highly significant activity that ought to characterize the Lord's Day is our witness. Do you do that on Sunday? You can do it on any day, of course. It is of the essence of our day that anything done on Sunday can and should be done on other days also. But do you at least bear a witness on Sunday? This is a day to invite your friends to go with you to hear God's Word proclaimed. At the least it is a day on which you should teach your children what you know about Christ.

Sunday should be characterized by a great spiritual *expectation*.

I love Sunday. One of the reasons why I love Sunday is that I never know in advance what will happen. As I leave my house on the way to the church, I never know precisely whom I will meet or what will take place. I do not know who will be present or who will respond to the preaching. I never plan messages to preach at problems that I imagine to be present in the congregation, and yet it is often the case that what I say is used of the Lord to speak precisely to some problem. Lives are changed. What is more, not infrequently that day is the turning point in someone's entire spiritual experience.

Do you go to the company of God's people with such expectation? If you do, it will increase your joy and cause you to work even harder. You will thrill to God's grace. And you will know in a personal way the burden of these words that summarize most of our Sunday activity: "So whether you eat or drink or whatever you do, do it all for the glory of God" (1 Cor. 10:31); "be prepared in season and out of season; correct, rebuke and encourage—with great patience and careful instruction" (2 Tim. 4:2); "pray continually" (1 Thess. 5:17); "be joyful always" (v. 16); "stand firm. Let nothing move you. Always give yourselves fully to the work of the Lord, because you know that your labor in the Lord is not in vain" (1 Cor. 15:58).

Jesus's Compassion
Mark 8:1–10

I have compassion for these people.
— MARK 8:2

The story of Jesus feeding the four thousand contains a lesson for anyone who feels that God has forgotten him or her. Do you feel that way? If you do, notice Jesus, out of compassion, had initiated the matter of feeding the people. That is an encouragement for us, both if we fail to show concern for others or if we are one of the multitude and so feel forgotten. Let us take our attitude toward others first. We often fail to see human need. We miss the cry of loneliness, despair, or frustration expressed by some poor soul. Jesus hears it. Our hearts may be cold, but the heart of Jesus is warm with compassion.

Or suppose you are one of the lonely ones. Even when there are other people who *are* interested in you, that interest still is always imperfect and partial. There are people in your home, office, or church who care for you, particularly if they are Christian people. But they are beset by all the sin and failure that is common to men and women. Only One will not fail you. There is only One whose interest does not waver. He created you. He planned the circumstances of your life. He knows your situation. It is this One who desires to supply all your need according to his abundant resources.

Do you say that you cannot see it? Consider Jacob. He was in his old age and complaining about the harsh blows that life had dealt him. Years before, his son Joseph had been killed by wild animals, so he thought. Then famine had come, and he had sent ten of his remaining sons to Egypt to buy food. He had kept Benjamin, the youngest, at home. The sons came back, but without Simeon, who had been left as a hostage. When the famine continued it became necessary to send the sons back to Egypt for more food, but they refused to go, saying they could not return without Benjamin. The man in charge in Egypt had told them that if they did not return with Benjamin he would treat them as spies. Jacob was greatly distressed. All things seemed against him. But it was at this moment that God was planning his greatest blessing for him. God knew the end from the beginning, and he cared about Jacob. He had actually sent Joseph to Egypt years in advance to prepare for this moment. Joseph was the man in charge. It was only when Jacob gave in to the situation that God brought to completion the blessing of a full reunion of all the brothers and their father in their new land.

Maybe you are going through a situation like that in your own life. Do not wring your hands and say, "God has forgotten." Trust him. He knows your need and where he is leading you.

Boice, *The Gospel of John*, Volume 2, Baker, 1999, 443–44.

Blessings and Persecutions
Mark 10:17–31

No one who has left home or brothers or sisters or mother or father
or children or fields for me and the gospel will fail to receive a hundred
times as much in this present age (. . . and with them, persecutions).
—MARK 10:29–30

Christ's words to the disciples are not just an encouragement to serve Christ, important as that may be. They are also an encouragement to trust him through difficult times. We can hardly escape this point since the Lord links his promise of blessings to the phrase "and with them, persecutions," thereby indicating that, although he undertakes to bless us abundantly with homes, brothers, sisters, mothers, children, and even fields, we will not enjoy these without the persecutions that inevitably come to any true follower of Christ. We will continue to have hardships until we come to possess our full inheritance in the presence of Jesus himself in heaven.

Most persecutions come from the world. The world hates Christ, so naturally it hates those who serve Christ and live like him. That hatred is increased when Christians are blessed by their heavenly Father.

Here the blessings of God on believers in this life are an encouragement to them to continue trusting him in spite of the difficulties. The Christian may reason, *It is true that the world hates me; Jesus warned that this would be the case. But though the world hates me and wishes me harm, it is evident that God loves me and wishes me good. He has blessed me a hundredfold—with homes, brothers, sisters, mothers, children, and fields. Every day I see further evidence of God's favor. So I will trust him to do me the further good of seeing me through these temptations and bringing me safe to heaven.*

Other persecutions come from the devil. We must not overly emphasize this source of temptations, for the devil is a finite creature and can therefore only tempt one individual in one place at one time. He has probably never persecuted either you or anyone you know personally. Still the devil has hosts of lesser demons who work with him, and he is capable of working indirectly through mere human beings. If persecutions come from this source, God's goodness is an encouragement to trust him through these times also.

Yet I say this: the promise is for the righteous, which means for those who have been made righteous through God's grace received in following after Jesus Christ. These are great promises. They are encouragement to trust God and serve Christ. But they are for those who have not turned back to their possessions, as the rich young man did, but who rather have turned from them, forsaking everything for the surpassing joy of the excellency of knowing Jesus Christ. To these alone God promises homes, parents, children, friends, and fields—with persecutions—and in the age to come eternal life.

Boice, *Christ's Call to Discipleship*, Moody Press, 1986, 155–57.

The Offered Pardon
Mark 15:6–15

Pilate released Barabbas to them.
—MARK 15:15

Suppose word had come to Barabbas that he was now free and that another prisoner, Jesus, would be dying. Suppose he replied this way: "What you are telling me cannot be true. It may apply to someone else, someone who has committed a lesser offense than I. But I am a great sinner and criminal. No, I cannot believe it. I must stay here." And suppose he had resisted when the guards attempted to remove his chains and release him? We can hardly imagine such a response. Yet this is the response of some to whom the gospel of the substitutionary atonement of the Lord Jesus Christ is preached. They think that it is for another and so do not respond to that which to them is life.

Suppose again that Barabbas had acted in this way. Suppose he had said, "I refuse to accept such a pardon, because what I have done was entirely justified. I was right to rob and murder and commit insurrection. I will not go unless the representative of Rome comes to apologize for the way I have been treated and provides me with a bill of absolution." In that case, Barabbas would have died, for it is a principle of law that a pardon is a gift and no man can ever be compelled to accept a gift. We might judge such a reaction foolish, as it is. But it is a possible one, and the consequences are certain.

Again, suppose Barabbas had responded to the announcement of his liberty that he would prefer to reform himself first of all: "By this means I will prove that I have earned my freedom and truly deserve it." The magistrates would have answered that however good a man he might yet become (or not become), this nevertheless has no bearing on the crimes he has already committed and for which he was condemned to die. Future reformation cannot atone for past sin. Consequently, Barabbas's only hope was in the pardon provided through the death of the innocent Christ.

Did Barabbas reply in any one of these ways? We know he did not. In fact, it is highly unlikely that any one of them even occurred to him, so anxious was he to leave the prison and return to a free life outside.

Why then should you do differently? A pardon is offered. Jesus has died. Will you not accept his death in place of your own and quickly go forth to serve him? If you have been languishing in the gloomy dungeon of your unbelief, you may do as so many others have done. Believe the gospel, and go forth to serve that One who out of the great measure of his love gave himself for your freedom.

Boice, *The Gospel of John*, Volume 5, Baker, 1999, 1462–65.

The Best News Ever Heard

Mark 16:1–7

You are looking for Jesus the Nazarene, who was crucified. He has risen!
—MARK 16:6

The resurrection of Jesus Christ is the best news the world has ever heard because it is true; it came after an apparent defeat; it proves many important things; and finally, it calls for a lifesaving response from each of us.

1. *It is true.* It is possible to have reports of events that sound like good news but later prove to be disappointments because the facts of the reports are wrong or because the events did not actually happen. That was not the case with news of the resurrection of the Lord. It is true, and as truth it is one of the most amazing and important facts in history.

2. *It came after an apparent defeat.* When Jesus died, his friends were plunged into sadness. It was an apparent defeat. But, then, on the third day he rose again. When Jesus died, men might have cried, "Christ is defeated; evil has triumphed; sin has won!" But after three days, the fog lifted, and the message came through to this world: "Jesus has risen; Jesus has defeated the enemy."

3. *It proves many important things.* It proves there is a God and that the God of the Bible is the true God. It proves the deity of our Lord, and thus that God loves you and came to be a ransom for your sins. It proves that all who believe in Jesus Christ are justified before God, because God showed through the resurrection that Christ was sinless and that he accepted his Son's atonement. The resurrection of Jesus Christ also proves that the believer in Christ can have a supernatural victory over sin in this life, for Jesus lives to provide the supernatural power to do it. Finally, the resurrection is also evidence for our own resurrection and of a life with Jesus in glory beyond the grave.

4. *It calls for a lifesaving response in faith from each of us.* Have you responded in faith to this one who died for you and rose again? There is some news that is by its very nature restricted. It applies to one or two individuals, but not to everybody. A promotion is good news to the man who receives it but not for the two or three others who failed to get the job. Almost all human news is restricted. But the good news of the resurrection is for all.

Have you heard the good news? Have you believed it? Have you trusted in the risen Lord? This is the heart of Christianity. It is not found in the liturgies of the churches, nor in the specific formulations of Christian theology, important as they may be. Christianity is Christ, the risen Christ. He died and rose again for you. Will you not come to him?

Boice, *The Christ of the Empty Tomb*, P&R Publishing, 2010, 125–35.

It's Absurd

Luke 1:26–38

"How will this be," Mary asked the angel, "since I am a virgin?"
—LUKE 1:34

The Christmas story seems absurd to many. It claims that the birth of Jesus is the birth of God, that is, the birth of one who was both man and God. How can that be?

But I want to ask, *why*? Why should God have saved us?

God is the holy God. God made us in his image, to have fellowship with him. We by our own wills have made a muddle of our lives in arrogant, willful rebellion against God. We have tried to build a world that is immune from God's good influence. We do not even want to hear the name of God acknowledged publicly. Why should God come to earth to save a race like that?

Why should God, the infinite God of the universe, take to himself the form of a helpless baby in the womb of a mother, be born in the pain of childbirth, be laid in a stable, be nailed to a cross and die an ignominious death? Why should God do that for us? Isn't that absurd?

There is an answer, of course. It may be an absurd answer, but it is still an answer. The answer is that God did it because he loved us.

God, why did you love us? Why did you send Jesus to be our Savior?

How is God going to answer that question in terms that we can understand? Can God explain his love to us? I don't think he can. God simply says, "I did it because I love you." And if we say to God, "But why did you love us? God answers, "It is because I loved you."

Let's apply this to us. 1 John 4:19 says, "We love because he first loved us." What that means is that if we have understood the Christmas story, we have understood at the most profound level that God has done this because he loves us. And then, because he has loved us—and loved us in this way—we must love others also. Some of the older versions wrongly add the word "him," saying, "We love *him* because he first loved us." But the text actually says, "We love . . ." We start by loving God, but we also love one another, even the unlovely, apart from "reason," loving them as God has loved us.

Isn't that absurd?

Yes, it is, if you are thinking about it as the world measures things. But that is Christianity, and it is that absurd but wonderful reality that is able to transform our wicked world.

Boice, *The King Has Come*, Geanies House, 1992, 84–86.

Christmas Paradoxes

Luke 2:1–7

She gave birth to her firstborn, a son.
—*Luke 2:7*

Why has the birth of this one man, Jesus Christ, so seized upon the minds and imaginations of men and women? Answers to that question are found in the paradoxes of the Christmas story.

One obvious paradox is of purity in the account of the birth of a child to an unwed mother. The birth of a child to a girl who is not married is not surprising or even remarkable, though it is tragic. It is a story known to any preacher—the girl, quite often deeply distressed; the parents, frantic with grief and indecision. But the tone of distress and grief we know is not the tone of this story. Rather, there is purity: the purity of Mary, who was troubled by the angel's announcement and asked in innocence, "How will this be . . . since I am a virgin?" (Luke 1:34); and the purity of Joseph, who was not the father but who believed the announcement of the angel and so shielded Mary by marrying her, though he did not have intercourse with her until after Jesus was born.

A second paradox follows that one. It is also a story of joy in what would normally be a tragedy. Under normal circumstances Mary would have been in danger of vicious public exposure and even death, for stoning was the penalty prescribed for fornication in Israel. She would have been distraught and in anguish. Yet when Mary came to Elizabeth her cousin, Elizabeth at once broke forth in praise to God and in ascriptions of blessings on Mary, and Mary responded with that great hymn of praise known as the Magnificat.

There are other contrasts in this story. There is the announcement of the birth of the baby to shepherds, those from the lowest levels of ancient Jewish society, by angels who are certainly figures of great stature and glory. There is the neglect of Jesus by his own people, while Gentile wise men came to worship him. Even the baby is a paradox. For unlike other babies, who are born to live, this child was born to die.

And yet, in this great story so filled with paradoxes, there is one paradox that stands out above the rest, and perhaps more than any other commends the account to many people. It is that the one born in such lowly surroundings—in a stable, of poor parents, laid in an animal's manger—was nevertheless the God of glory, whose splendor before the incarnation surpassed that even of those heavenly beings who announced his birth to the shepherds. Here is a baby. But he is the King of Kings and Lord of Lords. He is God in a stable. He is the supreme potentate of the universe among his own lowly cattle.

That is the paradox of the incarnation: Immanuel!

Boice and Ryken, *The Christ of Christmas*, P&R Publishing, 2009, 82–83.

Our Bethlehem

Luke 2:8–20

Let's go to Bethlehem.
—*LUKE 2:15*

On the way to the manger, the shepherds went through the city of Bethlehem, seeing it for what it was. When they came to the manger they saw a great contrast. When they left the manger to go back to their fields and their sheep, of necessity they passed through the town again. It was the same town. It was the same sinful, calloused, divided, sad city. In a certain sense, they must have perceived it to be even more sinful, more calloused, more divided, and sadder than when they had come in. Having looked into the face of Jesus Christ, they must have seen it for what it really was.

Yet when they had left the manger and gone back into the world, they must also have seen the city in a transformed light. It was indeed worse than they had imagined. But together with seeing it from God's point of view, they must have also begun to see it as a world God deeply loved and for which he was now sending his own beloved Son to die. "For God so loved the world that he gave his one and only Son" (John 3:16).

Love that world? That sinful, evil, wretched, God-hating, man-destroying world? Yes, God loved that world.

That world? That calloused, cruel, hard, indifferent world? A world so insensitive it would not even make a place for Mary who was about to give birth? A world that would crucify Jesus? Yes, God loved that world.

That world? That sad, grey, dismal, pathetic, miserable, dying world? Yes, God loved the world so much that he gave his Son to die for it.

I am sure that what happened is that, having seen Jesus and having, therefore, begun to see the world in God's way, the shepherds went out into that world and began to regard it a little more as God did. How do we know? We know because we are told that they "spread the word concerning what had been told them about this child" (Luke 2:17). They began to say, "The Savior of the world has been born. The hope of the world has come."

That world is our world too. It is the world in which we live, and that baby was the Christ we have come to believe in and worship. His very name means "Savior."

So when you are out in the world this Christmas, try seeing the world as those who have first seen Jesus. You will find that the world is everything bad you imagined it to be, and worse. It is sinful, hard, divided, sad, but it is the world for whom Jesus came, and he is its Savior. If you know him as your Savior, love the world and tell people about him. The world desperately needs to hear that message.

Boice, *The King Has Come*, Geanies House, 1992, 158–60.

Looking for Redemption
Luke 2:21–40

> She gave thanks to God and spoke about the child to all who
> were looking forward to the redemption in Jerusalem.
> —*LUKE 2:38*

Anna understood more about the full significance of the coming of Jesus Christ than any of the others who appear in the nativity narratives, for she understood that the infant Jesus was to become the Redeemer that God had promised to Israel. And we know this because she announced his birth to all in Jerusalem who, like herself, looked for that redemption.

I find this encouraging in the light of what seems to be so much indifference to the claims of Jesus Christ today. The world of Christ's day was filled with those who were unaware of, or indifferent to, his coming—just like today. But there were believers also waiting for the promised redemption. The Pharisees looked for a deliverer, but one who would enter the land of Canaan in power and who would drive out the occupying troops of the Roman army. Because of this fixed understanding of who the Messiah would be, the coming of Jesus as the Redeemer passed them by. There were also Essenes. These monklike figures looked for a teacher, a new Moses. But because Jesus did not come from their ascetic circles and teach their doctrines, they too passed him by. The Pharisees looked for a political Messiah. The Essenes looked for a teacher. The Sadducees looked for nothing. But—there were also believers. And these looked for a Redeemer in Israel.

And it was the same in all of the preceding ages. The Old Testament saints in heaven are there because they too looked for God's Redeemer. This has always been the faith of God's children. For this reason, the redeeming work of Jesus has always been found at the heart of the Christmas story. The angel said, "Thou shalt call his name Jesus, for he shall save his people from their sins" (Matt. 1:21 KJV). And in every age God has always had those who looked for such a savior. In ancient times there were Abraham, Jacob, David, Isaiah, Malachi, and more. In Christ's own time there were Zacharias, John the Baptist, Joseph, Mary, Simeon, Anna, and a host of others.

And there are scores of believers today. Are you one? Do you know Christ as your Savior? Is he your Redeemer? How sad it would be if you could manage to go through another Christmas season without coming to believe in him who came to earth, not to remain in a cradle, but to die for you, to enrich your life now through his own indwelling spirit, and eventually to bring you with great joy into heaven. If you do know him, will you be like Anna who spoke to her neighbors about Jesus? She became his first great witness in Jerusalem. If we really understand what Christmas is all about, we will speak of our Redeemer and do it with great joy.

Boice, *The Bible Study Hour*, December 1969, 5–9.

Losing Jesus
Luke 2:41–50

The boy Jesus stayed behind in Jerusalem, but they were unaware of it.
—LUKE 2:43

If Mary and Joseph could lose Jesus in a place like Jerusalem, you and I can certainly lose the sense of the presence of Christ wherever we may be. We can find ourselves drifting spiritually, and we can enter into a period where all that seemed rich, wonderful, and glorious fades away, and we even find ourselves wondering if what we had experienced before was real at all.

What is to be done if that has happened? You have to go back to where you lost Jesus. That is what his parents did. They went back to Jerusalem to seek him out. That is where they had seen him last. So that is where they went.

Where is it that you lost the presence of Christ? It may be that you lost him in your prayer life. You once were fervent and faithful in prayer. Yet as the days went by and the pressures of life closed in, those times got shorter, and when you did pray, your mind was not entirely on what you were saying. Eventually it seemed as if Jesus was no longer there. If that is where you lost him, you must go back and reestablish those times of prayer. You must cry out for him.

Perhaps you lost Jesus at the point of some sin. You know that fork in the road where Jesus was going ahead of you in one direction and sin was beckoning from another. You thought you would go down the other fork for awhile and return. But you never did go back. Sin captured you. If that is the case, you must go back to that sin, confess and relinquish it, and then turn again and go in God's way.

Maybe you have lost Jesus at the point of your study of the Scriptures. You know that it is through the Word of God that Christians grow. It is by Bible study that a Christian resists temptations. But you began to neglect Bible study until now you can hardly remember the last time you sat down and studied the Bible seriously. If so, you need to get back to serious Bible study, search out the mind of God, and when you have found it, conform your life to that teaching.

Let me encourage you as you seek to find the Lord once again. You may have gone a long, long way from Jesus and have lost him for a very long time. However far you have strayed and however long it has been, if you will determine to seek Christ, you will find that he is there to be found. He is not hiding. Moreover, when you find him, you will find him to be the same gracious, loving, merciful, wise, and sovereign Savior he has always been.

Boice and Ryken, *The Christ of Christmas*, P&R Publishing, 2009, 159–66.

Taking Up the Cross
Luke 9:18–27

If anyone would come after me, he must deny himself and take up his cross daily and follow me.
—LUKE 9:23

Christ's description of discipleship in Luke 9:23 includes the command "Follow me." Having heard of self-denial and cross-bearing, we may find ourselves looking about for some motivation that will bring us to that commitment. Knowing that the alternative is to lose our life or forfeit our very self helps. But the cost still seems high. In most cases, the only thing that will ultimately get us going along this path of self-denial and discipleship is following after Jesus, which means setting our eyes on him as he has gone before us.

Jesus is the model for our self-denial. He is the image of cross-bearing.

Seeing this was the turning point in the life of Count Zinzendorf, the founder of the Moravian fellowships. In a little chapel near his estates in Europe, there was a remarkable picture of Jesus Christ. The artist was a true child of God, and he had painted love for Christ and the love of Christ into his portrait as few have done either before or since. Underneath it were the lines, "All this I did for thee; what hast thou done for me?"

One day Zinzendorf entered the chapel and was arrested by the portrait. He recognized the love of Christ that had been painted into the face of the Master. He saw the pierced hands, the bleeding forehead, the wounded side. He read the couplet, "All this I did for thee; what hast thou done for me?" Gradually a new revelation of the claim of Christ on his life came upon him. He was unable to move. Hours passed. As the day waned the lingering rays of sunlight fell upon the bowed form of the young nobleman who was now weeping out his devotion to him whose love had conquered his heart. Zinzendorf left that chapel a changed man. He went to work through the Moravians, whose missionary interests and Christ-like service have encircled the globe.

This is what moves a person to follow after Jesus in the path of denial. It is what moves one to be a Christian in the first place—not the promise of rewards (though there are rewards) or an escape from hell (though following Christ does mean deliverance from hell). We are moved by the love of Jesus, for which he endured the cross.

People won by that love will never cease following after Jesus.

They "make every effort to enter through the narrow door" (13:24).

Boice, *Christ's Call to Discipleship*, Moody Press, 1986, 43–44.

Seeing the Light
Luke 11:33–36

See to it, then, that the light within you is not darkness.
—*LUKE 11:35*

Jesus had been talking to the crowds, among whom were some of his enemies. He had cast a demon out of a man, and they claimed that he had done it by the power of the devil—that is, that Jesus was an agent of Satan. Later they asked for a sign, and he replied that no sign would be given to that wicked generation except the sign of his coming resurrection. Those people had been seeing his miracles and would see the even greater miracle of the resurrection. But they were not believing—they were actually opposing him—and the reason for their disbelief was not a lack of evidence but rather their own warped vision that prohibited their seeing Christ clearly. His challenge was for them to change their outlook so that they would not stumble on in spiritual darkness forever.

This is what Jesus meant when he applied the image of a lamp to their eyes. It is as though he were talking of trimming the wick or polishing the glass. The light is shining; *he* is the light. But they needed to polish up their perception of him.

Here were people enveloped in spiritual darkness so that they could not perceive the light of the Lord Jesus Christ. They were so blind to him that they imagined his works were done by Satan's power. Jesus told them to take heed to their eyes, to see that the light within is not darkness. Does that mean that they could regenerate themselves, that they could give themselves the spiritual vision they did not have? No. But it does not mean that they were to sit back and do nothing. Here we think of Christ's teaching in John 3. "This is the verdict: Light has come into the world, but men loved darkness instead of light because their deeds were evil. Everyone who does evil hates the light, and will not come into the light for fear that his deeds will be exposed" (vv. 19–20). Those men were doing evil. They did not see the light because they did not *want* to see it and thus be exposed as the sinners they were. To such people Jesus says, "Turn from your sin. Repudiate your evil way of life. Seek righteousness. And the light of the gospel will flood your soul and bring you to faith."

You cannot have sin and Jesus too. Sin will keep you from him. But if you want the light and will turn to it, you will find that he's already shining and that God is already at work to save you through the gospel of our Lord and Savior Jesus Christ.

Boice, *The Parables of Jesus*, Moody Press, 1983, 145–46.

Rich toward God

Luke 12:13–21

A man's life does not consist in the abundance of his possessions.
—*LUKE 12:15*

To be "rich toward God" means that one is to be rich in spiritual things, which will last, as opposed to being rich only in material things, which will not last.

What must we do to achieve such riches? There are two prerequisites. First, we must determine that we really want them and that we, therefore, are willing to serve God first and foremost, rather than our possessions. The Lord himself said, "You cannot serve both God and Money" (Matt. 6:24). The word translated here as "money" is the Hebrew word *mammon*, meaning "material possessions." It came from a root meaning "to entrust" or "to place in someone's keeping." Mammon, therefore, meant "the wealth entrusted to another."

As time passed, however, the meaning of the word shifted away from the passive mood ("that which is entrusted") to the active ("that in which one trusts"). Now the word, whose original meaning was best represented by a small *m*, came to be spelled with a capital letter as designating a god.

That development repeats itself in anyone who does not have his eyes fixed on spiritual treasures. Have things become your god? Do they obscure God? It may not be so, but if you think more about your home, care, vacation, bank account, clothes, makeup, or investments than God, then you are serving Mammon and building treasure on earth. According to Jesus, "Where your treasure is, there your heart will be also" (v. 21).

The second necessary thing if we are to become rich toward God is that we must empty ourselves of anything that would take the place of those spiritual riches. We must become poor in spirit before we can become rich in spiritual blessings (see 5:3). We must empty the heart of greed, pride, and other sins so that the riches of God can flow in.

That is what God's children have found. Before his conversion, Augustine was proud of his intellect and knowledge, and his pride kept him from believing on Christ. It was only after he had emptied himself of his pride and the sense of being able to manage his own life perfectly that he found God's wisdom through the Bible. Martin Luther's experience was similar. When the future reformer entered the monastery at a young age, it was to earn his salvation through piety and good works. Nevertheless, he had an acute sense of failure. It was only after he had recognized his own inability to please God and had emptied himself of all attempts to earn salvation that God touched his heart and showed him the true way.

An empty vessel is what you must be if God is to fill you with the life of Christ and enable you to live for him—even in the use of your possessions.

Boice, *The Parables of Jesus*, Moody Press, 1983, 108–10.

The Real Question
Luke 13:1–9

But unless you repent, you too will all perish.
—Luke 13:3

Whenever we talk about evil things happening to the "righteous" we are talking only from a human point of view and are actually asking the wrong question. We are asking, "Why did God let that happen to him or her?" when, actually, the question should be, "Why doesn't God let it happen to us all?"

The Lord dealt with that issue in the incident found in this passage. Some people had pointed to a recent tragedy: Herod's soldiers had fallen upon a group of Galileans who were at the temple offering sacrifices. Here were devout men and women in the very act of worship—that is, if they were ever right with God, it was then when they were standing before the altar with their sacrifices. But at that very moment Herod's soldiers had fallen upon them and had slaughtered them. How could that happen? Or again, there was the matter of the tower of Siloam that fell over and killed many innocent people. How could God let that happen? If God is all-powerful and can therefore do as he wants and if he is loving and therefore cares about us, how can situations like these occur?

A philosopher said, "Either God is all-powerful but he does not care. Or he cares but he is not all-powerful."

What did Jesus reply? He said, "Do you think that these Galileans were worse sinners than all the other Galileans because they suffered this way? I tell you, no! But unless you repent, you too will all perish. Or those eighteen who died when the tower in Siloam fell on them—do you think they were more guilty than all the others living in Jerusalem? I tell you, no! But unless you repent, you too will all perish" (vv. 2–5). What is Jesus saying? He is saying that whenever we ask a moral question of God—"God, how can you let this happen in your universe?"—we are on dangerous ground, because we are asking the wrong question. We are saying, "God, how could you let this happen to them?" When the real question should be, "God, why hasn't it happened to me? Why am I still living, sinner that I am? Why am I not in hell this very minute?" Our problem is that we have forgotten how sinful we are. It generally takes a disaster to awaken us from sin's lethargy.

Abraham argued with God and said, "Will not the Judge of all the earth do right?" (Gen. 18:25). A very good argument! But when the Judge of all the earth did right in that story, judgment fell on Sodom and Gomorrah, annihilating those cities. It is not justice that we want from God. It is grace!

Boice, *Dealing with Biblical Problems*, Christian Literature Crusade, 1986, 19–21.

Counting the Cost

Luke 14:28–33

In the same way, any of you who does not give up everything he has cannot be my disciple.
—LUKE 14:33

What must I pay to be a Christian? I must pay the price of my self-
righteousness, no longer counting myself a good person but rather
one who has transgressed God's righteous laws and is therefore under the
sentence of his wrath and condemnation. But when I pay the price of my self-
righteousness, I gain Christ's righteousness, which is perfect and imperishable.
In that righteousness I can stand before the very throne of God and be unafraid.

I must pay the price of those sins I now cherish. I must give them up, every
one. I cannot cling to a single sin and pretend that at the same time I am following the Lord Jesus Christ. But in place of my sins I find holiness, without
which no one can see the Lord (Heb. 12:14). I come to know the joy of holiness
rather than the empty mockery of transgressions.

I must pay the price of my own understanding of life, of what it is all about
and of what ultimately matters. I must surrender my confused and contradic-
tory opinions to the revelation of God in Scripture. I must never attempt to
correct or second-guess God. But when I do bring every thought into captivity
to Christ, I find true liberation. As Jesus said, "You will know the truth, and
the truth will set you free" (John 8:32).

I must pay the price of this world's friendship. I will be in the world but not
of it. I will know that the world is no friend of grace to lead me on to God,
but that it will always keep me from him. Indeed, I must not only forsake the
world; I must despise it for the sake of following after God. A hard price? Yes,
but in place of the friendship of this world, I have the friendship of Christ
(15:15). Jesus is the Friend that sticks closer than a brother.

I must pay the price of my plans for my life. I have many ideas for what I
want to do and be, but I must give them all up. I cannot both run my life and
also have Jesus run it. Jesus is Lord of all, and unless he is Lord of all my life,
he is not Lord at all. If he is not Lord, he is not Savior. My plans must go.
Yes, but in place of those flawed plans, Jesus has a perfect plan that will both
bless me and help others.

I must pay the price of my own will. That sinful, selfish will must go entirely. But in its place comes that "good, pleasing and perfect will" of God
(Rom. 12:2).

Boice, *Christ's Call to Discipleship*, Moody Press, 1986, 112–13.

Like God or Like Satan?

Luke 15:11–32

> But we had to celebrate and be glad, because this
> brother of yours . . . was lost and is found.
> —LUKE 15:32

In the parable of the lost son, many find it easy to sympathize with the older son. I know I do. But I also know that in sympathizing with him I am showing how little like the Father and how much like Satan and the other fallen angels I am. We sympathize with the older son because we think of ourselves as being like him. We are not like the prodigal—so we imagine. We are like that faithful, hardworking, obedient son—so we suppose. But we are not! Or if we are, it is not entirely because we are regenerate but because we have within us the spirit of a hired servant, who works for money, rather than the spirit of a son, who works because he loves his father. What was wrong with the older son? Several things: first, he loved property more than people. He would have been quite happy if the *money* had come back and his *brother* had been lost. As it was, he was angry that the property was lost and his brother recovered. Second, and as a result of his first error, he had an inflated estimate of his own importance and a scorn of others. He was loyal, hardworking, obedient—or so he thought. So low was his opinion of his brother that he would not even acknowledge his relationship to him, calling him only "this son of yours" (v. 30).

This brings the parable back to the point where it began (vv. 1–2). The Pharisees are the older son. They are those "who were confident of their own righteousness and looked down on everybody else" (18:9). That also brings the parable back to us, if we consider ourselves better than others or imagine that we are children of the Father because of our character or supposed good works and not purely because of God's good favor.

Will we fault God for acting according to his own gracious nature? If so, he will not accept our accusation. He will acknowledge no wrong on his part. It is right that heaven should rejoice over the repentant sinner; and if we would be like our Father in heaven, we should rejoice also. For the prodigal is our brother, whether or not we acknowledge it. The older son referred to the prodigal as "this son of yours," but the father replied, "We had to celebrate and be glad, because *this brother of yours* was dead and is alive again; he was lost and is found." We are never so like God as when we rejoice at the salvation of sinners. We are never so like Satan as when we despise those who are thus converted and think ourselves superior to them.

Boice, *The Parables of Jesus*, Moody Press, 1983, 55–56.

Hopelessness or Hopefulness
Luke 16:19–31

Between us and you a great chasm has been fixed.
—LUKE 16:26

Consider this contrast between the *hopelessness* of the rich man's condition after death and the *hopefulness* of his condition before. After death there is no possibility of change. But in this life there is, and therefore we can rightly say, "where there's life, there's hope," spiritually speaking.

This is the note that I make: the opportunity that all who hear this parable of the rich man and Lazarus still have. No matter who you are or what you may or may not have done, you are not yet in the position of the rich man who prayed but who, because he prayed in hell, prayed too late. For you it is not too late. You can pray; you can find God now. You can turn from sin and believe in the Lord Jesus Christ as your Savior. You can come to Christ in many ways, but it is only through Christ that you can come to heaven (John 14:6).

One of the great writers of the Elizabethan age was Christopher Marlowe, who wrote what is probably the classic treatment of the Faustus legend in English. Faustus was the character who, according to the story, sold his soul to the devil for secret knowledge and intense pleasure on earth. The devil gave him those things. But in the story there comes the moment when Faustus's earthly time runs out and the devil comes to take him away to damnation. In Marlowe's *Doctor Faustus*, Faustus, in despair, begs time to stop:

> O lente, lente, currite noctis equi!
> [The line means, "Run slowly, slowly, horses of the night!"]
> The stars move still, time runs, the clock will strike,
> The Devil will come, and Faustus must be damned.

Those words chill the heart. They paralyze the will. But praise to the God of all grace, those words are wrong. Why? Because it is not possible to sell your soul to the devil. The devil owns no one, and while we yet live, it is not necessary that anyone be damned. Christ is preached. The door is open. Jesus himself says, "Whoever will may come."

Do not wait for signs. Do not wait for miracles. Abraham said that the brothers of the rich man would not believe "even if someone rises from the dead" (Luke 16:31). You have the Scriptures, the Bible, and the story says, "They have Moses and the Prophets; let them listen to them" (v. 29). Listen to that word. Jesus said, "These are the Scriptures that testify about me" (John 5:39).

If you are not yet a believer in Jesus Christ, I commend that Word to you. I urge it on you for your soul's sake.

Boice, *The Parables of Jesus*, Moody Press, 1983, 215–16.

Mercy-Seated

Luke 18:9–14

God, have mercy on me, a sinner.
—LUKE 18:13

The word translated "have mercy on" is the verb form of the word for the "mercy seat" on the ark of the covenant in the Jewish temple. Therefore, it could literally (but awkwardly) be translated "be mercy-seated toward" or "treat me as one who comes on the basis of the blood shed on the mercy seat as an offering for sins."

The ark of the covenant was a box about a yard long, containing the stone tables of the law of Moses. The lid of that box was the mercy seat, having on each end of it angels whose outstretched wings went backward and upward, almost meeting over the center of the mercy seat. Between those outstretched wings, God was imagined to dwell symbolically. As it stands, the ark is a picture of judgment intended to produce dread in the worshiper through a knowledge of his or her sin. For what does God see as he looks down from between the wings of the angels? He sees the law of Moses that we have broken. He sees that he must act toward us as Judge.

But here is where the mercy seat comes in, and here is why it is called the *mercy* seat. Upon that covering of the ark, once a year on the Day of Atonement, the high priest sprinkled blood from an animal that served as a substitute. It was an innocent victim dying in the place of the sinful people who deserved to die. Now, when God looks down between the outstretched wings of the angels, he sees, not the law of Moses that we have broken, but the blood of the innocent victim. He sees that punishment has been meted out. Now his love goes out in mercy to save the one who comes to him through faith in that sacrifice.

That is why the prayer of the tax collector was so profound. Not only did it embody his faith in the way of salvation by sacrifice, it actually expressed the idea by its form. That is to say, between "God," whom we have offended, and "me, a sinner," which describes us all, comes the mercy seat.

When the tax collector prayed, "God, have mercy on me, a sinner," he was thinking of these animal sacrifices because, although Jesus was then present, he had not yet died. When we pray the tax collector's prayer, we think of Jesus and the way in which God has provided a full and perfect salvation through him.

Do you think of Jesus? Have you prayed that prayer? No one will ever be justified who has not prayed it, nor will anyone be received by God who has not first of all taken his stand with sinners in need of the mercy that God alone provides.

Boice, *The Parables of Jesus*, Moody Press, 1983, 90–91.

Weeping for the Lost
Luke 19:41–44

As he approached Jerusalem and saw the city, he wept over it.
—*LUKE 19:41*

Is this not an insight into the very heart of God? God wants the wicked to repent. He wants you to repent. Jesus would have been pleased by the conversion of Jerusalem. Can you not then weep for others, as your Master did? Doesn't the fact of the final judgment move you? Or if not that, how about the mess unbelievers are currently making of their lives?

Jesus wept for Jerusalem. Should we not weep for our cities? Is there nothing about Philadelphia that might cause us to weep? Or New York? Or any place? Can you not weep for just one who is perishing?

Perhaps you are not yet a Christian and perhaps you say, "No one has ever wept for me." You cannot be sure that is true. There may be many who have prayed for you with tears that you do not know about. But even if your claim is true, there is still the picture of Jesus weeping that I leave you.

Christians are not what their Master is. They fall short. They do not weep or love as he does. But there is one thing they do. They point to Jesus, as I point to him now. See him sitting on that dry hill overlooking the great city of Jerusalem. He has not come in triumph, a warrior riding upon some great steed. He has come humbly, a king riding on a donkey. He has come to save you, to die in your place. The crowd is cheering him. They want a king who will drive out the Romans and resurrect the fallen throne of King David. But he is not thinking of that. He is thinking of you, and he is crying. He is saying, "If you, even you, had only known on this day what would bring you peace—but now it is hidden from your eyes."

Ah, but it may not be hidden long. It has been. That has been true of us all. But Jesus comes to bring light. It may be that he is bringing light to you at this moment. What will you do with the light now beginning to shine into the dark recesses of your heart and mind? Will you repress it? Do you prefer the darkness?

Never let that be said of you. Embrace the light! Run to it! God will illuminate the path, and he will draw you to the One who died for you and bind you to him with ties that can never be broken either in this life or eternity. And one day, when he comes to that new Jerusalem spoken about in Revelation, the city of the saints in which there will be no crying and in which all tears will be wiped away, you will be with him.

From an unpublished Palm Sunday sermon.

Herod's Downfall
Luke 23:6–12

[Herod] plied him with many questions, but Jesus gave him no answer.
—*LUKE 23:9*

These were the steps in Herod's fall, beginning with his encounter with John the Baptist: First, there was conviction of sin (see Matt. 14:1–5). But Herod did not welcome this conviction, being unwilling to part from his sin. He wished to be religious and keep his sin too. Therefore, second, he attempted to still the voice of conscience which, in this case, meant stilling the voice of John the Baptist. At first he tried prison. But once launched upon this course, he soon came to the position of murdering John both to satisfy Salome and also to rescue his own imagined honor (vv. 6–12). Third, having silenced the voice of conscience, which always insists upon the indispensible place of morality in true religion, Herod's religious instincts turned to superstition. He thought that Jesus was John the Baptist raised from the dead (v. 1). Fourth, superstition turned to raw unbelief, for when Herod finally did have Jesus before him, he looked upon him only as one who might be prevailed upon to do a trick for the amusement of himself and his court (Luke 23:8). Fifth and finally, when Jesus declined to perform for this by now rank profligate and unbeliever, Herod's interest turned to derision, and he and his soldiers viciously scoffed at Jesus (v. 11). Having silenced him who was the Voice, it was no marvel that Herod now failed to hear or appreciate the Word.

You cannot treat God lightly. You cannot mock him. If you would meet him, you must be serious about the encounter, more serious than you have ever been about anything in your life before, and you must be ready to be changed profoundly by him.

What is God anyway? An intellectual curiosity? Someone who exists to provide you with free entertainment or free blessings? Is he as idle as you? Is he as frivolous? He is the great, holy, omnipotent God of the universe who takes the business of being God seriously. "I am the LORD your God," he says. "You shall have no other gods before me" (Exod. 20:2–3). "Be perfect, therefore, as your heavenly Father is perfect" (Matt. 5:48). "Be holy" (1 Peter 1:16; cf. Lev. 11:44). Jesus said, "If anyone would come after me, he must deny himself and take up his cross and follow me" (Matt. 16:24).

This is what God requires. If you will not do that, then your religious sensibilities will decline, as did Herod's. And the time will come when Jesus will depart from your presence, never to return. On the other hand, if you will repent of your sin and turn to him, then you will find that he has already received you and is at work to lead you in the way of righteousness. Will you come? Will you not turn your back on that sin that holds you in its grip and follow Jesus?

Forgiveness at a Great Cost
Luke 23:32–38

Father, forgive them, for they do not know what they are doing.
—LUKE 23:34

This was a prayer for forgiveness and a great forgiveness at that. It was also a forgiveness prayed for at an enormous cost. This is because forgiveness does not come cheap. And the reason it does not come cheap is because God is God, the holy and just ruler of the universe, and a just God must act justly. Even God, especially God, must do what is right.

What is right? The right thing is that sin should be punished, evil must be judged. What we should expect if God were to act justly in this situation and do nothing else is that Pilate who judged, the soldiers who killed, the leaders who plotted, and the people who cried out for Jesus's death should have been punished. Because their sin was the great one of murdering the only beloved Son of God, they should have been punished for their sins in hell.

We can understand how God might want to forgive at no cost. We would like to do that too. Who does not want to be forgiving? But how can a just God both forgive and be just at the same time? The answer is the cross. And it is why these particular words were spoken from the cross and not before or in some other situation. It is because Jesus was taking the place of sinners in his death, taking your place and mine, that he was able to pray, "Father, forgive them." God was able to forgive because he was not simply forgetting about or overlooking sin. He was dealing with it. He was providing for its just punishment. But he was punishing it in the person of his Son rather than in the person of the sinner.

This is the very heart of God—forgiving but at a tremendous cost.

That does not always sound right to ears that are more accustomed to the thinking of our secular world than to the teachings of the Bible. But it had better be right, since it is our only hope of being able to stand before God when we ourselves die and are required to give an accounting for our lives. We will not be able to plead innocence of sin, because we are not innocent. Our only hope will be the death of Jesus Christ on our behalf.

Can we believe that? We can, since God himself encourages us to do so. The Bible says, "God demonstrates his own love for us in this: While we were still sinners, Christ died for us" (Rom. 5:8). This is not only the heart of God. It is the heart of Christianity.

Boice and Ryken, *The Heart of the Cross*, Crossway, 1999, 17–18.

The Believing Thief
Luke 23:39–43

Jesus, remember me when you come into your kingdom.
—LUKE 23:42

The story of the believing thief is our story too if we have truly believed on the Lord Jesus Christ as our Savior. The believing thief did three things. First, he recognized his own need, and by that I mean his spiritual need and not merely his physical one. On the physical side there were many things he needed. He needed deliverance, medical attention, drugs. He at least needed sympathy knowing that he was about to die. But this is not what he recognized and confessed so openly. What he recognized was that he was a sinner and that he needed a Savior. He confessed to his fellow criminal, "Don't you fear God, since you are under the same sentence? We are punished justly, for we are getting what our deeds deserve" (vv. 40–41).

Second, having recognized that he was a sinner and that he needed a Savior, he recognized that Jesus was that Savior. He may not have been able to explain the theology of justification but he knew that Jesus was the innocent Son of God and the Savior. He showed this by saying, "This man has done nothing wrong" and by referring to the coming of Christ in his "kingdom" (vv. 41–42).

Finally, having recognized his need of a Savior and that Jesus was that Savior, he committed himself to him personally. He said, "Jesus, remember *me* when you come into your kingdom." And the Lord did remember him. He remembered him on the spot, for he accepted him right then and promised that on that very day, after each had died, they would be together in paradise.

If you would be like that thief—if you would have your sin on Christ rather than on yourself and therefore be able to receive the promise of being with Christ and God the Father eternally—you need to do what he did. First, admit your sin. Second, see Jesus as your Savior. Third, commit yourself to him personally. You need to say, "Lord, I know that I cannot get to heaven on my own record, for I am a sinner, and my record condemns me. I need you as my Savior, and I ask you to accept me as one for whom you died. Receive me. Remember me in the day of your judgment." If you will pray that prayer, you can be certain that Jesus has received you just as he received the repentant thief. From a human point of view everything was against him. Yet he called upon Jesus, and Jesus, in what was his last interview upon earth, heard him, received him, and promised him an entrance into paradise.

Will you call upon him? You can never be too sinful or call so late that Jesus will not hear. He is listening for that call now.

Dying Well

Luke 23:44–49

Father, into your hands I commit my spirit.
—*LUKE 23:46*

As Jesus died, commending his spirit to God, so may we die in like faith. We can echo Jesus's words, knowing that as we pass from this life trusting Jesus's death on our behalf, we pass into the loving hands of the Father who is waiting in heaven to receive us to himself. This is how the saints of all ages have died, many with these very words on their lips.

We can also learn, in spite of our fears about death, how to die well. Have you noticed that when Jesus said, "Father, into your hands I commit my spirit," he was quoting Scripture, just as we do when we say the same words? The words come from Psalm 31, which says, "Into your hands I commit my spirit; redeem me, O LORD, the God of truth" (v. 5).

This shows what Jesus was doing on the cross, particularly in these last moments. He was reflecting on Scripture. And not only on Psalm 31! "My God, my God, why have you forsaken me?," the fifth of Jesus's seven words from the cross, comes from Psalm 22:1. In my opinion, the words "it is finished," the sixth of these sayings, come from the end of the same psalm, since the words "he has done it" (v. 31) can be equally well translated, "it is finished." Even the words "I am thirsty" were spoken, according to John who records them, so that Psalm 69:21 might be fulfilled (see John 19:28). That verse says, "They put gall in my food and gave me vinegar for my thirst."

Four of these seven last words were from the Old Testament. Only Jesus's direct addresses to God on behalf of the soldiers, to the dying thief, and to his mother and the beloved disciple were not. This means that Jesus was filling his mind and strengthening his spirit not by trying to keep a stiff upper lip or look for a silver lining, as we might say, but by an act of deliberately remembering and consciously clinging to the great prophecies and promises of God. If Jesus did that, don't you think you should do it too? And not only when you come to die.

You need to fill your head with Scripture and think of your life in terms of the promises of Scripture now. If you do not do it now, how will you ever find strength to do it when you come to die? You must live by Scripture, committing your spirit into the hands of God day by day, if you are to yield your spirit into God's loving hands trustingly at the last.

Boice and Ryken, *The Heart of the Cross*, Crossway, 1999, 64–66.

Christ's Threefold Office

Luke 24:19; Hebrews 2:17; Revelation 19:16

Jesus of Nazareth . . . a prophet, powerful in word and deed.
—*LUKE 24:19*

It has been common to speak of the work of Christ under three general heads: prophet, priest, and king. These refer to his teaching office, his role as Savior, and his function as ruler over the universe and over his people within the church. This threefold division of Christ's work has good scriptural support and, at least equally important, applies particularly well to human need.

As far as Scripture goes, Christ is acknowledged to be a prophet in Luke 24:19. In this passage Jesus is interrogating the Emmaus disciples, asking what had happened during the last tumultuous days in Jerusalem. They reply that these events concern "Jesus of Nazareth . . . a prophet, powerful in word and deed before God and all the people."

Jesus is declared to be a priest throughout the book of Hebrews as, for example, in Hebrews 2:17: "For this reason he had to be made like his brothers in every way, in order that he might become a merciful and faithful high priest in service to God, and that he might make atonement for the sins of the people."

Similarly, Revelation 19:16 declares, "On his robe and on his thigh he has this name written, KING OF KINGS AND LORD OF LORDS." This verse comes at the culmination of the extensive development of this theme through the Word of God.

The notion of the threefold office of Christ also applies well to human need. What is our spiritual need? One need is for knowledge; for we do not know God naturally, nor do we even understand spiritual things apart from a special divine illumination to us. God does this in three ways: through his own person, in whom the Father is fully revealed, through the gift to us of the written Word of God, and by the particular illumination of our minds by the Holy Spirit.

Again, we have a need for salvation. For it is not just that we are ignorant of God and of spiritual things; we are also sinful. We have rebelled against God and like sheep have all gone our own way. Jesus meets this need as our priest. Here he functions on two levels: first, he offers up himself as a sacrifice, thereby providing the perfect atonement for our sin; and second, he intercedes for us at the right hand of his Father in heaven, thereby guaranteeing our right to be heard and heard rightly.

Finally, we have a need for spiritual discipline, guidance, and rule. We are not autonomous, even after our conversion. We do not have the right to rule ourselves, nor can we rule ourselves successfully. Christ meets this need by his proper and loving rule over us within the church. He is our Master, our King.

Boice, *The Bible Study Hour*, January 1978, 4–5.

Three Openings
Luke 24:13–35

Were not our hearts burning within us while
he . . . opened the Scriptures to us?
—LUKE 24:32

Jesus opened the Scriptures; he also opened eyes and understanding. Each of those three openings had an important consequence. When Jesus opened the Scriptures to Cleopas and Mary, we are told that their hearts burned within them. They were saying, "Isn't this exciting? Isn't it thrilling?"

There was a different consequence when Jesus opened their eyes. Though it was the end of the day and the way to Jerusalem was long and dangerous, nevertheless, they experienced an immediate desire to tell others about the risen Lord. So they set out for Jerusalem the same night and there told their story.

Finally, as Jesus opened their minds to understand the Scriptures, they doubtless entered into a phase of their lives in which they understood both the Scriptures and the Lord differently. Before, much of the Word of God was a mystery. Hereafter, when they would turn to the book of Genesis and read about the seed of the woman who should bruise the serpent's head, they would know that the seed was Jesus. Genesis would be new for them, and they would understand the Lord himself better. They would read a bit further and find that he is not only the seed of the woman, he is the seed of Abraham also, the one who was to bring blessings to the nations. They would recognize the fulfillment of this prophecy in the subsequent proclamation of the gospel to the Gentiles. Cleopas and Mary would see Jesus prefigured in the life of Joseph. In Exodus he would be perceived as the Passover Lamb. In Numbers he is the rock in the wilderness from whom we receive the water of life freely. He is also the cloud who guides his people and covers them with his protection. Deuteronomy pictures Jesus Christ as the righteous one and defines that righteousness. In Joshua he is the captain of the Lord's hosts. In the psalms and prophets we are told of his suffering, death, and resurrection. In some of them—Ezekiel, Daniel, and others—we learn of his second coming in glory. The last book of the Old Testament, Malachi, portrays Jesus as the sun of righteousness risen with healing in his wings.

These three openings are three great blessings that we should all desire of the resurrected Lord. When the Bible is opened and we see the Lord Jesus Christ as he is interpreted to us by the divine operation of the Holy Spirit, we will never be the same again. The Word itself will be different. It will not be a mystery. It will make sense. What is more, it will be a great blessing. For it will be the place where we meet with Jesus, who died for us and who now lives to be known by his followers.

Boice, *The Christ of the Empty Tomb*, P&R Publishing, 2010, 120–21.

Jesus Christ Is God
John 1:1–13

In the beginning was the Word, and the Word was
with God, and the Word was God.
— *JOHN 1:1*

To say that Jesus Christ is God is to say that we can now know *the truth about God*. We can know what he is like. The counterpart to this statement is that apart from Jesus Christ we really cannot know him. Is God the god of Plato's imagination? We do not know. Is he the god of Immanuel Kant, the German philosopher? Is he the god of other philosophers? Is he the god of the mystics? The answer is that apart from Jesus Christ we do not know what God is like. But if Jesus Christ is God, then we do know, because to know the Lord Jesus Christ is to know God. There is no knowledge of God apart from a knowledge of the Lord Jesus Christ, and there is no knowledge of the Lord Jesus Christ apart from a knowledge of the Bible.

One of the saddest stories in the Word of God concerns this theme. It is in John's Gospel. Toward the end of his ministry, Jesus explained carefully that he was going away from the disciples but that he was going to prepare a place for them and would one day return. The disciples were depressed at the thought of his leaving them. He went on to say that if they had really known him, they would have known the Father. At this point Philip, who was one of the disciples asked him, "Lord, show us the Father and that will be enough for us" (14:8). In other words, Philip was saying, "If I could just see God, I would be satisfied." How sad! The disciples had been with Jesus for almost three years and now were nearing the end of his ministry. Still they had not fully recognized that Jesus is God and that they were coming to know God through him. Jesus then had to answer by saying, "Don't you know me, Philip, even after I have been among you such a long time? Anyone who has seen me has seen the Father. How can you say, 'Show us the Father'?" (v. 9).

If you want to know what God is like, study the life of Jesus Christ. Read the Bible! The things recorded there of Jesus Christ are true. What is more, if you read them, you will find that the Holy Spirit of God, who is the Spirit of truth, will interpret and explain them to you.

Beholding Christ's Glory

John 1:14–18

We have seen his glory.
—JOHN 1:14

When Jesus Christ pitched his tent among us, he did so in order that men and women might see him and thus come to know God. John indicates this when he observes: "We have seen his glory."

This happened in a very literal way with the first disciples about whom John is certainly speaking in this verse, for they saw the glory of Jesus during the days of his flesh. We must not miss the point that John has constructed his account of the first momentous week in the earthly ministry of Jesus Christ to emphasize this great truth. This was the reason for his coming. He came that men might see his glory and believe on him.

It is also true, however, that the experience of the early disciples is duplicated in all who believe in the Lord of glory today, for Paul writes of the experience of all Christians when he says that "we, who with unveiled faces all reflect the Lord's glory, are being transformed into his likeness with ever-increasing glory, which comes from the Lord, who is the Spirit" (2 Cor. 3:18).

Is that your experience? Have you beheld the glory of the eternal Son of God who tabernacled among us and who is revealed to us today by means of his Holy Spirit? If it is, then you are called upon to bear a witness to him, as John and the other disciples did. Can you testify to what he has done for you and in your life? I can testify to what Christ has done for me. I look at the second chapter of Ephesians and find myself placed among those who were "dead in . . . transgressions and sins . . . gratifying the cravings of our sinful nature and following its desires and thoughts" but of whom it can now be said, "But because of his great love for us, God, who is rich in mercy, made us alive with Christ even when we were dead in transgressions" (Eph. 2:1–5). He lifted my vision to see Christ, who is altogether lovely, and has drawn me toward himself with bonds of love, so that now I seek to serve him and exalt his name before men.

You say, "Is that something special?" Not at all. It is merely the experience of every true believer. To the giving of such a testimony each of us is called. What a vision! The glory of Jesus Christ! What a task! To make him known to a darkened and sinful world!

Cups Overflowing

John 2:1–11

You have saved the best.
—JOHN 2:10

Jesus, of course, knew that his times were in the hands of his Father in heaven. He would not be manipulated. And yet—this is a wonderful part of this story—he had no desire to allow a lack of joy or embarrassment either. So he moved quietly. There were six great water jars of stone standing by, used to hold water for Jewish purifications. He commanded the servants to fill them with water, which they did—to the brim! Then he told them to draw from the pots and carry the water (now made wine) to the master of the banquet, whom we would call the best man or the master of ceremonies. They did so; when the master of the banquet had tasted the wine he said to the bridegroom, "Everyone brings out the choice wine first and then the cheaper wine after the guests have had too much to drink; but you have saved the best till now."

That too is significant. It was *good* wine! It was the *best*! No wonder the Bible tells us that "every good and perfect gift is from above, coming down from the Father of the heavenly lights, who does not change like shifting shadows" (James 1:17). Jesus himself said, "If you, then, though you are evil, know how to give good gifts to your children, how much more will your Father in heaven give good gifts to those who ask him!" (Matt. 7:11).

Moreover, have you ever reflected on the quantity of wine Jesus produced? John tells us, probably as an eyewitness, that there were six stone water jars, each containing two or three firkins apiece. That makes twelve to eighteen firkins. Each firkin was the equivalent of nine or ten gallons. Consequently, Jesus must have produced between a hundred eight and a hundred eighty gallons of the very best wine. William Barclay is so startled by the amount of wine that he thinks it should not be taken with "crude literalness." But I think the amount is literal and, what is more, that Jesus intentionally produced the wine in abundance.

Do not think, if you come to Jesus, accepting him as your Savior, that the day will come when you will find yourself empty of joy, or disappointed. If that ever happens, it will be because you have drawn away from him, not because he has failed you. Certainly the Christ who produced the abundance of wine, who oversupplied with the loaves and fishes, who said, "He who comes to me will never go hungry, and he who believes in me will never be thirsty" (John 6:35)—certainly such a Christ is able to supply all your need "according to his glorious riches in Christ Jesus" (Phil. 4:19).

God's Greatest Gift
John 3:16–21

For God so loved the world that he gave his one and only Son.
—JOHN 3:16

One reason Jesus Christ is the greatest of God's gifts to fallen man is that he is perfectly suited to the needs of fallen man. Nothing else is! What are the needs of man? What are your needs?

Your first need is for a sure word from God, for *knowledge* of God. Jesus is the answer to that need, for it is Jesus alone who brings us the knowledge of who God is, what he is like, and what he desires for mankind. This is why Jesus is called *the* Word so many times in John's writings. Do you want to know what God is like? If so, do not spend your time reading the books of men. Do not think that you will find out by meditating. Look to Jesus Christ. Where will you find him? You will find him in the pages of the Bible. There you will find the strength, mercy, wisdom, and compassion that are the essence of God's character.

Your second great need is for a *Savior*. We do not merely have a need for sure knowledge. We have knowledge of many things but we are unable to live up to our knowledge. We are sinners. Consequently, we not only need a sure word from God, we need a Savior. Jesus is the Savior. He died to save you from sin and from yourself. Do you know him as Savior?

Finally, we have those needs that are part and parcel of living a finite sinful life. Psychiatrist Erich Fromm suggests that man is confronted with three dilemmas. The first is the dilemma of life versus death. We want to live but we all die. Jesus is the answer to that problem, for he gives eternal life to all who believe on him (John 11:25–26). The second of Fromm's dilemmas is the dilemma of the individual and the group. Jesus answers that problem too, for he has come to break down all walls and to make of his followers one new man, which is his mystical body (Eph. 2:14–16). The last of Fromm's dilemmas is the one arising from the conflict between our aspirations and our actual achievements. We all fall short of what we would like to be and believe ourselves intended to be. Jesus promises to make us all that God created us to be in the first place. We are to be conformed to Christ's image (Rom. 8:29).

The Lord Jesus Christ is the greatest gift that God has ever offered or could ever offer to the human race. Are you indifferent? Or do you respond to the offer, joining the millions of others who have believed in Christ with all their heart and mind and who now say, "Thanks be to God for his indescribable gift!" (2 Cor. 9:15)?

Facing the Gospel
John 4:4–26

I can see that you are a prophet.
—JOHN 4:19

In the city of Basel, Switzerland, there is a carnival each year called *Fashnacht*. It is much like the Mardi Gras, but it is held during the first week of Lent instead of before it, presumably to show that Basel is Protestant. Whatever the case, *Fashnacht* certainly does not show the city to be Christian in the biblical sense, for the carnival is always a time of riotous behavior in which the normally restrained and stolid Baselers let themselves go morally. Everyone knows what goes on. But no one knows precisely who is doing what because the revelers wear masks. Each year, however, the Salvation Army makes an attempt to challenge people to a higher standard of conduct by placing posters around the city bearing the German inscription "*Gott sieht hinter deine Maske*"—"God sees behind your mask." The point is that God knows what is going on within and who is doing it.

The Lord Jesus Christ is looking into your heart and mind. What does he see? Does he see all that you have done and are doing, unconfessed and demanding his judgment? Must he say of you, "There is no one righteous, not even one; there is no one who understands, no one who seeks God. All have turned away, they have together become worthless; there is no one who does good, not even one" (Rom. 3:10–12)? And is there no more to say? Or can he look at you as one who is indeed a sinner, but whose sin has been judged in his death and who now stands before him clothed in God's own righteousness?

This is the gospel. All indeed "have sinned and fall short of the glory of God" (v. 23). But "there is now no condemnation for those who are in Christ Jesus" (8:1).

You may be one who has seen something of your own sinfulness. I know that the first reaction upon seeing one's sin is to back off in despair. "If I am really so sinful," you ask, "how can God love me? How can he have anything to do with me?" Look at one more phrase in Christ's words to the Samaritan woman. What did Jesus say to the woman? He said, "Go, call your husband"— that is true; it was an attempt to establish her sinfulness—but he finished the sentence by saying, "and come back" (John 4:16).

"Go, call your husband." That was a word for her conscience. "Come back." That was a word for her heart.

In the same way he speaks to you. You must see your need. You need to face the truth about your own condition. Yet you must also hear his warm invitation. "Come to me" (Matt. 11:28). The way is open. Say, "Yes, I am coming, Lord Jesus."

Come!

John 4:27–42

Come, see a man who told me everything I ever did.
—JOHN 4:29

I wonder if you have ever thought about the specific invitation to the men of the city offered by the Samaritan woman. There are three great words, each beginning with the letter *C*, that are the evidences of the fact that she had been born again—a *confession* of faith in Christ, a *change* of values, a *concern* for the lost. Three great words beginning with C! But here is a fourth, the word *come*. This was the heart of her invitation, and she had learned it (as she had learned everything else) from Jesus. What had Jesus said to her? Jesus had said, "Go, call your husband, and come back" (v. 16). Now she, who had come, repeated the invitation, "Come, see a man who told me everything I ever did. Could this be the Christ?"

Come! This is a great word of the Christian gospel. It has brought peace to millions of restless hearts and satisfaction to many that were empty and lonely.

Think of the great verses that contain it. It was God's word to Abraham, "*Come* into the land which I shall show thee" (Acts 7:3 KJV). It was God's call to Moses to be Israel's deliverer, "*Come*, I will send you to Egypt" (v. 34). David wrote, "*Come* and see the works of the LORD, the desolations he has brought on the earth" (Ps. 46:8). God spoke through Isaiah, saying, "*Come* now, let us reason together. . . . Though your sins are like scarlet, they shall be as white as snow; though they are red as crimson, they shall be like wool" (Isa. 1:18). The angels spoke the word to all skeptics as they pointed the disciples to the empty tomb, "*Come* and see the place where he lay" (Matt. 28:6). It was Christ's invitation, "*Come*, follow me" (Mark 10:21). "*Come* to me, all you who are weary and burdened, and I will give you rest" (Matt. 11:28). Finally, it will be the song of the angels as they invite the redeemed to the marriage supper of the Lamb (Rev. 19:17) and of Jesus himself as he says to his own, "Come, you who are blessed by my Father; take your inheritance, the kingdom prepared for you since the creation of the world" (Matt. 25:34).

If you have heard this invitation from the lips of the Lord, it is your privilege and duty to pass that word on. As in the case of the woman of Samaria, God's "Come!" must become our "Come!" Come! It is the greatest invitation in the universe. Won't you come? If you have already come, won't you share the invitation with another?

Healing the Spiritually Disabled
John 5:1–15

Here a great number of disabled people used to lie.
—JOHN 5:3

The scene of the disabled by the pool is a desperate picture if we take it seriously. Yet it is the glorious prelude to the gospel of God's grace, for it is to such people—blind, lame, and paralyzed—that Christ came.

We read that the Lord Jesus Christ walked into that vast collection of sick people and saw there a man who had been disabled for thirty-eight years. No one recognized Christ as he moved among them, for they were blind spiritually. Besides, they had their hopes set on the superstition about the moving of the water. No one rose to meet him, for they were lame. No one reached out a hopeful hand; they were paralyzed. Yet Jesus moved among them and healed this most helpless of sinners.

"Do you want to get well?" Jesus asked him.

The lame man answered, "Sir, I have no one to help me into the pool when the water is stirred. While I am trying to get in, someone else goes down ahead of me."

Jesus commanded, "Get up! Pick up your mat and walk" (v. 8). At once the man was made well and did as Jesus commanded.

That is how God saves sinners today. If our salvation depended upon our recognizing him or reaching out a hand toward him, who would be saved? The answer is: no one. Yet instead of waiting for us to come—instead of waiting to "help those who help themselves"—Christ comes to us and speaks the words that give life.

He came to find you. Will you argue that you are not helpless, that you are not blind, lame, or paralyzed? If you will argue God's verdict upon your spiritual capabilities, you will not be saved. The Bible teaches that God will not debate his verdict upon the spiritual condition of the human race. God declares that the creature is not the Creator. You are not as perfect as the Lord Jesus Christ, and that makes you a spiritual paralytic or any other name for a handicap that you may wish to apply to it. Yet—this is the glory of the gospel—it is for such that Christ died.

As soon as I am able to accept the fact that I am an ungodly man by nature and therefore completely unable to rise to meet God by any inborn effort, then I can also know that my sins have been dealt with in Christ and that he gives new life to all who trust him for their salvation.

Missing the Christ
John 5:31–47

Yet you refuse to come to me.
—JOHN 5:40

The Bible was given by God to point a person to the Savior, and he must come to the Savior if he is to find life. This is necessary, for unless the life of God takes possession of our hearts, even the Word of God will be incomprehensible.

Has the Word of God done that for you? Has it pointed you to the Savior? One time in preparing a Christmas message, I became impressed with the large number of men who missed Christmas even though there was no real need for them to have missed it. The innkeeper was one. He was too busy. Herod was another. But by far the most interesting of all those who missed the birth of Jesus were the religious leaders, the chief priests and the scribes, who missed it even though they had the Old Testament and knew where Christ should be born. You remember the story. The wise men had come to Jerusalem. Herod inquired of the scribes. The scribes said that the Christ was to be born in Bethlehem. It was on their word that the wise men started out to Bethlehem where they found him. These men had the Scriptures. They knew them well enough to have the right answers. But they did not leave their own homes or the palace to investigate the Savior's arrival.

On the other hand, the Christmas story also tells of some who did find Christmas. They were not the kings of this world. They were not the religious leaders. They were not the thousands who were entirely engrossed in the countless minutia of materialistic lives. They were just poor folk who were looking to God and to whom God came.

Who were they? Some were shepherds. They were not important in the social structure of the ancient east. Yet they saw the angels. The wise men also found Christmas. They were not even Jews. Yet they saw the star. Finally, there were the poor but saintly folk like Simeon and Anna. These could well have been discounted either because of their means or social position or age. Some would dismiss them. Yet they saw and even held God's treasure. Why did these people find Jesus when the important of the world, as the world judges importance, so clearly missed him? There are two answers. First, they were honest enough to admit their need of a Savior. Second, they were humble enough to receive him personally when he came.

The Bible calls for this honest confession of sin and this humble commitment to the Lord Jesus Christ. You can read the Bible as the leaders of Israel did. You can misuse it out of pride. Or you can use it properly and come yourself to the Savior. Will you come in a spirit of humility?

The Significant Life
John 6:37–40

All that the Father gives me will come to me.
—JOHN 6:37

If you are a Christian, the fact that it is because God has chosen you and accomplished the work of your salvation is a great truth for you, for it is a truth that gives tremendous importance to what you become in Christ and to what you do. God has a plan. So if he has chosen you and called you to himself in the course of his day-by-day unfolding of that plan, then where you are and what you do where you are matters. The most important thing in this entire universe is, not what is happening in the halls of our heads of state or in the laboratories of the world's most brilliant scientists, but what is happening in you now. This gives importance to whatever you do. It means you matter.

Are you saying, "But I am far too insignificant; I am not important"? In the world's eyes, yes, that may be true. But it is not true for God. In Shakespeare's *King Lear* there is a dungeon scene in which a number of selfish nobles are about to put out the eyes of an old man named Gloucester. It is a wicked deed, and they are doing it for their own selfish ends. On the stage with them is an exceedingly minor character in the play. He does not even have a name. In the list of *dramatis personae,* he is just called a servant. No one has been paying any attention to him. Nevertheless, in this one scene he rushes across the stage to defend Gloucester. At once one of the nobles turns about and simply cuts him down with his sword. Then they go on and blind the old man anyway. Who is important in this scene? The world answers, "the noble." But if this were real life and we were looking at the play from God's perspective, the right answer would be, "the servant." For he did the right thing at the right moment.

We do not see this great drama of life clearly. God is the only One who knows the end from the beginning. We do not know the importance of our role, but we do know that he has created us and called us so that at this particular moment in the drama, in the play called "Time," we might take the part he has given in a way that is honoring to Jesus Christ. Will you take that role? Will you live for him? This is the spiritual meat of the text that tells us that all whom the Father has given to Jesus shall come to him and that no one who comes will be cast out.

Going Forward
John 6:66–69

Lord, to whom shall we go?
—JOHN 6:68

If you have believed on the Lord Jesus Christ as your Savior—if you are truly united to him through the miracle of the new birth—then there is no way for you to go but forward. A threefold cord binds you to him. Peter speaks of it.

First, there is nowhere else to go. Peter acknowledged this in the tone of his question. Who will have you after you have been with Jesus? Jesus was not wanted. He was killed. His followers down through the centuries have been killed. Who will take you in when the door has already been shut against your Master?

Second, you have learned that there is satisfaction in the words of the Lord Jesus Christ and that true satisfaction can be found in him only. Peter said, "You have the words of eternal life." It was said by the Greeks that that man would always be unsatisfied with human food who had once tasted the nectar of the gods. That is a description of your case if you are a Christian. Jesus said, "Drink of me, and I will satisfy your thirst; feed on me, and I will satisfy your hunger." You have done that. You have had heavenly food. Now anything else will seem flat by comparison.

Finally, as Peter says, "We believe and know that you are the Holy One of God" (v. 69). Thus, to go back now would be not only a crisis of faith but intellectual suicide and dishonesty. It cannot be done. We know too much to prove faithless.

I wish I could tell you what the future holds for you but I cannot. It may be that the future is bright. I often think this, for the trends of our day (in my opinion) are opening wide, wide doors for Christianity. It is a day of opportunity. The next generation may be the generation of the widest possible opportunity for the proclamation of the gospel and for witnessing and growth in history. If our day is the day of opportunity, we shall advance. We shall go forward. I am also aware, however, that days of opportunity often are followed by days of harsh persecution and that the chaff may be greatly winnowed out in our lifetime. The time may come when you and I may be persecuted. What shall we do then?

If the time should come when you or I should find ourselves in that position, I trust that we too shall be strong. We cannot turn back. There is no place to go but forward.

A Great Invitation
John 7:37–39

If anyone is thirsty, let him come to me and drink.
— JOHN 7:37

Have you heard it? Have you listened to that great invitation? I wonder if you have noticed that in this verse Jesus does not even detail the nature of the thirst. He was not specific. There were no limitations. Is there a thirst? Then come! You are the one to whom the Lord Jesus Christ is speaking. You say, "I do not know whether I thirst or not." Well, find out. Turn your eye inward and ask, *Is there no thirst within me? Am I not dissatisfied about something? Is there not some area of my life in which I am unfulfilled?* If you are such a one, then God has placed that hunger and thirst within you. Rejoice! And come to Jesus! He said, "If anyone is thirsty, let him come to me and drink. . . . Streams of living water will flow from within him."

Here in these words are directions that point you to Jesus. Do not say, "But what am I to believe? What doctrines must I accept?" That will come in time, but it is not the step for you to take now. If you are thirsty, come to Jesus. He said, "Come to me."

Do not make the mistake of coming to the church as an institution or become preoccupied with its rites and ceremonies. Ceremonies are intended to point you to Christ. If you look to them in themselves, they will deceive you.

Do what Christ's invitation requires. First, you are to "come." That is not hard, especially when the One to whom you are to come is so lovely. And it need not be lengthy, for Jesus has already taken the greatest part of the journey in coming to you. "Come" means to believe, to have faith in him, to commit yourself to him. Will you do that? If you come to Jesus, you will be coming to the One who came to this earth to redeem you, who died on the cross for your sin, and who then rose again and was glorified by God, his Father.

Second, you are invited to "drink" from Christ, as you would from a fountain. All that has been said about coming applies to this word too, but drinking involves one further idea. It involves appropriation. That which you drink becomes a part of you. If it is wholesome, it helps you grow. Thus does Christ want to become part of your life and personality.

Will you come? Will you drink? There is no other prescription for the thirst of the human soul. There is no other drink but Jesus. Do not delay in coming. You have not come before, and that was wrong. But you may come *now*. That is the great invitation.

Because of the Cross
John 8:1–11

Then neither do I condemn you.
—*John 8:11*

When we ask, "Why did the Lord Jesus Christ not pronounce judgment on the woman caught in adultery?" the only substantial and ultimately satisfying answer we get is that he did not pronounce judgment against the woman for precisely the same reason that he does not pronounce judgment against those who come to him in faith. It was because of the cross upon which he was about to bear the full penalty of God's wrath against every sin ever committed by those whom the Father had given to him. He did not give forgiveness easily. He did so only because he was about to make forgiveness possible by the costly act of suffering in place of the sinner. He would bear the justified wrath of God against the sinner. This is the gospel. This is the only solution to the problem of how God can remain just and also excuse the sinner. To us, salvation is free. But it is free only because the Son of God paid the price for us.

Finally, Jesus told the woman to stop sinning. This always follows upon divine forgiveness, for we cannot be saved by God and then continue to do as we please. We must stop sinning. At the same time, we can be glad that the order is as Jesus gave it. For if he had said, "Go, sin no more; and I will not condemn you," what hope would there be? We all sin, so there would be no forgiveness. Instead he says, "I forgive you on the basis of my death. Now, because you are forgiven, stop sinning."

I hope this has been your experience. I hope you have heard and understood these words of Jesus.

You must place yourself at some place in this story. Are you like the crowd, who stood watching? They witnessed forgiveness but they did not enter into it. Are you like the rulers? They were sinners, like the woman, but they went away from Jesus without even hearing the words of forgiveness. Or, finally, are you like the woman, who not only heard but also received the gospel message? Of all who were there that day by far the best one to be is the woman. The crowd was indifferent, as crowds always are. The rulers went out from Christ into darkness and six months later were killing the sinless Son of God. But the woman—well, the woman was forgiven through Christ, who died for her sin and for yours, whoever you may be.

Passed By

John 8:48–59

Jesus hid himself, slipping away from the temple grounds.
—JOHN 8:59

This verse indicates the sad result of the action of those who try to get rid of Jesus. What does it mean when we are told that Jesus hid himself? First, it means that although these men could not harm Jesus, nevertheless, they could not benefit from him either. It will be the same for you if you try to keep him out of your life. If you do not allow Jesus to be God in your life, you will not harm him. You cannot harm the invincible and omnipotent God. But you will not benefit from him either. The Lord Jesus Christ came to bring those divine benefits to you. He is the life. He came to give you life, abundant life. He is the light. He wants to shine upon you, to illuminate your darkness and guide you. He is the bread upon whom you may feed and grow. He is the living water who can quench your spiritual thirst. You forfeit these benefits if you refuse him his rightful place in your life.

Second, the verse tells us that there are some from whom Jesus does slip away or "pass by" as the King James Version states it. Notice that Jesus has not been trying to convert these religious leaders. He has merely been exposing their sin. Moreover, Jesus eventually passed by and went his way. There are some people whom God gives up (see Rom. 1:24, 26, 28). God gives up nations, if they will not live by righteous standards. God gives up churches, when they depart from their first love. God gives up individuals. Woe to the person whom the Lord Jesus Christ passes by! Finally, the verse leads us to see that there are some whom God saves anyway. I say "anyway" because even those who become Christians deserve to be passed by.

Notice this. In the King James text of John 8, the last words are "passed by." It is a tragic note, a tragic end to the contacts of Christ with these religious leaders. But in the opening verse of the very next chapter, the words occur again in a story that tells us that "*as Jesus passed by*, he saw a man who was blind from his birth" and saved him. Here was a man who in his blindness could not even see the Lord Jesus. Yet Jesus saw him and gave him both physical and spiritual sight. He could not seek Christ, yet he was found by him. How wonderful! What a great hope for the sinner! "Jesus passed by." Yes. But "as he passed by," he saw this one and saved him. With people such as these, he began to build his church. Are you such a one? Why should you not be? Why should you not be one who finds Jesus?

Able to Save

John 9:1–34

He saw a man blind from birth.
—JOHN 9:1

This is the gospel. It is the truth of God concerning the hopeless state of the lost and of the power of God to save such as he wills to save. God's purposes are not frustrated by either the hatred of men or the sin of the lost.

Let me apply these truths in this way. First, if you are a Christian and have been witnessing to another person concerning Christ, you can be encouraged by knowing that God will never be frustrated by human sin. There may be much in the situation to frustrate you. You may seem to get nowhere. In fact, in a given witnessing situation, there may be more to frustrate you than in any other situation in life. Still, God is not frustrated, and you should not be either. Instead, you should be encouraged by knowing that if God is working, nothing will hinder that working. If the light of God is shining, his light will make seeds grow. So, be bold! Witness boldly and expect God to bring forth his harvest!

Second, if you are one who has not yet believed in the Lord Jesus Christ as your Savior, you too can take heart by seeing what he did in the life of the man who had been born blind. Think of what Jesus Christ did for him. For one thing, the story tells us that he saw him, that is, that he took notice of him. The blind man could not see Jesus, but Jesus saw the blind man; and that was the important thing after all. Moreover, when he saw him, he saw him as a man who needed his help. Jesus alone saw him in this way. The disciples looked at the man and saw him as a sinner. "Who sinned," they asked, "this man or his parents?" (v. 2). The passersby looked at him as a beggar. "Isn't he the man who sat and begged?" (v. 8). The Pharisees saw him as a tool, for they wanted to maneuver him to trap Jesus. But Jesus—well, Jesus saw him as a man who needed help and he saved him.

Moreover, Jesus took him in when all others had cast him out. His family had cast him out. His neighbors had no use for him. Even his pastors rejected him. Eventually, because of the excommunication, the nation had no room for him either. No family, neighbors, pastors, nation! Who was left? Only Jesus! It was Jesus who sought him out and received him when no one else would receive him or even rejoice in his healing.

Are you one whom this world has cast out? Do you feel alone and rejected? Come to Jesus! Jesus is the One who is altogether lovely. Let Jesus be yours. Say, "O Lord Jesus, I want you to be my Savior."

The Dividing Rock

John 9:35–41

So that the blind will see and those who see will become blind.
—JOHN 9:39

Jesus is speaking of the indirect moral effect on everybody of his presence in the world, according to which some believe on him and others reject him.

The sun's light illustrates this. It warms things and makes plants grow. At the same time, however, the light will also drive away the creatures of darkness, so that bugs and crawly things will slither away into dark places if it is suddenly made to shine upon them. These were precisely the effects that Christ had on his contemporaries. He was the light of the world that caused faith to sprout and that which was alive spiritually to grow. On the other hand, he also repelled the religious leaders who, as creatures of darkness, hated him and wished to extinguish his light.

This is all the more true of the effect of his death by crucifixion; for it is at the cross that the division concerning Christ is most apparent. Most persons do not have trouble accepting Jesus of Nazareth as a teacher. But Jesus crucified—well, that is another matter. For a Jesus crucified speaks of man's inability to save himself, of the supremacy of Jesus by which he alone is able to make atonement for sins, of the truth that there is only one way of salvation, and that there is a future judgment against sin for any who reject him.

There is a point along the Continental Divide high in the Rocky Mountains of Colorado at which the waters of a small stream separate in order to begin two long and very diverse journeys, one leading to the Atlantic Ocean, the other to the Pacific Ocean. The dividing point is a rock in the middle of the stream. One drop of water striking that rock might turn west, with the result that it would flow into a small stream that in turn flowed into another one and another one until it entered the White River of Utah, then the Grand River, followed by the Colorado, the Gulf of California, and eventually the Pacific Ocean. Another drop, turning east, would flow through various small streams into the North Platte River and from there into the Missouri, Mississippi, Gulf of Mexico, and the Atlantic. The destinies of the two drops are entirely different, though the turning point is a very small one at the rock. In the same way, the cross of Jesus is the rock that is the true turning point in man's destiny. Those who believe enter into eternal life and go on to eternal happiness in the presence of God. Those who reject Christ reject God and go on being separated from him forever.

Take heed to your relationship to Christ. Your relationship to him is not inconsequential. How you respond to him determines your destiny.

Saved, Safe, and Satisfied
John 10:7–10

I am the gate for the sheep.
—JOHN 10:7

Jesus speaks of three great benefits of entering into God's flock through him. First, Jesus says that anyone who enters in will be *saved*. This promise is about not only future, but also past and present. It affects who we are and what happens to us from beginning to end. A better way of talking about it is in terms of sin's penalty, power, and presence. By entering in through Christ, we immediately escape sin's penalty, so that we need not fear our sins will ever rise up against us. This is justification. Then, too, we also enter into a life in which we are increasingly delivered from sin's power. The Bible calls this sanctification. Finally, we look forward to a day marked by the return of Christ or else our passing into his presence through death, in which even the presence of sin will be gone and our salvation will be perfected. The Bible calls this glorification.

Second, Jesus promises that anyone who enters in will be *safe*. This is the point of his reference to going "in and out." To be able to go in and out means security (see Deut. 28:6; Ps. 121:8), for in Christ's day, when a man could go in or out without fear, it meant that his country was at peace and that the ruler had the affairs of the nation under control. When danger threatened, the people were shut up in the cities under siege. Thus, Jesus promises safety for those who trust him.

Third, he also promised that they would be *satisfied*—saved, safe, and satisfied—for he said that they would be able to go in and out and "find pasture." Palestine is a barren land for the most part, and good pasture was not easy to find. Consequently, to be assured of good pasture was a wonderful thing. It spoke of prosperity and contentment, of health and happiness. It was in this sense that David wrote of the care of his Good Shepherd: "He makes me lie down in green pastures, he leads me beside quiet waters, he restores my soul" (23:2–3). It was this that Paul wrote of when he told the Philippians, "And my God will meet all your needs according to his glorious riches in Christ Jesus" (Phil. 4:19). This last verse does not speak of all our desires, of course. We often desire that which is wrong or is not good for us. It speaks only of our needs, but even in that form, it is a great promise. It is the promise that the one who enters in by Christ will not lack any good thing.

The Lord Jesus Christ is the Great Shepherd, our Savior. He leads us in and he leads us out. Under his care we find pasture.

Safe in Jesus's Hands
John 10:27–30

They shall never perish.
—JOHN 10:28

Jesus speaks of God's perseverance with his saints. That is, that none whom God has called to faith in Christ will be lost. Indeed, how can they be, if God is responsible for their salvation? Jesus says, "I give them eternal life, and they shall never perish; no one can snatch them out of my hand."

"But," says someone, "suppose they jump out of their own accord?"

"They shall never perish," says the Lord.

"Never?"

"No, never," says Jesus. "They shall never perish; no one can snatch them out of my hand."

This does not mean that there will not be dangers, of course. In fact, it implies them; for if Jesus promises that no one will succeed in plucking us from his hands, it must be because he knows that there are some who will try. The Christian will always face dangers—dangers without, from enemies, and dangers within. Still the promise is that those who have believed in Jesus will never be lost. We may add that the Christian may well be deprived of things. He may lose his job, his friends, his good reputation. Still, he will not be lost. The promise is not that the ship will not go to the bottom, but that the passengers will all reach shore. It is not that the house will not burn down, but that the people will escape safely.

Do you believe this promise, that you are safe in Jesus's hands, that you will never be lost? Are you able to trust God for this as you have for other truths? I suppose there is a way of explaining away almost everything, but I must say that I do not see how the opponents of eternal security can explain away this text. Am I Christ's? Then it is he who has promised that neither I nor any who belong to him shall perish. I wish that all God's children might come to know and love these truths. I wish that many might be saved by them.

I wish it might be the same with you! I do not preach a gospel that has a shaky foundation. I do not proclaim a religion of percentages and probabilities. I proclaim the message of Christ, Paul, Augustine, Luther, Calvin, and all others who have found God to be their pure hope and salvation. It is the message of man's complete ruin in sin and of God's perfect remedy in Christ, expressed in his election of a people to himself and his final preservation of them. God grant that you might believe it wholeheartedly.

Three Choices

John 11:45–53

What are we accomplishing?
—JOHN 11:47

Let me turn the story of the Jerusalem council around in order to address you personally. It began with a question: "What are we accomplishing? Here is this man performing many miraculous signs." Make this your question. *What am I accomplishing—what am I doing—with the Miracle-worker?*

There are only three choices for you, so far as I can see. The first is to try to ignore him. Many try this, of course. You may be trying it too. But if this is your choice, I do not believe that you get very far with it. Why? Because he does too many miracles. He did them then; he does them today. Do you not fear that if you "let him alone, all men will believe on him"? And if they do, what will you do? How will you survive in such a Christ-centered world? How will you ignore him when your daughter believes, your son believes, your husband believes, your wife believes, your father believes, your mother believes, your friend believes? How will you ignore him on that day when, as we are told, every knee will bow and every tongue confess that Jesus Christ is Lord to the glory of God the Father (Phil. 2:10–11)? Can he be ignored? Is Jesus really One whom you can thus put down?

Your second choice is to oppose him. Many have taken this course too, as we know. Caiaphas was the first but certainly not the only or even the worst persecutor of the Nazarene. History is full of those who opposed the Lord Jesus Christ. But where are they? The church remains, but what has happened to the persecutors?

Can you oppose him? If you do, do you really believe that you will be successful? Will you not rather be in the deplorable company of those rulers who "take counsel together against the LORD and against his Anointed One, 'Let us break their chains,' they say, 'and throw off their fetters,'" of whom we are told, "The one enthroned in heaven laughs; the Lord scoffs at them" (Ps. 2:2–4)?

The last of the three choices is the only sensible one. You can believe on Jesus and follow him. "Follow him?" you say. "But he went to the cross. He was crucified. What is desirable about that?" That is true; his way is the way of the cross. But the cross is the way to victory, for it is only by losing life that a man can save it. It is only by following Jesus that the victory is won. If you reject him, you will not win. In fact, you will lose all that you have, as did the Jewish rulers. But if you believe on Jesus and follow him, though you may lack some things now, you will pass beyond that and share his glory.

Living Witness
John 12:1–11

On account of him many . . . were putting their faith in [Jesus].
—JOHN 12:11

Many, we are told, believed on Jesus because of Lazarus. Here was a man so much alive because of Jesus and so identified with him in discipleship that others believed on Jesus just because of him. The application is obvious. Has anyone believed on Jesus because of you? Can it be said of you, "On account of him (or her), many put their faith in Jesus"?

One year the missionary conference of Tenth Presbyterian Church in Philadelphia was attended by four veteran missionaries. Two were a couple who had given more than thirty years of their lives to working in unevangelized fields in Africa. Another, together with her husband, has done pioneer Bible translation work in Mexico. The last had spent over forty years in Spain. These presented their work to the church and then eventually returned to their fields. After they were gone, I received this letter from a woman who had been a member of the church for many years and had attended the conference. She wrote, "In 1936, I started attending Tenth Church while in college and have followed ever since then the work of these three missionaries, who had just then left for missionary service. The Wolls have evangelized Kenya in that time. They have trained and sent out workers. They have established churches and Bible schools. Maria Bolet in that same time has been training Spanish missionaries in a Bible school and has sent those trained throughout Spain. She has operated summer camps. She has been persecuted, several times been put out of Spain, and then allowed to return. Now the children of her earlier converts are attending camps, and the mothers are crying out for more camps. In that time the Lathrops have reduced a language to writing, have translated the New Testament into that language, and have evangelized the entire Tarascan area of Mexico. They have established an indigenous church there. I have pursued my profession at home and overseas and have a few years remaining, a satisfying career. But who will greet me in heaven when I arrive there and say, 'I am here because you gave your life to proclaim the gospel of the Lord Jesus Christ'? Who will count me such a blessing?"

I know this person well enough to know that she has been a blessing. Quite a few have come to know and trust in Christ as a result of her testimony. But the question still stands—for me and for you. Have you been brought to spiritual life by Jesus? Can others tell that you have been with Jesus? Have any believed on Jesus because of your testimony? God grant that this might be true of each of us, or that we will allow God to make it true as we spend more time with him.

Drawn to Jesus

John 12:28–36

I . . . will draw all men to myself.
—JOHN 12:32

To whom does Jesus promise to draw people? The answer is: to himself. It is not said that Jesus will draw men and women to the visible church, still less to one particular expression of it. It is not said that he will draw them to a particular denomination, sect, movement, or program. It is possible that he may bless these endeavors and even raise up leaders for them but he does not promise that he will draw men and women to any of these. The promise is only that they will be drawn to Jesus. "Himself to himself!" That is the heart of the text. Is it your desire that those you know might indeed be drawn to him?

I apply this principle first to believers and then to unbelievers.

First, to believers involved in serving Christ. If you are serving Christ, you undoubtedly are trying to lead others to him; if you are, learn first that if you would win men and women for Jesus, you must draw them rather than drive them to him. Some think that people are won by black looks and scowls, but few come to this kind of preaching or witnessing. Do not scowl at people. Do not seek to condemn them. Love them for Christ's sake, and draw them through his love and by gentle invitations.

Second, learn even as you seek to draw them that, nevertheless, it is Christ who draws and who must therefore be the great and sole attraction. Would you win people? Then do not deal too much with more peripheral matters. Of course, you must cover the whole counsel of God in time in your preaching, if you are a preacher. You must also deal honestly with whatever questions are asked you as a result of your witnessing, regardless in what direction they tend. But to win men and women, it must be the case that Christ, rather than these other matters, is central. And, more than this, it must be Christ crucified. Speak of the Christ who died for sinners, and that very Christ will draw sinners to himself in abundance.

If you are not yet a Christian, learn that if Jesus said he will draw men and women to himself, then he will draw them now as much as at any point in history. He has not changed. The value of his death has not changed. People have not changed. The problems have not changed. The attraction of the Lord Jesus Christ is always present, and he will draw people now. Do you sense that he is drawing you? If so, do not ask, "May I come to Jesus?" Of course you may come, if you are drawn to come. If he is drawing you, come! Resist no longer. Turn from all that might hold you back and fly to Jesus.

Love to the End

John 13:1–17

> He now showed them the full extent of his love.
> —JOHN 13:1

What do we know about the love of God the Father and of the Lord Jesus Christ in the past? First, we can see the love of God in the creation of ourselves to an existence that is the highest existence possible, namely, communion with the One who created it. Second, God's love is seen in the fact that he, by the Holy Spirit's regenerating power has called us to himself and we cannot be lost. Third, we see God's love in Jesus's death for his people by which he has atoned for our sin.

The King James Version translates the phrase "the full extent" as "unto the end." It raises the question: Unto the end of what?

First, it means unto the end of Christ's earthly life. Though Jesus knew that he was about to die, such knowledge did not deter him, nor did the worldly and dull manner in which his disciples responded to him. He loved them, fully and unselfishly, to the end of his life. Second, he loved them to the end of their lives. As the risen Lord, he returned to bestow his own Spirit upon the disciples and then guide them and preserve them until the time when each would go to be with him in glory. Finally, the phrase also means "to the very end," that is, "to the end of ends" or "without end." Having loved his own who were in the world, he loves them to the end.

If this is the way in which God has loved us, then should we not love one another and also fervently love him? If you are not yet a believer in Christ, let me ask you, if God loves like this, how can you afford to be without such a great love? There is no love on earth like it. Your husband or wife will not love you like this. Your children and parents will not love you like this. Your neighbors and friends will not love you like this. Only Jesus Christ loves with a perfect and everlasting love! Moreover, one day you must stand before the judgment seat of his Father, whom you have offended by your ungodly conduct and by your rejection of his great grace. What will you do in that day—if you refuse the love of the Lord Jesus Christ? What will you do without having him to stand by you and say, "This is one of my own; this is one for whom I died; this is one whose debt I undertook to pay; this is one I love unto the end"? Without such love you will be lost forever. Fortunately, the day of God's grace is still present; you may yet come to Jesus Christ as your Savior.

Boice, *The Gospel of John*, Volume 4, Baker, 1999, 1003, 1005–6.

The New Commandment
John 13:31–38

As I have loved you, so you must love one another.
—*John 13:34*

Jesus is himself our example as we obey his command to love one another. It is not just that we are to love. It is that we are to love *as he loved us*. His love is to be the full measure of our love for one another.

How can we speak about this practically? One way is to turn to 1 Corinthians 13:4–8 and substitute "love" with the word "Jesus." "Jesus is patient, Jesus is kind. He does not envy, he does not boast, he is not proud. He is not rude, he is not self-seeking, he is not easily angered, he keeps no record of wrongs. Jesus does not delight in evil, but rejoices with the truth. He always protects, always trusts, always hopes, always perseveres. Jesus never fails." Clearly, the substitution of "Jesus" for "love" is quite proper, for Jesus is obviously the embodiment of such love. Our hearts acknowledge it to be so, and we rejoice in the fact.

Now make another substitution. We are told in our text that we are to love as Christ loves. But since 1 Corinthians 13 reveals the way that Christ did love, we (if we love in that way) should be able to substitute our name for his. We should be able to put "I" where "love" is printed. "I am patient, I am kind. I do not envy, I do not boast, I am not proud. I am not rude, I am not self-seeking, I am not easily angered, I keep no record of wrongs. I do not delight in evil, but rejoice with the truth. I always protect, always trust, always hope, always persevere. I never fail." When we read it this way, the result is humbling, for we recognize that we do not love as Jesus loves. We do not even understand such love. And we find ourselves praying, "Oh, Lord Jesus, teach me to love others as you love."

When we pray this way God will help us, and we will begin to grow in the love and knowledge of the Lord Jesus Christ.

Do those who are not yet Christians see God in you? It is a breathtaking thought. But this verse teaches that they can and will, if you will love others. Will you? Remember, this is not a divine invitation, as if Jesus had said, "Won't you please love others?" It is not even one of a series of steps to successful living, as if he had said, "You will be happier if you love one another." It is Christ's new command. "Love one another!" God grant that we shall and that, in doing so, we may truly be his disciples.

I Am the Life

John 14:1–14

I am the way and the truth and the life.
—JOHN 14:6

The third part of Christ's claim in this verse is to be "the life"—for all who believe on him, the emancipator from death. According to Scripture, the natural man is spiritually dead. But Christ can make such persons alive. Indeed, he promises to give life to all who will come to him.

This makes for great encouragement in the living of the Christian life, for if the life Christ gives is God's life, then that life is eternal life. And the Christian can no more perish than can God the Father. This is what is taught in John 3:16, the verse that so many know: "For God so loved the world that he gave his one and only Son, that whoever believes in him should not perish but have eternal life."

Does it really mean everlasting life? Yes, it does. And in case we are still inclined to doubt it, Jesus adds just a few chapters later, "My sheep listen to my voice; I know them, and they follow me. I give them eternal life, and they shall never perish; no one can snatch them out of my hand" (10:27–28).

Christ came that you might have life. Will you come to him right where you are? You *can* come. You can come *now*. Jesus does not require you to do anything. What could you do, even if you wished to do something? Would you seek to find the way to God and then walk in it? How can you? He is the way and he has come to you rather than making you come to him. Would you study to find out the truth before you believe in God? How can you do that? He is the truth; Scripture presents him fully to your eyes. Would you attempt to awaken yourself out of your spiritual lethargy by self-effort? How can you do even that? He is the life you need; he offers himself to you freely.

There is nothing to do, except to receive him by faith. There is nothing to achieve, no improvements to be made, no lessons to learn. Just believe on Jesus. Accept him for what he claims to be—the way to God, the truth about God, the life of God. Jesus did not say, "I am one of an indefinite number of equally valid ways to God, an aspect of truth, or a phase of life." He said, "I am *the* way and *the* truth and *the* life; no one comes to the Father except through me."

The Holy Spirit as Teacher
John 14:15–27

The Holy Spirit . . . will remind you of everything I have said to you.
—JOHN 14:26

The Lord's emphasis on remembering teaches us two separate truths. First, it teaches us that the wisdom of God is not a new thing. It is that which God has revealed in the past and that is the same because he is the same. Second, it teaches that we tend to forget these doctrines and need to be continually reminded of them.

This verse also tells us that the object of the teaching is Christ. We have a danger of making the Scriptures an end in themselves, forgetting that the purpose of the Scriptures is to reveal Christ to the seeking heart and mind. The verse also makes the point that the Holy Spirit is the One who enables us to teach these truths to others. Teaching spiritual truths cannot be done in the power of the flesh.

Thus three things are necessary if God's truth is to be properly communicated. There must be the revelation of the truth to the apostles by the Holy Spirit. This has been done. There must be the teaching of the Holy Spirit to our hearts, so that, as we read their words, we come face-to-face with the Lord Jesus Christ about whom they wrote. And there must be the continuing work of the Holy Spirit to take our testimony concerning this Word and carry it home to the hearts of those who have not yet heard or understood it. Three stages!

But there can be error in each. There are some who do not begin with the Scriptures. They consider the Bible to contain the words of men rather than the very words that the Holy Spirit taught to the apostles. There are others who accept the Bible as the Word of God but who do not allow the Holy Spirit to teach them. Then there are those who accept the Bible as the Word of God and who do meet with Jesus Christ, but they testify in their own power in a way that brings glory to themselves, and few are won.

We do a farmer's work. First, we prepare the soil. Then we take a seed and plant it. We water it and we wait for it to grow. But we do not give life to the seed. The seed already has life in it. Moreover, we can scratch a furrow and put the seed in it, but the ground must have the nutrients that God has placed there. And even then the work of God is not finished, for the seed will not grow unless the sun shines upon it. The Holy Spirit must be the sun in our witnessing. We must be faithful in scratching the furrows, watering, even pulling out weeds. But we must look to God to give life.

No Greater Love

John 15:9–17

Greater love has no one than this, that he lay down his life for his friends.
—JOHN 15:13

It may not happen often, but sometimes one human being will voluntarily die for another; still, this gift never equals or even parallels Jesus's sacrifice. We see this when we reflect on Jesus's death.

First, when we begin to reflect on Jesus's death, we recognize that his death was exceptional if only because *Jesus did not have to die*. That is not true of us. We are mortal. We must die. But Jesus was immortal and therefore did not have to die. He could have come into this world, performed a full and varied ministry, and then returned to heaven without ever having experienced death.

Second, the death of the Lord Jesus Christ is exceptional in that *he knew he would die*. Again, this is not usually the case when a mere man or woman gives his or her life for another. Few who die in this way do so knowing in advance that they will die. Rather, it is usually the case that, although the act is a risk and death is possible, they nevertheless think they may escape death while yet saving their friend. People take calculated risks and sometimes die but they do not often die deliberately. Jesus by his own testimony deliberately went to the cross to die for our salvation.

There is another area of Christ's exceptional love. The text says that we are Christ's friends. But if we think of this closely and honestly, we must recognize that, when the Lord Jesus gave his life for us, strictly speaking *we were not exactly his friends*. When he died for us, or when in eternity past he determined to die for us, he did so while we were yet enemies or were foreseen to be enemies. It was "while we were still sinners, [that] Christ died for us" (Rom. 5:8).

There is one more reason why the love of the Lord Jesus Christ for his friends, seen in his death for us, is superior to all human loves. *The death of the Lord was a spiritual death*, whereas ours, if we are Christians, is only physical.

If we were to give our life for someone else, the death we would endure would be only physical. We cannot die spiritually in the place of another person. But that is precisely what Jesus Christ did. Spiritual death is the separation of the soul and spirit from God. This is the separation that Jesus endured for us. He died physically also. But the truly horrible aspect of his death was his separation from the Father when he was made sin for us and bore sin's punishment.

Do you know him as the One who demonstrated his love and friendship for you by thus dying? Is he your friend in that sense?

The Work of the Holy Spirit
John 15:26–16:16

> The Spirit of truth . . . will testify about me.
> —JOHN 15:26

When we say that the Holy Spirit speaks through the Bible to the individual heart, precisely what does the Holy Spirit do?

First, the Holy Spirit gives *comprehension*. Apart from the ministry of the Holy Spirit there is no understanding of spiritual things. The Bible is taught, but men and women do not comprehend it. The gospel is proclaimed forcefully, but the unregenerate consider it nonsense. What is wrong? What is wrong is that the Holy Spirit has not yet granted understanding. This is what Paul is speaking about in 1 Corinthians 2 when he says, "The man without the Spirit does not accept the things that come from the Spirit of God, for they are foolishness to him, and he cannot understand them, because they are spiritually discerned" (v. 14). Without the internal witness of the Holy Spirit, the unregenerate comprehend nothing of the gospel. On the other hand, where the Holy Spirit is at work, understanding follows. This is true regardless of the obstacles to comprehension.

The second thing the Holy Spirit brings is *conviction*. This is necessary too because it is not enough merely to have a comprehension of spiritual things. Comprehension is necessary. But if we have a proper comprehension, this will involve an understanding of our own sin and we will need to be convicted of our sin. Jesus says, speaking of the Spirit, "When he comes, he will convict the world of guilt in regard to sin and righteousness and judgment: in regard to sin, because men do not believe in me; in regard to righteousness, because I am going to the Father, where you can see me no longer; and in regard to judgment, because the prince of this world now stands condemned" (John 16:8–11). It is the Holy Spirit's work to bring such conviction.

Third, the Holy Spirit will also bring *commitment* to the Lord Jesus Christ. Having comprehended the gospel and having been convicted of sin to the point of repentance, the one to whom the Holy Spirit bears his witness then commits himself to Christ as Lord and Savior.

Is he at work in your heart? Do you know that Jesus Christ is indeed the Son of God, as he claimed to be, and do you understand that he died in your place, the just for the unjust, that he might save you from sin? Are you convicted of sin so that you are sorry for sin and willing to turn from it? Have you reached the point of committing yourself to Jesus? If you have, say, "Lord Jesus Christ, I am a sinner but I believe that you are the Son of God and that you died for me. Accept me now as one of your children and help me to follow you faithfully until my life's end."

The Christian's Peace
John 16:17–33

I have told you these things, so that in me you may have peace.
—*JOHN 16:33*

The Christian's peace is not an absence of conflict or any other kind of trial. Rather it is contentment and trust in God in spite of such circumstances. But it is not automatic. The conditions he lays down in this passage are two.

First, the peace Christ gives is for those who are "in him." This is a conscious dependence on him and staying close to him that are the prerequisite to joy and fruitfulness in the Christian life. The gift of peace is appropriated only by those who depend on him, trust him, and remain close to him in their living of the Christian life.

Moreover, Christ's peace requires that the words of Christ be in his followers. Jesus indicates this when he says, "*I have told you these things*, so that in me you may have peace." What things are these? He has spoken of his love for the disciples; that he would guarantee a personalized place in heaven for his followers; that he would himself send the Spirit and that he would come to be in them and work through them; that they would be given work to do in this world, making their lives meaningful; that their prayers would be answered and he would be interceding for them.

Finally, Jesus adds another teaching: "But take heart! I have overcome the world." Christ overcame the world in three areas: in his life, in his death, and in his resurrection. He overcame it in life because, in spite of abundant griefs and temptations, he pursued the course God had set before him without deviation, sin, or error. He overcame the world in death because his death was the price of sin and thus broke sin's hold upon us. He overcame the world in his resurrection because by his resurrection he began his return to the throne of heaven from which he now rules the church and from which he will one day come again to put down all authority and power.

"I have overcome the world." These words were spoken within the shadow of Golgotha, at the very foot of the cross. They were spoken on the verge of what surely seemed a defeat. But they were true then. And if they were true then, it is even more abundantly demonstrated that they are true now. Do you believe them? Is Christ the victor? If you do and if he is, then stand with him in his victory. Possess the peace that he dispenses, and in your turn also overcome the world. Does the world deride Christ's gospel? So much the worse for the world. Do circumstances press us down? He has overcome circumstances. Stand with him then. He is the King. He is God over all, whose name is blessed forever.

The Preeminence of Love

John 17:1–26

That the love you have for me may be in them.
—JOHN 17:26

We see the preeminence of love readily if we look at it in reference to the other marks of the church. What happens when you take love away from them? Suppose you take joy and subtract love from it? What do you have? You have hedonism. You have an exuberance in life and its pleasures, but without the sanctifying joy found in relationship to the Lord Jesus Christ.

Subtract love from holiness. What do you get? You get self-righteousness, the kind of hypocritical virtue that characterized the Pharisees of Christ's day.

Take love from truth, and you have a bitter orthodoxy, the kind of teaching that is right but that does not win anyone.

Take love from mission, and you have imperialism. It is colonialism in ecclesiastical garb. We have seen much of that in recent history.

Take love from unity, and you soon have tyranny. This develops in a hierarchical church where there is no compassion for people nor a desire to involve them in the decision-making process.

That is one side of it. On the other hand, express love in relation to God and man and what do you find? You find all the other marks of the church following. What does love for God the Father lead to? Joy! Because we rejoice in God and in what he has so overwhelmingly done for us. What does love for the Lord Jesus Christ lead to? Holiness! Because we know that we will see him one day and will be like him; therefore "everyone who has this hope in him purifies himself, just as he is pure" (1 John 3:3). What does love for the Word of God lead to? Truth! Because if we love the Word, we will study it and therefore inevitably grow into a fuller appreciation and realization of God's truth. What does love for the world lead to? Mission! We have a message to take to the world. Again, where does love for our Christian brothers and sisters lead us? To unity! Because by love, we discern that we are bound together in that bundle of life that God himself has created within the Christian community.

Is it any wonder that Jesus ends his final discourses and prayer (undoubtedly spoken within the hearing of the disciples) with this emphasis? Hardly! Rather, we expect it, for it is as though Jesus, in anticipation of the writing of the fourth Gospel, could go back to the beginning of this fourth section in chapter 13, verse 1 (where we read, "Having loved his own who were in the world, he showed them the full extent of his love"), and then conclude, "Yes, and here at the very end of my discourses and prayer, I am going to talk about precisely that, for love is the most important characteristic."

Boice, *The Gospel of John*, Volume 4, Baker, 1999, 1348–49.

Understanding Jesus's Death
John 18:1–11

Now Judas, who betrayed him, knew the place.
—JOHN 18:2

Jesus was in control of the events leading to his death. They did not come upon him by accident, but rather he willed them in conformity to his knowledge of the will of his Father. On the final night, it was he who dispatched Judas on his errand of betrayal.

Historically, there has been a heated discussion as to who killed Jesus. Gentiles who have not known their Bible too well (or the evil of their own hearts) have tried to blame the Jews. Jews (and others) have blamed the Gentiles; for it was Gentiles in the person of Pilate, the Roman governor, who actually pronounced the death sentence. Sometimes these views have led to fierce anti-Semitism or an opposite anti-Christian feeling. But these are not the most important details. In fact, they are relatively insignificant. By contrast, the most important thing that can be said about the death of Christ is that God the Father willed it. It was God who ordained that he should be killed for our sin. The second important fact is that Jesus also willed his death out of love for us and in obedience to the revealed will of his Father.

Moreover, he ordered the events of this last Passover week to indicate the meaning of what he was doing. For just as he ordered his entry into Jerusalem to correspond to the exact time at which the Passover lambs were being led up to the city, so also did he time his death to coincide with the killing of those same lambs. He was the great Passover Lamb of which they were but shadows. It was his blood, rather than theirs, which was to take away the sins of the world.

It is comforting to know of the Father's and the Son's sovereign work, but there is also a sobering lesson. It concerns Judas, who was so close to Christ and yet was unsaved. Think how close he was. He had been with Jesus for at least three years. He had heard his teaching. He had even understood his teaching; for although he had not understood the meaning of Christ's death, he had at least understood Christ's warning that he was to die. Judas was that close to Jesus. Yet he was unsaved. I put it to you: it is possible to be quite close to Christ, to sit in a Christian church listening to good sermons, to hear good Bible teaching by radio, even to understand what you hear, and yet fail to make that personal commitment to Christ that is the necessary human response to God's work of salvation.

How foolish it is to come that close and yet be lost. How much wiser, by contrast, to put your faith in that One who is altogether lovely and who willingly died for your salvation.

Jesus's Claims
John 18:19–24

Meanwhile, the high priest questioned Jesus.
—JOHN 18:19

The Jewish trial exposes the true nature of the hearts of men and women. Jesus was not condemned under a primitive, barbaric, or even inadequate judicial system, but under the best. He, the righteous One—the One who on one occasion demanded which of his enemies was able to convict him of sin and left them speechless—was condemned to death by the most merciful and careful system of judicial processes known to our race. If we ask, as we must, "But how could that happen? How could the very Son of God be condemned?" the answer is simply that the problem, then as now, is not so much in the system itself as it is in the hearts of those who interpret and implement the system and its codes. The human heart is "deceitful above all things and beyond cure," as Jeremiah once wrote (Jer. 17:9). It is this that circumvents the law or (as in this case) actually uses the law to destroy the innocent. Understand that the roots of even the most heinous crimes ever perpetrated in the history of the world are within us and that, being placed in a situation similar to that of others who did these things, we have nothing within to hinder us from doing likewise.

The trial of Jesus also reminds us of his claims and promises. True, Jesus was condemned illegally. But still, the issues themselves were the right issues, and the claims for which he was convicted were real claims. He had made three of them. He had claimed to be God. He had claimed that he would rise from the dead after three days. He had claimed that he would return again in judgment. Are these claims true? The resurrection was true. If it was true, Jesus was also obviously who he claimed to be, for God would not have vindicated his claim to be the unique Son of God if this were blasphemy. Indeed, the final judgment is proved by the resurrection. For as Paul said to the Greeks in Athens, "[God] has set a day when he will judge the world with justice by the man he has appointed. He has given proof of this to all men by raising him from the dead" (Acts 17:31).

So the question is not whether the claims of Jesus of Nazareth are true but rather how we ourselves will respond to them and therefore also how we will greet him when he comes. Will we greet him as those who, like the rulers of his day, attempted to banish his presence from their lives? Or will we greet him as those for whom he died and who trust him as the only wise God and our Savior?

What Is Truth?

John 18:36–38

I came into the world, to testify to the truth.
—JOHN 18:37

The statement of Christ is preeminently a word to our own disillusioned culture.

First, it says that there *is* such a thing as truth and that *truth is an entity.* That is, truth is singular. It is not in fragments that would require us to speak of "truths" in the sense of unrelated facts or items. Truth holds together. Therefore, there is no phase of truth that is not related to every other phase of truth. All things that are true are part of the truth and stand in a proper and inescapable relationship to God, who is himself the truth.

Second, truth is not only an entity, it is *objective.* That is, it is there to be observed and discussed, and we can observe it and discuss it without prejudice. This is involved in Christ's statement that he has come to bear witness to the truth, as one might to any fact submitted in a court of law. If truth is an entity and truth is objective, then religious truth is not something to be reached by a great "leap of faith." Rather, it is something that may be studied and that will therefore inevitably throw light upon our natures and the nature of the universe. We look through the microscope of the Word to see our true condition. In that Book we find that God has done what needs to be done by sending his Son as our Savior. Jesus died for us. He rose for us. He reigns for us. That is objective truth, which may be studied and applied to our lives as any other truth can.

Third, *truth must come from above*, for when Jesus says that he has come to bear witness to the truth, he implies that, in the ultimate sense, truth is not of this world but rather must come to this world by revelation.

This is so of all truth, even for scientific truth. For it is God who has given us minds capable of perceiving the revelation of himself in nature and actually leads the mind to discover what is to be found there.

Fourth, in the ultimate sense *the truth that comes from God has been embodied in a person.* No one would ever imagine this. To us truth is abstract and may be supposed always to remain abstract. But God says that truth is personal. More than that, it is a person and this person is the Lord Jesus Christ, the Word that was with God and is God. That Word has now come. The Lord is that Word. He is the One who has come to reveal all mysteries and make everything plain to those who will come to him.

Jesus the King

John 19:19–22

JESUS OF NAZARETH, THE KING OF THE JEWS.
—JOHN 19:19

What does it mean for Jesus to be Lord? I think there is an answer to that question in the significance of the languages in which the caption of the cross was written (see v. 20 KJV). The first language mentioned by John is Hebrew. Hebrew was the language of religion and morality. Proclaiming Jesus King in Hebrew suggests that he is King of religion. He is himself the only true representation of God and the only sure and certain proclaimer of the way to be just before him. Jesus is Lord in this area. Consequently, if he is your Lord, he must be the One who determines what you believe concerning God and salvation.

Greek is the second language. This was the language of science, culture, and philosophy. It was the language of beauty. If Jesus is Lord in this area, then his outlook must prevail as you look out upon our culture. Is what you see what he desires? Is our culture's world-and-life-view his view? If it is not—and it is certain that it is not—then you must side with your Lord regardless of the world's opinion either of him or of you.

Finally, there is Latin, the language of law and good government. This reminds us that Jesus is the supreme lawgiver and law administrator. His laws must govern your conduct, and you must be obedient to him, even though his commands may be countermanded by the state or any other human authority.

The cross reveals the place of Jesus in your life. Pilate put his inscription on the cross primarily to irritate the leaders of the Jewish people, and it did irritate them, so much so that they requested that the wording be changed. These leaders hated Jesus so much that in his death they did not want to give even the appearance of recognizing his kingship. The inscription revealed their nature as it truly was. But it did that for Pilate too, for in response, the cowardly recalcitrance of Pilate emerged clearly so that the one who did not have courage to acquit One whom he knew to be innocent nevertheless stupidly dug in his heels over this.

The cross always reveals men as they are. It reveals the soldiers' nature, the nature of the crowds, that of the faithful women and John who was present. It reveals our hearts as well. We cannot be hypocrites before that cross. It is too great, its scope too universal. What does the cross show you to be? Does it show you to be a sinner—without hope, under condemnation—because you have no part in the Savior? Or does it show you to be his follower? God grant that if you have not yet done so, you might find him as Savior and begin to follow him as your rightful King and Lord.

Christ Our Passover
John 19:31–37

They did not break his legs.
—JOHN 19:33

The fact that Jesus's bones were not broken points to him as *the Passover Lamb* slain for the sins of his people. Psalm 34:20 tells us, "He protects all his bones, not one of them will be broken." This is the verse John refers to. But if we are candid, we must admit that a careful reading of this psalm does not at once suggest that this verse should be applied to the Messiah. It refers rather to the righteous man about whom David is writing. What is wrong then? Is this a case of invention on John's part? Not at all. It is true that he is referring to this psalm, but he is thinking of something greater. He is remembering that in the institution of the Passover it was explicitly indicated that not a bone of the Passover lamb should be broken. Exodus 12:46 declares, "It must be eaten inside one house; take none of the meat outside the house. Do not break any of the bones." Again Numbers 9:12 says, "They must not leave any of it till morning or break any of its bones." This seemingly pointless detail in the Passover ritual and this seemingly pointless detail in the death of Jesus combine in God's providence to identify Jesus as the Passover Lamb through whom we have a spiritual deliverance.

Every Jew knew the significance of the Passover. This was the event in which God delivered the people from their slavery in Egypt. God had said that on this night he would bring the last of his ten great judgments upon Egypt, a judgment in which the firstborn of every household would be killed. God would send his angel to slay the firstborn throughout the whole land. The Jewish homes would be spared only if they followed these instructions. They were to take a lamb, which was to have been kept in the home for three days and was to be without blemish or spot, and were to kill it. Then they were to take the blood of the lamb and spread it upon the doorposts and lintel of the house. The angel of death would come, but wherever he would see the blood he would "pass over," and the inhabitants of that house would be spared. This was the great national event and festival that the Jews were beginning to remember the day that Jesus of Nazareth was killed. What John is indicating (and God who speaks through him) is that Jesus is the perfect fulfillment of that important Old Testament figure. We are sinners. We deserve to die. The angel of God's judgment is coming. But Jesus has died in our place. His blood has purged our sin; now, because of his death, the angel of judgment will pass by all who trust in him.

For Love
John 19:38–42

Joseph of Arimathea asked Pilate for the body of Jesus.
—JOHN 19:38

Will not love generated at the cross draw you to Christ?

It was obviously the death of Christ that brought cowardly Joseph and weak Nicodemus from their places of hiding. Much to their shame, during the days of his ministry, they had failed to profess Christ openly. But in his death—when even the other, bolder disciples had fled—these came forward, touched by the loving sacrifice that Jesus made for our salvation. They awoke to their cowardice—and to God's love. They were not necessarily believers. Guilty consciences have done as much on similar occasions. But the death of Christ obviously awakened something within them, and they seemed willing at last to identify themselves as his followers.

God can do that with you, if you will but look on Christ's passion. The Bible says, "God demonstrates his love for us in this: While we were still sinners, Christ died for us" (Rom. 5:8). It is in Christ's death that we see God's love. Does that not move you? You may have held back before, hardly knowing whether you were a true believer or not. But you *can* come forward. He died for you. He paid the price for your sin. He bore the anguish of the cross for your salvation. How can you fail to love him? If you love him, how can you fail to confess him?

I will give you one more incentive. Notice that in his burial Jesus is already taking the first step toward the exaltation at God's right hand that is now his, from which he shall come forth in power at the end of the age. There was a true day of the jackal when men cursed and laughed and hated and spit upon him. There was a day of humiliation, but that day is now past. It ended with his death. Now even in his burial he is attended with love as those who have the means to care for his body and bury him honorably wait upon him. It was prophesied. Isaiah tells us that, although he was to die in the company of the wicked, he was to be attended by the rich in his death (Isa. 53:9). Besides, this is now followed by resurrection victory and the ascent to heaven.

The Christ you are asked to follow is not a humiliated Jewish preacher but the Lord of glory. Indeed, he does not merely ask you to come to him; he commands it. He tells you to turn from your sin and come to him openly for salvation. Will you do that? Will you come? "The Spirit and the bride say, 'Come!' And let him who hears say, 'Come!' Whoever is thirsty, let him come; and whoever wishes, let him take the free gift of the water of life" (Rev. 22:17).

Resurrection Lessons

John 20:1–9

He saw and believed.
—*John 20:8*

There are a few lessons that arise out of the narrative of the empty tomb. The first is that God has provided perfectly adequate evidence of the resurrection of Jesus Christ from the dead. The evidence consists of the claims of those who saw Jesus between the day of his resurrection and the day of his ascension into heaven, the empty tomb, the changed character of the disciples, the authenticity of the records, and the evidence of the undisturbed burial garments. The evidence is there, and the evidence of the grave clothes alone was sufficient to quicken faith in John. We conclude that if men fail to believe, it is because they will not believe, not because the evidence is lacking.

Second, the experiences of Peter and John at the tomb indicate that the body of the Lord was glorified. It was sown a natural body and was raised a spiritual body. In this body Jesus lives, seated at the right hand of God where he intercedes for his own until the moment when he will return again in judgment. Today we need not think of Jesus as the vulnerable Jesus of history. Jesus died but he died once for all. He was buffeted and spat upon and cursed, but that will not be repeated. We pray today to a powerful Lord, to an exalted Lord. This Lord will return one day to take his own to be with him in glory.

Finally, the transformation of the body of Jesus Christ points to a new mode of life for all believers. He is the first fruit. We, the harvest, shall be like him in our bodies as well as in his traits of character. Our resurrection bodies will be better than our old physical bodies. They will not be our physical bodies resuscitated. Our bodies hamper us. They tie us to earth, to habits, even to traits of character that we have inherited from our parents through their genes. They slow our thought processes. When we are sufficiently tired, they carry us away in sleep. Eventually they die. But we are to gain by death. The resurrection body will not hamper us. The body of the risen Christ is the forerunner of our bodies, and it was and is wholly subservient to his wishes. It did not hamper him. It freed him. In that body he knew no pain, no suffering, no want. For us there will also be freedom. There will be no want. There will be unlimited wakefulness and unlimited opportunities for service.

Privileged Adoption
John 20:10–18

I am returning to my Father and your Father.
—JOHN 20:17

Our new relationship to Christ provides a new relationship to God the Father. What is involved here is our adoption into the family of God. We are not naturally born into God's family. We are alienated from God and are born outside it as heirs of sin and death. But God is gracious; therefore, by the death of Christ and by the application of that death to us by the Holy Spirit, God brings us back into fellowship with himself and grants us family privileges.

Could anything be more utterly unexpected or overwhelming than the new relationship with God that is bestowed on his children? It is hard to think so. Justification is overwhelming enough, for it is all of grace. God did not need to justify us. Having justified us he could still have left us on a much inferior level of status and privilege. But he has gone far beyond what we could ever conceive of or expect by taking us into his own family where our status and privilege are that of daughters and sons. So great is God's condescension in this act of adoption that we would be inclined to dismiss this relationship, thinking it presumption, were it not that God has made a special effort to seal these truths to our hearts. As Paul has written, "No eye has seen, no ear has heard, no mind has conceived what God has prepared for those who love him—but God has revealed it to us by his Spirit" (1 Cor. 2:9–10).

What are these privileges? One is prayer, for access to God is based on our adoption. It is only because of our adoption that we can approach God as "Father," and it is only through the Spirit of adoption that we can be assured that he is indeed our Father and that our prayers are heard by him. This is what Paul is speaking of when he says, "For you did not receive a spirit that makes you a slave again to fear, but you received the Spirit of sonship. And by him we cry, 'Abba, Father'" (Rom. 8:15).

A second and related privilege of our new relationship to God is that we can have confidence before him. We are his children and we can know that nothing can ever destroy that relationship. If God is our Father, he will help us in the days of our spiritual infancy, teaching us to walk spiritually and lifting us up when we fall down. If he is our Father, he will care for us throughout the days of our earthly pilgrimage and will abundantly bless us. As our Father, he will guide us in the way we should go and eventually bring us home to heaven to be with him forever.

From Doubt to Faith
John 20:24–31

My Lord and my God!
—*JOHN 20:28*

What convinced Thomas that Jesus had risen from the dead? What finally got through to him was the presence of Christ, identified by the wounds in his hands, feet, and side. It was the Christ of the cross who reached Thomas. This is the greatest proof of all: the love of Christ revealed in his wounds. Do not misunderstand me here. If you have honest intellectual questions about Christianity, God will provide intellectual answers for them. He gave you a mind as well as a heart. He will provide what you need. But the thing that will ultimately win you is not so much the reasoned arguments, though they are often important stepping stones, but the love of Christ demonstrated by his death for you.

Here is some encouragement. Thomas was the most doubting of all Christ's apostles. But notice that when the Lord revealed himself to Thomas, Thomas moved from doubt to the greatest testimony of faith in Christ recorded by this or any other Gospel. He said, "My Lord and my God." "Lord" was sometimes used of Christ by others, often with less than its full meaning. But here it must have all the content it will bear—"Jehovah, Master, Sovereign." "God" is a new form of address; no one had previously addressed the Lord in this way. It represents a great insight of faith, perhaps even greater than that similar confession of the apostle Peter for which he was commended by Christ (Matt. 16:13–17). Then, lest all this should be thought insufficient, Thomas uses the personal pronoun, saying, "*My* Lord and *my* God." It was not enough that Jesus be both God and sovereign. He was now to be that for Thomas personally.

This is the high point of the Gospel. It is the climax. John shows here how one who began as a great doubter came by the grace of Christ to that confession with which the Gospel began: "And the Word was God" (John 1:1). The book was written to lead people to this conviction (20:30–31).

No case is hopeless. Your case is not hopeless. God took Abraham, the pagan, and made him into a pillar of faith and the father of his people. He took Moses, the stammerer, and made him into the greatest vehicle for the communication of the word of God until Paul. He made the shepherd boy David into a king; Peter "the weak" into Peter "the rock"; John the Son of Thunder into the apostle of love; Paul the persecutor of Christians into a faithful ambassador and martyr. He can do that for you. Allow him to do it. Believe on Christ. Rather than being faithless, may you be one who, like Thomas, was found "faith-full."

Trusting Christ's Knowledge
John 21:15–19

You know that I love you.
—JOHN 21:15

As Christ questioned him, consider Peter's repeated appeal to Christ's knowledge. In each case he answered Christ's question by affirming his love and then saying, "You know that I love you" (vv. 15–17). He might have said, "As I know my own heart, I swear that I love you." But Peter had said something like that once and had been dead wrong. Obviously there could be no confidence in his self-knowledge. What confidence there could be would have to be in Christ's knowledge of him—warts and all.

This seems illogical, of course. Peter was weak and sinful. He now knew this. Christ knew all things, as Peter had come to discover. How with that combination could Peter possibly be encouraged by an appeal to Christ's knowledge? It seems illogical, but this is actually the strength of one who has met Christ and known himself to be loved by him. Peter was a sinner. Yes! But a forgiven sinner. Therefore, though conscious of sin, Peter nevertheless knew that Jesus could look beneath the surface of his denial to see a heart that had been made new and truly loved him.

There is joy in an awareness of God's omniscience—for two reasons.

First, God knows the worst about us and loves us anyway. If God did not know all things, we might fear that someday something evil in us would spring up to startle God and turn his affection from us. He would say, "Oh, look at that horrible sin! I didn't know that was there. How terrible! That changes everything. I won't have anything to do with that person anymore." If God were not omniscient, that might well happen. But God knows all things. He knows the worst about us and loves us anyway. The Bible teaches that it was "while we were still sinners, Christ died for us" (Rom. 5:8). Second, since God knows all things, he also knows the best about us, though others do not. The disciples might have been startled by Peter's defection. They might have said, "If Peter is capable of denying Jesus like that, who knows what other sins are lurking within him. He might even be a false disciple." But Jesus knew better. He knew Peter's heart and love. It is not surprising in view of this knowledge that Peter appeals to him.

Never say, "I can do it, Lord. I know I can. I know my heart." Say rather, "Lord, you know what is there. You put it there. You know what love I have for you. Take it and make it into something that will abound to your glory."

The First Forty Days

Acts 1:1—11

This same Jesus, who has been taken
from you into heaven, will come back.
—*Acts 1:11*

We know that the Lord Jesus Christ is returning to judge the world, because we are told about it elsewhere in the New Testament. The disciples also had been told that one day Jesus would return to render judgment. But when the disciples were told that "this same Jesus" would be coming back, they would have thought of the Jesus they loved, not a judge. It was this gentle, loving, gracious but sovereign, holy, and majestic Jesus who would come back. He would stand with them and would say, Well, brothers, how have you done? What have you accomplished during all these years that I have left you to carry out my Great Commission? Have you done the work well? Or have you let your opportunities slide? The disciples, as they thought of Jesus's return, would have been encouraged for the task at hand.

In the summer of 1986 I was in England taking part in the great Keswick convention, and one of my blessings at that convention was meeting Derrick Bingham, an Irish preacher. He had a great work in Belfast, where every Tuesday night he taught more than one thousand young people. He shared with me how he was called into the ministry. His dying mother said to him, "Derrick, my boy, you have the gift of gab. But you don't know the Word. If you'd learn the Word, the Lord might be able to use you." That was how Derrick Bingham received his call to the ministry. Within three weeks of his mother's death, Derrick Bingham was preaching.

Bingham was greatly impressed with the Keswick convention, as was I. One evening, as we were walking home late at night after speaking to perhaps five thousand or more people, he said, "You know, as I was sitting there on the platform, I was thinking about my mother. And I was thinking that if my mother could come back from heaven for a moment and walk in here and see this great convention and me sitting there on the speaker's platform, I'd say to her, 'Look what we're doing, Mom. Here we are. We're doing what you wanted us to do all the time.'" Derrick was encouraged by that thought.

If that was an inspiration to him, if that kept him going, if that fired him for the task at hand, how much more should we be inspired by the thought that one day the Lord Jesus Christ himself is going to return. He is going to say to us, "How are you doing, my brothers? How are you doing, my sisters? Have you carried out your assignment?" Jesus will not be harsh but he will come expecting that we will have carried out the task.

Boice, *Acts*, Baker, 1997, 20.

That Incendiary Fellowship

Acts 2:1–13

All of them were filled with the Holy Spirit.
—Acts 2:4

Christianity is meant to be a spreading flame. When Jesus said that he had come to pour fire on the earth, he meant a fire that was destined to sweep over all the earth. How do we know? We know because of the way he spoke in giving the Great Commission. He said, "You will receive power when the Holy Spirit comes on you; and you will be my witnesses in Jerusalem, and in all Judea and Samaria, and to the ends of the earth" (1:8). This prophesied expansion of the Christian gospel began at Pentecost. That is why the second paragraph of Acts 2 talks about the many different people who were present in Jerusalem and who heard the gospel in their own language on that day: "Parthians, Medes and Elamites; residents of Mesopotamia, Judea and Cappadocia, Pontus and Asia, Phrygia and Pamphylia, Egypt and the parts of Libya near Cyrene; visitors from Rome (both Jews and converts to Judaism); Cretans and Arabs" (vv. 9–11)—people from all over the world, all the way to Rome and even beyond it. These individuals, reached for the first time at Pentecost, spread out in all directions like ripples on a pond.

When the Holy Spirit comes in power, what we are to have is not necessarily some particularly intense experience. We don't have to speak in tongues so that in a miraculous way everybody will hear our words in his or her language. Rather, we need to have a widespread speaking about Jesus. Everyone will hear as the gospel spreads through the testimony of those who are obeying the Great Commission. That is what you and I are called upon to do. That is the task to which the Lord Jesus Christ sends us.

In his book *The Incendiary Fellowship*, Elton Trueblood describes the character and company of those who are filled by the Holy Spirit. "Incendiary" means "set ablaze." It refers to Christians themselves. But "incendiary" also means the act of setting other people ablaze. It refers to those in whom the fire of the Holy Spirit is so intense and so meaningful that they just cannot keep the message of the Spirit to themselves. So they speak of Jesus, and, as a result, here and there little fires spring up. And pretty soon there is a great raging fire of revival that spreads across the world. I do not think we have a raging fire in our time, though there are some places in the world where it may be beginning. But there is a fire. The Holy Spirit is working. We need to be part of that working and see the flames spread.

Boice, *Acts*, Baker, 1997, 45.

A Model Church

Acts 2:42–47

They broke bread in their homes and ate together
with glad and sincere hearts, praising God.
—ACTS 2:46–47

Consider some of the things that are said about this model church.

It was a Bible-studying church. A Spirit-filled church is always going to be a Bible-studying church. And what is true of the church is true for individuals also. If you are Spirit-filled, then you will be drawn to this Book. The Holy Spirit, whose chief task is to bear witness to Jesus Christ, inevitably draws the people of God to Jesus through the Scriptures.

Evangelical, Spirit-filled, Bible-oriented churches should offer many ways for people to get to know the Bible. It must be done through the preaching. It may be done through Bible classes and home Bible studies. We are going to see that the early Christians worshiped in their homes. So I am sure they studied the Bible in their homes.

It was a church that practiced fellowship. Christian fellowship means "common participation in God." These early Christians had all participated in God the Father and in Jesus Christ, so they quite naturally participated in a common life and shared everything with one another. Fellowship with God and true fellowship with others go together. If you find yourself out of fellowship with God, you will begin to find yourself out of fellowship with other Christians. But if you come close to God, you will inevitably find yourself being drawn close to other Christians. And it works the other way too. If you spend time with other Christians, that fellowship will help to draw you closer to the Father.

It was a church that worshiped. "Breaking of bread" (v. 42) stands for the communion service, and prayer here is the formal exercise of prayer in the assembly. The Greek text actually says, "to the prayers." They devoted themselves "to *the* breaking of bread and to *the* prayers." Obviously, that is a reference to something formal. There is also a reference to formal worship by the phrase "in the temple courts" (v. 46), probably referring to the courtyard of the Gentiles. Then, not only did the Christians worship in a formal setting, but *they worshiped informally as well,* as the phrase says: "They broke bread in their homes." It means that they observed communion in the court and in their homes. They had formal worship and they had informal worship.

It was a witnessing church. This is why we find that the Lord added "to their number daily those who were being saved" (v. 47). We know that the way God reaches people is through the spoken word and that when the Holy Spirit came at Pentecost, those who received the Spirit immediately began to speak about Jesus. How could they do otherwise? They had experienced something wonderful, the ministry of God's Son. They had to share it with other people. How could they not?

Boice, *Acts*, Baker, 1997, 56–61.

Inducements to Repent

Acts 3:11–26

Repent, then, and turn to God.
—Acts 3:19

The inducements that Peter gave to his hearers to repent and believe on Jesus are the same offered to you. The first is forgiveness of sin. Forgiveness is what people need, and the only place anyone will ever really find forgiveness is in Christ. Most people carry heavy loads of guilt. This may be true of you. You may not have told anybody what you have done. Nevertheless, you remember what you have done and you carry the guilt of your actions around with you day by day, week by week, and year by year. Moreover, you do not find forgiveness in the world. The world is not capable of that. The world can judge you for your sin or pretend to overlook it. But it is not capable of forgiving it. Only God can forgive sin. That is why the world is so unsatisfactory in this respect. Peter is saying that God can forgive your sin; he can lift that great load of guilt. Clearly this is one great inducement to turn from sin and believe in Jesus Christ.

Peter has another inducement too. It is the "times of refreshing [that] come from the Lord." This probably concerns a future day of blessing. On the other hand, there are also "times of refreshing" for all God's people even now. Many of us go through much of life feeling pretty stale in what we do. Many people find, especially if they are in an unrewarding job, that life is often quite dreary. And sometimes even their Christianity becomes stale. Well, that happens. We all go through dry spells. Times like that do not necessarily mean that we are far from God. They only mean that we *feel* far from God. What we are told here is that in Christ there will be times of refreshing.

There is another inducement here to Peter's hearers indicated in verse 26: "When God raised up his servant, he sent him first to you to bless you by turning each of you from your wicked ways." First to you! To whom? Well, to the very ones who had been instrumental in the death of Jesus. And he comes to them *first*. It is God's way of saying, "I know what you have done but I do not hold it over you. I love you anyway. It is precisely for people like you that I caused Jesus to die."

You and I cannot say that God sent his servant to us first of all. Many have come to Christ before us in former ages of human history. But the principle is the same. Regardless of the guilt you may carry, God proclaims his Son to you. And the reason the gospel is proclaimed to you is because God says it is for you that Jesus died.

Boice, *Acts*, Baker, 1997, 69–70.

On Guard

Acts 5:1–16

Ananias, how is it that Satan has so filled your heart
that you have lied to the Holy Spirit?
—ACTS 5:3

In the early days of the church, Satan was outraged by what was happening in this Christian fellowship. Satan, the one who wants everything for himself—who makes people as selfish as he possibly can make them—must have hated the spirit of generosity and unity among the early Christians. So with devilish wisdom he must have said, "I'll turn this around. I'll use the spirit of sharing to break down the very generosity it is supposed to be expressing. I'll get them to lie and introduce chaos to the church."

Years later Peter would write, "Be self-controlled and alert. Your enemy the devil prowls around like a roaring lion looking for someone to devour. Resist him, standing firm in the faith" (1 Peter 5:8–9). This is an important warning. If we go through periods of special blessing, as these early Christians had, personally or in our church, we can expect Satan or one of his demons to attack us. It is because Satan does not want the church of Jesus Christ to thrive. If you are only going through the motions of serving Jesus, Satan will not worry about you very much. If you are not attempting anything important for God, if you are not breaking new ground, not witnessing, not serving in any particularly effective way, Satan will probably leave you alone. On the other hand, if you really are trying to do something for God—if your church is effective, if you have a strong missions program, if you have people out witnessing, if you are trying to embody the gospel in social programs that minister to the needs of real people and demonstrate the real love of Jesus Christ—Satan will attack you. You will have to be on your guard against him.

How can you do it? Satan is stronger than we are. He was stronger than Ananias, a man who even sat under the apostolic preaching. James tells us: "Submit yourselves, then, to God. Resist the devil, and he will flee from you" (James 4:7). But how do we first submit to God? We do it through prayer and a devotional life of which prayer is a part. Our example here is Jesus, who resisted and overcame the devil in his temptation. Jesus had just spent forty days in close fellowship with God, so he was utterly submissive to God's will, as of course he always was anyway. Then, when Satan came, he responded by quotations from Scripture. It is in Scripture that God has expressed his will.

Boice, *Acts*, Baker, 1997, 98–99.

The First Deacons

Acts 6:1–7

> Brothers, choose seven men from among you who are
> known to be full of the Spirit and wisdom.
> —ACTS 6:3

By electing deacons as the first administrative officers in the church other than the apostles, the church was electing people to do what above all else is most essential to true Christianity. This is because their service was patterned on the servant ministry of Jesus Christ. *Deacon* means "servant." And Jesus was the servant of everybody.

When we think about success, we have to remember that the Bible's evaluation of success is completely different from the world's evaluation. If you ask people of the world, Who are the really important people? Where are those who are really great? the world answers that it is those at the top of the administrative pyramid. It is those who have a lot of people under them. If we are talking about a person's private circumstances, it is those who do not need to work. People work for them.

That is not the way Jesus spoke of greatness. Jesus said: "The kings of the Gentiles lord it over them; and those who exercise authority over them call themselves Benefactors. But you are not to be like that. Instead, the greatest among you should be like the youngest, and the one who rules like the one who serves. For who is greater, the one who is at the table or the one who serves? Is it not the one who is at the table? But I am among you as one who serves" (Luke 22:25–27).

Jesus also said, "If anyone wants to be first, he must be the very last, and the servant of all" (Mark 9:35).

If you want to be great in God's sight, try serving people. Be a true deacon. If you want to be even greater in God's sight, serve even more people. The more people you can serve, the greater you will be. And that includes doing things for them that the world would call menial.

Remember Jesus. When he was about to be crucified and wanted to give his disciples a graphic demonstration of what true greatness was, he removed his clothes, wrapped himself with a towel, knelt before them, and washed each of the disciples' feet. The Lord of the universe—the Lord of glory, the King of Kings—knelt before Galilean fishermen and performed a servant's task. Peter understood how incongruous this was, at least from his point of view. He told his Master, "You shall never wash my feet" (John 13:8). But notice that he did not say, "No, Lord, let *me* wash their feet." He just didn't want the Lord to wash him. The Lord taught him how to be a servant.

Boice, *Acts*, Baker, 1997, 117–18.

Stephen: The First Martyr

Acts 7:54–60

> But Stephen . . . looked up to heaven and saw . . .
> Jesus standing at the right hand of God.
> —ACTS 7:55

Jesus is standing. Why? There have been two valid suggestions. One is that Jesus stood up to receive his martyr, Stephen. Sometimes we hear stories like that of the death of Christians. They are lying on their beds, but as they die they lift their arms and rise upward, sometimes even saying something like, "Look, I see Jesus." Then they fall back and die. My own great grandfather died that way, reacting in astonishment to what he saw of the heavenly glory as he died. Perhaps that is the explanation of why Jesus stood when Stephen died.

But there is another valid explanation. Jesus said in Matthew 10:32: "Whoever acknowledges me before men, I will also acknowledge him before my Father in heaven." In view of this verse, it may be that we have a case of Jesus standing to plead Stephen's cause as his advocate. That is, Jesus takes the position of a defender and witness before the Father's throne.

If this is the case, then what Stephen caught a glimpse of was that second and much greater trial in which he was involved. Up to this moment he had only been able to see the earthly trial. He was condemned by the earthly court. But at the moment of his death, he caught a glimpse of that greater, heavenly trial, in which he was acquitted. In this trial the Lord Jesus Christ took his side, pleaded his case, and prevailed. I find that immensely encouraging.

In this life we go through many situations in which we are on trial, and although we try to do our best, we often fail and are even misunderstood. We get discouraged. But we have to remember that the trials we go through in this life are not the final trial of history. They may be important. We want to do as well in them as we possibly can. That is why we have to be strong and bear a faithful testimony in all circumstances. But the trial that really matters, the verdict that counts, is the verdict that is given by the Lord Jesus Christ and by God the Father.

I do not know what the Lord Jesus Christ says when he looks down, sees us, and pleads our case before the Father, though I am sure it varies in every case. But I do know that, if we are his, he owns us and pleads our case in heaven. He says in effect, "This one is mine. That one is mine. I died for these people. My death covered their sin. They are clothed in my righteousness." As long as that is true, we can carry on. We can fight the good fight of faith, stand firm to the end, and bear a victorious testimony.

Boice, *Acts*, Baker, 1997, 126–27.

Owning Repentance

Acts 8:9–25

Pray to the Lord for me.
— ACTS 8:24

It is possible, just possible, that Simon was a believer. Nevertheless, this seems rather to be a case of one who had been exposed to strong preaching, was impressed by the miracles, and wanted to tap into the evident blessings of the gospel, but who did not have that genuine change of heart that would have meant that he was born again. We can apply the story either way.

It ends with Peter's words to Simon. Peter tells Simon, "Repent of this wickedness and pray to the Lord. Perhaps he will forgive you for having such a thought in your heart. For I see that you are full of bitterness and captive to sin" (vv. 22–23).

Simon replied, "Pray to the Lord for me."

Does that sound pious to your ears? "Pray to the Lord for me." That is the sort of thing ministers hear all the time. We talk to somebody about spiritual things, and he or she says, "Well, pray for me. Pray for me."

I do not want to be misunderstood: it is good to pray for people. If somebody says, "Pray for me," I try to do it. But Peter had told Simon to pray. He was to repent of his wickedness and pray to God. So when Simon replied by saying, "Pray for me," he was not being pious at all but rather disobedient. His words were what we would call in colloquial English "a cop-out." He was refusing to do what he had been told he should do and was passing the buck to Peter.

Do you do that? Do you pass the buck for your spiritual growth to other people? Do you pass it to your minister? Lots of people try to pass the buck to me. They think that somehow I can solve their problems. I cannot. I cannot even solve my own problems, let alone their problems. If you are sinning, *you* are the one who must repent of the sin. If prayer is needed, *you* are the one who must pray.

The Bible says that it is our "iniquities" that have separated us from God. It is because of our "sins" that "he will not hear" us (Isa. 59:2). If you have sinned, you must confess it and repent of the sin; then you can pray. You must come to God like the prodigal, saying, "Father, I have sinned against heaven and against you" (Luke 15:21) or like the tax collector at the temple, "God, have mercy on me, a sinner" (18:13). It is hard to pray in that fashion. But if you do it, you will find, as Peter suggested to Simon, that God will forgive your sin, cleanse and restore you, and save your soul.

Boice, *Acts*, Baker, 1997, 135, 137–38.

Biblical Religion
Acts 9:36–43

Tabitha . . . was always doing good and helping the poor.
—ACTS 9:36

Christianity has a gospel of salvation from sin, and flowing from that is a practical calling to help and serve other people. Yes, Christianity calls people to turn from sin and respond to Jesus Christ in saving faith. But if they have done that, it then calls them to serve others also.

Before the coming of Jesus Christ, there were no hospitals in the world. If somebody got sick at home, there would have been family members to take care of them. There were doctors, but there were no hospitals. Nobody established institutions to take care of those who were ill, certainly not those who were poor and unable to pay for their treatment. But where Christianity came, the light of medicine followed and hospitals were founded everywhere.

Before Jesus Christ came, there were no orphanages in the world. People did not care for children who had no parents. Letting orphans die was considered the best thing. Even worse, good Greek and Roman families would expose their own children to perish from the elements if they thought they had enough children. That is the way the people of those days treated children. If by some means some rejected child should manage to grow up to a reasonable age, even then nobody would take the child in. Generally, such children fell into male or female prostitution.

There were no leprosariums in the world before the coming of Jesus Christ. Everyone feared leprosy and fled at a leper's approach. There was no compassion or humanitarian care for those who were suffering as a result of this disease.

There were no disaster relief organizations in the world before the coming of Jesus Christ. You never in all of ancient literature read, for example, of the community in Rome getting together to take up an offering to send to the starving poor in Egypt. Yet at even this very early stage, when the Christians were for the most part quite poor themselves, you find the apostle Paul going around the Greek communities collecting money to send to the poor in Jerusalem because there had been a famine there. Christians felt a tie to one another and to other men and women because of a common humanity.

There were not even any great schools in the ancient world. There was education, of course. But there was nothing like common education. There was no concern for those who did not have means. Christians brought that concern. It is Christians who have gone into the cities of the world and have hunted out the poor, the young, the sick, the uneducated and have brought them into schools to train them and give them skills that enabled them to be something other than destiny would seem to have chosen for them.

This is just biblical religion.

Boice, *Acts*, Baker, 1997, 170–71.

Accepted by God

Acts 11:1–18

When they heard this, they had no further objections and praised God.
—ACTS 11:18

The results of Peter's explanation and defense of his ministry to the Gentiles were all good. Verse 18 says, "When they heard this, they had no further objections and praised God, saying, 'So then, God has granted even the Gentiles repentance unto life.'"

I notice two things about this response. First, the Jews of Jerusalem were convinced that this had been of God. Peter had explained the situation, and they were intellectually convinced. Second, because they were convinced, they praised God. What God had done was perhaps not what they would have preferred. It certainly was not what they expected. Nevertheless, there was evidence that this was truly God's work. And if God was working, then God was to be praised.

However, although the Jews were convinced by Peter's presentation, it was only for a time. They praised God, but not for long. Not very long after this, a party began to grow up in the Jerusalem church that rejected this position. These people said in effect, "We must not allow the Gentiles to ignore the law of Moses. If we let down the barriers in this way, pretty soon everyone will start acting like Gentiles. And we all know how the Gentiles act. We have to preserve the law of Moses (and our traditions). We have to insist that Gentiles be circumcised, come under the law of Moses, and then keep the regulations that we have been keeping for centuries." So these questions had to be battled out again and again. Acts 15 tells about one such struggle, and the matter appears again in Paul's writings, particularly in his letter to the churches in Galatia.

Prejudice dies hard. But we need to learn from these early lessons regarding the scope of God's grace in the gospel. Often we find it difficult to believe that God can accept other people without these others first becoming like us. Yet God does accept them. And it is good he does, because if he did not, you and I would never have become Christians. We would have been excluded. The only reason we are believers is that God does not show favoritism. That is why we are "in." Therefore, we must not show favoritism ourselves. We must reach out to everyone, and we must not count it a threat when God brings into our fellowship somebody who from our perspective just doesn't seem to fit.

What matters is not whether other people fit in with us. What matters is that they have been accepted by God.

Boice, *Acts*, Baker, 1997, 194–95.

Gospel Advancement

Acts 12:1–25

But the word of God continued to increase and spread.
—ACTS 12:24

I think of those who have tried to oppose the gospel over the centuries. There were times when Christ's enemies tried to oppose the expansion of the Word of God by the sword, just as Herod did when he executed James. The powerful said, "If you continue to preach this gospel, we will take away your lives." And they did. There have been countless martyrs in the history of the church. Yet the Word of God has not been bound. The more the enemies of Christ have killed his followers, the more the gospel has spread outward like ripples on a pond.

Others have tried to suppress the Word of God by ridicule. They laugh at us, saying, "Who in his right mind would ever believe a foolish thing like that? No enlightened, no modern person can believe such foolishness." The French agnostic philosopher Voltaire tried to destroy the church by ridicule, predicting that within fifty years people would have forgotten even who Jesus Christ was. Fifty years after his prediction, the Geneva Bible society was running off thousands of Bibles on presses that had been set up in Voltaire's former home in Geneva.

Others have tried to bind the Word of God by neglect, by pretending it no longer matters, just getting on with their utterly secular lives. Yet the gospel spreads.

People have tried to bind the gospel by creating substitutes for it, counterfeits. They say, "Well, all right, we'll have religion, but we'll have it without Christ. We don't need this business of the cross and an atonement. We'll just take the beautiful things like Jesus's ethics." That kind of religion, a Christ without the cross, has no power and appeals to no one except those seeking a substitute for the true thing. Thus do people fight, oppose, and ridicule the gospel we hold dear. Yet that true gospel of God goes on from strength to strength while the other secular gospels and their advocates fade along the way.

But though the Word of God is always advancing, it does not do so without human channels. God has also decreed that it is to advance by human messengers, like Barnabas, Saul, and even young John Mark, who once seemed to have abandoned the missionary call. Do you look to others who have been in the faith a long time and think they are the ones to carry the gospel on? They are, of course. They are doing it to the best of their ability. But you, like Mark, are also called by Jesus to the same assignment. Will you do it? You must, because God has determined that the Word of God shall "increase and spread" through you, as it has through other normal people in earlier generations of the church.

Boice, *Acts*, Baker, 1997, 220–21.

Appointed for Eternal Life

Acts 13:42–49

And all who were appointed for eternal life believed.
—ACTS 13:48

This verse expresses the doctrine of election: that those who believe are those who are appointed to eternal life by God. Isn't it interesting that we should have this statement of the doctrine of election right in the middle of this great evangelistic story? There are people who cannot imagine how anybody can be an evangelist if God decides who will be saved and then saves them. The argument goes, "If God is going to save certain people, God will save them regardless. What I do doesn't matter."

Actually, those who have had the greatest faith in God's electing power are also those who, by the grace of God, have proved to be the most effective evangelists. Virtually all the famous missionary pioneers were believers in election.

Why did they go out to evangelize, then, if they believed God was going to save people anyway?

That isn't quite the way to put it. If God is going to save someone, God will save them. That is true. But it is not quite correct to say that God will save them *anyway*, because when we say, "God will save them anyway," we mean that God will save them apart from our (or another's) witness, and that is not true. The God who appoints the ends also appoints the means, and the means he has appointed in the evangelization of other people is our witness.

We are to take the gospel into all the world. But as we go we are to know that God will work through that witness to bring to faith those he has appointed.

Suppose conversion does not depend on God; suppose it depends on you. Suppose people are saved because you are eloquent or because you have the right answers or because you happen to be in the right place at just the right time—entirely apart from God's election. If that is true, it means that if you do not have the right answers, if you are not in the right place, if you do not present the gospel in just the right way, then these people will perish and it will be your fault. I do not know how anybody can live with that.

On the other hand, if you believe that God has appointed some for eternal life and that, as you testify, God will use that testimony to bring those persons to faith, the burden is removed and witnessing becomes what it was meant to be: a joy, as it obviously was for Paul and Barnabas. Persecution? Yes, they had that. But in spite of the persecution, a church was founded and it was not subdued. On the contrary, it prevailed and went on to become one of the strongest churches of the ancient world.

Boice, *Acts*, Baker, 1997, 248–49.

Continuing the Work

Acts 14:21–28

Then they returned . . . strengthening the disciples.
—*ACTS 14:21–22*

In the very last section of chapter 14, we find Paul and Barnabas retracing their steps, going back through the cities where they had been persecuted and from which they had been ejected. They went to strengthen those left behind. They did a number of things.

1. *They gave encouragement.* It was a hostile, pagan community in which citizens of these cities were called to live for Jesus Christ, and they didn't even know much about him. So the apostles went back to encourage them.

2. *They taught the believers.* Paul taught that "we must go through many hardships to enter the kingdom of God" (v. 22). He taught other things as well.

3. *They organized the church.* Here for the first time in the book of Acts, we find the appointing of elders (v. 23), which we learn later was to become Paul's natural pattern of church organization. I do not know how "elderly" these elders were, but I know they had not been Christians very long, since the gospel itself had not been known to them very long. Was that any way to establish a church? Most Presbyterians wouldn't do it that way. We want to be slow, careful, dull, and (maybe) ineffective. But Paul had faith in what God was doing, and if there were to be churches in these cities, they obviously needed sound organization. So Paul appointed elders, more than one, and the churches thrived.

4. *They prayed.* The last thing Paul did (and possibly the first thing too) is that he prayed for them (v. 23). We should be praying too, praying for those to whom we witness and for the church.

When we get to the very end of this chapter, we find something marvelous. Verse 26 says, "From Attalia they sailed back to Antioch, where they had been committed to the grace of God for *the work they had now completed.*" This was only one stage in Paul's lifelong ministry, the end of the first missionary journey. There were going to be two more, but this was the first stage. It had been clearly defined, they were commissioned to do it, and they completed it. So they went home, reporting, "The task is done."

That is a great thing to be able to say. How many Christians have started out in some work but have not finished it! Many have been given a task to do, but because of the hardships, divisions, persecutions, and such things, they have said, "I think I had better quit." The victory is not to those who start. It is to those who finish.

Boice, *Acts*, Baker, 1997, 257.

Why Missions?

Acts 16:1–10

Come over to Macedonia and help us.
—ACTS 16:9

This call of God to Paul and his missionary team teaches some important lessons about missions. Why do we engage in world missions? There are a number of reasons.

1. *Jesus Christ has told us to do it.* We call this "The Great Commission," and we find it five times in the New Testament—once in each of the four Gospels, toward the end, and once at the beginning of Acts. If God says something once, we should pay attention. If he repeats it, we should give rapt attention. How, then, if he says it three, four, five, or more times? Obviously, it is something we dare not overlook and to which we must give the most intent, sustained, and obedient scrutiny.

2. *Christ's love constrains us.* Paul talks about this explicitly in 2 Corinthians 5:14, saying, "Christ's love compels us." It would be important for us to go into all the world with the gospel if for no other reason than Jesus has told us to do it. But it would be sad if the only motivation we had were mere obedience. Paul, who understood the marching orders of Jesus Christ, also understood the compulsion of Christ's love, saying, "Christ's love compels me."

Christ's love involves the love of Christ for the lost; he loves them. But it also involves our love, as the love of Christ works its way out through those who know him. Paul loved those to whom he was sent. So must we. In fact, there is nothing that so commends the gospel to the lost as love for them by the one who proclaims it.

3. *The world is in need.* The world is perishing in its sin apart from the gospel of Jesus Christ, and it also has other needs—social and physical. I find it significant that it is largely in these terms that the call to come to Macedonia was given. "Come over to Macedonia and help us." That is, *we* need help and *you* are the one who can help us.

I wonder if you have thought of your church's missionary effort or your witnessing to a neighbor in those terms. You say, "It is difficult to witness today because so many people in our day don't want the gospel." That is true. They don't. They very seldom do. Most people today are self-satisfied. They do not want anything that might upset their lifestyle. But if that is the case, why not refocus your witnessing for a time at least on those who *are* hurting and *do* have needs.

This is what life is about. It is about God's calling out a people to himself, a people who will know him. His purpose for us is to assist in that great call and work.

Boice, *Acts*, Baker, 1997, 274–76.

Laborers for the Harvest
Acts 18:18–28

They invited him to their home and explained to
him the way of God more adequately.
—ACTS 18:26

Apollos's story is rich with practical spiritual lessons. Here are three of them.

1. *Learning and fervor, though valuable gifts, are not in themselves enough for Christian workers.* We must know Jesus Christ. Even knowledge of the Scriptures and skill in presenting them are not enough. There are always people in churches who are not saved but who know a great deal. They know the Scriptures well. But they do not know Jesus. They do not know him personally as their Savior and Lord. They are not his disciples. It may be true of you. Although you may have gone to church for many years and may know a great deal about the Scriptures, the mere learning and even fervent teaching of these things is not enough. You must know Jesus Christ.

2. *Different kinds of people are needed in Christ's work.* Aquila and Priscilla were different from Apollos, and Apollos was different from Paul. Paul was a feisty Jewish rabbi. Apollos was a man of polish, erudition, and learning. Aquila and Priscilla, Apollos, and Paul were all needed in the church. How do we know? We know because God called them: Paul, with his energetic missionary fervor; Apollos, who watered the seed that Paul had sown; Priscilla and Aquila, who settled down, opened their home, and were hosts to the developing church. Each one was necessary.

So are you, if you are Christ's disciple. God has given you a distinct spiritual gift. That gift is needed where you are. If you think, *I am not needed, because someone else is more eloquent or someone else is more hospitable or someone else has more energy or is a better evangelist than I am*, you are making a great mistake. If you neglect to use your gift, the church will be impoverished.

3. *If you lack workers for Christ where you are and feel the need, you should pray about it, asking God for help.* Paul must have been praying strongly for these churches, and knowing that he was unable to do all that needed to be done himself, he must have been asking God to send new workers into the missionary field. And God did.

The Lord Jesus Christ said, "The harvest is plentiful but the workers are few. Ask the Lord of the harvest, therefore, to send out workers into his harvest field" (Matt. 9:37–38).

Those words are true for us. The harvest is plenteous. Just outside our doors are many people who need to hear the gospel. They are resistant. No one left to himself or herself is going to come to God. That is why you must pray for God to send more workers into his vineyard. It is by many that God works to save some.

Boice, *Acts*, Baker, 1997, 317–18.

Eyes on Our Inheritance

Acts 20:17–38

Now I commit you to God and to the word of his grace,
which can build you up and give you an inheritance.
—*Acts 20:32*

Paul reminds us that if we are faithful to our task, as Paul was urging the Ephesian elders to be, there will be laid up for us "treasures in heaven, where moth and rust do not destroy, and where thieves do not break in and steal" (Matt. 6:20).

I suppose that is why Paul went on in an unexpected way to speak about himself again. He had already given his testimony; he had spoken directly to the elders. At first glance it seems strange that Paul should then have begun to talk about himself some more, saying, "I have not coveted anyone's silver or gold or clothing" (Acts 20:33).

It may be a bit unexpected but it is not hard to understand how he got there. He had just urged them to deny themselves for the sake of God's kingdom, concluding, "God [will give you] an inheritance among all those who are sanctified." Then, having said that, he reminded them that what he was urging on them he had himself done. He said in effect, "I have not tried to build an earthly fortune. I have not coveted anyone's gold. I have not been in this religion business to become wealthy. The reason I have not done that is that I have had my eyes set upon the inheritance laid up for me in heaven."

What a difference it would make if we would all learn to think like that. I know it is hard. The world bombards us with its values and with a philosophy that says, "You only go around once. Now is the time to make it. If you do not lay up treasure for yourself now, you'll never have it."

By contrast, the Word of God says, "You can lay it up now. But when you die, it will be gone forever; on the other hand, if you live for God now, you will have treasure forever." It is literally true that you cannot take it with you into heaven. But if you are obedient to God and try to serve him wholeheartedly now, spiritual treasures will be waiting for you in heaven when you get there. These treasures are the eternal well-being of the soul, eternal felicity, basking in and enjoying the favor of God forever. Compared with those spiritual treasures, the things for which we sell our souls here are worse than trifles. They are nothing. They are literally the refuse of this disintegrating world. Learn to lay up treasures in heaven, as Paul did.

Boice, *Acts*, Baker, 1997, 350–51.

Through Christ Alone

Acts 21:40–22:22

Go; I will send you far away to the Gentiles.
—ACTS 22:21

Paul had been doing everything possible to stress how Jewish he was, but as soon as he uttered the word "Gentiles," the mob reacted violently and would have killed him if it could have.

Why did they object to that word? They were objecting to Paul's persuasion that Gentiles could be saved without adhering to the law of Moses, without becoming Jews.

But God saves people his way, and his way is through Christ.

If you are a Gentile, you can come as a Gentile. But it must be through Jesus Christ alone.

If you are a Jew, you can come as a Jew. But you must come through Christ alone.

If you are an Englishman, you can come as an Englishman. But you must come through Christ.

If you are Japanese, you can come as a Japanese. But you must come through Christ.

Why must we come in this way and not in some other way? Why can't we invent our own way? It is because God sent Jesus Christ to be the Savior. This is how God has done it. So when we talk about the gospel today, we are not talking about a religious opinion, though the world would like to make it that. We are talking about reality, about truth. Once I talked to a woman on an airplane about spiritual things, and every time I said something about the gospel, she said, "But that's just your opinion."

I replied, "That's true, it is my opinion. But that's not the point. Whether it is my opinion or not does not matter. What matters is, is it true?"

When I explained something else, the same thing happened. "But that's just your opinion," she said.

I replied, "Yes, that is my opinion. But the point is not whether it's my opinion. The point is, is it true?" We went on that way for about an hour, and at the end I knew even she was beginning to get it, because she was laughing. She knew what was coming.

Paul had met Jesus on the road to Damascus, and that meeting turned his life around. God sent Jesus Christ to be the Savior. If you rebel against that fact, you are doing exactly what the Jews did. You are saying that you have to do something first and you want others to do it your way. If you are thinking like that, it is no wonder you despise and even hate a gospel as humbling as this gospel is.

It may be simple and it may be humbling, but it is still the gospel, and it is the way to be saved. May God give you grace to embrace it wholeheartedly.

Boice, *Acts*, Baker, 1997, 369–70.

The Peril of Pride

Acts 26:19-32

Do you think that in such a short time you can persuade me to be a Christian?
—*Acts 26:28*

Festus might have been willing to hear Paul talk about some future resurrection, particularly if it could be thought of metaphorically. Most people are at least willing to consider the possibility of some future state in which we will all possibly have to answer for our misdeeds. But Paul was talking about a literal, bodily resurrection that had happened in history and that had made all the difference in his life and in the lives of others who had met Jesus Christ. It was this resurrection that was incredible and intolerable to Festus. "You must be crazy," was Festus's response. He perished because of it.

Paul then turned to Agrippa saying, "The king [that is, Agrippa] is familiar with these things, and I can speak freely to him. I am convinced that none of this has escaped his notice, because it was not done in a corner. King Agrippa, do you believe the prophets? I know you do" (vv. 26–27). Agrippa was no Roman. He would have had some acquaintance with what Moses and the prophets had written. He may even have had considerable understanding of the Jews' religious books. Agrippa would have known something of the events surrounding the life of Jesus of Nazareth too. Yes, but Agrippa still had his position in life to think about and he perished because of that.

Festus probably perished through the pride of intellect. How could a Roman governor believe anything as crazy as a literal resurrection? That was not the case with Agrippa. Agrippa probably believed in the resurrection. But he had his position, and he just could not humble himself, acknowledging himself to be a sinner like anybody else, and receive Jesus Christ as his Savior. He was put on the spot—embarrassed, no doubt, before the governor. So he dodged the question, saying, "Do you think that in such a short time you can persuade me to be a Christian?"

This is precisely what men and women do today. When the supernatural gospel of a crucified but risen Savior is proclaimed, a gospel that demands that we turn from sin and begin to show our conversion by good works, the world puts up barriers and rejects it for precisely these reasons: pride of intellect and pride of position. If you are not a Christian, isn't it true that, when you look into your heart, you find that those are the things that keep you from bowing to Jesus Christ? Think how foolish that is, since both intellect and position will eventually pass away. Jesus said, "What good will it be for a man if he gains the whole world, yet forfeits his soul?" (Matt. 16:26).

Boice, *Acts*, Baker, 1997, 407–8.

Preaching Christ
Acts 28:17–31

Boldly and without hindrance he preached the kingdom of God and taught about the Lord Jesus Christ.
—*Acts 28:31*

Notice a few last points at the end of Acts.

1. *The gospel Paul preached in the twenty-eighth chapter of Acts is the same gospel preached by Peter in the second*. It was not a different gospel because it was being preached to different people, by a different person, or in a different setting. No matter who is preaching or where, it is always the same gospel. It is the gospel of salvation through Jesus Christ. It is our gospel today.

2. *The results of the preaching of that gospel are the same*. Some reject it, and some respond to it. It was that way when Peter preached at Pentecost. It was that way when Paul preached at Rome. It is that way when we teach about Jesus Christ today. We are not to think that if we experience rejection or resistance we are any different from those who have preceded us.

3. *Christ's plan for the expansion of the gospel and the founding of his church has not altered*. As Acts closes, the Great Commission is being fulfilled. We may be frustrated by what we regard as the slow progress of the gospel, but Jesus is not frustrated. His plans are not sidetracked.

What happened to the apostle Paul? From God's perspective there is a sense in which it does not really matter. What happens to his servants does matter to God, of course. "Precious in the sight of the LORD is the death of his saints" (Ps. 116:15). What happens to you matters to him. But there is a sense also in which what happens to us is incidental to the greater story, which is the expansion of the gospel. At one period of history there may be a great moving of God's Spirit, and everything will seem to be going well. At other times, times more like our own, the response to spiritual things will be superficial or people will be hostile. But in a sense, it does not matter.

What does matter is whether we are faithful in the calling to which God has called us. The Lord Jesus Christ told his disciples, "This gospel of the kingdom will be preached in the whole world as a testimony to all nations, and then the end will come" (Matt. 24:14). That end has not yet come. So you and I still have the task of preaching the gospel.

Will we? Will we be found faithful?

That is the final question for us from Acts. The Word is not hindered. We are its messengers. Will we take the gospel to the ends of the earth beginning with our Jerusalem, as we have been instructed to do? If we will, God will bless it to the praise of the glory of his great grace.

Boice, *Acts*, Baker, 1997, 430–31.

God's Grand Old Gospel

Romans 1:1–17

Set apart for the gospel of God.
—*ROMANS 1:1*

The gospel is *God's* gospel. It is something God announced and accomplished and what *he* sent his apostles to proclaim. It is something God blesses and through which *he* saves men and women. The grammatical way of stating this is that the genitive ("of God") is a subjective rather than an objective genitive. It means that God creates and announces the gospel rather than that he is the object of its proclamation.

Note how prominent this point is in these early verses of Romans. God the Father has "promised [the gospel] beforehand through his prophets in the Holy Scriptures" (v. 2). He has sent his Son, the Lord Jesus Christ, to accomplish the work thus promised, with the result that the gospel, then as now, is "regarding" him (v. 3). Finally, it is "through him and for his name's sake" that Paul and the other apostles, exercising a calling received by them from God, were in the process of proclaiming the gospel to men and women everywhere (v. 5).

If God is concerned about his gospel to this extent, will he not bless it fully wherever these great truths are proclaimed?

Let me tell you one story of such a blessing. In the year 1816 a Scotsman by the name of Robert Haldane went to Switzerland. Haldane was a godly layman who, with his brother James Alexander, had been much used of the Lord in Scotland. In Geneva, on this particular occasion, he was sitting on a park bench in a garden in the open air and heard a group of young men talking. As he listened, he realized two things. First, these were theological students. Second, they were ignorant of true Christianity. As a result of this encounter and after a few encouraging conversations, Haldane invited the students to his room and began to teach them the book of Romans. God honored this work, and the Holy Spirit blessed it by the conversions of these young men. They were converted one by one, and in turn they were instrumental in a religious revival that not only affected Switzerland but also spread to France and the Netherlands.

Why should it be any different today? If it were *our* gospel, we could expect nothing. But it is not our gospel. It is "the gospel of God," that grand old gospel that was "promised beforehand through his prophets in the Holy Scriptures" and achieved for us by the Lord Jesus Christ through his substitutionary death and resurrection. We should proclaim it fearlessly and with zeal, as did Paul.

Boice, *Romans*, Volume 1, Baker, 1991, 35–36.

The Angry God
Romans 1:18–32

The wrath of God is being revealed from heaven against
all the godlessness and wickedness of men.
—ROMANS 1:18

Where do most people begin when making a presentation of Christian truth? Many begin with what is often termed "a felt need," a lack or a longing that the listener will acknowledge. The need may involve feelings of inadequacy; a recognition of problems in the individual's personal relationships or work or aspirations; moods; fears; or simply bad habits.

Here is the way Paul speaks of a felt need in another letter: "For the time will come when men will not put up with sound doctrine. Instead, to suit their own desires, they will gather around them a great number of teachers to say what their itching ears want to hear" (2 Tim. 4:3). "What their itching ears want to hear" is a classic example of a felt need. In this passage the apostle warns Timothy not to cater to it. Another way we present the gospel today is by promises. Through this approach, becoming a Christian is basically presented as a means of getting something. We also commonly offer the gospel by the route of personal experience, stressing what Jesus has done for us and commending it to the other person for that reason.

The point I am making is that Paul does not do this in Romans, and in this matter he rebukes us profitably. Paul was God-centered, rather than man-centered, and he was concerned with that central focus. Most of us are weak, fuzzy, or wrong at this point. Paul knew that what matters in the final analysis is not whether we feel good or have our felt needs met or receive a meaningful experience. What matters is whether we come into a right relationship with God. And to have that happen, we need to begin with the truth that we are not in a right relationship to him. On the contrary, we are under God's wrath and are in danger of everlasting condemnation at his hands.

Our hope, then, is in Jesus, the Son of God. His death was for those who deserve God's wrath. And his death was fully adequate, because Jesus did not need to die for his own sins—he was sinless—and because, being God, his act was of infinite magnitude.

The place to begin for salvation is not with your own good works, since you have none, but by knowing that you are an object of God's wrath and will perish in sin at last, unless you throw yourself upon the mercy of the One who died for sinners, even Jesus Christ.

The Long-Suffering God
Romans 2:1–16

> Or do you show contempt for the riches of his kindness, tolerance and patience?
> —ROMANS 2:4

There are two ways we can go in responding to God's kindness, tolerance, and patience. Paul is clear about them. One way is repentance, the way Scripture urges. The other is defiance, or spite toward God's goodness.

Which will it be for you? You can defy God. You can set yourself against his goodness, tolerance, and patience. But why should you do that? Why should you "show contempt for the riches of his kindness, tolerance and patience"? These are winsome qualities. A kind, tolerant, and patient God is a good God. Why should you fail to realize that God's exercise of these attributes toward you is for a good end?

I want to give you three reasons why you should allow these attributes to lead you to repentance and should no longer despise the goodness of God.

First, if God is a good God, then whatever you may think to the contrary in your fallen state, to find this good God will mean finding all good for yourself. You do not normally think this way. You think that your own will is the good. Can you not see that it is your own sinful way that is the cause of your miseries? God is not the cause. God is the source of all good. If you want to find good for yourself, the way to find it is to turn from whatever is holding you back and find God. God has provided the way for you to turn to him through the death of his Son, the Lord Jesus Christ.

Second, if God is tolerant of you, it is because he has a will to save you. If he wanted to condemn you outright, he could have done it long ago. If he is tolerant, you will find that, if you come to him, he will not cast you out.

Third, if God is patient with you in spite of your many follies, it is because he is giving you an opportunity to be saved. The apostle Peter wrote, "The Lord is not slow in keeping his promise, as some understand slowness. He is patient with you, not wanting anyone to perish, but everyone to come to repentance" (2 Peter 3:9). If God is good in his patience, his reason for being so must be to do good. His patience must be to give you opportunity to turn to him. If he has allowed you to live twenty, forty, or even eighty or ninety years, it is so that you might come to him now—before you die and the opportunity for salvation is gone forever.

Silence at Last

Romans 3:9–20

So that every mouth may be silenced and the
whole world held accountable to God.
—ROMANS 3:19

Some years ago there was a dance instructor who had been out late on a Saturday evening. In the wee hours of the morning, he staggered back to his hotel room, fell into bed, and went to sleep. The next morning he was suddenly jolted awake by his clock radio. A man was speaking and he was asking this question, "If in the next few moments some great disaster should happen and you should be killed and if you should find yourself before God and he should ask you, 'What right do you have to come into my heaven?' what would you say?"

The dance instructor was amazed and confounded by this question. He realized that he did not have an answer. He had not a single thing to say. He sat silently on the edge of his bed as Donald Grey Barnhouse explained the answer to him. That dance instructor was D. James Kennedy, author of the evangelism program known as "Evangelism Explosion." Kennedy believed on Jesus Christ that day, and the question that had been used to save him became the chief tool in his evangelism strategy.

I ask that same question of you. Someday you will die. You will face God, and he will say to you, "What right do you have to come into my heaven?" What will your response be?

Perhaps you will say, "Well, here is my record. I know that I have done some bad things, but I have done a lot of good things too. All I want from you is justice." If you say that, justice is exactly what you will get. You will be judged for your sin and be condemned. Your good works will not save you. For God has said: "There is no one righteous, not even one . . ." (v. 20).

Perhaps you will not plead your good works, but instead will stand before God silenced. This is better. At least you will have recognized that your goodness is not adequate before God. You will know you are a sinner. But it is still a most pitiful position to be in: silent before the one great Judge of the universe, with no possibility of making a defense, no possibility of urging extenuating circumstances, no hope of escaping condemnation.

So what will you say? I trust you will be able to answer, "My right to heaven is the Lord Jesus Christ. He died for me. He took the punishment for my sin. He is my right to heaven, because he has become my righteousness."

Amazing Grace
Romans 3:21–26

And are justified freely by his grace through the redemption that came by Christ Jesus.
—*ROMANS 3:24*

When a person is first presented with the pure core of Christianity, the reaction is usually revulsion. We want to save ourselves, and anything that suggests that we cannot do so is abhorrent to us. But Christianity is not only the religion we *need* so desperately. It is also the only religion *worth having* in the long run. Let me explain.

1. *If salvation is by the gift of God, apart from human doing, then we can be saved now.* We do not have to wait until we reach some high level of attainment or pass some undetermined future test. Many people think in these terms, because they know that their lives and actions are far from what they should be now and they keep striving. But this means that salvation can never be a present experience but is something always in the future. It is something such persons hope to attain, though they are afraid they may not. It is only in Christianity that this future element moves into the present, because of what God has *already* done for us in Christ.

2. *If salvation is by the gift of God, apart from human doing, then salvation is certain.* If salvation is by human works, then human works (or a lack of them) can undo it. If I can save myself, I can unsave myself. I can ruin everything. But if salvation is of God from beginning to end, it is sure and unwavering simply because God is himself sure and unwavering. What he has begun he will continue, and we can be confident of that.

3. *If salvation is by the gift of God, apart from human doing, then human boasting is excluded, and all the glory in salvation goes to God.* I doubt any of us would want to be in a heaven populated by persons who got there, even in part, by their own efforts. The boasting of human beings is bad enough in this world, where all they have to boast of is their own good looks, their money, their friends, or whatever. Imagine how offensive it would be if they were able to brag about having earned heaven through works, even the work of faith.

But it is not going to be like that! Salvation is a gift. It is receiving God's righteousness—apart from law, apart from human doing. It is, as Paul wrote to the Ephesians, "not by works, so that no one can boast" (Eph. 2:9). No one in heaven will be praising man. In heaven the glory will go to God only. *Soli deo gloria!*

Thank God it is that way.

Never!

Romans 4:1–8

Blessed is the man whose sin the Lord will never count against him.
—ROMANS 4:8

There is a word in Paul's citation of David's testimony that deserves special consideration. It is the word *never*: "Blessed is the man whose sin the Lord will *never* count against him."

Never means never, and it must be taken at full value here, even though the opposite is almost always the case in human relationships. We all know the kind of forgiveness in which a person reluctantly accepts our apology and says that he will forgive us. But we know, as he says this, that he is not forgetting what happened, that our offense will linger in his mind and will probably be brought out against us in the future.

This text tells us that God is not like that. It tells us that, once he has forgiven us for our sin through the work of Christ, he will *never, never* bring it up to us again. He will not bring it up in this life, never remind us of something in the past. He will always begin with us precisely where we are in the present. And he will never bring it up at the day of judgment. Why? Because it is truly forgiven. It will *never* be remembered anymore.

That is real "blessedness," which is the terminology David uses. And my concluding question is this: Why trade away that blessedness for the false blessings offered by this world?

The world does offer its blessings, of course. It is how it holds its victims. It offers material things chiefly, but it also offers intangibles, such as a good reputation, success, happiness, and such. Let me remind you that you can have all these things and more and still be miserable—if the burden of your sin is not lifted. David is an example. He was the king of a most favored nation. He had wealth and reputation. But the very psalm from which our key verse is taken describes what he was like before his sin was forgiven. He wrote that, when he kept silent about his sin, trying to hush it up, "my bones wasted away through my groaning all day long. For day and night your hand was heavy upon me; my strength was sapped as in the heat of summer" (Ps. 32:3–4). But because David found forgiveness with God, the burden of his sin rolled away, his strength was restored, and he could write: "Blessed is the man whose sin the Lord will never count against him."

I commend that very great blessing to you.

Boice, *Romans*, Volume 1, Baker, 1991, 451–52.

God's Love Demonstrated
Romans 5:1–11

But God demonstrates his own love for us in this:
While we were still sinners, Christ died for us.
—ROMANS 5:8

How can any merely human words sufficiently express the greatness of God's love for us? Did you know that the love of God seemed so great to the biblical writers that they invented, or at least raised to an entirely new level of meaning, a brand-new word for love?

The Greek language was rich in words for love. There was the word *storgē*, which referred to affection, particularly within the family. There was *philia*, from which we get "philharmonic" and "philanthropy" and the place name "Philadelphia." It refers to a love between friends. A third word was *erōs*, which has given us "erotic," and which referred to sexual love. This was a rich linguistic heritage. Yet when the Old Testament was translated into Greek and when the New Testament writers later wrote in Greek, they found that none of these common Greek words was able to express what they wanted. They therefore took another word without strong associations and poured their own, biblical meaning into it. The new word was *agapē*, which thereby came to mean the holy, gracious, sovereign, everlasting, and giving love of God that is expressed here.

If you do not yet fully appreciate (or perhaps have not even begun to appreciate) the greatness of the love God has for you, the explanation is probably that you have never really thought of yourself as God saw you in your fallen state.

Perhaps you have never thought of yourself as someone who was utterly without strength or powerless before God saved you.

Perhaps you have never considered yourself to have been ungodly.

Nor a sinner.

Nor God's enemy.

But that is what you were—and still are if you have never come to Christ in order to be justified. It is only if you can recognize the truth of these descriptions that you can begin to appreciate the love that God holds out to you through the death of his Son.

If you have never responded to this great overture of the divine love, let me encourage you to do that, assuring you that there is no greater truth in all the universe. Can you think of anything greater? Of course, you can't. How could anybody? God loves you. Jesus died for you. Let those truly great thoughts move you to abandon your sin, love God in return, and live for Jesus.

Reigning in Life

Romans 5:12–21

> How much more will those who receive God's abundant provision of grace and of the gift of righteousness reign in life.
> —ROMANS 5:17

Adam fell, because he was not able by his own strength to confirm himself in righteousness. Similarly, were we to attempt to stand in our own righteousness, assuming that we could attain to it in the first place, we would fall also. But we do not fall. We stand instead, and the reason we stand is that we do not stand in our own righteousness. So we sing:

> Jesus *thy* Blood and righteousness
> My beauty are, my glorious dress;
> 'Midst flaming worlds in these arrayed,
> With joy shall I lift up my head.

Moreover, it is not only that we will stand in that final day of divine judgment. We stand now, which is what the phrase "reign in life" refers to. It means that by the grace of the Lord Jesus Christ, the love of God, and the communion and empowering of the Holy Spirit, we are victorious *now*. In this way, the gift of God in Christ far surpasses the effects of Adam's and all other transgressions.

We were in Adam once, and we fell in him. What then? Good news! We can escape the effects of Adam's fall. More than that, we can rise above the position in which Adam first stood. We can stand in a divine righteousness, which is perfect and which can never be taken away from us. It enables us to reign in life, triumphing over sin, as Adam, in his own human (though once perfect) righteousness, could not. Therefore we can sing:

> On Christ the solid rock I stand;
> All other ground is sinking sand.

Are you "in Jesus"? Adam was not "in Jesus," and he fell, even from his high pinnacle of human perfection. If he who was once humanly perfect fell, what chance do *you* have to stand, you who are corrupted by many sins and wholly disposed to unrighteousness? Your only hope is to believe on Jesus and be joined to him. It is to stand in him, as you originally stood (but also fell) in Adam.

Dead to Sin
Romans 6:1–14

We died to sin; how can we live in it any longer?
—ROMANS 6:2

A reigning monarch is a triumphant monarch. If grace is reigning in us, grace is advancing its conquest over sin. Christians sin. But they are not defeated by sin and they do not continue in it.

Do you understand the absurdity of the objector's question—"Shall we go on sinning so that grace may increase" (v. 1)? If you understand the nature of grace, you will understand that for grace to increase, sin must decrease, not increase. The goal of grace is to destroy and vanquish sin. Therefore, if a person goes on sinning, as the objection suggests, it shows that he or she actually has no part in grace and is not saved.

I give two warnings.

The first is directed particularly to the many people in religious circles who have much head knowledge about doctrine and who suppose, just because they know such things and give mental assent to them, that all is therefore well with their souls, that they are saved. That is not necessarily the case. If you are such a person, I need to warn you that it is not enough for you only to believe these things. Salvation is not mere knowledge. It is a new life. It is union with Christ. Therefore, unless you are turning from sin and going on in righteousness, as you follow after Jesus Christ, you are not saved. It is presumptuous to believe you are. So examine your life. Make sure you are saved. The Bible warns you to "make your calling and election sure" (2 Peter 1:10).

The other warning is to all Christians, and it is in the words of an old Puritan preacher who asked in relation to our passage from Romans: "Is there anyone here who, by his conduct, gives occasion for this objection?" Is your life so careless that an unsaved person looking on might reasonably conclude that this is precisely where the doctrine of justification by grace leads Christians?

If that is the case, correct that impression at once. The writer to whom I was referring says, "It is a lamentable fact that one man who dishonors the gospel by an unholy walk does more injury to the souls of men than ten holy ones can do them good." I urge you to be part of the solution, part of the ten, rather than part of the problem. Let your life be marked by righteousness, not marred by sin—for your own soul's good as well as for the good of other people.

Our Fruitful Union

Romans 7:1–6

You also died to the law through the body of Christ, that
you might belong to another, to him who was raised from
the dead, in order that we might bear fruit to God.
—*Romans 7:4*

God's object in saving us is *so that we, who beforehand were lost in sin and wickedness, might live a holy life.* Our new marriage to Jesus Christ produces holiness by bringing us into a love that will never fade and a relationship that will never end. We died to our unfruitful first marriage to the law when we died in Christ. That marriage ended. But now, having been raised in Christ, who will never die, and having been joined to him, we are assured of a love that will last forever.

"But suppose my love is weak?" you ask.

Don't say "suppose." As a new bride of Christ, your love for him *is* weak, but it will grow. It will grow here on earth and it will go on growing throughout eternity.

"Suppose my love should grow cold?" you wonder.

That is a sad thing to imagine since there is no excuse for it, but it is true that this sometimes happens. We get involved in the affairs of this world and forget the Lord for a time. Ah, but he is still seeking us. He has only used our neglect of him to show us how much his love means and how empty our lives are without it.

"But suppose I betray his love, as Gomer betrayed the love of Hosea?" God forbid that you should ever do that! But even if that should happen, Jesus's love is greater even than your betrayal. He died to deliver you from the condemnation of the law and purchase you for himself. Do you think he will abandon you now? The Bible tells us, "If we are faithless, he will remain faithful, for he cannot disown himself" (2 Tim. 2:13).

One day the great God of the universe is going to throw a party. It will be the most magnificent party that has ever been held. The banquet will be spread in heaven. The guests will be numbered in the billions. The angelic legions will be there to serve these honored guests. Jesus, the Bridegroom, will be seated at his Father's right hand. And you will be there too, for this is the great marriage supper of the Lamb. You will be there. Do you understand that? *You will be there.* Nothing is going to keep you from that great celebration—if you are really joined to Jesus Christ.

If you know where you are headed, you will be preparing for that day with every spiritual thought you have and with every deed you do. You will be bearing fruit for God, because on that day of celebration you will be able to lift it up and offer it to him with pure hands and with joy unspeakable.

The Incomparable Glory
Romans 8:18–25

I consider that our present sufferings are not worth comparing with the glory that will be revealed in us.
—*ROMANS 8:18*

If we can appreciate what Paul is saying in this text and get it fixed in our
minds, we will find it able to change the way we look at life and the way
we live—more than anything else we can imagine. It will provide two things
at least.

1. *Vision.* Focusing on the promise of glory will give us a vision of life in
its eternal context, which means that we will begin to see life here as it really
is. We have two problems at this point. First, we are limited by our concept
of time. We think in terms of the "threescore years and ten" allotted to us, or
at best the few years that have led up to our earthly existence or the few years
after it. We do not have a long view. Second, we are limited by our material-
ism. Our reference point is what we perceive through our senses, so we have
the greatest possible difficulty thinking of "the spirit" and other intangibles.
We need to be delivered from this bondage and awakened from our spiritual
blindness.

In *The Weight of Glory*, C. S. Lewis addressed the objection of those who
might consider his talk about glory as only fantasy, the weaving of a spell.
He replied by admitting that perhaps that is what he was trying to do. But he
reminded his listeners that spells in fairy tales are of two kinds. Some induce
enchantments. Others break them. "You and I have need of the strongest spell
that can be found to wake us from the evil enchantment of worldliness which
has been laid upon us for nearly a hundred years."

2. *Endurance.* "Breaking the spell" will give us strength to endure whatever
hardships, temptations, persecutions, or physical suffering it pleases God to
send us. Suppose there were no glory. Suppose this life really were all there is.
If that were the case, I for one would not endure anything, at least nothing I
could avoid. And I would probably break down under the tribulations I could
not avoid. But knowing that there is an eternal weight of glory waiting, I will
try to do what pleases God and hang on in spite of anything.

Paul writes, "I consider that . . . ," meaning that he has thought it through
and concluded that "the sufferings of this present time are not worthy to be
compared with the glory which shall be revealed in us" (KJV). By using this
word he invites us to think it through also. If you are a Christian, I ask, Isn't
what the apostle says in this verse true? Isn't the glory to come worth anything
you might be asked to face here, however painful or distressing?

Boice, *Romans*, Volume 2, Baker, 1992, 866–68.

The Love of God in Christ Jesus
Romans 8:31–39

For I am convinced that neither death nor life . . . nor anything else in all creation, will be able to separate us from
the love of God that is in Christ Jesus our Lord.
—ROMANS 8:39

What does "anything else in all creation" include? The answer is that it includes everything that exists except God, since God has created all these other things. Thus, if God is for us and if God controls everything else, since he has made it, then absolutely nothing anywhere will be able to separate us from his love for us in Christ Jesus.

Paul is *convinced*. This is Paul's personal testimony but it is a testimony based on the soundest evidence, evidence that had persuaded Paul and should persuade us also. What are the grounds of this persuasion? Paul's conviction is not based on the intensity of his feelings or a belief that the harsh circumstances of life are bound to improve or that any of these separating factors will somehow be dissolved or go away. Rather, it is based on the greatness of God's love for us in Christ, and that awesome love has been made known in that God sent his Son to die in our place.

There is nothing in all the universe greater or more steadfast than that love. *Therefore*, nothing in all the universe can separate us from it:

> Not death, not life
> Not angels, not demons
> Not the present, not even the future
> Not any power
> Not height, not depth
> Not anything else in all creation

I do not know of anything greater than that. So I ask of you: Is this *your* testimony? Have you been persuaded of these truths, as Paul was? Can you say, "I no longer have any doubts. I know that salvation is entirely of God and that he will keep me safe until the very end"? If you are not certain of these truths, it is because you are still looking at yourself. You are thinking of your own feeble powers and not of God and his omnipotence.

As far as I am concerned, I am persuaded and I am glad I am. There is nothing in all of heaven and earth to compare to this assurance.

True Israel

Romans 9:6–12

For not all who are descended from Israel are Israel.
—ROMANS 9:6

How can we be sure we are Christians? There are a number of specific questions to be answered as we examine ourselves.

1. *Do I believe on Christ?* The first requirement is faith, because faith is our point of contact with the gospel. Ask yourself, *Have I believed on Jesus?* Not, *Have I believed on him in broad cultural terms?* But rather, *Have I been touched by the knowledge of Jesus's death for me and have I committed myself to him? Am I serious about following after Christ, obeying his commands, and pleasing him?*

2. *Am I following after Christ?* The first question leads to the next: *Am I actually Jesus's follower?* The way Jesus called his followers was by the words, *Follow me.* And when they did follow him, their lives were inevitably redirected. Nobody who has begun to follow Jesus Christ has ever been entirely the same or walked in the same paths afterward. So ask yourself: *Has my life been redirected? Is there anything I am doing now that I did not do before or would not be doing were I not committed to Jesus? And are there things I have stopped doing? Is Jesus my very own Lord and Savior?*

3. *Do I testify to Christ?* This is a harder point for true self-examination, because it is easier for some to talk about Jesus than for others. Nevertheless, this is an important question and one worth asking. If you never speak to anyone about Jesus, how can you suppose that you really care about him and love him, not to mention caring about and loving the other person, who needs to receive the Savior?

4. *Am I learning about Christ? Am I trying to learn more and more about Jesus Christ? Do I know more about him today than I did at the time of my conversion? Or at this time last year?* How can you think of yourself as a Christian when you have no interest in learning about the One who gave himself for you?

Christian leaders say we need a revival. But what is a revival? A revival is the reviving of the alleged people of God, and it is preceded by an awakening in which many who thought themselves to be Christians come to their right senses and recognize that they are not new creatures in Christ and that all is not well with their souls. Revival begins in the church, not in the world. It begins with people like you. I too think we need a revival. But if it happens, why should it not begin with us? With you? May God grant it for his mercy's sake.

God's Beautiful People
Romans 10:5–15

How beautiful are the feet of those who bring good news!
—ROMANS 10:15

Do you know how the gospel came to Hugh Latimer (ca. 1485–1555), that great bishop who became one of the brightest lights of the Protestant Reformation in England? Hugh Latimer was a "beautiful" man, strikingly good-looking and brilliant. But he did not know Christ and he was using his learning to oppose the teachings of the Reformers, especially that of Melanchthon, Martin Luther's co-worker and friend. Latimer was at Cambridge at this time, and there was at Cambridge a little monk whose name was Thomas Bilney. No one paid much attention to Bilney. But Bilney had discovered the gospel, and he wanted the great Hugh Latimer to come to Christ too. *What a tremendous influence he would have, if only he would discover the gospel of God's grace in Christ,* Bilney thought.

So he hit on a plan. One day after Latimer had been preaching, Bilney caught his arm as he was coming out of the church and asked if he would hear his confession. That was a prescribed duty of a priest. So Hugh Latimer listened to Bilney, and the little monk who had found Christ "confessed" the gospel, sharing how it had changed his life. Latimer later said that he was converted by Bilney's gospel "confession." As for Latimer, he became a great reformer in England and is best known for his encouragement of Nicholas Ridley as they were being led to the stake in Oxford at the height of the English persecutions in 1555: "Be of good comfort, Master Ridley, and play the man; we shall this day light such a candle by God's grace in England as (I trust) shall never be put out."

Bilney was not a beautiful person as we generally think of beauty. But he was the bearer of the gospel to Hugh Latimer, and that means that he was beautiful in the sight of God, just as are all those who obey the Lord Jesus Christ in carrying out the Great Commission.

May I suggest that you start thinking of beauty the way God does. What you think is beautiful now is going to be a thing of the past in just a few short years. Those you think beautiful now will no longer be beautiful in physical terms. But the beauty of the bearers of the gospel will last forever. What is more, they will go on getting more and more beautiful, as they use not only this life but eternity to praise the Lord Jesus Christ more fully.

Beauty really is as beauty does. I invite you to value others not by their outward appearance, but by their service to Jesus Christ and the gospel. And I invite you to become one of God's beautiful people yourself.

Holy Destiny

Romans 11:13–22

> If the part of the dough offered as firstfruits is holy, then the
> whole batch is holy; if the root is holy, so are the branches.
> —ROMANS 11:16

Our destiny as Christians is the same as that of the nation of Israel. We too are to be "holy to the Lord." And if that is the case, if that is what we will surely be one day—since "without holiness no one will see the Lord" (Heb. 12:14)—we must strive to be holy now.

Have you ever thought of your destiny in terms of holiness? If you are a Christian, you have been set apart to God to be wholly his. But you are not holy now. You are sinful now, and the more you live, the more you will be aware of it. Your *destiny* is holiness. That is why we read about this so often in the Bible. God told the people through Moses, "Be holy, because I am holy" (Lev. 11:44–45; cf. 19:2; 20:7). And Peter picks up on the theme, writing, "But just as he who called you is holy, so be holy in all you do; for it is written: 'Be holy, because I am holy'" (1 Peter 1:15–16). This is not only a command. It is our sure end. If we belong to Jesus Christ, God, whose purposes do not change, will make us like him in holiness one day.

We usually think of salvation relationally today. That is why we think of God's attributes as being, first of all, love, then perhaps mercy, kindness, goodness, and such things. This is not wrong, of course. God is love, and we are being enabled to love him and others because he first loved us and so showed us what love is like.

But this is not the way the Bible speaks of our destiny. It is not the love relationship that is emphasized. We are not told that we will spend our time in heaven loving God and others, though we undoubtedly will. The Bible emphasizes holiness. And the reason it does is that a lack of holiness is what accounts for our inability to love rightly and, in fact, to do anything else well. The reason our relationships to God are not all they should be is that we are not holy. The reason why our relationships to others are not all they should be is that we are not holy. We need to be holy.

But praise God, one day we shall be holy. "We shall be like [Jesus], for we shall see him as he is" (1 John 3:2).

So why not be holy now? That is what John concludes. For immediately after telling us that we will be like Jesus one day, he says, "Everyone who has this hope in him purifies himself, just as he is pure" (v. 3). Do you? You will, if you have your eyes fixed on that great destiny.

Soli Deo Gloria

Romans 11:33–36

To him be the glory forever! Amen.
—ROMANS 11:36

Romans 11:36 is the first doxology in the letter of Romans. But it is followed by another at the end, which is like it, though more complete: "To the only wise God be glory forever through Jesus Christ! Amen" (16:27). It is significant that both doxologies speak of the glory of God, and that forever. Here are two questions to help us understand them.

1. *Who is to be glorified?*

The answer is: the sovereign God. For the most part, we start with man and man's needs. But Paul always started with God and he ended with him too.

2. *Why should God be glorified?*

The answer is that "from him and through him and to him are all things," particularly the work of salvation. *Why is man saved?* It is not because of anything in men and women themselves but because of God's grace. It is because God has elected us to it. God has predestinated his elect people to salvation from before the foundation of the world. *How is man saved?* The answer is by the redeeming work of the Lord Jesus, the very Son of God. We could not save ourselves, but God saved us through the vicarious, atoning death of Jesus Christ. *By what power are we brought to faith in Jesus?* The answer is by the power of the Holy Spirit through what theologians call effectual calling. God's call quickens us to new life. *How can we become holy?* Holiness is not something that originates in us, is achieved by us, or is sustained by us. It is due to God's joining us to Jesus so that we have become different persons than we were before he did it. We have died to sin and been made alive to righteousness. Now there is no direction for us to go in the Christian life but forward. *Where are we headed?* Answer: to heaven, because Jesus is preparing a place in heaven for us. *How can we be sure of arriving there?* It is because God, who began the work of our salvation, will continue it until we do. God never begins a work that he does not eventually bring to a happy and complete conclusion.

"To him be the glory forever! Amen."

So let us give God the glory, remembering that God himself says: "I am the LORD; that is my name! I will not give my glory to another or my praise to idols" (Isa. 42:8). And, "For my own sake, for my own sake, I do this. How can I let myself be defamed? I will not yield my glory to another" (48:11).

Transformation

Romans 12:1–2

Be transformed by the renewing of your mind.
—ROMANS 12:2

Note what Paul says we are to be: not *conformed* but *transformed* by the renewing of our minds. There is a deliberate distinction between these two words. Conformity is something that happens to you outwardly. Transformation happens inwardly. The Greek word translated "transformed" is *metamorphoô*, from which we get *metamorphosis*. It is what happens to the lowly caterpillar when it turns into a beautiful butterfly.

This Greek word is found four times in the New Testament: once here, once in 2 Corinthians 3:18 to describe our being transformed into the glorious likeness of Jesus Christ, and twice in the gospels of the transfiguration of Jesus on the mountain where he had gone with Peter, James, and John. Those verses say, "There he was transfigured before them" (Matt. 17:2; Mark 9:2). The same word used by Paul to describe our transformation by the renewing of our minds so that we will not be conformed to this world is used by the gospel writers to describe the transfiguration of Jesus from the form of his earthly humiliation to the radiance that Peter, James, and John were privileged to witness for a time.

And that is why Paul writes as he does in 2 Corinthians, saying, "We, who with unveiled faces all reflect the Lord's glory, are being transformed into his likeness with ever-increasing glory, which comes from the Lord, who is the Spirit" (3:18).

In 2 Corinthians Paul says, "It is happening." In Romans 12 he says, "Let it happen," thus putting the responsibility, though not the power to accomplish this necessary transformation, upon us. How does it happen? Through the renewing of our minds; and the way our minds become renewed is by study of the life-giving and renewing Word of God. Without that study we will remain in the world's mold, unable to think and therefore also unable to act as Christians. With that study, blessed and empowered as it will be by the Holy Spirit, we will begin to take on something of the glorious luster of the Lord Jesus Christ and become increasingly like him.

The Debt of Love

Romans 13:8–10

Let no debt remain outstanding, except the continuing debt to love one another.
—ROMANS 13:8

Besides refraining from doing harm to our neighbor, real love is also positive. It "does" for the other. This is involved in the very first thing Paul
says, for he writes of the "continuing debt to love one another."

Let's think about this "continuing debt" positively, and ask, What does it
mean to discharge this debt honestly? Here are some extremely simple but
important and often neglected ways.

1. *Listen to one another.* We live in an age in which few people really listen
to one another. We talk to or at one another, of course. To really love another
person, we must listen. If we do not know how to listen, we must learn how.
And we must take time to do it.

2. *Share with one another.* The second thing we need to do is share ourselves
with each other. The problem is that sharing ourselves makes us vulnerable,
especially if we are trying to share with a person we care deeply about. We
are afraid to be vulnerable. Sharing is the reverse side of listening. We listen
to the other person as he or she shares. Then we share ourselves. This is the
only way to show real love and build real relationships.

3. *Forgive one another.* None of us is without sin. Therefore, we are all
guilty of sinning against others. For this reason, listening and sharing also
involve forgiveness. Sharing means expressing our hurts, and listening means
hearing how we have hurt the other person.

4. *Serve one another.* The fourth practical expression of what it means to
love one another is service. This does not come to us naturally, which is one
reason the Bible mentions and illustrates it so often. This was practically the
last lesson Jesus left with the disciples when he washed their feet. Jesus was
giving an example of menial service, teaching that we are to serve others.

What the world needs is the sincere, selfless, sacrificial, serving love of God
displayed in those who know him and are determined to obey him faithfully.
If you know Jesus, you will not follow after the world's selfish ways but instead will love as God loves. You will keep the law: "Love is the fulfillment of
the law" (v. 10). But you will also go out of your way to listen to, share with,
forgive, and serve all other people.

Where Is the Chasm?

Romans 14:1–4

Accept him whose faith is weak, without passing judgment on disputable matters.
—*ROMANS 14:1*

Let's allow God to deal with each of his servants how, when, and as kindly as he will. And while we are at it, let's be thankful that he has dealt as kindly as he has with us. If he had not, we would all be in deep trouble.

Take notice here that Paul has two initial points of advice. In fact, what he says is stronger than advice—these are commands, and the whole sentence is made up of them: Accept him whose faith is weak and Do not pass judgment in disputable matters.

1. *Accept him whose faith is weak.* This means that we are to accept other Christians as Christians and that, as John Murray says, "There is to be no discrimination in respect of confidence, esteem, and affection."

Accept is a strong term, because it is used of God's acceptance of us in verse 3 and of Christ's acceptance of us in 15:7. Verse 3 says, "The man who does not eat everything must not condemn the man who does, for God has accepted him." The other verse says, "Accept one another, then, just as Christ accepted you." If God has accepted the other person, who are you not to accept him?

2. *Do not pass judgment in disputable matters.* Recognize that some standards of right conduct are unclear and that other matters really do not matter. In those areas, let the matter drop and get on with things that do matter. Above all, accept the other believer for what he or she has to offer to the whole body of Christ. And do your own part too! Tell someone about Jesus. Certainly you have better things to do than to hunt out the speck in the eye of your fellow Christian while overlooking the plank in your own.

Francis Schaeffer used to talk about "the chasm." He said that we put it in the wrong place, dividing ourselves from other Christians. It shouldn't be there. True, there is a chasm between those who know Jesus Christ and those who do not, between Christians and the world, and it is a deep one. But that is where it lies, between Christians and the world, not between Christians and Christians. All who know Jesus Christ are on this side of the chasm, and we must stand with them for Christ's kingdom.

Building Up or Tearing Down
Romans 15:1–6

Each of us should please his neighbor for his good, to build him up.
— ROMANS 15:2

Is all this worth it? Is it worthwhile sharpening our skills and developing our Christian character so that others might grow to be like Jesus Christ? Of course, it is. The problem is not that we doubt the ultimate value of the work we are given to do but that we get bogged down in the hard, daily task of fashioning the stones of this building and fitting them to the overall structure. We get our eyes off the blueprint and get bogged down in the rubble.

It helps to remember that what God is building is a temple. Here is an illustration. We are told in 1 Kings 6:7 that when the great temple of Solomon was constructed "only blocks dressed at the quarry were used, and no hammer, chisel or any other iron tool was heard at the temple site while it was being built." To my knowledge, no other building in history was ever built in this way. Its construction was so well done it was almost silent. Silently, silently the stones were added, and the building rose.

So it is with the church. We do not hear what is going on inside human hearts as the Holy Spirit creates new life and adds individuals to the temple he is building. We do not even fully realize the part we are playing as we seek to build these other people up by focusing on the important matters, laying aside petty differences, and teaching the Word of God to each of them faithfully. But God is working, and the temple is rising. In the days of the apostles God was adding Gentiles to his church. Paul was his chief instrument in carrying the gospel to them. God added the high and low, slaves and freemen, Greeks, Romans, and barbarians. He added many at the time of the Reformation and in the days of the Great Awakenings and revivals.

He is still building his church today, and we are his workmen, laborers together with Jesus Christ. We have a responsibility to do the work well.

Glory to the Only Wise God

Romans 16:25–27

To the only wise God be glory forever through Jesus Christ! Amen.
—ROMANS 16:27

Think carefully about this last word of the letter. What does it mean to say, "Amen"?

Amen is a wonderfully rich word. It is found in nearly half the languages of the world, and it refers to what is true, firm, or faithful. In its intransitive form it means to be shored up—to be firm, unshaken. It means to be faithful, trustworthy, sure, something that one can lean on or build upon. In this sense it is used as a name for God in Isaiah 65:16, though the New International Version translates it by the word *truth*. The verse says, "Whoever invokes a blessing in the land will do so by the God of truth." But the Hebrew text actually says "by the God of the Amen." It is a way of saying that God is a sure and solid foundation for those who lean upon him. He is utterly reliable.

We use this word at the end of something God says. In other words, when God says something, he begins with "Amen, amen": "What I am about to say is true; pay attention." For our part, we hear the words, repeat them, and then say, "Amen," meaning that we agree with God's declaration. We set our seal to our belief that the Word of God is true and that he is faithful.

That is what Paul is doing as he comes to the end of Romans and offers these last words of doxology. He is setting his seal to God's truth, saying that he believes God's Word. Can you do that? Can you add your "Amen" to what Paul has written?

For my part that is what I am determined to do. There is much in this world that I do not understand. There is much even about the ways of God that I do not understand. But what I do understand I believe, and to God's declaration of these eternal truths I say a hearty, "Amen." "There is no one righteous, not even one" (Rom. 3:10). Amen! "For all have sinned and fall short of the glory of God" (v. 23). Amen! "For the wages of sin is death, but the gift of God is eternal life in Christ Jesus our Lord" (6:23). Amen! "Neither death nor life, neither angels nor demons, neither the present nor the future, nor any powers, neither height nor depth, nor anything else in all creation, will be able to separate us from the love of God that is in Christ Jesus our Lord" (8:38–39). Amen!

"Then all the people said, 'Amen'" (1 Chron. 16:36).

Foolish Things Wisely Chosen
1 Corinthians 1:26–31

But God chose the foolish things of the world to shame the wise.
—*1 Corinthians 1:27*

As you think about what is needed to live a Christian life, to live in a way that is honoring to the Lord Jesus Christ, you naturally feel inadequate to such things; and indeed you are. You say to yourself, *Even with my wisdom I am still foolish; even with my strength I am weak; even with my nobility I feel like a nobody; I still fail to achieve; I still have no status in God's sight.* So you say to yourself, *Of what use am I? How can I be useful?* Each of these questions is good, and the insights are excellent. But at this point God speaks to you further and says, "Yes, yes, all these things are true. It is true that I have not chosen the wise, the mighty, the noble. I have chosen people just like you. But look, even though in yourself you are inadequate, I am adequate. I want to become your wisdom so that, in your newfound wisdom, you can make the wisdom of this world look foolish. I want to become your strength so that, in your new strength, you can tear down strongholds. I want to become your status so that, in your new status, you might stand high and speak my word to those who are without it."

Here I can do no better than direct you to the apostle Paul, the very man who wrote these verses in 1 Corinthians. Here was a man who seemed to have it all—the wisdom of education, the power of a good Roman family, the credentials of a Hebrew birth. But what did this educated rabbi, this powerful figure, this pure-blooded Jew, have to say when he spoke spiritually? He said, "All these things that I once counted as being so important, I learned were actually worse than nothing. For not only did they not help me to God, they were actually a hindrance because I was trusting them rather than trusting Jesus Christ. Moreover, I was using my talents to persecute the church. But God intervened. He spoke from heaven with a blinding light. He said, 'Saul, Saul, why persecutest thou me?' Then he turned my life around. And I learned to count all these things—wisdom, power, and status—as refuse, in order that I might win Christ, and find him to be my all."

Is Christ your all? Is he wisdom to you? He can be. Paul says that he "is made unto us wisdom, and righteousness, and sanctification, and redemption" (v. 30 KJV). Is he your strength? Paul claims "I can do all things through Christ, who strengtheneth me" (Phil. 4:13 KJV). Is he your status? He can be that too. For in him we become children of God and can be all that he wants us to be.

By Revelation
1 Corinthians 2:6–16

But God has revealed it to us by his Spirit.
—*1 Corinthians 2:10*

It is entirely possible that God could give an inspired writing and yet have that writing be unappreciated by us because we do not have the ability to identify with the things that are found there. It is why Paul can say, "No eye has seen, no ear has heard" (v. 9). Even if the words are spoken, even if the words are infallible, even if word by word they come from God, men still do not understand them. Something more is needed. So God in his grace and by the same Spirit that caused the Bible to be written also moves us to understand and accept what is written. If you are a Christian, you have this enabling by God's grace, and it is on that basis alone that you can say, as Paul does in verse 10: "But God has revealed it to us by his Spirit."

What has God revealed? What about the cross? Who would have invented the cross of Jesus Christ as the solution to human sin? Obviously, it would not have entered the mind of any Greek thinker. For, says Paul, they considered it foolishness. To think of the infinite God, the incorporeal God, becoming flesh and dying for us was incomprehensible to the Greek mind. The Jewish people too failed to think of it, for they failed to understand it even when the Lord came. The disciples whom he taught failed to understand it. It was only by the Holy Spirit that it came to them. And yet, what could be more simple—that God should find reconciliation between his love and his justice in this, that God himself in the person of his Son would die and by his death take the penalty for human sin? So God the Father punishes God the Son and thus saves the sinner. Simple? Yes, but also profound, and hidden until God reveals it unto us by his Spirit.

Or again, Paul talks about the church. I mention this because the church is the great mystery that has been hidden—that God should make unto himself one people from all walks of life and from all positions in society, mold them into one, and then should begin to work in that people so that Paul can say that we are fellow workers with God. Who would have guessed that? No one! Yet this has been revealed to us by God's Spirit. It is simple, and at the same time profound.

The Holy Spirit, the emissary of the Lord Jesus Christ, his representative on earth during his absence from us, opens our understanding of such things which God has revealed. As we come to understand the Scriptures we come to know him better and to love him better. By the grace of God we may serve him better also.

Boice, *The Bible Study Hour*, January 1976, 24–27.

Escaping Temptation
1 Corinthians 10:1–13

But when you are tempted, he will also provide a way out.
— *1 CORINTHIANS 10:13*

The way of escape is different in different kinds of temptations. First, there are the sins of the *flesh*. When we think of fleshly sins, we think of drunkenness, overeating, and sexual sins. Yet there are other sins in that category that we do not think of so often, such as laziness. What is the solution? The way of escape for these sins is simply to flee from them. There are some things that we simply must face by running away. If you are an alcoholic, you must stay away from bars. If you are lazy, you must get yourself away from the television set. If you are tempted to sexual sins, you must simply remove yourself from the place of temptation. It is as simple as that.

Second, there are temptations that come to us from the *world*. These are temptations that come to us in order to make us conform to the world's value system. We fall into this whenever we find ourselves striving to be important, whenever we want to be the one who is most noticed. The way of escape for this type of temptation is found in Romans 12:2: "Do not conform any longer to the pattern of this world, but be transformed by the renewing of your mind. Then you will be able to test and approve what God's will is." This tells us that the cure for worldliness is by being gradually transformed from within by the renewing of our minds as we feed upon the Word of God.

Third, some temptation comes to us from the *devil* or, more likely, by demonic influence. How do you overcome the devil? The answer is found in James 4:7: "Submit yourselves, then, to God. Resist the devil, and he will flee from you." There are two key words in that verse. The first is "submit," the second is "resist." If we are to submit ourselves unto God, we must consciously submit our will to his will. That is to be done largely through prayer. On the other hand, resisting is to be done through using the Word of God, the sword of the Spirit. So these two things, prayer and Bible study, are to be central in our lives if we are to be able to resist temptation from this demonic source.

God has provided a way of escape in temptations, and these are the primary provisions: the Word of God and the privilege of coming to him in prayer. When we learn to pray, as the Lord Jesus Christ prayed, and when we know Scripture and learn to apply it as the Lord Jesus Christ applied Scripture, then we will be victorious in our temptations. And glory will come, not to feeble men and women, but to God, "who is faithful."

Boice, *The Bible Study Hour*, January 1976, 32–34.

Start with Love
1 Corinthians 13:1–13

And now these three remain: faith, hope and
love. But the greatest of these is love.
—1 CORINTHIANS 13:13

You may be one who has never known any of these three responses to the
Lord Jesus Christ—neither faith nor hope nor love. You say that you cannot believe, that you have no grounds for hope, that you do not see how you
can love him. If this is your case, may I suggest that you begin with love. And
if you say, "But how can I love?" I answer that the way to come to love him
is to begin with the knowledge that he loves you. That love is shown by his
death for you. Moreover, he commends his love to you by this fact. The book
of Romans says, "But God demonstrates his own love for us in this: While we
were still sinners, Christ died for us" (5:8).

Can you not focus on his death on your behalf and love him for that? I am
convinced that if you truly focus on that death and respond to it—how can
you fail to?—then the matter will not stop there. I am convinced that you will
hear him call your voice and that, when he does, you will recognize him and
respond to him gladly. In that moment, faith will be born in you and hope
will triumph. You will be his forever.

Then too there is an application for those who already are Christians.
You have believed in Christ; you love him. Your hope is centered in him. But
it may have happened, as it does to nearly all of us at one season or another,
that tragedy has come into your life, and faith and hope have both suffered
from it. It may be death, perhaps that of a close friend or loved one. It may
be suffering. It may even be just extremely bad news. The circumstance has
confused you, and you have been wondering if you have ever really believed
as you ought or if your hope for the future was ever a realistic one. If that is
the case, do not despair. It has been the case of many. Instead, allow your love
for Christ, which can never be destroyed by circumstances, to blossom. Draw
near to him. For when you have done so, you will know the sweet communion
that causes even faith and hope to grow also. You will learn to keep your faith
and hope moving in the same direction as your love.

Faith, hope, and love! These three! "But the greatest of these is love."

Boice, *The Bible Study Hour,* March 1977, 18–19.

Victory through Christ
1 Corinthians 15:51–58

Listen, I tell you a mystery: We will not all sleep, but we will all be changed.
—*1 Corinthians 15:51*

When Paul talks about the new body we are going to receive, he begins to think of our bodies' transformation, and it occurs to him that transformation is to be seen not merely in the resurrection of those whose bodies have died, but also in those who will still be living when the Lord comes. Paul calls this a "mystery" because it was not known beforehand. One can imagine his saying, "But now it is known: Jesus is going to return, and when he returns he is going to usher in the consummation of all things. Some will be dead; their bodies will be transformed and raised to meet the Lord in the air. Some will be living; their bodies will be changed, apart from death, so that their status will be exactly the same as those who have died. When that happens, death will be swallowed up in victory, and sin will be defeated."

Paul is not thinking of the kind of victory over death that we talk about when we talk only of Jesus's resurrection. We say that because Jesus was raised from the dead, death was therefore defeated where he was concerned. He will not die again. That is true, but that is not what Paul is saying. He is saying, "True and glorious as that may be, when we talk about the saints being transformed at the final resurrection, there is an even greater truth, because at that time, death will be abolished forever. It will no longer exist."

The conclusion is this: "Therefore, my dear brothers, stand firm. Let nothing move you. Always give yourselves fully to the work of the Lord, because you know that your labor in the Lord is not in vain" (v. 58).

If there is no resurrection, our labor in the Lord *is* in vain. There is no point to it. There is no point in serving a dead Lord, and there is no point in serving other people. But if there is a resurrection, then it makes sense to do what Paul concludes.

Stand firm; you stand upon the rock of God's truth. Let nothing move you; there are things that will try. Give yourself fully to the work of the Lord; your labor is not in vain. So long as I know that—that my labor in the Lord is not in vain—then I will keep at it no matter what the difficulty, no matter what the persecution, no matter what the ridicule. I am going to keep at it no matter what the obstacles may be. The victory does not lie with the world; it lies with Jesus and the kingdom of God.

Boice, *The Christ of the Empty Tomb*, P&R Publishing, 2010, 160–61.

A New Creature

2 Corinthians 5:11–21

Therefore, if anyone is in Christ, he is a new creation.
—2 CORINTHIANS 5:17

As a new creation in Christ, God has planted a new spiritual life within the heart of every Christian, and this spiritual life is the same life that we will be living a thousand years from now in heaven. No child of God will ever enter into the fullness of his relationship with God until he becomes certain that he possesses this new life and that he possesses it forever. As a new creation the Christian has also received a new Spirit. The Holy Spirit enables us to live righteously in this world.

And the Christian has a new master. The thought is expressed significantly in our passage: "that those who live [who have been made alive spiritually] should no longer live [physically] for themselves, but for him who died for them, and was raised again" (v. 15). Do you see the importance of this point? Buddhism has a founder who is an example to his followers. But Gautama died. Islam has a teacher for its founder. But Mohammad died. Christianity has both an example and a teacher in its founder, but Christianity has something more. Christ died but he also rose again. And as a result of his resurrection, every Christian is confronted with a living master, as well as a teacher and example, to whom he owes obedience and whose glory he must exhibit to the world.

The sun rises in the east and sets in the west. And when the sun goes down, the moon comes up. During the night we see the moon and not the sun, and the moon seems to glow in the heavens. But the moon does not glow with its own light. It is seen only by the light of the sun. Here we have an illustration of the Christian's relationship to his Lord. There was a time when our master, the true light, was himself on earth; but ever since his ascension into heaven, we see his light only as it is reflected in the lives of those who acknowledge him as Savior and Lord. But Christians do not always reflect this light with maximum brilliance. Whenever they keep their faces turned toward Jesus, they are "full moon" Christians, and Christ is seen in them. Whenever they turn their faces away, they are "new moon" Christians, and they become indistinguishable from the dark world in which they dwell. There are times when Christians are at the quarter, and it is difficult to tell whether it is a waxing or a waning quarter. But whether they are at the full, at the quarter, or at eclipse, they still are servants of a Master who is the same yesterday, today, and forever, and whose glory it is their responsibility to reflect to those about them.

From an unpublished Watch Night Service, December 31, 1964.

Sufficient Grace

2 Corinthians 12:7–10

My grace is sufficient for you, for my power is made perfect in weakness.
—*2 CORINTHIANS 12:9*

Paul's point here is that grace, which provides the power, is seen in us, not when we are strong, but when we are weak. But if that is so, then, as Paul says, "I will boast all the more gladly about my weaknesses, so that Christ's power may rest on me. That is why, for Christ's sake, I delight in weaknesses, in insults, in hardships, in persecutions, in difficulties. For when I am weak, then I am strong" (vv. 9–10).

Do you see how different this is from triumphalism? This is not triumphalism, that is, glorying in how successful or victorious or favored a Christian I am. It is the very opposite of triumphalism. It is boasting, yes. But it is boasting in our weaknesses because we know that it is only in our weakness, not our strength, that the power and grace of the Lord Jesus Christ can be seen.

Who is it that you want to glorify? Who do you want to praise? If you want to praise yourself (and have others praise you), then tell us what a wonderful Christian you are. Tell us about your triumphs and victories and visions and revelations. But if that is not your objective, if you want to glorify Jesus rather than yourself, if you want other people to praise him, then do what mature believers in Christ have always done. They do not point to themselves. They point to Jesus. They tell others about his grace, his power, his majesty, his sufficiency, his glory. And when they come into the picture themselves, if they do, they confess only that they are sinners saved by grace. If they are called upon to suffer and do suffer, they do it, not by some great force of character within them, but by the grace and power of him who endured even greater suffering for them, even death on a cross.

"My grace is sufficient for you," God says. Is it sufficient? It is a privilege to be able to show others that it is. So instead of boasting, learn to glory in your weaknesses, since it is only in them that the grace of God is made fully known.

Boice, *Amazing Grace*, Tyndale, 1993, 183–84.

A Man of God

Galatians 1:11–24

And they praised God because of me.
— *GALATIANS 1:24*

Paul was a man of God. He had principles, but they were God's principles. This is why he wasn't an obstinate egotist. He was defending the standards that had been taught to him by God. He was also strong but he was strong with God's strength. It was Paul who said in Philippians: "I can do everything through him who gives me strength" (4:13).

What makes a man of God? Why was Paul the man he was? The first chapter of Galatians gives us a threefold answer. A man or woman must first be called of God. His message must be received from God. And he must fill his mind with Scripture. What is the result? Look at verses 23 and 24: "They only heard the report: 'The man who formerly persecuted us is now preaching the faith he once tried to destroy.' *And they praised God because of me.*"

What makes real character? There is a strong temptation in Christian circles to believe that the effectiveness of a minister or a Sunday school teacher or even of ourselves as witnesses to the gospel depends upon our natural abilities. There is no use going into the ministry, we hear, unless the young person has a "gift" with people or an aptitude for study. To be a successful witness, we must be able to speak fluently about spiritual things.

But this is absolutely wrong. Paul had great natural ability, more than you or I will ever have. But before his life had been changed by God, he was a persecutor of the church. Great abilities do not make a great Christian character. What makes a great man of God is his call, his message, and his book. If you have never received that call from God which can entirely change your life and make you live it with an entirely new purpose, you can hear it now. All God wants you to know is that he calls you through Jesus Christ and that you must come to him through Jesus. And if you haven't received a message that you are burning up inside to give, that will make a difference to those who hear it, God will give you a message. He will give it through a serious study of his written Word. With this basis each of us can begin to develop a character like Paul's. And we can say with all the strength of purpose that was his: "I want you to know, brothers, that the gospel I preached is not something that man made up. I did not receive it from any man, nor was I taught it; rather, I received it by revelation from Jesus Christ." And God can be glorified in us.

From an unpublished chapel message at Stony Brook, February 4, 1963.

Gospel Compromise
Galatians 2:11–14

> When Peter came to Antioch, I opposed him to his
> face, because he was clearly in the wrong.
> —GALATIANS 2:11

Here is the reason why Peter was in the wrong or stood condemned. It was not, it must be noted, a case of Peter's simply making an honest mistake. The Peter who had received the vision prior to going to the house of Cornelius and who had defended Paul at the council was not fooled by the arguments of the legalizers. The difficulty was that he gradually gave in to pressure exerted by the legalizers, even though he knew what was right. In other words, Peter played the hypocrite.

Unfortunately, conduct such as Peter's is not inconsequential, neither in his day nor now. So one is not surprised to read that other Jews, including Barnabas, were led away by his dissimulation. If Peter had been a lesser man or less prominent, the defection might have been less serious. But this was Peter, the pillar apostle, the companion of the Lord during his earthly ministry!

What Peter did moved others. It is obvious that any Christian must give heed to his actions and the greater the position or responsibility, the more important those actions become.

Paul has already shown that he opposed Peter to his face because he was wrong, but we are not to think that he did this because he loved exposing error or, even less, because he loved an argument or wanted to enhance his own prestige. Paul's real concern was for the truth of the gospel. It was not a matter of personalities. To the Corinthians he wrote, "What, after all, is Apollos? And what is Paul?" (1 Cor. 3:5). It is not a matter of trivial forms or ceremonies. What was at stake was the gospel itself. Hence, Paul acted out of the very concern that Peter lacked.

This is the second time that Paul has spoken of "the truth of the gospel" (Gal. 2: 5, 14)—the good news that men and women do not become accepted with God because of anything they have done or can do but solely on the basis of God's grace shown in the death and resurrection of Jesus Christ. Moreover, on the basis of this death, all who believe become fully accepted by God and are accepted equally. Peter's conduct compromised this principle, for it implied that there could be a superiority in some Christians based on race or traditions.

It is not enough merely to understand and accept the gospel, as Peter did, nor even to defend it, as he did at Jerusalem. A Christian must also practice the gospel consistently, allowing it to regulate all areas of his conduct.

Boice and Wood, *The Expositor's Bible Commentary: Galatians/Ephesians*, Zondervan, 1995, 40–41.

Justification by Faith Alone

Galatians 2:15–21

> [We] know that a man is not justified by observ-
> ing the law, but by faith in Jesus Christ.
>
> — GALATIANS 2:16

Justify is a forensic term borrowed from the law courts. It means "to declare righteous or innocent." The opposite of "to justify" is "to condemn" or "to pronounce guilty." Such a term involves an objective standard, and since righteousness is understood to be the unique characteristic of God, that standard must be the divine standard. In themselves, all persons fall short of this standard—"For all have sinned and fall short of the glory of God" (Rom. 3:23). But in Christ, God declares all righteous who believe, imputing divine righteousness to them. In this sense, justification expresses the judicial action of God apart from human merit according to which the guilty are pardoned, acquitted, and then reinstated as God's children and as fellow heirs with Jesus Christ.

This experience does not happen automatically to all men. God justifies only as he unites a man or woman to Christ, a union that takes place only through the channel of human faith. Faith is the means, not the source, of justification. Faith is trust. It begins with knowledge, so it is not blind. It builds on facts, so it is not speculation. It stakes its life on the outcome, so it is not impractical. Faith is trusting Christ and proving his promises.

It is also implied in this commitment that a person will turn his back on the only other apparent possibility—the attempt to be justified by works done in obedience to formal statutes from whatever source. The article "the," included in the NIV translation, is not present in the phrases "observing law" or "works of law." This means that Paul's emphasis is not on the Jewish law, the law of Moses, at all, though it includes it, but rather on any system of attempting to please God by good deeds. "Works of law" are "deeds of men."

Paul's threefold repetition of the doctrine of justification by faith in this one verse is important, because it shows the importance the apostle gives to the doctrine. Besides, the three phrases increase in emphasis. The first is general. Paul says, "A man is not justified by observing . . . law, but by faith in Jesus Christ." A man is *any* man, anyone. The second phrase is particular and personal. "We, too, have put our faith in Christ Jesus that we may be justified by faith in Christ and not by observing the law." This statement involves Paul himself, as well as all who stand with him in the faith. The final statement is universal: "By observing the law no one will be justified." The words are literally "all flesh," i.e., mankind without exception.

Boice and Wood, *The Expositor's Bible Commentary: Galatians/Ephesians*, Zondervan, 1995, 42–43.

Our Time to Trust God
Galatians 4:1–7

But when the time had fully come, God sent his Son.
—*GALATIANS 4:4*

There is a fullness of time in which Christ comes to each of us. God comes in the fullness of time to each heart.

Paul referred to this, using the illustration of planting, growth, and harvest. He said in reference to himself and Apollos, "I planted the seed, Apollos watered it, but God made it grow. So neither he who plants nor he who waters is anything, but only God, who makes things grow" (1 Cor. 3:6–7). This is the way it is in evangelism. God begins to work in a heart. He does so through sowing the seed of his Word. At the beginning it may be such a small seed that you hardly know the plant is there. But the Word of God is present and growing. Then somebody else comes along and waters it a little, and there is some more growth. From beginning to end the work is God's who causes each of his ministers to contribute what is needed in the proper fullness of time.

I wonder if that is the way it is with you. There may be somebody who has sown the seed of the gospel in your heart. One person has explained the gospel to you. Another has witnessed to the reality of Christ's power from his or her own experience with God. A third has answered your questions. A minister has taught you from the Bible through faithful exposition. But you have not yet come to the point at which you have made a personal, believing response to Jesus Christ.

I wonder if that time might be now.

What better time than now! I cannot say, in your particular case, that this is the time. But I can warn you against delaying beyond the time God has established. Perhaps God is saying, "Jesus, who came two thousand years ago and was born in a manger, also died on the cross. And the man who died on the cross died for you. He died in your place, for your sin. After that he rose again and now lives for ever and works to draw people just like you to faith in himself as the Savior. I want you to abandon your sinful way of life and follow him."

If God is saying those things to you and is calling you to follow Jesus, whom you have heard about and know a great deal about already, then this is the time, the fullness of time, for you to make a commitment.

Say, "Lord Jesus Christ, I acknowledge my need of you as my Savior and I commit myself to you. I promise to follow you from this time onward and for ever." I hope you will do that if you have never done it before.

Boice, *The King Has Come*, Geanies House, 1992, 109–11.

Spiritual Blessings
Ephesians 1:1–14

> [God] has blessed us . . . with every spiritual blessing in Christ.
> —*EPHESIANS 1:3*

Ephesians 1:4–14 is a listing of the spiritual blessings we have in Christ.

1. *Election* (v. 4). Paul says that "he [that is, God] chose us in him [that is, Christ] before the creation of the world to be holy and blameless in his sight." Election is what gives us a capacity for choosing that we did not possess previously as unregenerate persons. It guarantees that we are being sanctified for holiness. It teaches that "salvation comes from the LORD" (Jonah 2:9).

2. *Adoption* (v. 5). The second spiritual blessing in Christ is adoption. Adoption means becoming God's sons and daughters with all the privileges implied. On this basis we are said to be "heirs of God and co-heirs with Christ" (Rom. 8:17) and have the privilege of bringing all things to God in prayer and of being heard by him.

3. *Redemption* (v. 7). Redemption means being delivered from the slavery of sin by the death of Christ on the cross. Before, we were held captive and could not break free to do God's bidding. We did not even want to. Now we are freed by Jesus's death to serve God.

4. *Forgiveness of sins* (v. 7). Paul links forgiveness of sins to redemption in verse 7. They differ in that redemption means being freed from sin's power, so that it no longer rules over us. Forgiveness means having God wipe the slate clean.

5. *The revelation of God's purpose in history* (vv. 9–10). The disharmony of the world is not to go on forever, for the same God who has predestined us to salvation in Jesus Christ has also predestined all things to be brought together in submission to him.

6. *Sealing by the Holy Spirit* (v. 13). Seals authenticate documents and declare that the promises contained in them are good. This is what the Holy Spirit does for Christians. God's gift of the Holy Spirit is an authentication that believers are truly God's and that none of the promises God has made to them will fail.

7. *An inheritance* (v. 14). Paul terms the Holy Spirit "a deposit guaranteeing our inheritance until the redemption of those who are God's possession." This is a nice turn of phrase. According to this verse, Christians are God's inheritance. But the Holy Spirit, who is God, has been given to us as a down payment on the fullness of the inheritance, which is already ours in Jesus Christ.

What is the situation when we are "in" him? We have "every spiritual blessing" and so praise God the Father, as Paul himself does, exuberantly. We will ask for our daily bread here and other things besides. But if we suffer want here, in the final analysis it will be all right, because we still possess every spiritual blessing "in the heavenly realms."

Boice, *Ephesians*, Baker, 1997, 10–13.

But God

Ephesians 2:1–10

> But . . . God.
> —EPHESIANS 2:4

Our position as sinners (apart from God) is hopeless for three reasons. First, we are "*dead* in [our] transgressions and sins" (v. 1). We are no more able to help ourselves spiritually than a corpse is able to improve its condition. Second, we are *enslaved* by sin. Although we are dead in sin so far as our ability to respond to God is concerned, we are nevertheless alive enough to be quite active in the practice of wickedness. Third, we are under God's just sentence for our transgressions so that we are "by nature objects of wrath" (v. 3).

But God! Here is where the beauty and wonder of the Christian gospel comes in. We were hopelessly lost in wickedness. But God has intervened to save us and he has saved us by intervening sovereignly and righteously in each of these areas.

Notice how this works out. We were dead in sins, but God "made us alive with Christ even when we were dead in transgressions" (v. 5). Our experience as Christians is like that of Jesus's friend Lazarus. We were dead to any godly influence. But God can awaken the dead. Like Lazarus, we have heard the Lord calling us to "come out" (John 11:43); his voice brought forth life in us, and we have responded, emerging from our spiritual tomb. Now life is no longer as it was. Life is itself new, and in addition we have a new Master and a new standard of righteous living to pursue.

Again, not only were we dead in our sins, we were also enslaved by them. Even though we might have desired to do better, we could not. Instead our struggles to escape only drew us down, plunging us deeper and deeper into sin's quicksand. But God! God has not only called us back to life; he has also "raised us up with Christ and seated us with him in the heavenly realms in Christ Jesus" (Eph. 2:6). There are no slaves in heaven. So if we have been raised up with Christ and been made to sit in the heavenly realms in him, it is as free men and women. Sin's shackles have been broken, and we are freed to act righteously and serve God effectively in this world.

Third, God has dealt with the wrath question. In our sins we are indeed "objects of wrath" (v. 3). But since Jesus has suffered in our place for our sin and we have been delivered from it, we are no longer under wrath. Instead we are objects of "the incomparable riches of [God's] grace, expressed in his kindness to us in Christ Jesus" (v. 7).

The words "but God" show what God has done. If you understand those two words—"but God"—they will save your soul. If you recall them daily and live by them, they will transform your life completely.

Boice, *Ephesians*, Baker, 1997, 51–54.

No Barrier

Ephesians 2:11–22

For he himself is our peace, who has made the two one.
—EPHESIANS 2:14

Not only is fellowship with the Father restored, but fellowship between estranged human beings also—if they are in Christ. Jesus's death for sin opened the way to God for all who will come to God by him. And since the greater barrier (between God and man) is down, there is no need for the lesser barriers (between individuals). In fact, they inevitably fall with the large one.

The reason is that the veil between ourselves and God drops only for those who are in Christ. And if we are in Christ, then there can never be a barrier between us and others who are also in Christ, otherwise Christ would be divided. If we are in him, we are in the same place. We are members of the one body, and peace has been restored between all who are members of it.

Consider two points.

First, if you are in Christ, then in God's sight you are one with every other believer—whether Jew or Gentile, male or female, bond or free—regardless of any distinction whatever. Therefore, you must act like that. You may not see eye to eye with every other Christian on everything. But you must not break with them! You must realize that regardless of your differences of opinion, the unity that you have with them is greater than the unity you will ever have with anyone else in the world, even if the unbeliever is of the same class, race, nationality, sex (or whatever) as you are. Your duty is to live in harmony with these brothers and sisters in Christ, and to let the world know that you are members of one spiritual family. That in itself should be a large portion of your witness.

Second, if you are not yet "in Christ," you should learn that your most basic problem is to be found in your personal relationship to Jesus Christ. There is an objective side to Christ's work. It is described as his "making peace" between men and "reconcil[ing] both . . . to God through the cross" (vv. 15, 16). It is what Jesus did on Calvary by his death. But there is a subjective side as well. It is the part in which we are joined to him by faith as we hear and respond to the gospel. This is why verse 17 speaks of preaching: "He came and preached peace to you who were far away and peace to those who were near."

So the final question is this: Are you in him? If not, you remain divided from countless other human beings and, what is much worse, from God himself. If you come to him, he will remove the barrier and make you a part of that new humanity that he is uniting in himself.

Boice, *Ephesians*, Baker, 1997, 86–87.

The Great Drama

Ephesians 3:7–13

His intent was that now, through the church, the manifold wisdom of God should be made known.
—EPHESIANS 3:10

Here in a nutshell is what I think the purpose of history is, as demonstrated in the lives of those who have been saved from sin by Jesus.

Instead of annihilating Satan when he rebelled, God, to show his "manifold wisdom," took an entirely different path: "I have already determined to create a race called man and I know in advance, because I know all things, that Satan will seduce him from my righteousness and plunge him into misery. Satan will think he has won. But while Satan is doing that—turning the human race against me and setting individual human beings against one another and even against themselves—I will begin to create a new people who will glory in doing what is right, even when it is not popular, and who will delight in pleasing me, even when they suffer for it. Satan will say, 'Your people serve you only because you protect them, only because you provide for them materially.' But here and there in a great variety of ways, I will allow them to be greatly abused and persecuted, and I will show by their reactions that not only will they continue to praise me in their suffering, and thus bring glory to my name, but they will even be happier in their sufferings than Satan's people will be with their maximum share of human prestige and possessions."

So God let history unfold like a great drama upon a cosmic stage. The angels are the audience. We are the actors. Satan is there to do everything he can to resist and thwart God's purposes. This drama unfolds across the centuries as Adam and Eve, Noah, Abraham, Moses, David, Isaiah, John the Baptist, Jesus, Peter, Paul, and all the other *dramatis personae* of Christian history, both the great persons and the minor persons, are brought on stage to play the part God has assigned them and speak words that come from hearts that love him. Adam proved that God's way is the best way and he repented of his sin and trusted in the coming of Jesus. So did Eve and Noah and all the others. All these endured as seeing by faith him who is invisible, and they looked beyond the distresses of this life for their reward.

Now, you and I are the players in this drama. Satan is attacking, and the angels are straining forward to look on. Are they seeing the "manifold wisdom" of God in you as you go through your part and speak your lines? They must see it, for it can be seen in you alone. It is there—where you work and play and think and speak—that the meaning and end of history is found.

Boice, *Ephesians*, Baker, 1997, 105–6.

A Wondrous Prayer

Ephesians 3:14–21

To know this love that surpasses knowledge.
—EPHESIANS 3:19

If Christ's love surpasses knowledge, how are we to grasp or know it? Although we cannot exhaust the love of Christ by our knowledge, we can nevertheless know this love truly. It is the same with the knowledge of God generally. We cannot know exhaustively, but we can know truly. So although, in the same way, we cannot know all of Christ's love for us, we can know that what we perceive as Christ's love is truly love. The love of Christ that we know at the beginning of our Christian life is the same love that we will know (though more fully) at the end. And we are to grow in our awareness of that love, particularly through the routine hardships, sufferings, and persecutions of life.

The most audacious part of the prayer is that believers may be filled to the measure of the fullness of God. By the phrase "fullness of God," Paul seems to be praying that we (and all other Christians) may be filled up to or unto all the fullness that is in God himself.

How can this be? Here is the highest rung of the ladder, the highest step of the stairs. We are to be filled with all God's fullness, an infinite thing. But then, we have all eternity (an infinite time) to be so filled. I think Paul is praying that we will be filled and filled and filled and filled and filled—and so on forever, as God out of his infinite resources increasingly pours himself out into those sinful but now redeemed creatures he has rescued through the work of Christ.

I do not know how God is going to do that, and I will tell you something interesting: even though he talks about it, I do not think Paul understood it either. I say that because of the benediction that immediately follows this prayer. It is "to him who is able to do immeasurably more than all we ask or imagine, according to his power that is at work within us . . ." (v. 20). When Paul says "we" he includes himself. He is saying that even he, the great apostle, cannot fully understand or even imagine all that God is going to do for us. But Paul does know that God can do it. And not only is God *able* to do it, he is able to do it "immeasurably," which means indefinitely.

My mind stops at that, and I think that is where Paul's mind stopped too. Beyond that top step on the staircase is infinity. It remains only to say, as Paul does, "to him be glory in the church and in Christ Jesus throughout all generations, for ever and ever! Amen" (v. 21).

Boice, *Ephesians*, Baker, 1997, 111–12.

Spiritual Gifts
Ephesians 4:7–16

But to each one of us grace has been given as Christ apportioned it.
—*EPHESIANS 4:7*

How can you discover what your gifts are?

First, *study what the Bible has to say about spiritual gifts.* Without a knowledge of what God's Word teaches in this area, we can easily be led to desire experiences that are not his will for us or begin to think of spiritual gifts in secular terms. As we study the Bible's teaching, we must be careful to discern God's purpose in giving spiritual gifts. It is for the growth of the body and not merely personal growth or satisfaction.

Second, *you must pray.* This is not a matter to be taken lightly or one in which we may feel free to trust our own judgment. We may find ourselves wanting a gift that exalts our sense of self-importance but that God does not have in mind for us. We may find ourselves resisting the gift he has for us. Thus, we must lay the matter before the Lord in serious, soul-searching prayer and ask him, as he speaks through his Word, to show us his gift for us.

Third, *make a sober assessment of your spiritual strengths and abilities.* If we do not do this on the basis of a careful study of the Word of God and through prayer, we will be misled. But if we have first sought the wisdom and mind of God, we can then go back and look at ourselves through spiritual eyes.

We can ask, What do I like to do? This is not a sure guide to what our gifts are, but it is one indication, since God's leading is always toward that for which he has prepared us and which we therefore naturally find enjoyable and satisfying.

We can ask, What am I good at? If you are asking to fulfill a certain ministry in the church but are constantly failing and feel frustrated, it is likely that you are working in the wrong area and have assessed your gifts wrongly. If you are seeing spiritual fruit from your efforts, you are probably on the right track.

Finally, *seek the wisdom of other Christians where your gifts are concerned.* Where the church functions properly, one of the things that should happen is that others with the gift of insight or wisdom should be able to sense what your gifts are and point them out in terms of the needs of the particular congregation. Others are almost always more objective about ourselves than we are. We must cultivate the ability to listen to these other members of the family of God and follow their guidance as far as we are able. If others tell us of our gifts, we are at least freed from the presumption of assuming we have gifts that actually we do not have.

Boice, *Ephesians*, Baker, 1997, 143–44.

Love That Forgives

Ephesians 4:25–32

Forgiving each other, just as in Christ God forgave you.
—*EPHESIANS 4:32*

L ove is to be forgiving. Since God the Father forgave us through the work
of Christ, we are to forgive one another. This is love's nature.

This link between God's forgiveness of us and our forgiveness of others is
important, because it is only through knowing ourselves to be forgiven that we
are set free to forgive others lovingly. People are in desperate need of forgiveness. Some years ago I was talking with a friend who is a psychiatrist, and he
said, "As far as I am concerned, most of what a psychiatrist does is directly
related to forgiveness. People come to him with problems; they feel guilty about
their part in them; they are seeking forgiveness. In effect, they confess their
sins to the counselor and find that he forgives them. Then a pattern is set up
in which they can show their change of heart in tangible ways toward others."

That is what we have in Jesus Christ—forgiveness—and because we find
forgiveness there, we can in turn be forgiving. God's forgiveness is not a mere
overlooking of sin, as though he said, "Well, boys will be boys (or girls will
be girls). We'll overlook it for now; just don't let it happen again." God takes
sin with such seriousness that he deals with it fully at the cross, and it is on
that basis—the death of Jesus—that we can know we are forgiven.

Do you know this, really know it? So long as you think you are a pretty
good person who does not really need to be forgiven, you will naturally have
a very hard time loving and forgiving others. But if you know yourself to have
been a sinner under God's just wrath, all that is changed. God says that in his
sight even the best of us is vile to the extreme (see Rom. 3:10–18).

If we see ourselves through his eyes, knowing our vile rebellion against
his love and moral standards and yet finding ourselves forgiven on the basis
of Christ's death for us, then we will inevitably love and forgive others. For
nobody can act as badly toward us as we have acted toward God, and yet he
has forgiven us.

If we are not forgiving in our love, we really do not know the extent of
God's forgiveness of us. We still consider ourselves to be better than we are.
But if we see ourselves as forgiven sinners, then we will be set free to love oth-
ers in imitation of God.

Boice, *Ephesians*, Baker, 1997, 173–74.

Spiritual Warfare
Ephesians 6:10–18

Put on the full armor of God.
—*EPHESIANS 6:11*

The battle of the Christian is not simply against particularly evil men and women. Rather it involves "the spiritual forces of evil in the heavenly realms" (v. 12). The spiritual forces against which we struggle are not holy or beneficent. They are wicked and destructive. And their work of evil and error will carry the world into a new dark age unless Christians stand firm.

Thus, Paul admonishes us to "put on the full armor of God" and "stand [our] ground" against Satan. Where did Paul get his thoughts about this armor? I am inclined to think that in this case, as in many others, Paul got his ideas from the Word of God. He would have known that in Isaiah 59 there is a picture of God putting on his own armor. Part of it says, "He put on righteousness as his breastplate, and the helmet of salvation on his head" (v. 17).

This means that when Paul speaks of the "armor of God," he is not thinking of it only as the armor that God supplies, but rather God's own armor, that which he himself wears.

What do we need if we are to fight against Satan? Is it truth? Yes, we need truth, but not just any truth. We need God's own truth: the truth of God, which we find in Scripture. Do we need righteousness? Yes, but not just human righteousness. We need the righteousness of God. The gospel? It is God's gospel, God's Good News. Peace? It is God's peace. Faith? It is faith from God, a fruit of the Holy Spirit (Gal. 5:22). Is it salvation? God is salvation. We must be armed with him.

Furthermore, everything that is given to us to make our victory possible is from Christ. Is it truth (Eph. 6:14)? He is the truth; he is the one who said, "I am the way and the truth and the life. No one comes to the Father except through me" (John 14:6). Is it righteousness (Eph. 6:14)? He is our righteousness. Paul writes, "Christ . . . has become for us wisdom from God—that is, our righteousness, holiness and redemption" (1 Cor. 1:30). Is it the gospel (Eph. 6:15)? The gospel is the gospel of Christ (see Mark 1:1). Is it faith (Eph. 6:16)? It is faith in him (Gal. 2:20). Salvation (Eph. 6:17)? Christ is our salvation; he achieved it by his death on the cross (see Acts 4:10–12). Even prayer is by the channel that he has opened up for us (Heb. 10:19–20).

Not one of us can stand against the spiritual forces of evil in our own strength—not even for a moment. But in Christ, armed with God's armor, we can fight on to victory.

Boice, *Ephesians*, Baker, 1997, 228, 240.

Finishing His Work
Philippians 1:3–11

He who began a good work in you will carry it on to
completion until the day of Christ Jesus.
—*PHILIPPIANS 1:6*

When I was in grade school, I spent a number of summers at a Christian camp in Canada. One summer I spent several hours watching one of the campers learn to climb a telephone pole. This boy was one of these campers who partially pay for their vacation by working; and since the camp needed more adequate wiring, he had the job of stringing the wires. For that he had to learn to climb a pole.

The secret of climbing a telephone pole is to learn to lean back, allowing your weight to rest on the broad leather belt that encircles you and the pole, allowing your spikes to dig into the pole at a broad angle. Climbing a pole is easy—as long as you lean back. Of course, if you fail to lean back and pull yourself toward the pole, then your spikes will not dig in and you'll slip. It isn't very pleasant to slip because the pole is covered with splinters that easily dig into your body.

At first my friend would not lean at all, and as a result he never got off the ground. The spikes simply would not go into the wood. It was frustrating. After a while he learned to lean back a bit and got started, but as soon as he was a few feet off the ground he became afraid and pulled himself close to the pole. Down he would go with a bump, getting covered with splinters in the process. This practice went on until he learned that he had to lean fully into the belt that held him. When he learned this, he began to climb.

It is the same in the Christian life. God wants you to climb. This is his purpose in saving you. He wants you to rise to Christ's own stature. What is more, he is going to insist on it. He is going to teach you to climb by resting on him. There will be times when you think that you can hold on better by grasping the pole than by leaning on the belt, and when you do, you will slip spiritually and God will let you get covered with splinters. He will do it because he knows that is the only way you will learn to trust him, and to trust him is the only way to climb. What is more, he will keep at you; he will not let you quit. "He who began a good work in you will carry it on to completion until the day of Christ Jesus."

Boice, *Philippians*, Baker, 2000, 37–38.

No Disappointments
Philippians 1:12–30

Christ will be exalted in my body, whether by life or by death.
—*PHILIPPIANS 1:20*

Think of the scope of this statement in verse 20. In the first place, Paul knew that Christ would be magnified. Paul lived in an environment in which the pagan gods were worshiped and all power seemed to be on the side of pagan Rome. But he knew that Christ would ultimately be exalted and would rule in power until he had crushed all enemies beneath his feet. Second, Paul knew that God's determination to exalt his Son also extends to those who are united to him by faith. Paul did not merely say that Christ would be magnified. He said that Christ would be magnified in him. If you are a Christian, do you know that God the Father is determined to exalt his Son in you? Third, Paul recognized that Christ would be magnified in him whether he lived or died. This means Paul was so confident that God's will for him was perfect that he was able to accept it willingly even if it meant death.

When life is smooth, it is easy to say, "All things work together for good to them that love God" (Rom. 8:28 KJV). It is easy when you have everything you want, but it is not so easy at the grave or in the face of bitter disappointment and pain. If you are to have confidence in God in such moments, you must learn to trust him in the small disappointments of life.

I know a couple who are extremely fond of children and who early in their courtship planned to have a large family. They were married, and not long afterward there came sickness and an operation that left the woman unable to bear children. I have never met a couple for whom this was a greater disappointment and consequently a greater opportunity for bitterness. But they accepted it from God as his perfect will for them and asked instead that they might act as spiritual parents for those who needed them. God blessed them in this way, and they befriended many lonely people. Many became Christians. When I last saw them God had used them to found three different Christian congregations. In a very real sense they became a father and mother to many dozens of young Christians. They testify they have not been disappointed in God.

So it will be with you. You may not see it now. You may resist God's will and drown yourself in pity, even in legitimate sorrow. But the day is coming when you will see it as you stand before your loving heavenly Father. You will look back from a vantage point in eternity millions of years from now and will confess that God knew what he was doing in your life. You will see that Christ was certainly exalted and you will not be disappointed.

Boice, *Philippians*, Baker, 2000, 66–67.

Every Knee Shall Bow
Philippians 2:5–11

Every tongue [will] confess that Jesus Christ is
Lord, to the glory of God the Father.
—*PHILIPPIANS 2:11*

H ere we read that the confession that will be made—that Jesus Christ is Lord—will result in glory to God the Father.

This is not true of any honor given to humans. If you glorify human beings, you dishonor God. You do so if you exalt yourself or your merits as a means of salvation, or exalt human beings as mediators between yourself and God, as saints who win God's favor for you, or exalt human wisdom as that which is ultimately able to solve the world's problems, or place your hopes for the future in psychiatry, science, systems of world government, or whatever it may be. If you exalt the ability of mankind in any of these ways, you dishonor God, who declares that all of our works are tainted by sin and that we will never solve our own problems or the problems of others except by turning to Christ and depending upon his power to do it. The only way to honor God is to give honor to Jesus Christ.

Think of the terms by which we are privileged to give glory to Jesus. Think of his names. Jesus Christ is the Wonderful Counselor, the Mighty God, the Everlasting Father, the Prince of Peace. He is the Messiah, the Lord, the First and the Last, the Beginning and the End, the Alpha and Omega, the Ancient of Days, King of Kings and Lord of Lords, God with us, God our Savior, the only wise God our Savior, the Lord who is, who was, who is to come, the Almighty. He is the Door of the sheep, the Chief Shepherd, the Good Shepherd, the Shepherd and Bishop of our souls, a Lamb without spot or blemish, a Lamb slain before the foundation of the world. He is the Logos, the Light of the World, the Light of Life, the Tree of Life, the Word of Life, the Bread that came down from heaven, the Resurrection, the Way, the Truth, and the Life. He is Immanuel, God with us, he is the Rock, the Bridegroom, the Wisdom of God, our Redeemer. He is the Beloved. He is the head over all things, which is the church. He is the one who is altogether lovely, the one in whom the Father is well pleased.

Is Jesus Christ these things to you? He can be. He deserves to be. If he is these things to you, then in your own heart you praise him and in giving him glory you give glory to God our heavenly Father.

Boice, *Philippians*, Baker, 2000, 139–40.

Spiritual Sensitivity
Philippians 3:1–11

The righteousness that comes from God and is by faith.
—*PHILIPPIANS 3:9*

Will you accept God's verdict upon your goodness and turn to him for the righteousness he gives you by grace? Paul did this, for he says that his desire was to be found in Christ, not having his own righteousness, which is of the law, but having that which is through faith in Christ—righteousness from God by faith.

Quite a few years ago a man was brought into the emergency room in McKeesport, Pennsylvania, with a dislocated spine. My father, who was an orthopedic surgeon, was on duty, and he saw at a glance that the man had been partially paralyzed. He had been in a serious accident, and there was much wrong with him. His legs had been broken and there were deep lacerations over much of his body, but he could not feel these things because a nerve had been pinched by the spine. My father began to operate on him using a local anesthetic and occasionally asked if the man could feel anything from his injuries. The questioning went like this: "Do you feel anything?" "No." "Do you feel anything now?" "No." At last my father came to a piece of splintered bone that was pressing on the nerves. This time, as he removed the bone and asked, "Can you feel anything?" the answer came back loudly, "Yes, yes, I can feel it!" It was a cry of pain. But it was a pleasing cry, for it was the first step in the man's complete recovery.

It may be the same for you. God's verdict upon the human race includes all people—the hedonist, the moralist, the most religious person, and you, whatever you may be. It is one that declares all human righteousness unable to satisfy the righteous standards of God. You are included in that judgment, but you may not be able to feel that the things God is saying about you are true. Are you sensitive to God's verdict? Do you feel the truth of his statements? If not, there is a spiritual disorder in your life and God must begin to operate on it before you will come to him.

Perhaps he is doing that now! You may be feeling the most acute spiritual pain because of it, but you must know that your new sensitivity is the first step in your spiritual recovery. Your recovery will take place completely as you come to God to receive a righteousness that comes from God himself and is entirely untainted by sin. That righteousness comes by faith in Jesus Christ. You must come to God through him.

Boice, *Philippians*, Baker, 2000, 176–77.

No Regrets

Philippians 3:12–21

I press on to take hold of that for which Christ Jesus took hold of me.
— PHILIPPIANS 3:12

Mark Twain's *The Prince and the Pauper* tells the story of how a prince and a pauper exchange places. The pauper, mistaken for the prince, is taken to live in the palace, while the prince is turned back to the poor streets of London where he suffers great indignities before he eventually regains his rightful place and the throne.

In the same way, the Lord Jesus Christ took on our poverty, while we have been clothed in his finery. The Bible says, "For you know the grace of our Lord Jesus Christ, that though he was rich, yet for your sakes he became poor, so that you through his poverty might become rich" (2 Cor. 8:9). He became poor as we were so that we might be clothed in his righteousness. He endured suffering and death that we might become like him—sons of God and coheirs with him of God's glory.

It is true that the paupers must give up their rags, but there is no comparison between our rags and God's glory. Jesus has told us that there is nothing given up in this life that is not replaced a hundredfold by spiritual treasure, not only in this world but in eternity also.

Years ago the son of a wealthy American family graduated from Yale University and decided to go out to China as a missionary for Jesus Christ. His name was William Borden. Many of his friends thought him foolish to give up so much of this world's goods and his future to go there. But Borden loved the Lord Jesus Christ, and he wished to serve him. After only a short time on the field, and before he even reached China, Borden contracted a fatal disease and died. He had given up everything to follow Jesus. But at his bedside his friends found a note that he had written as he lay dying: "No reserve, no retreat, and no regrets." Borden had given up everything but he had found a treasure that was beyond words.

Perhaps there is something that God has been asking you to lay aside in order that you might be a more effective witness for him. I do not know what it is. The thing that is a hindrance for one disciple is often entirely different for another. But whatever it is, you know it. At this point in your life, for you it is the touchstone of your discipleship. Will you cast it aside to follow Jesus? If you do, you will grow in your Christian discipleship, and God will bring great blessing into your life and through you also into the lives of others.

Boice, *Philippians*, Baker, 2000, 194–95.

The Promise of Peace

Philippians 4:4–7

> In everything, by prayer and petition, with thanks-
> giving, present your requests to God.
> —*PHILIPPIANS 4:6*

God invites us to place our earnest requests before him. This is God's cure for anxiety. God invites you to place your request about these things that trouble you before him. The promise is that the peace of God will keep your heart and mind through Christ Jesus.

Notice that these verses do not say we shall necessarily receive the things we ask for. We would expect the passage to say, "Present your requests to God, and God will fulfill your requests." Instead it says, "And the peace of God, which transcends all understanding, will guard your hearts and your minds in Christ Jesus" (v. 7). Our prayers are often in error, and we pray for things that are not good for us. God does not promise to give us these things. All things work together for *good* to them that love God. However, God does promise to give a supernatural peace to those who share their real needs with him.

Paul was not recommending something for others that he had not found true for himself. Paul too had had this experience. Do you remember the prayer that Paul wrote in Romans 15:31–32? Paul was in Corinth and was about to go on to Jerusalem with the collection from the gentile churches. After that he had planned to travel to Rome as an ambassador of the Christian gospel. He asked prayer for three things:

1. "that I may be rescued from the unbelievers in Judea"
2. "that my service in Jerusalem may be acceptable to the saints"
3. "that by God's will I may come to you with joy and together with you be refreshed"

How were Paul's requests answered? We do not know every aspect of God's answers but we know that Paul's first request was not fulfilled literally. Paul fell into the hands of unbelievers and spent two years in prison in Caesarea as a result, although his life was spared. We have no information about his second request—that his collection might be received willingly by the saints in Judea—but there is no reason to think Paul received a warm welcome from anyone. Finally, we know that Paul's third request—for a joyous journey to Rome—was fulfilled, if it was fulfilled, only after long delays and through much hardship. When Paul arrived in Rome at last, he arrived as a prisoner in chains.

God certainly did not answer Paul's requests as Paul intended. But God did answer, and he answered exactly as Paul indicates in his words about prayer to the Philippians. He answered by giving Paul peace. Paul knew God's peace even in the most difficult of earthly circumstances and he writes out of these circumstances to tell us also to make requests of God, our heavenly Father.

Boice, *Philippians*, Baker, 2000, 242–43.

The Power of Remembering

Philippians 4:10–20

Not one church shared with me in the matter of giving and receiving, except you only.
—*PHILIPPIANS 4:15*

You only! Not only were the Philippians distinguished by the fact that they
had remembered Paul in his need—that was significant—they had also
been the *only* ones to remember him.

There is always a special aura about someone who does something for you
when only that one has remembered to do it. In his vastly successful book *How
to Win Friends and Influence People*, Dale Carnegie has a section in which he
tells of some of the devices he developed for pleasing business acquaintances.
One of them was to learn their birthdays. Each year the acquaintances would
receive birthday cards from Carnegie. In most cases he was the only one outside of the immediate family who had remembered the man's birthday. The
resulting goodwill was staggering.

I believe that if Dale Carnegie could do that for secular ends to win friends
and influence people, Christians ought to be able to do the same type of thing
for spiritual ends and to do so sacrificially to win them for Christ.

Do you want real joy in this world, real fruit in your Christian ministry?
If so, let me suggest this. Instead of wondering to yourself, as you often do,
why people do not treat you better or remember things that are important
to you, seek for ways in which you can help them, particularly in those areas
in which only you know the problem. God will show you how. The other
person will think that no one understands his need or no one is aware of his
problem. Then your gift or your word of encouragement will come. He will
be overjoyed; and if he is a Christian, he will see it as another way in which
God uses people as channels of his faithful provision and blessing.

I cannot tell you who the person is whom you could help. I cannot tell you
what the circumstances will be or even what you can do. That will vary. You
will have to find it out for yourself. It might be a person in your own family with
a unique need, perhaps one of your children who desperately needs someone
to do something special for him or her, or your wife or husband who needs
understanding. It might be someone at work who thinks that no one cares
about him. It might be someone at church. It might be a stranger. It might be
a financial need. It might be a word of encouragement. Whatever it is, God
will help you to find it if you ask him. And he will give you great joy in being
the one who, like the Philippians, did not forget, but remembered.

Boice, *Philippians*, Baker, 2000, 254–55.

Grace, Seasoned with Salt

Colossians 4:2–6

Let your conversation be always full of grace, seasoned with salt.
—COLOSSIANS 4:6

What should the Christian's conversation be like? This verse suggests five characteristics.

1. *Our words should be kind.* God is kind to us. Therefore, we should be kind when we speak to other people. God's words are gracious words. Ours should be gracious also. Words do hurt. Sometimes words kill. So do not harm by your words. Speak kindly.

2. *Our speech should be serious.* I do not mean by this that Christians should be humorless or grim. We are never told that Jesus laughed, but we know he was witty and that he was an enjoyable person to be with. Yet Jesus was not frivolous either, was he? He never engaged in stupid or mindless conversations. He could enjoy life and have a good time. But he also knew that what we say is important and that spiritual matters are of the utmost importance. Therefore, when speaking, Jesus always seemed to have the spiritual well-being of other people uppermost in his mind.

3. *Our comments should be discerning.* This is what Paul is speaking about when he tells us to "make the most of every opportunity" (v. 5). Not every moment of our day contains opportunities for sharing the gospel or speaking a timely or encouraging word. On the other hand, there are many more opportunities to speak about things that matter than most of us are conscious of, and a discerning person will pick up on them.

4. *Our statements should be wise.* How to speak, when to speak, and when not to speak are all matters that involve wisdom. But when we think of our conversations being wise, we should also think of the content of what we say and how true wisdom is found not in the world's insights but in the Bible. True wisdom comes from God through the instruction in the Bible, and the conversations of Christians should be filled with it.

5. *Our conversation should be interesting.* In Paul's reference to "seasoned with salt," he is alluding to salt's ability to contribute flavor to something that might otherwise be insipid. Is your conversation like that? Is it interesting? I am afraid that many Christians are dull in what they say because they are not thinking much about important matters. Yet it is also true that the most interesting of all people are Christians, particularly if they are studying God's Word and learning to think about life as Christians.

Let this be your daily prayer: "May the words of my mouth and the meditation of my heart be pleasing in your sight, O LORD, my Rock and my Redeemer" (Ps. 19:14).

Boice, *Amazing Grace*, Tyndale, 1993, 220–27.

Day of Judgment

1 Thessalonians 4:13–5:11

For the Lord himself will come down from heaven, with a loud command.
—*1 Thessalonians 4:16*

Christ's coming will be a joy for Christians, who will be raised to meet him. But it will also mean the beginning of Christ's judgments for those who have spurned the gospel.

Christians acknowledge this truth every time they recite the Apostles' Creed, for they say that Jesus will come again from heaven "to judge the living and the dead." This sobering fact tells us that history has an end and that this end involves accountability. We shall answer for what we have done, and we shall all be judged either on the basis of our own righteousness, which will condemn us, or on the basis of the perfect righteousness of him who is our Savior. Unfortunately, some will not face this reality and so go on in blissful ignorance of the day of reckoning.

Jesus spoke of this shortly before his crucifixion. In the sermon given on the Mount of Olives in the middle of his last week in Jerusalem, Jesus used three gripping parables to teach what the final judgment would be like for such people: the ten maidens who had been invited to a wedding banquet, the three servants left by their master to invest his money, and the separation of the sheep from the goats (see Matthew 25).

Each of these parables, though quite different from the others in detail, is nevertheless one with them in its essential features. In each case, there is a sudden return of the Lord, which demands an accounting. In each case, there are some who are prepared for his coming and others who are not. In each case, there are rewards and judgments. Most remarkable of all—and it is this for which I have recounted these parables—in each case, the lost are totally amazed at the outcome. The foolish maidens are astounded that the bridegroom will not open the door to them. The wicked and lazy servant clearly expected the master to be pleased with his zero-growth performance. The goats cannot believe that they have actually rejected Jesus.

Thus it will be with our generation. We have more opportunities to learn about Christ in our day than ever before in human history. The call has gone forth, "Behold the man! Look to this one for salvation! He loves you! He died for you! He rose again! Turn from your sin and place your trust in him as your Savior!" But many go blithely on and will be overwhelmed in the day of God's reckoning.

Today is the day of God's grace. The wisdom of the just in this day consists, as Paul expressed it, in knowing nothing among men except "Jesus Christ and him crucified" (1 Cor. 2:2).

Boice, *Foundations of the Christian Faith*, InterVarsity, 1986, 711–13.

Why Christ Became Man
1 Timothy 2:1–7

Christ Jesus . . . gave himself a ransom for all.
—1 TIMOTHY 2:5–6

The death of Christ on the cross is the true meaning of the incarnation. Christmas by itself is no gospel. The life of Christ is no gospel. Even the resurrection is no gospel. For the Good News is that sin has been dealt with, that Jesus has suffered its penalty for us and as our representative so that we might never have to suffer it, and that therefore there is nothing left for all who should believe on him but heaven.

Any gospel that talks merely of the Christ-event, meaning the incarnation without the atonement, is a false gospel. Any gospel that talks about the love of God without at the same time pointing out that this love led him to pay the ultimate price for sin in the person of his Son on the cross is a false gospel. The only true gospel is the gospel of the Mediator, who gave himself for our salvation.

Furthermore, just as there can be no gospel without the atonement as the reason for the incarnation, so also there can be no Christian life without it. Without the atonement the incarnation theme easily becomes a kind of deification of the human and leads to arrogance and self-advancement. With the atonement the true message of the life of Christ, and therefore also of the life of the Christian man or woman, is humility and self-sacrifice for the obvious needs of others. The Christian life is not indifference to those who are hungry or sick or suffering from some other lack. It is not contentment with our own abundance, whether that is the abundance of middle-class living with its home and cars and clothes and vacations, or whether it is the abundance of education or even the spiritual abundance of good churches, Bibles, Bible teaching, or Christian friends and acquaintances. Rather, it is the awareness that others lack these things and that we must therefore sacrifice many of our interests in order to identify with them and thus bring them increasingly into the abundance we enjoy.

Paul wrote of the incarnation, "For ye know the grace of our Lord Jesus Christ, that, though he was rich, yet for your sakes he became poor, that ye through his poverty might be rich" (2 Cor. 8:9 KJV). But this is also a statement of the atonement and of the Christian life. In fact, it occurs in a chapter in which Paul is speaking about the duty of the Christians at Corinth to give of their money for the relief of less fortunate brethren who lived in Judea. We will live for Christ fully only when we are willing to be impoverished, if necessary, in order that others might be helped.

Remember the Resurrection

2 Timothy 2:1–13

Remember Jesus Christ, raised from the dead . . .
—2 TIMOTHY 2:8

We are to remember the resurrection of Jesus Christ because, if we do remember it, we will always have a satisfying gospel. The truth of the resurrection of Jesus Christ satisfies.

There is much in life that is not satisfying. We may be satisfied for a time. But the pleasures soon pale and satisfaction fades. When we are young and life lies before us, the offerings of the world are not bad, it seems. There is an appeal to fame or wealth or companionship. The hunger of the imagination paints our goals in bright colors. We live on dreams. But what happens when the future doesn't bring what we ask for? What happens in the face of suffering, death, or sorrow? What happens in old age? If there is nothing more to life than the things that time takes from us, life becomes misery. On the other hand, if we are united to the living Lord Jesus Christ, who has gone before to prepare for us a place in his presence, then life retains its meaning and is filled with joy.

We find an illustration of this later in the chapter. Paul is writing to Timothy. But where was Paul? Paul was in prison. There had been times of great liberty when he was free to preach the gospel wherever he wished and to whoever would listen. But now he was confined. Those days were over. Soon his life would be ended. Is there bitterness? Does he regret his commitment to Christ? Not at all! He rejoices! We find him declaring, "Here is a trustworthy saying: If we died with him, we will also live with him; if we endure, we will also reign with him. If we disown him, he will also disown us; if we are faithless, he will remain faithful, for he cannot disown himself" (vv. 11–13).

Paul found that the gospel of the crucified and resurrected Lord was satisfying even at the end of life and in suffering.

Have you remembered the resurrection of Jesus Christ? If you have, you have a gospel that is simple, supernatural, scriptural, and satisfying. You have something that you will be able to communicate to those who need it desperately.

Boice, *The Christ of the Empty Tomb*, P&R Publishing, 2010, 184–85.

The Word of Truth
2 Timothy 2:14–15

A workman . . . who correctly handles the word of truth.
—2 TIMOTHY 2:15

The Bible is given by God in order to provoke a personal response in us. Consequently, if we do not allow that to happen, we inevitably misuse the Bible (even in studying it) and so pervert its intention and misinterpret it. We have an example of this from Christ's day in his words to the Jewish leaders, as recorded in John 5. On this occasion Jesus said, "You diligently study the Scriptures because you think that by them you possess eternal life. These are the Scriptures that testify about me, yet you refuse to come to me to have life. . . . How can you believe if you accept praise from one another, yet make no effort to obtain the praise that comes from the only God?" (vv. 39–40, 44).

No one could fault the Jews of Christ's day for any low opinion of the Scriptures, for they actually had the very highest regard for them. Nor could they be faulted for a lack of meticulous study. The Jews did study the Scriptures. They prized them. This was an acknowledged fact. The difficulty lay in the fact that in their high regard for the Bible they quite easily passed over its intention. Their lives were not changed. As a result, although they gained honor from men for their detailed knowledge of the Bible, they did not gain salvation.

We have a contemporary example of this error in those who have a high degree of biblical knowledge—those who can name all twelve apostles, the cities Paul visited, the list of the Hebrew kings, and so on—but who have missed what the Scriptures have to teach about sin, justification, the Christian life, and obedience. Many others make this precise mistake in a preoccupation with prophecy.

Jesus said that we will know the truth about him only if we are willing to do his will, that is, allow ourselves to be changed by the truths we find in Scripture. He said, "If anyone chooses to do God's will [that is, determine to do it], he will find out whether my teaching comes from God or whether I speak on my own" (7:17).

And we must pray. We must ask God the Holy Spirit to do his work of enlightenment in our hearts. The Spirit's presence is given to us to make the careful and diligent study of the Word of God effective. Without the Spirit, even with the best of minds, methods, and intentions, nothing is possible except error and unbelief.

In the Bible, God speaks. So we must allow him to speak; we must listen so that we may hear what he will say to us and we must be willing to be changed by it.

Word of the Living God
2 Timothy 3:14–17

All Scripture is God-breathed, and is useful.
—2 TIMOTHY 3:16

It is in the Bible alone that we can learn of God's redemption of sinners in Christ, and it is through the Bible and on the basis of the Bible that the Spirit speaks to individuals. Without the Scriptures our imagined wisdom runs to mere foolishness. With the Scriptures and under the guidance of the Holy Spirit, we are able to learn who God truly is, what he has done for us, and how we may respond to him in faith and live our lives in fellowship with him.

The importance of the Bible lies in its being the very Word of God written, and this is what it testifies of itself—"God-breathed." The question for us is: do we believe that the Bible is the written Word of God?

It is popular to doubt this teaching; hence, the great confusion that exists in theology and in the Christian church. But the doubt is not new. In fact, it is the most fundamental and original of all doubts, for it is found on the lips of Satan in the earliest chapters of the Bible: "[The serpent] said to the woman, 'Did God really say, "You must not eat from any tree in the garden"?'" (Gen. 3:1). This is the first question mark in the punctuation of the Bible; it marks an invitation to doubt the Word of God. The doubt is still heard. But the questions are: Can God be trusted? Is the Word he has given to us truly his Word? Do we believe this without any mental reservations? If we do question the Word of God and if we have mental reservations as to its authority, we will never be interested in true Bible study nor will we come into the fullness of that wisdom concerning God and ourselves that is God's desire for us. On the other hand, if we do accept these truths, then we will find the Bible to be our chief delight, we will want to study it, and we will grow in knowledge and devotion.

At the coronation of the king or queen of England, the Moderator of the Church of Scotland presents a Bible to the new monarch with these words: "The most precious thing this world affords, the most precious thing that this world knows, God's living Word." The saying is true. But if it is, then we must prize the Scripture, study the Bible, memorize the Bible, guard the Bible, believe the Bible, contend for the Bible, be thankful for the Bible, and allow our lives to be increasingly conformed to the Bible. We must begin at this point if we are to grow into a full knowledge of God's grace.

Strong in Grace

2 Timothy 4:1–8

I give you this charge: Preach the Word; be prepared in season and out of season; correct, rebuke and encourage.
—2 TIMOTHY 4:1–2

What a tremendous charge, especially in light of the situation in the church and world that Timothy lived in. How could Timothy possibly hope to carry it out?

It seems to me that there are three answers.

First, this is God's charge to Timothy and the charge of the Lord Jesus Christ, not merely Paul's charge. It is why Paul begins as he does, saying, "In the presence of God and of Christ Jesus, who will judge the living and the dead, and in view of his appearing and his kingdom." The work may be hard, but it is God who has given it to us. We cannot take his commissioning lightly. We must be faithful to the end.

Second, others have done it. Paul had an even more difficult time of ministry than Timothy, but Paul had come through, having "fought the good fight," "finished the race," and "kept the faith" (v. 7). When we are tempted to quit, let's remember that "no temptation has seized you except what is common to man"—even the temptation to quit—and that "God is faithful; He will not let [us] be tempted beyond what [we] can bear." And there is this too: "He will also provide a way out so that [we] can stand up under it" (1 Cor. 10:13), which leads us to the next point.

Third, God will provide the grace we need to be faithful. This is what the end of 2 Timothy says. It looks like mere personal notes, as in most of Paul's letters. But it is far more. It describes the situation Paul is in. Demas has deserted him. Everyone but Luke has departed. Alexander the metalworker did him great harm. At this first trial, no one came to his support. But the God of grace was with him. "The Lord stood at my side and gave me strength, so that through me the message might be fully proclaimed and all the Gentiles might hear it. And I was delivered from the lion's mouth" (v. 17).

There it is! If you determine to stand for God without quitting, you find that God will stand with you. He will rescue you from every evil attack and in the end bring you "safely to his heavenly kingdom" (v. 18).

Boice, *Amazing Grace*, Tyndale, 1993, 168–69.

The Christian's "Death Benefits"
2 Timothy 4:6–18

Now there is in store for me the crown of righteousness.
—2 TIMOTHY 4:8

The first great benefit of death for Christians is that death brings a permanent freedom from evil. The Christian who has tasted the delight of God's righteousness longs for a purity that he will never have on earth. He longs to be free of sin, pain, care, and anxiety. And he knows that death brings freedom.

The second great benefit of death to believers is that they will be like Jesus. John writes, "Dear friends, now we are children of God, and what we will be has not yet been made known. But we know that when he appears, we shall be like him, for we shall see him as he is" (1 John 3:2). It is not enough to say that death brings freedom from evil. Annihilation would be just as effective and death is better than that. The Bible teaches that death brings a final perfection of the sanctification of the believer that has begun on earth.

We shall be like him. That means that we shall be like him in *righteousness*, for Paul speaks of "the crown of righteousness, which the Lord, the righteous Judge, will award to me on that day—and not only to me, but also to all who have longed for his appearing." The thought is almost breathtaking. Crowned with righteousness! We do not know that righteousness now; we have only tasted it slightly. But the day is coming when we shall be what we should be.

We also shall be like him in *knowledge*. Now we see things imperfectly. We know in part, and our knowledge (even of spiritual things) is always mixed with error. In that day we shall know as God knows us, and all that has puzzled us in this life will become clear.

We shall also be like Christ in *love*. What a joy to be like him in this. There is so much of self in everything we do, but Christ's love was selfless and self-sacrificing. It was a love that reached to us when we were sinners and saved us for this life and for eternity.

Certainly the greatest benefit of the believer's death is that he or she will be with Jesus. Now we know him and he is with us in this life. We may trust in the fact that he will be particularly close to us in death. For we are told that "precious in the sight of the LORD is the death of his saints" (Ps. 116:15). But the day is coming when we shall be with him as never before, as the bride is with her husband on the evening of their marriage. In that day there will be no tears, no unfulfilled longings or disappointments, and no separation.

Boice, *Philippians*, Baker, 2000, 81–85.

The Trinity

Titus 3:4–7

> God our Savior . . . saved us . . . through . . . the Holy
> Spirit . . . through Jesus Christ our Savior.
> —*TITUS 3:4–6*

It is common among Christians to divide the work of God among the three persons, applying the work of creation to the Father, the work of redemption to the Son, and the work of sanctification to the Holy Spirit. A more correct way of speaking is to say that each member of the Trinity cooperates in each work.

One example is the work of *creation*. It is said of God the Father, "In the beginning you laid the foundations of the earth, and the heavens are the work of your hands" (Ps. 102:25); and "In the beginning God created the heavens and the earth" (Gen. 1:1). It is written of the Son, "For by him all things were created: things in heaven and on earth, visible and invisible" (Col. 1:16); and "Through him all things were made; without him nothing was made that has been made" (John 1:3). It is written of the Holy Spirit, "The Spirit of God has made me" (Job 33:4). In the same way, the *incarnation* is shown to have been accomplished by the three persons of the Godhead working in unity, though only the Son became flesh (see Luke 1:35). At *the baptism of the Lord* all three were also present: the Son came up out of the water, the Spirit descended in the appearance of a dove, and the voice of the Father was heard from heaven declaring, "This is my Son, whom I love; with him I am well pleased" (Matt. 3:16–17). All three persons were present in the *atonement*, as Hebrews 9:14 declares: "Christ, who through the eternal Spirit offered himself unblemished to God." The *resurrection* of Christ is likewise attributed sometimes to the Father (Acts 2:32), sometimes to the Son (John 10:17–18), and sometimes to the Holy Spirit (Rom. 1:4).

We are not surprised, therefore, that our salvation as a whole is also attributed to each of the three persons: "Chosen according to the foreknowledge of God the Father, through the sanctifying work of the Spirit, for obedience to Jesus Christ and sprinkling by his blood" (1 Peter 1:2). Nor are we surprised that we are sent forth into all the world to "make disciples of all nations, baptizing them in the name of the Father and of the Son and of the Holy Spirit" (Matt. 28:19).

But although we can say meaningful things about the Trinity (on the basis of God's revelation of them), the Trinity is still unfathomable. We should be humble before the Trinity. We believe the doctrine of the Trinity, not because we understand it, but because the Bible teaches it and because the Spirit himself witnesses within our heart that it is so.

Boice, *Foundations of the Christian Faith*, InterVarsity, 1986, 115–16.

Our Surety
Philemon 1–25

If he has done you any wrong or owes you anything, charge it to me.
—PHILEMON 18

I suppose that in that moment, Philemon's heart was conquered. He knew what Paul was saying. What is more, he knew that Onesimus had confessed his sin and had returned on Paul's recommendation and with confidence in Paul and in his relationship to Philemon. Paul was becoming surety for Onesimus. Although old and in prison, Paul was offering to pay. Onesimus had trusted him. Who can doubt that at this point Philemon freely forgave Onesimus and received him as he would have received Paul?

The connection between this story, the failure of human works, and the need to believe on the Lord Jesus Christ for salvation is obvious. This is a pageant, if we may so understand it. Philemon is playing the part of God the Father. Paul is Jesus Christ. You and I are Onesimus. What have we done? We have wronged God. We have stolen from him that which is rightly his—honor, worship, glory, obedience—and we have run from him in order to sin our fill. There is no chance of our ever being able to make up that which we owe, and beyond that there is the whole matter of forgiveness and of the good will of the Father.

What shall we do? Shall we trust to good works, moral reformation, ceremonies? None of these things will do. Instead we come to Christ and find him interceding on our behalf. "Father," he says, "this runaway slave has wronged you. He owes what he can never repay. But he believes in me. He has been changed. Therefore, I ask that you charge all that he has done to my account."

Do you see that great picture of salvation? Will you come to God on the basis of that great offer of the Lord Jesus Christ? You can run farther, if you will. You can try to escape the consequences of your sin, if you wish—though you will not succeed. Or you can accept the work of the Lord Jesus Christ on your behalf and trust in him as your surety. If you look to yourself, you may well tremble. But as you look to Jesus, you will hear that still, quiet voice of the Holy Spirit that speaks comforting words on your behalf:

> Arise, my soul, arise! Shake off thy guilty fears;
> The bleeding sacrifice in my behalf appears:
> Before the throne my Surety stands—
> My name is written on his hands.

On this basis no charge shall ever be raised against you. And you will know that the true work of God is done when you believe on Jesus.

Our Advocate

Hebrews 2:14–18

That he might be a merciful and faithful high priest.
—HEBREWS 2:17

Jesus fulfilled his priestly role, first, by the offering up of himself as a sacrifice for sin and, second, by interceding for his people in heaven. There is a wonderful word that is used for this mediatorial function of intercession, and it is doubly wonderful because it is also used of the earthly ministry of the Holy Spirit on our behalf. In the Greek language the word is *parakletos.* In English it is translated "comforter" or "counselor" or "advocate."

A *paraklete* is one called alongside another to help him, in other words, a lawyer, precisely the meaning for "advocate." The picture, then, is of something we might call a heavenly law firm with us as clients. It has a heavenly branch presided over by the Lord Jesus Christ and an earthly branch directed by the Holy Spirit. Each pleads for us. It is the Spirit's role to move us to pray and to intensify that prayer to a point of which we ourselves are not capable. Paul writes of this ministry, "Likewise, the Spirit also helpeth our infirmity; for we know not what we should pray for as we ought; but the Spirit himself maketh intercession for us with groaning which cannot be uttered" (Rom. 8:26 KJV). Similarly, it is the ministry of the Lord in heaven to interpret our prayers aright and plead the efficacy of his sacrifice as the basis of our coming to God.

The consequence of this is that we can have great boldness in prayer. How could we ever have boldness if the answering of our prayers depended either upon the strength with which we pray or upon the correctness of the petitions themselves? We could not. Our prayers are weak, as Paul confesses, and we often pray wrongly. But we are bold, nevertheless, for we have the Holy Spirit to strengthen the requests and the Lord Jesus Christ to interpret them rightly.

What things should we be bold about in our prayers? Certainly that we might grow and become strong in the faith. That God might do things in us individually and in his church that we have not dreamed possible. That he might work through us to our communities to do something really remarkable, memorable, and spiritually lasting for his grace. Let us pray these things boldly and ask the Lord to bless us as we do.

Boice, *The Bible Study Hour*, January 1978, 15–17.

The Throne of Grace
Hebrews 4:14–18

Let us then approach the throne of grace with confidence.
—*Hebrews 4:16*

Because of who God is and what Jesus Christ has done in dying for us, changing the throne of judgment into a throne of grace, we who trust Christ are to draw near the throne of grace in confidence. If we came in our own merit, we could have no confidence at all. The throne of God would be a place of terror. But since God has done what was needed to take away all judgment for our sin, it is now sin for us to come in any other way but with confidence. If we come in confidence, we can come knowing that God will do exactly what the author of Hebrews says he will do and we will indeed "find grace to help us in our time of need."

Whatever our need may be! Do you seek forgiveness for sin? You will find God's grace forgiving you for every sin. Do you need strength for daily living? You will find the grace of God providing strength. Do you need comfort because of some great loss? God will provide comfort. Direction for some important decision? You will receive direction. Encouragement? You will receive encouragement. Wisdom? That too.

Remember what Paul wrote in Romans 8. "If God is for us, who can be against us? He who did not spare his own Son, but gave him up for us all—how will he not also, along with him, graciously give us all things?" (vv. 31–32).

So pray! That is what we need to do. We do not need more lessons on prayer or elaborate instructions on how to pray. What we need to do is pray. So pray! The Bible says, "You do not have, because you do not ask God?" (James 4:2). Jesus said, "Ask and it will be given to you; seek and you will find; knock and the door will be opened to you" (Matt. 7:7).

God is not indifferent or hard of hearing or difficult to be entreated. He hears each and every one of our cries. He has opened the way and is easy to approach through Jesus Christ. He does not always answer as we expect or according to our timetables, of course. His ways are not our ways; nor are his thoughts our thoughts (see Isa. 55:8). But he welcomes our prayers and delights to answer them.

So why do we not pray? Can it be that we do not really believe that God is like this? Or do we just not believe we need his help? Abundant grace from the throne of grace. It is exactly what we need.

Boice, *Amazing Grace*, Tyndale, 1993, 196–98.

Priest and King

Hebrews 7:11—28

For it is declared: "You are a priest forever, in the order of Melchizedek"
—*HEBREWS 7:17*

The author of Hebrews stresses that Jesus is a priest forever in Melchizedek's order, as opposed to any other kind of priesthood. So we ask, What is it about Melchizedek that points to the superiority of Jesus's priesthood? Why is it important that Jesus be a priest in Melchizedek's order rather than in the order of Aaron (v. 11)?

One answer comes from the first thing the author of Hebrews says about Melchizedek: "This Melchizedek was king of Salem and priest of God Most High" (v. 1). The important word in that sentence is "and," for in Old Testament times the royal and priestly offices were kept apart, and it is only in Melchizedek and Christ that these two important functions are combined. Jesus is no mere human being. He is the God-man, as perfect in his divine as in his human attributes. He alone is able to be both priest and king.

F. B. Meyer writes, "How marvelously [these] blended in the earthly life of Jesus! As Priest, He pitied, and helped, and fed men; as King, He ruled the waves. As Priest, He uttered his sublime intercessory prayer; as King, He spoke the 'I will' of royal prerogative. As Priest, He touched the ear of Malchus; as the disowned King, to whom even Caesar was preferred, He was hounded to the death. As Priest, He pleaded for His murderers and spoke of Paradise to the dying thief; whilst His Kingship was attested by the proclamation affixed to His cross. As Priest, He breathed peace on His disciples; as King, He ascended to sit down upon His throne."

The kingship of Melchizedek is particularly significant in regard to Jesus's kingship, for it points to his superlative kingly qualities. "Melchizedek" may be just a name but it does mean "king of righteousness." The Salem of which Melchizedek was king may have only been the early and earthly Jerusalem (see Ps. 76:2), but Salem does mean "peace." Jesus is preeminently the King of Righteousness and the King of Peace. Moreover, he is both, and in that order. "First, his name means 'king of righteousness'; then also, 'king of Salem' means 'king of peace'" (Heb. 7:2). Not peace at any price or at the cost of righteousness, but righteousness first—the righteousness of his personal character—the righteous meeting, on our behalf, of the just demands of a divine and holy law. And then founded on and arising from this solid and indestructible basis, there sprang the Temple of Peace in which the souls of men may shelter from the shocks of time. "The work of righteousness will be peace; the effect of righteousness, will be quietness and confidence forever. My people will live in peaceful dwelling places, in secure homes, in undisturbed places of rest" (Isa. 32:17–18).

Our Great High Priest
Hebrews 8:1–6

We do have such a high priest, who sat down at the right
hand of the throne of the Majesty in heaven.
—*Hebrews 8:1*

Jesus fulfilled the Old Testament priestly function in two ways, by offering himself up as a sacrifice for sin (which the Old Testament priests could not do) and by interceding for his people in heaven.

That Jesus is himself the sacrifice for sins makes clear that his priesthood is different from and superior to the Old Testament priesthoods. There are other differences too. To begin with, the Old Testament priests were sinful and were required to offer a sacrifice for themselves as well as for those they represented. Furthermore, the sacrifices the priests of Israel offered were inadequate. They taught the way of salvation through the death of an innocent victim. But the blood of sheep and goats could not take away sins (Amos 5:22; Micah 6:6–7; Heb. 10:4–7). Finally, the sacrifices of the earthly priests were also incomplete. They had to be offered again and again.

In contrast to this earthly priesthood, *the sacrifice of Jesus is by one who is himself perfect* and who therefore has no need that atonement be made for him. Second, being himself perfect and at the same time the sacrifice, it follows that *the sacrifice made by Jesus was itself perfect.* Hence, it could actually pay the price for sin and remove it, as the sacrifices in Israel could not. They were a shadow of things to come but they were not the reality. Jesus's death was the actual atonement on the basis of which God declares the sinner righteous. Finally, unlike the sacrifices of the Old Testament priests that had to be repeated daily, *the sacrifice of Jesus was complete and eternal.* This is confirmed by the fact that he is now seated at the right hand of God. In the Jewish temple there were no chairs. This signified that the work of the priests was never done.

Teaching about priests and sacrifices is hard for most people today to understand. But it was not that easy to understand in antiquity either. That is why God gave elaborate instructions for the performances of sacrifices—to teach both the serious nature of sin and his provision for forgiveness. The sacrifices taught two great lessons. First, sin means death. It is a lesson concerning God's judgment. It means that sin is serious. Second, there is grace. The significance of the sacrifice is that by the grace of God an innocent substitute can be offered in the sinner's place. The goat or lamb was not that substitute. It could only point forward to it. But Jesus was and is, for all who will have him as Savior. He is the only, perfect, all-sufficient sacrifice for sin on the basis of which God counts the sinner justified.

Christ's Saving Work
Hebrews 9:25–28

So Christ was sacrificed once to take away the sin of many people.
—*HEBREWS 9:28*

J esus's offering of himself was the perfect and final sacrifice for sin. Therefore, nothing more needs to be done or can be done to reconcile sinful men and women to God. Jesus's sacrifice of himself was a real sacrifice for sin, not a symbol that merely pointed forward to something else, as the Old Testament sacrifices did. Those sacrifices pointed forward to the atonement Jesus would make, but they were not themselves that atonement. Jesus put away our real sin by his real death.

The author of Hebrews says very clearly, "[Christ did not] enter heaven to offer himself again and again, the way the high priest enters the Most Holy Place every year with blood that is not his own. Then Christ would have had to suffer many times since the creation of the world. But now he has appeared once for all at the end of the ages to do away with sin by the sacrifice of himself. Just as man is destined to die once, and after that to face judgment, so Christ was sacrificed once to take away the sin of many people" (vv. 25–28). This is why today we insist that there is no Savior but Jesus and that we must believe on him and commit ourselves to him if we are to be saved.

Because of Christ's saving work, it is now possible for those who believe on him to approach God directly. The people of God could not do this before Christ's death. They needed to approach God indirectly, asking a priest to intercede for them. But now the way is open for everybody. The author of Hebrews wrote, "Therefore, brothers, since we have confidence to enter the Most Holy Place by the blood of Jesus, by a new and living way opened for us through the curtain, that is, his body, and since we have a great priest over the house of God, let us draw near to God with a sincere heart in full assurance of faith" (10:19–22).

One man who approached God by faith was the Roman centurion standing at the foot of the cross when Jesus was crucified. When he and those with him saw Jesus die on the cross, they cried out with true faith, "Surely he was the Son of God!" (Matt. 27:54).

This may not have been a full confession. It lacked much that the centurion undoubtedly would come to know later. But it was correct as far as it went, and Matthew included it as an example of what is required of all who come face-to-face with Jesus. Have you made that vital confession, acknowledging that Jesus is both the Son of God and your Savior? You need to. It is the only way that anyone can be saved.

Boice and Ryken, *Jesus on Trial*, Crossway, 2002, 110–13.

Born for a Purpose

Hebrews 10:5–10

I have come to do your will, O God.
—*HEBREWS 10:7*

Our Lord came into the world for a purpose. That is important, for it is
uniquely true of him. It cannot be said of any other person that he or she
came into the world to do something. It is often true that there are purposes
parents have for their children. They hope that the child lying in a crib will
grow up to do something significant in this world. If the parents are Christians,
they want their child to be kept from sin and be able to serve Jesus Christ.
Parents have those and other aspirations. But the child does not have them.
The child has to acquire them. This is why, from a Christian perspective, the
child must be taught its destiny from the pages of the Word of God.

But Jesus was different. Our Lord says that he came (and was conscious of
coming) for a specific purpose. Moreover, he spells that purpose out: "I have
come *to do your will, O God.*"

What was that will? God willed Christ to be our Savior.

I do not know why it is, but we often lose a sense of that purpose in telling
the Christmas story. We focus so much on the birth of the baby and on the
sentiment that goes with that story—and there is a certain amount of legitimate sentimentality that goes with it—that we miss the most important things.
Actually, the story is treated quite simply in Scripture, and the emphasis is
always on the fact that Jesus came to die. The Lord Jesus Christ, the eternal
Son of God, took a human body in order that he might die for our salvation
When our Lord speaks of his coming, it is therefore highly understandable
that he is thinking along those lines.

In the tenth chapter of Hebrews the author contrasts the sacrifices that
took place in Israel before the coming of Christ—the sin offerings and burnt
offerings, by which believers testified of their faith that God would accept them
on the basis of the death of an innocent substitute—with Christ's great and
perfect sacrifice. It is in the context of that contrast, between the former things
and that which has now come, between the shadow and the reality, that he
brings in this quotation from Psalm 40. The Lord Jesus Christ came into this
world with a purpose, and that purpose was to do God's will: to be our Savior.

Boice and Ryken, *The Christ of Christmas*, P&R Publishing, 2009, 18–20.

What Is Faith?

Hebrews 11:1–7

Now faith is being sure of what we hope for.
—*HEBREWS 11:1*

Faith is believing God and acting upon it. But let me break this down into faith's three elements. Faith has an *intellectual element*. Biblical faith is faith in God and in the promises of God. So we do not have faith in the biblical sense until we begin to enter into these things intellectually. Now faith involves not merely intellectual content, but also that intellectual content seeping down in *the heart* so that it moves us and stirs our emotions. The third element of faith is what we would call *commitment*. We understand, respond, and then because of what God has done say, "Henceforth, I am going to follow the Lord Jesus Christ as my Lord and Savior."

I think we have an illustration of this in courtship and marriage. When a man and woman first get to know one another, fall in love, and get married, they go through a series of stages. The first corresponds to the intellectual element in faith. If they are wise, they spend time getting to know one another. Next comes what we call falling in love. It corresponds to the heart element. You do not marry somebody merely because you think you might be able to live with him or her for forty years. You marry because you are in love with that person.

But even that is not marriage. So the time comes when the man and woman come to the front of the church, stand before the preacher, and exchange their vows. They make a commitment to one another "before God and these witnesses." And that is the marriage! This last step corresponds to the commitment we make when we promise to serve the Lord Jesus Christ, who has already made his commitment to us.

And when that commitment is made, we experience a name change. Let's carry this illustration of marriage further. The woman comes to the service as Miss Jones, let us say, and she marries Mr. Smith. She goes out Mrs. Smith. In the same way, you and I come to God as Miss Sinner. And God, in that marvelous marriage union of ourselves to Christ changes our name. We become Mrs. Christian and go out with the name of Christ.

If that has not happened to you, you have to do what one does in the marriage service. The Lord Jesus Christ is there, and he takes his vows first, promising to be your loving and faithful husband. You must promise to be his loving and faithful wife. When you do that, God pronounces the marriage. You then take the name of Christ and bear it from that time on before the watching world. God grant that we might all bear it honorably to the glory of him who deserves all our honor and all our praise.

Boice, "Faith: Believing God," *Tenth: An Evangelical Quarterly*, July 1980.

Benediction of Peace
Hebrews 13:20–21

The God of peace . . . through the blood of the eternal covenant brought back from the dead our Lord Jesus.
—*HEBREWS 13:20*

This benediction tells how God has become a God of peace to us rather than a God of wrath. It has three parts.

1. *The blood of the eternal covenant.* This refers to the death of Jesus by which our Lord by his death on the cross fulfilled the terms of a covenant made between God the Father and himself before the creation of the world, and then received the promise of the covenant, which was to have a great company of people for his own, that is, the church.

This covenant is eternal—established in eternity past, before you or I or the world or any other part of the created order came into being and will endure forever. It is also important because of the parties involved. In the case of this "eternal covenant," the parties are the persons of the Godhead. God the Father covenants to give to his Son a people who will be the objects of the Father's love and whom he will forgive of sin. The Holy Spirit covenants that he will regenerate all those whom the Father gives to the Son and will cleanse them of unrighteousness. The Son covenants that he will make atonement for the sins of his people, will intercede for them, and bring them safely to the Father.

2. *The resurrection of the Lord Jesus Christ.* The second work of God that is mentioned is God's raising Jesus Christ from the dead. It is part of the covenant, since the Father committed himself to do this even before the incarnation. But it is more. It is a demonstration and proof of the great power of God, which has worked not merely to bring Jesus back from the dead, but also to save us from the penalty of our sins, keep us from sin, and lead us into an abundant and fruitful Christian life. It is an encouragement to us as we try to serve God and do good works.

3. *The Shepherd work of Christ.* Jesus is referred to as a Shepherd in three separate passages. In John 10:11 Jesus is called "the *good* shepherd" because he "lays down his life for the sheep." In 1 Peter 5:4 Jesus is called "the Chief Shepherd" to whom the elders of the church must give account. Here Jesus is called "the *great* Shepherd" because he has triumphed over death and now lives to guide, nourish, and protect the flock that the Father has given him.

When we put these descriptive phrases together we are assured that God, who brought back Jesus Christ from the dead, is able and most certainly will save us from all our sin and take us to heaven to be with him forever.

From an unpublished Easter sermon, 1996.

Judgment and Mercy

James 2:1–13

Speak and act as those who are going to be judged by the law.
—*JAMES 2:12*

James says that the favoritism we practice but think of as unimportant is actually a very serious sin. It is a sin that will bring us into judgment. If you break the law to "love your neighbor as yourself" (Lev. 19:18)—and you do break it if you show favoritism—then not only have you broken that law and stand condemned by it, but you have also broken the entire law as well.

He reminds us that there is such a thing as judgment and that judgment will fall on those who break God's law. In the light of the coming judgment, James urges us to reexamine our relationships with other people as well as with God. Of course, James is not teaching salvation by works. He is not saying that if you keep this law and the next law and the law after that, you will be saved by keeping the law. What he is teaching is this: If you are showing favoritism, consider carefully what you are doing, because you are breaking God's law, and stop doing it. Knowing what you are doing should cause you to reexamine your relationship to God and start to behave differently. And you will behave differently if you are a Christian!

If you are related to God the Father, as you should be in Jesus Christ, something of the spirit of Christ that went out to those who were destitute, needy, poor, and unimportant should be in you, and you should find yourself showing mercy to them, even as Jesus did. This is how Christians must behave and operate. Therefore, if you are not doing this, you should reexamine yourself to see if you are really saved. If we are believers, each of us must be living a life that matches our profession.

This is really the bottom line. We read the Word; we know the teaching; we can give discourses on what the doctrine says. But James asks, "Does your life match the things you teach and, in particular, does it match up in this very important matter of choosing who are to be your friends?"

Who are your friends? They should be those who are friendless, those who do not attract the attention of the world, those who would be neglected if it were not for Christian people. Jesus reached out to such people. You also should reach out to them and include them for the sake of the Lord Jesus Christ and the gospel.

Boice, *Sure, I Believe—So What!* Geanies House, 1994, 51–53.

Tongue Control
James 3:1–12

No man can tame the tongue.
—*JAMES 3:8*

You and I cannot control our tongues, but God by the power of his Holy Spirit within us can control them. Let me give you three helpful principles, based upon the fact that the tongue speaks what the mind thinks.

1. *Present your mind to God.* In Romans 12:1–2 the apostle Paul speaks of mind control: "Offer your bodies as living sacrifices, holy and pleasing to God. . . . Do not conform any longer to the pattern of this world, but be transformed by the renewing of your mind." If anything good is to develop in our lives, there must first be the transformation of our minds since what we think will always determine what we do. Moreover, it is only as we present our minds to God that we can be kept from thinking according to the world's standards. Only when we give our minds to God can they be channeled to think according to Christ's standards.

2. *Begin to obey Christ's teachings.* Paul says in 2 Corinthians 10:5, "We take captive every thought to make it obedient to Christ." We must be serious about seeking out what Christ has said and striving to obey it. You are not Christ's unless you are obeying Christ, and you are not obeying if you do not pay attention to what Jesus taught. As we search the Scriptures to see what the Lord would have us do and then set about to obey it through the power of his Holy Spirit, God will begin to change our way of thinking. We will start thinking the thoughts of God after God; and as we begin to think differently, we will begin to speak differently and the matter of tongue control will become a reality.

3. *Practice speaking helpfully.* We must also control our tongue positively, so we say the things we ought to say. That will take conscious effort. Why not set some personal goals in this area? You might determine to say one good thing in praise of God to someone every single day. You might determine to memorize a Bible verse each week, so you can recite it to others. You might want to say something good about someone else. There are dozens of possibilities.

It may be helpful to remember that God tells us that he hears what we say and takes note of it himself. Malachi 3:16 says, "Those who feared the Lord talked with each other, and the Lord listened and heard. A scroll of remembrance was written in his presence concerning those who feared the Lord and honored his name." If we use our tongues in a disciplined way to praise God, not with speech only but with the mind that goes behind it, God will bless our words and remember them and give us the ability to be a blessing to other people.

Boice, *Sure, I Believe—So What!* Geanies House, 1994, 75–79.

Submitting to God

James 4:1–10

Submit yourselves, then, to God.
—JAMES 4:7

James calls us "adulterous people" (v. 4) because we have committed spiritual adultery against God. He speaks of a friend of the world being God's "enemy." What James has in mind here is the fact that we have rebelled against God's rightful rule over us and now fondly believe that we are masters of our own fate.

In verses 7 and 8 he speaks of a cure for this adultery against God. "Submit yourselves, then, to God. Resist the devil, and he will flee from you. Come near to God and he will come near to you."

How do we draw near to God? Is James saying that the first move is up to us? If we seek God, then God will seek us? No, that is not what James is saying at all.

We draw near to God at the cross, and we draw near to God as the Holy Spirit draws us to him. It would be correct to say that as God has drawn near to us, so God draws us to him. "Submit to God" means "submit to the drawing power of God." If you do this, if you allow God to draw you to him, you will find God to be the one you need. He will restore the broken Creator/creature relationship and subdue your pride.

This is the truth that Isaac Watts conveyed in his great hymn of the atonement.

> When I survey the wondrous cross
> On which the Prince of glory died,
> My richest gain I count but loss,
> And pour contempt on all my pride.

Submission to God happens in no other way and in no other place, for only as we see what God has done for us is our pride subdued and we find ourselves being brought near to him.

So long as we think we are contributing spiritually to what God is doing, we will be proud of what we have done. But when we see the matter as God portrays it in Scripture, when we see the cross, we will recognize how desperate our state is and that there is nothing in us to commend us to God. We are the kind of men and women who crucified Jesus. Yet God still sent his Son to pay the price of our sin and then by the power of his Spirit open our eyes to see what we have done and draw our wills so that we might come and receive the Lord Jesus Christ as our Savior.

When we recognize what God has done for our salvation, we are truly humbled and are able to ask God to do with us what needs to be done.

Boice, *Sure, I Believe—So What!* Geanies House, 1994, 86–88.

Regeneration and God's Word

1 Peter 1:22–25

For you have been born again, not of perishable seed, but of imperishable, through the living and enduring word of God.
—*1 PETER 1:23*

God exalts his Word in the saving of men and women. For it is by his Word and Spirit, and not by testimonies, eloquent arguments, or emotional appeals, that he regenerates the one who apart from that regeneration is spiritually dead. There are many moving images for the Word of God in the Bible, but none is so bold as the one Peter used in this passage: the Word is like human sperm. Peter uses this image, for he wishes to show that it is by means of the Word that God engenders spiritual children.

In the first chapter of his epistle, Peter has been talking about the means by which a person enters the family of God. First, he has discussed the theme objectively, saying that it is on the basis of Christ's vicarious death that we are redeemed. "For you know that it was not with perishable things such as silver or gold that you were redeemed from the empty way of life handed down to you from your forefathers, but with the precious blood of Christ, a lamb without blemish or defect" (vv. 18–19). Second, he has discussed the theme subjectively, pointing out that it is through faith that the objective work of Christ is applied to us personally. "Through him you believe in God, who raised him from the dead and glorified him, and so your faith and hope are in God" (v. 21). Finally, having mentioned these truths, Peter goes on to discuss the new birth in terms of God's sovereign grace in election, this time showing that we are born again by means of the Word of God, which he then likens to the male element in procreation.

What does this teach about the way in which a man or woman becomes a child of God? It teaches that God is responsible for the new birth and that the means by which he accomplishes this is his living and abiding Word. We might even say that God does a work prior to this, for he first sends the ovum of saving faith into the heart. Even faith is not of ourselves, it is the "gift of God" (Eph. 2:8). Afterward, when the sperm of the Word is sent to penetrate the ovum of saving faith, there is a spiritual conception.

The point of these verses is that it is by means of the very words of God recorded in the Scriptures and communicated to the individual heart by the Holy Spirit that God saves the individual.

Is it really the Word that God uses in the salvation of the individual? If it is, then you should revere that Word as the supernatural gift without which nothing spiritually will happen within your life.

Boice, *The Foundations of Biblical Authority*, Zondervan, 1979, 139–40.

Persevering Grace
1 Peter 5:8–11

The God of all grace, . . . after you have suffered a little while, will
himself restore you and make you strong, firm and steadfast.
—1 PETER 5:10

The suffering Peter has in mind is that which Satan causes. How can we
resist Satan's powerful onslaughts? In ourselves we cannot resist him even
for a moment. We can only do it by the grace and power of God.

Peter had learned this from Jesus. You will recall how Jesus told Peter at
the Last Supper that "Satan has asked to sift you as wheat" (Luke 22:31). The
devil must have meant, "I know you are placing a lot of hope in these twelve
disciples that you will be leaving behind when you return to heaven. But it is
a hopeless gamble, and I will show you how hopeless it really is. If you will
just let me get at Peter, your leading apostle, I will shake him so badly that all
his faith will come tumbling out like chaff at threshing time, and he will be
utterly ruined." Satan must have remembered how easy it had been for him to
ruin our first parents in Eden, and he concluded that if he had brought Adam
and Eve to ruin when they were in their unfallen and pristine glory, it should
have been easy to knock down Peter, who was already sinful, ignorant, brash,
and ridiculously self-confident. And he was right. Peter had boasted that he
would never deny Jesus. But when Satan blew upon him, he fell.

Yet what Satan had not counted on was what Jesus also told Peter. He
warned him that Satan would indeed attack him and that he would fall, but he
added, "I have prayed for you, Simon, that your faith may not fail. And when
you have turned back, strengthen your brothers" (v. 32). If Peter could explain
that statement to us, he would probably say something like this: "When Jesus
told me he had prayed for me, he was telling me that I could not stand against
Satan alone. And neither can you! Satan is much too powerful for us. So do not
make the mistake I made, assuming that because I loved Jesus I could never
be led by Satan to deny that I ever knew him. Satan can bend us any way he
wishes. But if we are joined to Jesus, we will find that he is able to keep us
from falling, or if he allows us to fall, he is able to keep us from falling the
whole way and will in any case forgive us, bring us back to himself, and give
us meaningful work to do."

If we are to stand against Satan, it must be by the persevering grace of
God, who has promised to restore us and make us strong, firm, and steadfast.

Boice, *Amazing Grace*, Tyndale, 1993, 236–38.

The Certain Word

2 Peter 1:12–21

We have the word of the prophets made more certain.
—2 PETER 1:19

The way we listen to Jesus today is by hearing what he has already said to us in the Bible. "But that is so commonplace, so prosaic," you might say. "It is not much of a mountaintop experience. I want to see the bright light, be enveloped by the cloud, and hear the rolling thunder of God's voice. I want a personal revelation."

Consider, then, Peter's wise observations on his own experience seeing the transfiguration of Christ. He claimed that he was one of the "eyewitnesses of his majesty" and that he heard the voice that came to Jesus "from the Majestic Glory." He heard God say, "This is my Son, whom I love; with him I am well pleased" (vv. 16–17). But then he adds, "And we have the word of the prophets made *more certain*, and you will do well to pay attention to it, as to a light shining in a dark place, until the day dawns and the morning star rises in your hearts."

This means that Peter's experience on the mountain was an important one; he bears testimony to it. But he adds that there is something "more certain" even than this: the testimony of Scripture to which we must pay the most deliberate and rapt attention. He is saying that the Bible is more certain even than a voice from heaven.

We live in an age when people appeal to their experience as the only sure measure of anything, not realizing that our experiences can be wrong or misleading. We hear people justifying all types of unbiblical teaching or behavior by words such as, "God told me this is all right" or "I feel at peace with what I'm doing." But here is Peter—a prominent apostle of the Lord, a man who had a visual experience of Christ's transfiguration as well as having heard an audible word of God from heaven, experiences confirmed as true by the other apostles who were with him at the time—speaking of God's revelation in the Bible as being "more certain" even than his exceptional experience. He does it to remind us that we must evaluate our experiences by the Bible's teaching, rather than the other way around.

Do you do that? Or are you still longing for experiences that are being reserved for that future day when you are with the Lord in heaven? That day will come. You can be encouraged by it. But for now your duty is to read, mark, learn, and digest the words of God we have been given. If you do so and do so faithfully, carefully obeying what you read and understand, God will teach you all you need to live for him and serve him in this life until you die.

Boice, *Gospel of Matthew*, Volume 1, Baker, 2001, 324–25.

God of Patience
2 Peter 3:1–13

They will say, "Where is this 'coming' he promised?"
—2 PETER 3:4

Peter responds to the scoffing that God's judgment is long in coming by relating it to the previous judgment of the world by flood. He makes the following points.

First, the views of scoffers are based on ignorance, and a willful ignorance at that. That is, they have willfully closed their minds to the abundant evidence that God does not tolerate evil and that he eventually does intervene to judge wickedness. It is not that the evidence for a coming judgment is not there. It is. It is because people willingly close their minds to what is coming. Why do they do this? Peter does not hesitate to say that it is so they can follow "their own evil desires" (v. 3). They reject warnings of judgment in order to continue on their own evil way.

Second, Peter explains God's delay in sending judgment. It is true that from our standpoint the judgment is slow in coming. But this is not because God is indifferent to sin or, worse yet, because he does not exist. It is because God's timing is not our timing and because he delays his judgment in order to give people opportunity to repent. Peter says, "But do not forget this one thing, dear friends: With the Lord a day is like a thousand years, and a thousand years are like a day. The Lord is not slow in keeping his promise, as some understand slowness. He is patient with you, not wanting anyone to perish, but everyone to come to repentance" (vv. 8–9).

Peter's third point is that the judgment is inevitable. It may be delayed but it is no less certain for that fact. How can Peter be so certain? It is because God has said that this is what he will do and because he has already done it once in destroying the earth by flood in Noah's period.

Peter's last point is an application: "Since everything will be destroyed in this way, what kind of people ought you to be? You ought to live holy and godly lives . . ." (v. 11).

We do not know when God's second and final judgment will come, but it is coming closer hour by hour, minute by minute. It could be at any time. These are serious thoughts. Allow them to move you to faith in Jesus Christ, our ark of salvation, and to live a godly life for him.

Walking in God's Light

1 John 1:1–10

God is light; in him there is no darkness at all.
—*1 JOHN 1:5*

John contrasts the nature of God ("God is light") with the nature of man; and he begins to show the characteristics of those who walk in the light as opposed to those who walk in darkness. It is not enough that a man should claim to be in the light. He must actually walk in it. He must be a child of the light.

What will be true of the individual if God is actually the light of his life? Obviously, the light of God will be doing for him what light does. For one thing, the light will be exposing the darkness so that the dark places are increasingly cleansed of sin and become bright and fruitful places for God's blessing. This does not mean that the individual will become increasingly conscious of how good he or she is becoming. On the contrary, a growth in holiness will mean a growth in a true sensitivity to sin in one's life and an intense desire to eliminate from life all that displeases God. Instead of boasting in his progress, the person will be increasingly ready to acknowledge sin and seek to have it eliminated.

It will be a genuine acknowledgment. It will not be as it was in the case of a woman who once asked Charles Wesley to pray for her because, as she said, "I am a great sinner." She added, "I am a Christian but I sometimes fail so dreadfully. Please pray for me."

Wesley replied, "Yes, Madam, I will pray for you; for truly you are a great sinner."

She answered, "What do you mean? I have never done anything very wrong."

If God's light is really shining on us, we will rather say, as did Isaiah, "Woe to me! . . . I am ruined! For I am a man of unclean lips, and I live among a people of unclean lips, and my eyes have seen the King, the LORD Almighty!" (Isa. 6:5); or with Peter, "Go away from me, Lord; I am a sinful man!" (Luke 5:8); or with Paul, "I am the worst [of sinners]" (1 Tim. 1:15).

Second, if God is our light and if we walk in the light, we will be growing spiritually. The Bible will be becoming more precious, for God is revealed in it. We will love godliness. And we will be finding fellowship with God's people more and more delightful and valuable.

Finally, we will also be finding it increasingly desirable to serve the Lord Jesus Christ. Indeed, we will yearn to serve him, for we will know him more and more as the one who brought us out of the bondage of our darkness into his marvelous light. To follow Christ is the natural desire of the one whose life has been illuminated by him.

Boice, *The Epistles of John*, Baker, 1979, 33–34.

Righteousness: The Moral Test

1 John 2:1–6

We know that we have come to know him if we obey his commands.
—1 JOHN 2:3

It often happens that shortly after a person believes in Christ, doubts set in. The initial experience of the Christian is usually one of great joy. He had been lost in the darkness of his own sin and ignorance; now he has come into the light. Formerly he had not found God; now he has found him. But then, as time goes by, the new Christian may begin to wonder if, in fact, anything has really changed. He thought that he was a new creature in Christ; but, to speak frankly, he is really much as he was. The same temptations are present; they may even be worse. There are the same flaws of character. Even the joy, which he once knew, seems to be evaporating. At such a time the new Christian often asks how it is possible to be certain that he is saved by God. He may ask, "How can I truly know that I know God?"

To answer this question is one of the major purposes, perhaps the major purpose, of 1 John. There are three answers or tests. There is the moral test, which is the test of righteousness. The second test is social, the test of love. Finally, there is the doctrinal test.

John introduces the first of the tests for Christian assurance in verse 3. But he does so, not by saying, or "By this we may know that we are Christians," but rather by the idea of knowledge. John is saying, "What is it that characterizes the one who truly knows God?" The answer is "righteousness."

Do we say we are Christians? Then "whoever claims to live in him must walk as Jesus did" (v. 6). The call is to emulate Jesus in our conduct. To walk as Christ walked is to live, not by rules, but by an example. It is to follow him, to be his disciple. Such a discipleship is personal, active, and costly. It is *personal* because it cannot be passed off to another. To walk as Christ walked is also *active* because the Lord himself is active. To be inactive is to be left behind.

Finally, it is *costly* as well, because the path that Jesus walked is the path to crucifixion. It leads to glory, but before that, it leads to the cross. Such a path can be walked only by the one who has died to self and who has deliberately taken up the cross of Christ to follow him.

Such a one, whether in John's day or our own, will always have confidence before God and will be sure that he knows him. By the test of righteousness we may know that we know God and may assure our hearts before him.

Boice, *The Epistles of John*, Baker, 1979, 44–49.

Truth: The Doctrinal Test

1 John 2:18–27

All of you know the truth.
—1 John 2:20

Christians must learn that questions concerning truth matter. Unfortunately, there is a tendency in some Christian circles to minimize thought and to substitute for it either ethical demands, sometimes conceived quite legalistically, or subjective experiences, such as so-called "second blessings" or "tongues" or the mere obligation to "love." Not all of these substitute items are bad, of course. In fact, the tests of life, which John is giving, include the test of obedience and the test of love. But in addition to these there is also the very important test of truth; and it is so important that John can even declare that those who do not hold to the truth concerning Jesus are of the antichrist. Truth, as it is contained in the Scriptures and as it is revealed in Jesus Christ, is an objective standard. It provides a basis for making judgments and it reveals error. Consequently, Christians should be concerned with truth, should seek to understand it with increasing fullness, and should proclaim it to the world.

Second, there is the matter of Christian responsibility where truth is concerned. It is true that believers have an "anointing" and have no need that anyone should "teach" them. But this only means that any valid and therefore useful teaching of the Lord's people must be done by those who are themselves among the Lord's people and that, if Christians are confronted by the false teaching of unbelievers, they have within themselves the means of exploring the Scriptures and thus dividing truth from error. But this may not be construed as an excuse for failing to remain in the truth by conscious effort and determination. Here the key term is "abide" or "remain" (*menō* in Greek), which occurs five times in the last verses of this section and with which the passage closes. True, the Word abides in all Christians, but for this reason they are to allow it to abide in them increasingly. The Holy Spirit also abides in them, but they are also to abide in him or Christ.

Third, there are the means by which every Christian should achieve victory over error in life: the Word of God and the indwelling of the Holy Spirit. Both are necessary. Without the Spirit, knowledge of the Word becomes but a bitter orthodoxy. Without the Word, the experience of the Spirit can lead to the most unjustified and damaging of excesses. The only safeguard against either and therefore the only sure defense against heresy is to have abiding within us both the Word from which we learn and the Holy Spirit who teaches it to us.

Boice, *The Epistles of John*, Baker, 1979, 74–75.

Love: The Social Test

1 John 4:7–21

Everyone who loves has been born of God and knows God.
—1 JOHN 4:7

Of the three tests for Christian assurance, we might ask which is most important. In one sense this obviously is an illegitimate question, for any approach to the tests is illegitimate if it allows us to minimize one of them. On the other hand, there are senses in which a question about the most important test is valid. We can ask it in terms of our need, for instance: which do we most lack? Or we can ask it in terms of John's interests: upon which does John lay most emphasis as he writes this letter? Interestingly enough, the answer to both these forms of the question is love, for we need to love, and it is upon love that John himself seems to lay the greatest emphasis. There are several reasons for this.

The first reason is obviously that we need love most, particularly in the so-called evangelical churches. These have sound doctrine, at least to a point. There is a measure of righteousness. But often, sadly, there is very little love. Without it, however, there is no true demonstration of the life of Christ within or true worship of the Father. The second reason is that Jesus himself made love the first and second of the commandments. The first commandment is love for God (Deut. 6:5). The second is love for one another (Lev. 19:18). The two properly belong together. As Jesus said, "All the Law and the Prophets hang on these two commandments" (Matt. 22:40). The third reason is that it was the realization of this double love in us for both God and man that was the object of Christ's coming. This is what John seems to speak about in the opening verses of the letter when he says, "We proclaim to you what we have seen and heard, so that you also may have fellowship with us. And our fellowship is with the Father and with his Son, Jesus Christ" (1 John 1:3). That is, the coming of Christ is proclaimed so that those who hear of his incarnation and death might believe in him and thereby learn to love both God and one another.

The devil is the one who disrupts. The Lord Jesus Christ is the one who draws together. Moreover, in the drawing together into fellowship, love is the key factor. Little surprise, then, that we have this commandment from him: "Whoever loves God must also love his brother" (4:21).

Boice, *The Epistles of John*, Baker, 1979, 113, 121–22.

The Victory of Faith

1 John 5:1–5

This is the victory that has overcome the world, even our faith.
—1 JOHN 5:4

John has talked about the content of the Christian's faith several times before. The new element in these verses is that of victory, expressed as an overcoming of the world. This is found three times: once in the first half of verse 4, in the statement that whatever is born of God overcomes the world; once in the second half of verse 4, in the statement that the active ingredient in this victory is faith; and once, finally, in verse 5, in the rhetorical question "Who is it that overcomes the world? Only he who believes that Jesus is the Son of God."

These three statements express three important principles. First, that which is victorious over the world is that which has its origins in God. Indeed, if it were not for the reality of that new life that springs from God and that is implanted within the Christian, no victory would be possible. The Christian could not resist the world were it not for the fact of the new birth and for the truth that he who is within the Christian is greater than he who is within the world.

The second principle involved in the Christian's victory is faith, which John defines as faith in Jesus as the Christ and as the Son of God. This confession is important for our age. No one would deny that other points of doctrine are important. But since Jesus is the center of Christianity, obviously the truth about him is most important and, in fact, determines what is to be believed in other areas.

The third principle of victory is faithfulness, which is, indeed, always involved in the idea of "faith" as the Bible defines it. It is not just a past overcoming that John is thinking of therefore, but also a present overcoming through a continuing and persevering faith in Jesus Christ. John is not thinking of a superior class of Christians that is involved, nor those who do some great work as the world might evaluate it. It is rather those who remain faithful to the truth concerning Jesus as the Christ and who continue to serve him.

This all who truly know the Lord will do. Indeed, in the broadest view, the faithfulness is not theirs, but rather his who has brought them to spiritual life and who, as a result, has also led them to faith in Christ, a pursuit of righteousness, and love for other Christians.

Boice, *The Epistles of John*, Baker, 1979, 128–19.

The Christian Walk
2 John 1–13

It has given me great joy to find some of your children walking in the truth.
—2 JOHN 4

The unique feature of this letter's opening salutation is John's surprising emphasis upon truth and his linking of the truth he thus emphasizes to love. Indeed, the word *truth* occurs four times in these first three verses and one more time in verse 4. In these verses John claims to love the elect lady and her children "in the truth," that these are also loved by all others who "know the truth," that this is precisely "because of the truth," and that in this they are all following the way of the Father and Son, who indeed dispense the great blessings of grace, mercy, and peace "in truth and love." These phrases are of importance, for they are expressions of the fact that Christians are bound to other Christians primarily by the special bond of truth and that this is the foundation of genuine Christian love. Why do Christians love one another after all? It is not on the ground of some special but imagined compatibility, for they are often highly incompatible. It is not merely on the ground of some deeply shared goals or programs, as would be true, for example, of some voluntary social service agency, though Christians do have many goals in common. What binds the Christian community together is a common commitment to the truth, out of which love rises. This means that Christians will differ fundamentally from the false teachers in their midst or from outright heretics. For a time false teachers and Christians may share common goals. For a time the false teachers may even be indistinguishable from those who are truly born again. But the false teachers will leave and go out into the world, as John said earlier, while on the other hand, the Christians will demonstrate that they are true Christians by remaining with one another in truth and by walking in love.

John goes on to encourage Christians to walk in truth, obedience (i.e., righteousness), and love. The Christian is obliged to "follow along" in them or "walk" in them. In other words, by a deliberate and disciplined choice he is to pursue that path upon which he has been set by the very God of grace who saved him. It may be objected by some that this is not possible, that a person cannot be *commanded* to love, to follow truth, and to pursue righteousness. But this is precisely what we are commanded to do. Belief in God's truth is not optional. It is commanded. Similarly, love is the expression of a self-sacrificing service to others, which can be deliberately undertaken. And righteousness is that into which, by the grace of God but, nonetheless, by conscientious choice and deliberate action, a believer may grow.

Boice, *The Epistles of John*, Baker, 1979, 161–63.

Right Imitation

3 John 1–14

> Do not imitate what is evil but what is good.
> —3 JOHN 11

John attributes Diotrephes's bad conduct, not to a difference of opinion about who should have the final word, but to obvious sin; for John argues that the struggle came about because Diotrephes "loves to be first" (v. 9). This is the original and greatest of all sins. It is the sin of Satan, who was unwilling to be what God had created him to be and who desired rather to be "like the Most High" (Isa. 14:14). It is the opposite of the nature of Christ "who, being in very nature God, did not consider equality with God something to be grasped, but made himself nothing, taking the very nature of a servant, being made in human likeness. And being found in appearance as a man, he humbled himself and became obedient to death—even death on a cross" (Phil. 2:6–8). For Satan's attempt to exalt himself, he shall be made low (Isa. 14:15). For his humility and obedience, God "exalted [Christ] to the highest place and gave him the name that is above every name" (Phil. 2:9).

In 3 John 11 we have what seems to be a general exhortation to do good and not evil. In this context the evil example is most obviously Diotrephes, and the good example, Demetrius, whom John commends (v. 12). The Greek word for "imitate" is *mimeomai*, which is always translated "follow" in the KJV. Paul speaks three times of the need of Christians to imitate "us," that is, the apostles (1 Thess. 1:6; 2 Thess. 3:7, 9). Twice he says "me" (1 Cor. 4:16; 11:1). Once he speaks of being "imitators of God's churches in Judea, which are in Christ Jesus" (1 Thess. 2:14). The author of Hebrews twice speaks of imitating those whose lives are characterized by faith (Heb. 6:12; 13:7). These tests convey a great lesson, for this is as much as to say that men and women will always imitate other men and women, and that this is all right. However, Christian people must be careful whom it is they imitate. Even in Christian circles there are bad examples, like Diotrephes; and there are good examples, like Demetrius. So choose your example carefully, John seems to be saying. Moreover, he gives the reason. For in attempting to imitate the good we indicate that we are of God, just as by imitating the bad those who do so indicate that they are not God's children.

Boice, *The Epistles of John*, Baker, 1979, 170–73.

God or Man

Jude 1–25

Enoch, the seventh from Adam, prophesied about these men.
— JUDE *14*

Jude tells us that Enoch was a preacher who lived in the time before the flood and who preached against the ungodliness of his generation. Enoch had a message of judgment that centered on the ungodliness of his contemporaries. The text uses the word *ungodly* four times. It was a true message, since his was a particularly wicked culture, but the message was also unpopular.

Genesis tells the secret of Enoch's success in such a dismal time. Genesis 5:24 says, "Enoch walked with God." This was an age in which hardly anyone else was walking with God. Certainly his ungodly cousins (Irad, Mehujael, Methushael, Lamech and his sons), of whom we read in Genesis 4, were not. Like Joseph, Enoch lived in a time and place when sin was ascendant. People were undoubtedly saying, "Why should you stand apart? Why should you think you're better than other people? Come down off your high horse! Do what others do!" Enoch did not yield to that argument because he was walking with God, and this was the most important factor in his life. As long as he was walking with God, well—not *everyone* was sinning. As long as he was standing for righteousness, others might stand for righteousness too.

Hebrews 11:5 adds: "By faith Enoch was taken from this life, so that he did not experience death; he could not be found, because God had taken him away. For before he was taken, he was commended as one who pleased God." Enoch pleased God!

As long as you and I are in this world, we must serve God first and hope that in pleasing him and receiving his blessings we also please men and women and find their favor. For most of us this is the story of a lifetime. But let us observe that there are times when it is not possible to serve or please both God and man. When that happens, we must be clear in our minds that we are to please God first of all and then actually choose for him, whatever the consequences. Enoch was undoubtedly despised by his contemporaries; he was certainly ridiculed. But he stood for God and was vindicated in due time.

We need a generation of men and women like that today. We need Christians who serve humanity as they serve Jesus, but who serve Jesus above all and listen for his commendation: "Well done, good and faithful servant! You have been faithful with a few things; I will put you in charge of many things. Come and share your master's happiness!" (Matt. 25:23).

Boice, *Genesis*, Volume 3, Baker, 1998, 910–11.

Faithful Like Jesus
Revelation 1:4–8

Jesus Christ, who is the faithful witness, the firstborn from
the dead, and the ruler of the kings of the earth.
—*REVELATION 1:5*

The faithful witness. Jesus was a faithful witness to all God instructed him to teach. Before Pilate at the time of his trial, he told Pilate, "For this reason I was born, and for this I came into the world, to testify to the truth" (John 18:37). Paul refers to this testimony specifically in his charge to Timothy: "In the sight of God, who gives life to everything, and of Christ Jesus, who while testifying before Pontius Pilate made the good confession . . ." (1 Tim. 6:13).

When we remember that Revelation was written to Christians who might soon be facing persecution and even death for the sake of their testimony to Christ, we can understand how John's description of Jesus would be a source of encouragement for them. Jesus bore a faithful witness before the rulers of this world and suffered for it. They should do the same, even though persecution or death might be the consequence.

The firstborn from the dead. The Christians would need to remember that although Jesus died once, he also triumphed over death by the resurrection. That is the reason for this important title. Jesus bore his witness and died for it, but he was also raised from the dead by the Father; and so would Christians be, if they also would remain faithful.

The ruler of the kings of the earth. In a context that reminds us of Jesus's trial before Pilate and of his triumph through the resurrection, we cannot help but contrast what is ascribed to Jesus in this last phrase with the offer made to him by the devil at the time of his wilderness temptation. The devil offered him "all the kingdoms of the world and their splendor," if only Jesus would bow down and worship Satan (Matt. 4:8–9; see Luke 4:6–7). Jesus was not uninterested in the kingdoms of this world. They are his, and he was promised a thorough and everlasting possession of them. But he would not take them on the devil's terms. He would not rule with Satan. Jesus knew that the way to the kingdoms of this world was the cross, followed by the resurrection, and that only if he pursued that path would he reign with the blessing of the Father and with those given to him by the Father from before the creation of the earth.

This is also the path that is set before us. Many want the kingdoms of the world without suffering. They want it by the world's own means, by political manipulation, and by compromise. It does not come that way. It comes by the faithful testimony and suffering of those who are the disciples of the Lamb.

From an unpublished sermon, November 28, 1999.

The Sure Road Home

Revelation 2:1–7

Repent and do the things you did at first.
—REVELATION 2:5

Jesus prescribes two things for this church's spiritual cure.

1. *Remember.* Any true church or any true believer has experienced the grace of God in the past, or it or he would not exist today. Therefore, the first step in a genuine spiritual recovery consists in remembering what was once known and experienced. This is especially true if what we have lost is our "first love." The Prodigal Son had known the father's love and at one time had probably loved him back. But he had forgotten this love when he took his share of the inheritance and fled to the far country. His spiritual recovery began when he remembered his father's house. If we have forgotten the Father and Jesus Christ, we need to remember the joy of our conversion and our spiritual heritage and recover our first love.

2. *Repent.* We also need to repent, for our spiritual declension is not merely a falling away; it is a sin against God whose love we have forsaken. We tend to think of repentance as something we did in the past when we first believed on Jesus but which we do not need to repeat and have now forgotten to practice. But we never cease to be sinners, even when we are justified by God's grace. Therefore, we must be always repenting and never more so than when we have forsaken our first love for the love of the world, for the world's way of doing things, and for worldly success.

Jesus's last word to the church is a blessing for those who heed his commands and overcome. The blessing is to "eat from the tree of life, which is in the paradise of God" (v. 7), an obvious reference to the Garden of Eden and the loss Adam and Eve sustained when they turned their backs on God. The tree appears again in Revelation 22:2 as part of the glorious consummation of Christ's return.

Ever since Adam and Eve lost Paradise because of their sin, sinners have tried to build their paradise on earth. Cain tried it first by constructing the city of Enoch in the land of Nod. Some tried to do it at Babel by building a tower that they hoped would reach to heaven. The Greeks tried to make Athens a paradise. The Romans tried to do it in Rome. We do it too, supposing that we can have our paradise here, even in our churches. But the cities of men are doomed to destruction. They will all fall away. The only true paradise is in heaven, where it has been prepared only for those who love God. For they alone are able to overcome "by the blood of the Lamb and by the word of their testimony" (12:11).

From an unpublished sermon, January 2, 2000.

Measuring Success
Revelation 3:7–13

Yet you have kept my word and have not denied my name.
—*REVELATION 3:8*

How do you measure success as a Christian? The investment firm of Morgan Stanley Dean Witter measures success "one investor at a time." Their customers measure success by the return on their portfolios. Others measure success by the size of their houses, by what they pay for their cars, or by their bank accounts. How should a Christian measure success? One answer is Jesus's commendation of the church in Philadelphia: "You have kept my word and have not denied my name." This is the only real measure of success in the Christian life. The church in Philadelphia was not famous. It was not large or rich or prominent. It had only a small amount of strength. But because it had kept Christ's word and had not denied his name, Christ's letter to the church is one of unqualified commendation.

But there is another way of looking at the question. Jesus goes on to say to the church in verse 11: "Hold on to what you have, so that no one will take your crown." How does a Christian measure success? It is to be still standing when the battles of life are over or when Jesus comes.

I have always remembered a line from the first of the many popular Rocky movies. Because of a promotional fluke, Rocky Balboa has come out of oblivion by being given a chance to fight the heavyweight champion of the world, Apollo Creed. No one thinks Rocky has a chance, and he doesn't really, though he loses the fight in the end only by a close decision. But Rocky takes the challenge seriously and goes into rigorous training. He gives it everything he has. Yet as the day of the fight draws near, in a reflective mood, he confides to his girlfriend, Adrian: "There's no way I can beat Apollo Creed. I just want to go the distance." He meant he just wanted to last the fifteen rounds.

That is not a bad approach for Christians. How do you measure success? One way is just to go the distance. Jesus Christ says, "Hold on! Don't give up! Don't let anyone take your crown! And remember, I am coming soon!" Can you remember that? Can you hang on? Jesus doesn't ask for heroics. He just wants those who are his to persevere. But to those who do persevere, who endure to the end, he promises his own new name, the name of a conqueror, and a crown of glory that will never tarnish or be snatched away.

From an unpublished sermon, February 6, 2000.

How Should We Worship?

Revelation 4:1–11

Holy, holy, holy is the Lord God Almighty, who was, and is, and is to come.
—REVELATION 4:8

How should we worship? We can notice a number of important features is this passage.

1. *True worship is the worship of God alone.* Here, in its worship, the entire creation is focused utterly on God. And so must we be focused, if we are really worshiping. We must have our attention fixed on God himself and no other. In a sense, this is merely our obedience to the first and second of the Ten Commandments: "You shall have no other gods before me. You shall not make for yourself an idol. . . . You shall not bow down to them or worship them" (Exod. 20:3–5). Or our obedience to what Jesus called the first and greatest commandment, which he drew from Deuteronomy 6:5: "Love the Lord your God with all your heart and with all your soul and with all your mind" (Matt. 22:37). If we are concentrating on something else, however good it may be in itself, we are not worshiping.

2. *True worship honors God for his godlike attributes.* This is what worship actually is. It is assigning to God his true worth. We will never do this exhaustively, of course, for we are finite beings and God is the infinite One. We will never probe God's attributes to their depth nor be able to cease our awestruck worship of God throughout the infinite duration of eternity. But the fact that we cannot praise God exhaustively does not mean that we cannot praise God rightly or that our praise is without eternal value. Here God is praised for three great attributes: holiness ("Holy, holy, holy"), sovereignty ("is the Lord God Almighty"), and eternity ("who was, and is, and is to come").

3. *The best worship is ceaseless worship.* It is continuous, for it is rendered to God day and night. We cannot do this ourselves, of course, except in the sense that our entire lives should be ordered to God's glory. But we can worship ceaselessly, literally, along with others. And we are. It is happening right now as around the world, in every land and by countless Christian congregations, praises are given to God continuously by his redeemed and grateful people.

4. *The fullest worship is with others, with the entire creation.* Should we worship God individually, when we are by ourselves in our own times of prayer and Bible study? Of course. But we must not forsake worshiping God with others either, for there is something in the corporate worship of God by the assembled people of God that is right, enhanced, and beneficial. Especially beneficial! For worshiping with others keeps us on track and reminds us that God is God, that he is in control of history, that we are his people, and that our chief end is to glorify and enjoy him.

From an unpublished sermon, March 5, 2000.

Worshiping the Redeemer
Revelation 5:1–14

You are worthy . . . because you were slain.
—*REVELATION 5:9*

The hymn in Revelation 5 explains why Jesus is worthy.

1. *Jesus is worthy because he was "slain."* This is a fact of history and an amazing fact at that, when you consider who Jesus Christ is. It is amazing that God, the immortal God, could become man in order to accomplish our salvation by his death. How can the immortal die? Or even become a man for that matter? The Greeks considered it the height of foolishness to think that God could even appear in human flesh, not to mention dying on a cross. But that is exactly what Jesus has done, and it is what he is praised for in this hymn. It is what he will be praised for eternally.

2. *Jesus is worthy because he "purchased men for God."* This is an interpretation of the fact, for it explains what Jesus's death was about. Jesus's death was no mere fluke of history, even less a meaningless tragedy. On the contrary, it was the very essence of what God was doing in him for our salvation. Jesus was purchasing men and women for God at the cost of his own precious blood or life. Later in Revelation Jesus will be hailed as "King of Kings and Lord of Lords" (19:16) but he is not being praised as "King of Kings" here by the elders. On the contrary, one thing for which he is praised is that he has made *us* kings or "a kingdom" (5:10). Jesus is our high priest too but he is not praised for being a priest in this chorus. Instead, he has made *us* "priests" (v. 10). The elders are remembering that Jesus died to redeem them personally, and the greatness of the cost.

3. *Jesus is worthy because he made those he purchased "a kingdom and priests."* This is the end result of the fact that Jesus died for their salvation, and it is also a repeated theme in Revelation.

At this point John looks out, beyond the immediate vicinity of the throne, and sees "many angels, numbering thousands upon thousands, and ten thousand times ten thousand" (v. 11). Having noted what Jesus accomplished by this death, the heavenly armies now ascribe to him the glory that is his just due, first to Jesus alone, then to Jesus together with the Father. Nature joins in the singing of the final song, along with the redeemed, because God and the Lamb are responsible for both creation and redemption, and nature can certainly give God honor for the first of those two acts.

What is left after that? Nothing, but to do what the four living creatures and the twenty-four elders do. "The four living creatures said, 'Amen,' and the elders fell down and worshiped" (v. 14).

From an unpublished sermon, April 2, 2000.

Christ in Control

Revelation 6:1–17

They were given power over a fourth of the earth to kill.
—REVELATION 6:8

Some writers on Revelation have trouble believing that Jesus is actually controlling war, bloodshed, famine, plague, and death and sends the woes portrayed by these horsemen. They do not want to make him the immediate cause of these judgments, arguing that he only permits or tolerates what unfolds. But the message of Revelation is that Jesus Christ is totally sovereign over all things, including the forces of evil in this world and that he uses these things for God's purposes, as he always has. As far as the wicked are concerned, Revelation teaches that it is Jesus himself who is the judge and executor of the judgments that are these persons' due.

Moreover, the judgments depicted here will get worse, which is what the unfolding series of seals, trumpets, and bowls of God's wrath that follow the four horsemen and their judgments portend. For after all, this is a just war. The Four Horsemen of the Apocalypse release only what human beings unleash against each other every day. Yet in the days still to come, God will exercise his just judgments by the breaking up of nature and its destructive forces and by the unleashing of the Antichrist, Beast, and False Prophet who will strike the world with their satanic evil. In the days of Abraham, when God foretold the history of Jewish people, he said that "the sin of the Amorites had not yet reached its full measure" (Gen. 15:16). They were to be spared four hundred years. But the four hundred years did pass, their sin did reach its fullness, and they were destroyed by the Jewish invasion of Canaan under Joshua's command.

The pictures painted by John in this last book of the Bible are not for our amusement or puzzles merely to exercise our minds. They are warnings of how seriously God takes sin and of how he is going to judge it fully in time.

Let me make this personal. The evil that is portrayed by the Four Horsemen is not merely something that is out there somewhere in the world being practiced by other people. It is in ourselves, because the seeds of all this destruction are in ourselves. What the Four Horsemen do, we do, or at least are very capable of doing. And the meaning of this is that we need to repent of our sin and turn to Jesus Christ where alone salvation can be found. Do not blame others for the evil. Blame yourself. An early edition of the Anglican Prayer Book has a prayer that begins: "By my fault, by my own fault, by my own most grievous fault. . . ." That is it exactly. It is where you must start, because it is only when you turn from your own self-righteousness that you can find God's mercy in Jesus Christ.

From an unpublished sermon, April 16, 2000.

The Seal of God

Revelation 7:1–8

Then I saw another angel coming up from the
east, having the seal of the living God.
—*REVELATION 7:2*

The Bible speaks of seals in several ways. First, a seal protects against tampering, as the seal placed upon the tomb of Jesus (Matt. 27:66). The leaders of the people wanted the seal so the disciples could not come and steal the body and then say that Jesus had been raised from the dead. We do not use seals so much today, but we have an example of this use in the great seal of the United States that appears on a passport so the document cannot be altered. It has the effect of validating the passport and indicating that the one possessing it is a United States citizen. Second, a seal marks ownership. In ancient times a merchant would seal a shipment of goods to indicate that it belonged to him, and the owner of a vineyard would seal his amphora of wine to show that it came from his vineyard and bore his guarantee. Third, a seal certifies something as genuine. A contemporary example would be the seal of a notary public. It confirms the oath taken by the person who signs the document and authenticates it.

The wonderful thing about the Bible's use of the word *seal* is that it is used to show how Christians have been marked as God's possession by the Holy Spirit. One example is 2 Corinthians 1:21–22. It is a particularly good example in respect to Revelation 7, because it links our being sealed to God's ownership of us and our standing firm in Christ until the end. "Now it is God who makes both us and you stand firm in Christ. He anointed us, set his seal of ownership on us, and put his Spirit in our hearts as a deposit, guaranteeing what is to come." This is exactly what the sealing of the servants of God in Revelation is about.

Do you have the mark placed on the 144,000? It is not your baptism. It is not a certificate of membership in a particular church. It is the Holy Spirit who is the agent of your conversion and faith. Are you born again? Do you have the assurance of that within your heart?

If not, come to Jesus now. The angel holds God's seal and is waiting to stamp its impress on your forehead: this one belongs to God. This one has been purchased by the Lamb.

Draft of a sermon not preached, Spring 2000.

Christ's Rewards

Revelation 22:12–17

My reward is with me, and I will give to everyone according to what he has done.
—*REVELATION 22:12*

Someday we will see each other rewarded for faithful service in this life, for the Bible speaks of crowns that will be given to those who are faithful. There is a right way to think about rewards, for the prospect of rewards is set before us as one reason why the patriarchs and other biblical characters were faithful. They had much to discourage them. Often there were severe trials, hardships, beatings, pain, and ridicule. But they endured because they were "looking ahead to [their] reward" (Heb. 11:26).

One of our great hymns, written by Heinrich Schenk early in the eighteenth century and translated into English by Francis Cox, speaks of these rewards:

> Who are these like stars appearing,
> These before God's throne who stand?
> Each a golden crown is wearing;
> Who are all this glorious band?
> Alleluia! Hark, they sing,
> Praising loud their heavenly King.

> Who are these of dazzling brightness,
> These in God's own truth arrayed,
> Clad in robes of purest whiteness,
> Robes whose lustre ne'er shall fade,
> Ne'er be touched by time's rude hand?
> Whence come all this glorious band?

> These are they who have contended
> For their Savior's honor long,
> Wrestling on till life was ended,
> Following not the sinful throng;
> These, who well the fight sustained,
> Triumph through the Lamb have gained.

In the day of our heavenly reunion, we shall have those rewards, if we are faithful. And we shall rejoice in the triumphs of other Christians. Do you not think, since this will be true, that you could rejoice with them now? We tend to be critical of one another and, of course, sometimes there are grounds for it. We do sin; we are unfaithful. But by God's grace we are also, at times, faithful, for which we shall be rewarded. If only we could see this, we would regard one another differently. We would rejoice in the triumphs, rather than bemoan the faults. We would pray for one another fervently.

So let us pray and work. Let us do so until the day when the entire ransomed church of God is raised to be with Jesus and is made like him.

Topical Index

Topics are referenced by date (month/days).

The Church

Knowing God

Knowing Jesus Christ

his character, 5/10
his cleansing work, 4/2
the cross, 9/9, 9/10
his death, 8/6, 9/6
his divinity, 6/24, 7/1
God's gift, 8/12
his glory, 11/16
his incarnation, 6/15, 7/21, 11/23
as king, 9/9, 12/3, 12/24
as Lord, 9/9
his love, 8/29, 9/2, 9/11, 11/10
as Messiah, 6/26, 7/10
his names, 6/15, 11/16
as Passover Lamb, 9/10
his presence, 7/24
as priest, 12/3, 12/4
as redeemer, 2/28, 3/15, 12/28
our refuge, 4/6
his resurrection, 7/13, 7/19, 9/12
as sacrifice, 2/6, 2/12, 12/4, 12/5,
our Savior, 6/22, 8/22, 10/2, 12/6

as shepherd, 4/18, 6/11, 8/24, 12/8
his trial, 7/11
as the way to God, 1/9, 1/22, 2/11, 8/31

Knowing the Holy Spirit
Holy Spirit, 9/1, 9/3, 12/1, 12/30

Way of Salvation
adoption, 9/13
assurance of salvation, 8/25, 10/16
belonging to God, 12/30
confession, 1/27
conversion, 6/9, 6/27, 7/3, 8/5
faith, saved by, 6/16, 6/22, 7/19, 12/7
forgiveness, 2/4, 5/1, 8/4, 10/10
gospel, 10/4, 10/5, 11/3, 11/24
gospel call, 1/29, 6/25, 8/14, 8/19
grace, 1/5, 1/7, 10/9, 12/13
regeneration, 12/12
repentance, 1/28, 9/19, 9/23, 10/7
salvation, 7/31, 10/8, 10/12, 11/30

Scripture Index

Scripture is referenced by date (month/year). Those in roman type are the primary references, and those in italics are secondary references.

aerate
verb
(<u>ehr</u> ayt)

to supply with air

Every spring, Solomon used his tiller to *aerate* the compact soil.

Synonyms: oxygenate, carbonate

40 DAYS OF WISDOM FROM A BELOVED PREACHER AND BIBLE TEACHER

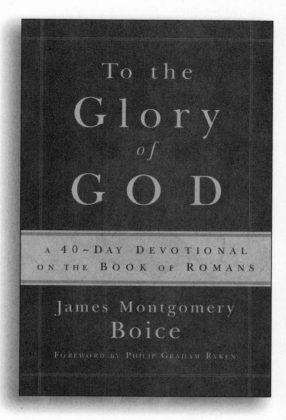

Believers have looked to the book of Romans for both doctrine and encouragement. Many Christian readers have long trusted James Montgomery Boice to guide them through the Scriptures through his preaching ministry and his writings.

Now these two much-loved sources of wisdom come together in *To the Glory of God*, an inspiring devotional drawn from Boice's classic commentary on the book of Romans. Offering rich reflections on Romans, this meditative book contains forty days of selections, daily devotional challenges, and the complete text of the book of Romans.

To the Glory of God is your forty-day journey toward strengthened faith and a greater encounter with the power of God's Word.

"The reader is taken stanza by stanza through Psalm 119 and encouraged to learn and work out the practical dimensions of it. The Psalm, by virtue of its length, may be off-putting to some. If so, this little book will help them to get into it and love it."

—*The Banner of Truth* (February 1999)